ETHIOPIAN

JOURNEYS

ETHIOPIAN JOURNEYS

TRAVELS IN ETHIOPIA 1969-72

by

PAUL B. HENZE

ERNEST BENN LIMITED

LONDON & TONBRIDGE

First published 1977 by Ernest Benn Limited
25 New Street Square, Fleet Street, London EC4A 3JA
& Sovereign Way, Tonbridge, Kent TN9 1RW

Distributed in Canada by
The General Publishing Company Limited, Toronto

Printed in Great Britain

ISBN 0 510-44220-X

DEDICATED TO

My companions

on these journeys,

Ethiopian and Ferenji

Contents

List of Plates

[in one section between pages 224 and 225]

Acknowledgement

All photographs were taken by the author, except for 6b and 43a, which are the work, respectively, of Miss Virginia Hazzard and Miss Ann Anielewski.

List of Maps and Plans

Abbreviations

used frequently in the text

CADU Chilalo Agricultural Development Unit
EAL Ethiopian Air Lines
EO *Ethiopia Observer*, a quarterly journal published in Addis Ababa and in England
ETO Ethiopian Tourist Organization
HIM His Imperial Majesty, i.e. Haile Selassie I
HSI Haile Selassie I
HSIU Haile Selassie I University, Addis Ababa
IEG Imperial Ethiopian Government
IES Institute of Ethiopian Studies, HSIU
IHA Imperial Highway Authority
JES *Journal of Ethiopian Studies*, a scholarly quarterly published by the IES
PC American Peace Corps
PCV Peace Corps Volunteer

Introduction

Shortly before I left Ethiopia in August 1972, after living more than three years
there, I delivered an illustrated lecture to a large audience in Addis Ababa.
Calling my talk 'Faces of Ethiopia', I summed up impressions of the country by
describing people I had met in my travels around it. When I finished, a group of
university students came up to ask questions. 'I was surprised that most of the
people you showed were smiling', one said; 'what did you do to make them
laugh when you photographed them?' I replied I did nothing except talk to them.
On the whole, I added, I had found Ethiopians a rather happy people. The
student scowled, reflected a moment, then declared, 'You may be right. They
look happy. But they shouldn't be!'

He has had his wish. Since 1974 Ethiopia has been in turmoil and there is no
end in sight. To an extent I could not have envisioned when I wrote this book
in 1973, it has turned out to be a record of an Ethiopia that has vanished. The
final years of Haile Selassie's rule from the old Solomonic throne now look to
some like a lost golden age, though in the fashionable jargon of Ethiopia's
current military rulers, it was an era of feudal oppression. It was neither.

Change did not begin in Ethiopia the year before last. In the final decades of
the nineteenth century, the great emperor Menelik II reunified the empire and
consciously began moving it into the modern world. After a brief, confused
interregnum, Haile Selassie I took up where Menelik left off. Even the tragedy
of the Italian invasion had its good side. Both economic and political gains came
of it. After the 1941 Liberation, the old feudal magnates were never able to
challenge the central government for long and Haile Selassie was able to lay
the basis for a modern system of administration and a development programme
that gained steady momentum through the 1950s and the 1960s.

The groups that now vie for power in Ethiopia were all deliberately created
and encouraged by Haile Selassie: the officers and soldiers of the armed forces
and police, the students, teachers, technicians, civil servants, labour leaders.
As Edward Ullendorff has observed in his preface to the last emperor's autobiography, 'For two thirds of his life all the problems Haile Selassie had to
face arose from the fact that he was in advance of his time . . .'[1]

Without the progress that the old Lion of Judah had fostered – in roads and
means of communication alone – I could never have travelled as widely as I did
in Ethiopia to observe both what was changing and what had remained
unchanged. More than most countries, Ethiopia carries an enormous burden of
history and tradition. It is by no means all disadvantageous. There is probably
no place in the world where primitive, ancient, medieval, and modern are as
intermingled as they are here. They are intermingled not only in the landscape
and the language, but in the minds of the people. I have tried in this book to
provide a picture of Ethiopia as I found it in all its variety, not only historic

sites, scenery, and wildlife, but above all people in groups and people as individuals living their daily lives and reacting to political, social, and economic processes affecting them.

Haile Sclassie's Ethiopia will never return again, but when the current commotion has subsided, more of the fundamentals of Ethiopian life, traditions, habits, and attitudes will have survived than now seems likely. This has been true of all empires that have undergone great upheavals: Russia, Turkey, China.

The first comprehensive account of travel in Ethiopia was written by the Portuguese Father Francisco Alvares, who spent more than six years in the country in the 1520s. There is a two-volume English translation of his book known as *The Prester John of the Indies*.[2] I found it still a useful guide on journeys in many parts of the northern and central provinces. The works of three twentieth-century travellers stand out above all others: Cheesman's *Lake Tana and the Blue Nile*,[2] Nesbitt's *Desert and Forest*[2] and Buxton's *Travels in Ethiopia*.[2] They all served me as practical reference works on the road as well as models and sources of inspiration in writing this book. Other good travel books and specialized studies on Ethiopia are cited in the footnotes and listed in the Bibliography.

There is no standard system for transliterating Ethiopian languages into the Latin alphabet. To avoid adding to the confusion, I refrained from inventing my own. In reproducing names of places and people I have used forms which are simple and familiar in current international usage or which approximate local pronunciation. All dates are Gregorian calendar unless specifically identified as Ethiopian Calendar (EC). Dates after emperors' names are the years of their reigns (not their lives) as given in Pankhurst's *Ethiopian Royal Chronicles*.[2] After the first citation, books are cited only by author's last name and abbreviated title. Heights and other geographical data are from the new 1 : 250,000 map series resulting from the joint surveys of the U.S. Army Mapping Mission and the Imperial Mapping and Geography Institute which were completed in 1971. For areas which these new maps do not yet cover, I have used the old Italian/British 1 : 500,000 series based on data from the 1930s. Population statistics are from the Ethiopian Central Statistical Office.

Though practically all the travel described in this book originated from Addis Ababa, I have included almost no description of the capital or of journeys in Shoa, modern Ethiopia's central province. It is a microcosm of the country as a whole and deserves separate treatment. I plan another book devoted to Shoa alone.

Washington, D.C.   P. B. H.
April 1977

NOTES

1 Edward Ullendorff (ed.), *My Life and Ethiopia's Progress, the Autobiography of Emperor Haile Selassie I*, Oxford, 1976, p. xiii.
2 See references in Bibliography, pp. 275–6.

1 The Hidden Empire

Travel in Ethiopia

Space and Time

In Ethiopia one travels in broadened dimensions of both space and time. In terms of space, travel is not only horizontal but vertical. When you become accustomed to living at 2,500 m. in Addis Ababa, you come to think of the central Rift Valley as *low, only* 1,200 m. around Awash station and much lower farther north. To cross the Blue Nile, the road to Gojjam descends 1,500 m. in less than an hour from the cool Shoan highlands to the sultry bottom of the gorge and it is a relief to climb up again to the plateau. Not only temperature and vegetation change with altitude, but the whole way of life and the people themselves. Amharas and Tigreans do not like to live in low country. Given a choice, they will move up beyond 3,000 m. and endure frosty nights and bitter winds rather than settle in damp or dry lowlands. Until recent times the low country of Ethiopia was always sparsely populated. Even now few people live in the great gorge systems of the Blue Nile, the Takazze and the Omo which occupy perhaps 20 per cent of the surface of the country. Malaria control programmes have made the lowlands less dangerous to health and improved roads have opened large areas to agricultural development, but basic attitudes change more slowly.

Time is less tangible than space and more than merely three-dimensional, so the contrasts are even greater. In Addis Ababa or Asmara or Diredawa one can live in the twentieth century. The twentieth century has penetrated Ethiopia in many ways and places: power stations, port facilities, factories, hospitals, radio and TV broadcasting, schools, airlines, and modern highways. But many highways end in trails and one steps quickly from the twentieth century back into the tenth or into Biblical times. The quality of Ethiopian rural life in the highlands still has more in common with the European Middle Ages than it has with any period since. In the lowlands and in the south and west one moves even farther back in time. Here forest and island tribes are just beginning to abandon primitive ways. In the south-east life revolves around herding of cattle and camels, sheep, and goats. True nomadism can still be found in Ethiopia, as well as all the stages of evolution to settled agriculture.

Only a few cities and towns have more than a hundred years of history. At least three provincial capitals have been in existence less than a quarter-century. Almost all country towns have an air of impermanence and a feel of the frontier about them. In Addis Ababa and Asmara a large proportion of the population is only a generation or two from the countryside. Their way of life is a mixture of old country and new city habits.

Roads, Tracks, and Trails

Until modern times the wheel was almost unknown in Ethiopia. There was no need for wheels because there were few places where they could be used. Carriages, carts, wagons, wheelbarrows did not evolve. The Amharic word *mangad* combines all the meanings of the English road, route, way, path, track. It is now used for paved highways as well as for the rutted tracks that climb up the side of gorges at 45° angles and the dusty trails that lead for miles through savannah country. Only a few decades ago the only kind of *mangad* Ethiopia knew was the simple, unimproved track. The Italians began building good roads in Eritrea at the end of the nineteenth century. Roads were built and improved elsewhere in Ethiopia in response to the coming of the motor car. By the time the Italians invaded the country in 1935, several motorable routes existed. The Italians extended them energetically. One of their main purposes, of course, was to facilitate military control, but the greatly improved highway system made it easier for the Ethiopian and British Commonwealth forces to liberate the country a few years later. In remote areas some Ethiopians had come to equate motor roads with foreign invaders and let Italian-built highways fall into neglect. By the time the Imperial Highway Authority (IHA) was established in 1951, Ethiopia's road system had declined badly.

IHA has benefited from foreign money and advice, but is now essentially Ethiopian-run. Considering the obstacles it has had to overcome, its performance is remarkable. Except in the Ogaden, where a track can be cleared over flat landscape, there are few places where the highway engineer does not have to bring all his skills to bear on designing routes. Gorges and escarpments, mountain ranges, swamps, expanses of shifting sand, and great lava flows confront roadbuilders in all parts of the country. A creek with a trickle of water in the dry season rages with hundreds of thousands of gallons per minute after the heavy rains. No matter how carefully maintenance men reinforce retaining walls, each rainy season brings landslides in the northern highlands and traffic can be held up for hours or days. The effect of heavy rain on blacktop is like that of frost: potholes form and the road-bed absorbs moisture; heavy traffic soon causes the surface to disintegrate; temporary repairs with rocks make travel possible but at a crawl. It is not surprising, therefore, that a route which takes only two hours under good conditions, can take three or four times as long at the end of the rains. Each year during my time in Ethiopia, IHA maintenance improved and it is now usually possible to drive in a day from Addis Ababa to Bahr Dar, Arba Minch, Jimma, or Diredawa even during the big rains.

Secondary and tertiary routes can be deceptive. In the dry season what is marked as a broken line on the map (or not even shown at all) may turn out to be a track which can be travelled for miles as easily as a paved highway. Then it turns down into a valley and splits into several rock-strewn paths. Hours and a good deal of backtracking may be needed to determine which path leads on to where you wish to go. In the rainy season the same track may be a mass of muddy ruts and pools, too much even for a sturdy landrover. But most of the year, in most of Ethiopia, these tracks are dry and, stones and fords and other obstacles notwithstanding, they are intriguing routes to travel for they lead to places where outsiders seldom penetrate, to isolated settlements where people still lead lives unchanged since medieval times, to churches and holy sites, past unusual vegetation and concentrations of birds and animal life. Travel on such routes is safe enough if you have a 4-wheel-drive vehicle in good repair, jerricans of fuel and water, and, preferably, someone along who speaks Amharic.

Road signs are rare in Ethiopia, even on main highways.

Much of Ethiopia is still not accessible by vehicle at all, but can be reached only by horse, mule, donkey, or on foot. And, though roadbuilding programmes are now going well, some sections of the country are bound to remain roadless for decades to come. In the gorge country, shelves of cultivated land and isolated mesas (Amh. *amba*) exist as worlds apart, reachable only on foot over unbelievably rocky trails.

There are two railroads in the country, the Franco-Ethiopian line from Djibouti to Addis Ababa and the shorter Eritrean line from Massawa up the escarpment to Asmara and then on to Agordat. Both still have an aura of romance about them and both are still economically important.

While journeys that look simple on even a good map may turn out to require days, there is hardly any part of the country with an airfield that cannot be reached in two or three hours from the capital. Ethiopian Air Lines (EAL) were established in 1946 with TWA assistance and have been a success from the beginning. A good balance has been kept between international routes and internal service. EAL's flights from Europe and Asia are dependable and comfortable. The company has a safety record equalled by few other airlines in the world. Domestic flights are reliable and colourful but not always smooth. As a result of EAL's continually expanding internal services, it is now possible to fly to Lalibela, unreachable by all but the hardiest travellers only a decade ago, and then spend further hours or days visiting ancient sites in the hinterland on muleback or horse. The traveller can no longer expect to be the first European to visit most of these places, but he may even yet be only the thirty-ninth or fortieth.

Thirteen Months of Sunshine

The Ethiopian Tourist Organization's (ETO) colourful advertisements are honest. Ethiopia has one of the best climates in the world. I cannot recall a day when the sun did not shine. It shines less during June, July, August, and September, for this is the period of the big rains, *kremt* in Amharic, usually translated by Ethiopians as 'winter'. And winter it is, compared to the rest of the year. It is the coolest and dampest season in the highlands; colds and fevers are common and much vegetation is dormant. But even during *kremt* several days of continual rain are rare; enormous thunderstorms and cloudbursts are frequent.

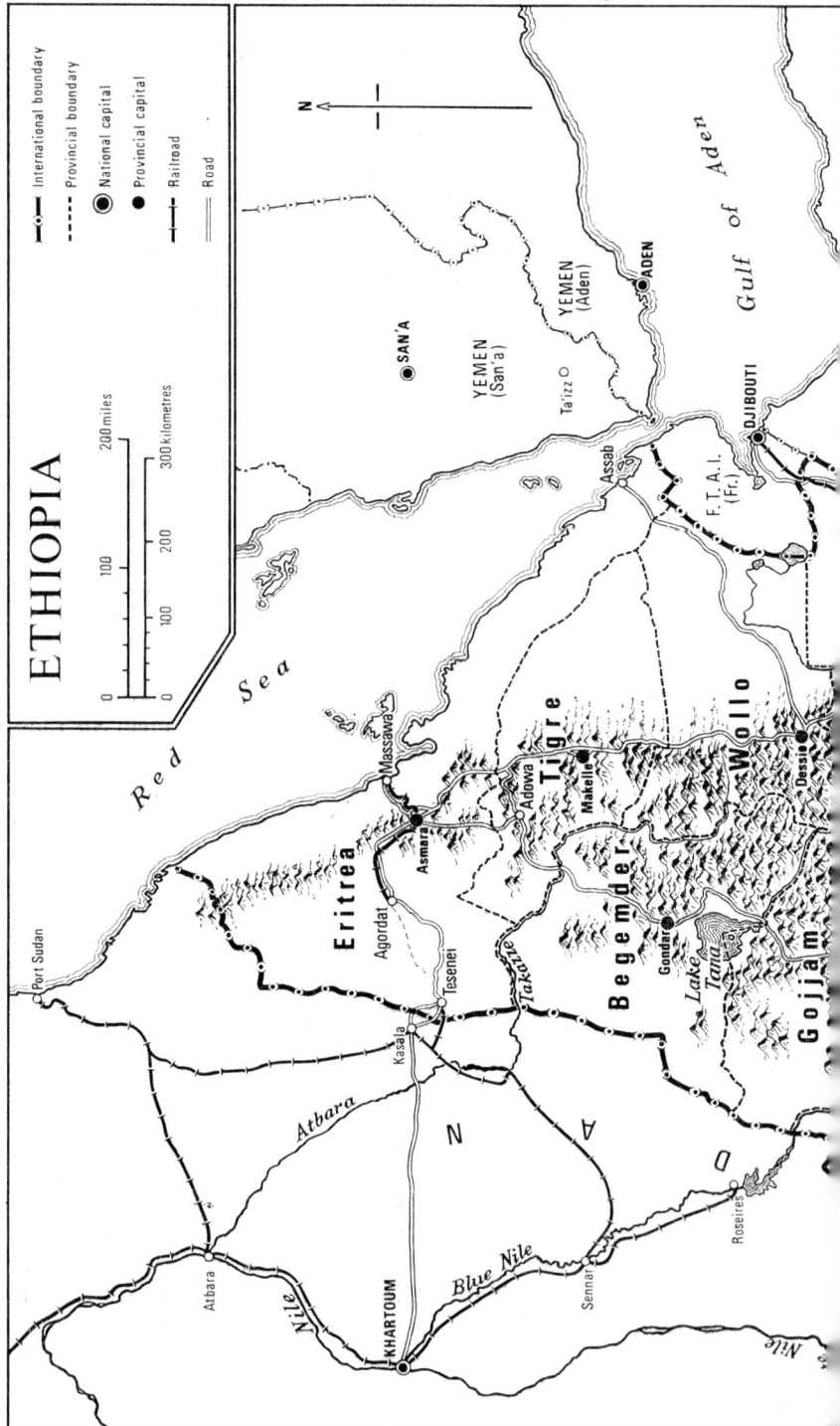

Fig. 1   Ethiopia: General Map

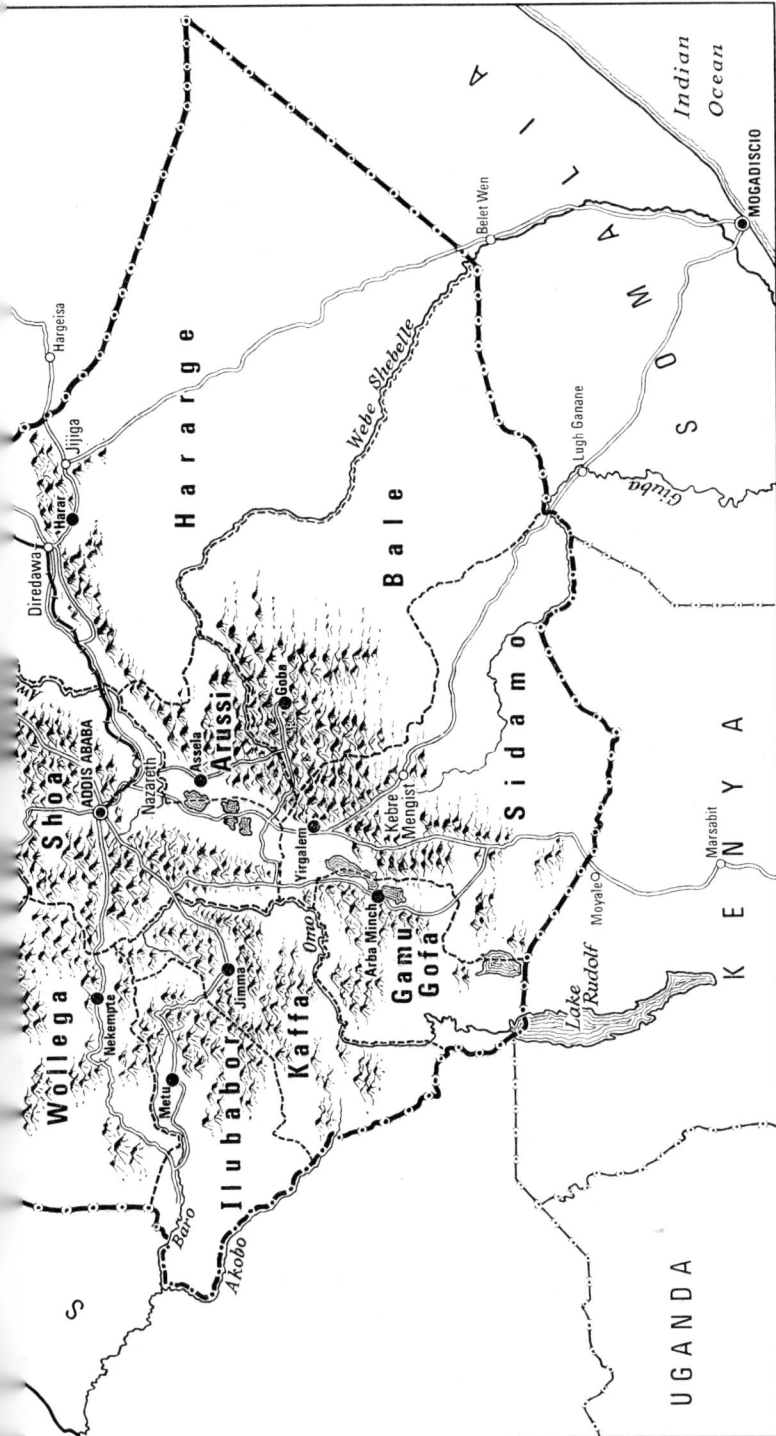

Hail sometimes accumulates to a depth of 8–10 cm. In between spells of violent weather there are hours and sometimes days of sunshine when the vivid blue sky is decorated by billows of sparkling white cloud. The big rains start erratically in June, but they usually end about the time of the Feast of Maskal on 27 September. This festival derives from pre-Christian practices and, like Easter in Europe, is a celebration of rebirth after a season of cold and dormancy. It is said to commemorate the finding of the True Cross by St Helena in the fourth century. All over the country people sing and dance at sundown around bonfires on hilltops and in town squares.

From October through December, and usually well into January, the weather is sunny and rain uncommon. The nights become cooler in late November and frost occurs at heights above 2,500 m., but the days are dependably dry, warm, and fresh. This is the best time of the year for travelling in the highlands.

The little rains are less predictable than the big rains. Some years they never come; other years they begin in January and merge into the big rains at the end of May. They are not as copious as those of *kremt* and there are always intervals of a week or two when no rain falls. Thunderstorms and hailstorms also occur. The best kind of little rains last for only six or seven weeks in March and April. These green up the countryside, settle the dust, and enable farmers to plant an extra grain crop. Then there is a May and early June period of full summer. With or without rain, the time from late April to early June is always the warmest time of the year in the highlands with daytime temperatures 3°C warmer than in November and December and night temperatures 6–8°C higher. But even at this time of the year a day that could be called truly hot by American or European standards is rare.

It is easy to vary one's weather in Ethiopia. Everything that has been said above applies to the central and northern highlands. Lower country is never far. In the far north, along the Red Sea and in the Danakil Depression, lies some of the hottest, driest country in the world. Travel here is comfortable only in the period October–March. The central and southern Rift Valley lake country is pleasant the year around. Averaging 1,600 m. around Lake Zway, it declines to 1,200 m. in Gamu Gofa. Throughout southern Ethiopia the rainy seasons are less distinct than in the northern highlands and some rain falls during most months of the year. Nevertheless, even in these regions, the thirteen months of sunshine principle still holds – there is more sun than rain, the rain falls, mostly in squalls, showers, and thunderstorms, and overcast days are rare.

The Ethiopian calendar has thirteen months and lags seven or eight years behind the Gregorian calendar.[1] It is based on the old Egyptian system of dividing the year into twelve thirty-day months with an extra month of five days (six in leap year) at the end of the year. This thirteenth month, called Pagumen, comes in early September. The years are dedicated to the four Evangelists in turn: Matewos, Marcos, Lucas, and Yohannes. Leap year is always the year of St Luke. Like the Feast of Maskal, the practice of beginning the new year at the end of the rainy season corresponds to the basic climate pattern of the highlands and undoubtedly has roots in the pagan past. It may also reflect ancient Jewish and south Arabian links.

Though Ethiopian months do not match those we are accustomed to, the days of the Ethiopian week match those of the rest of the world. The system of reckoning the hours of the day is different. It is based on the sunrise-to-sunset principle and has been used since ancient times. The new day begins at 6 in the morning. One o'clock Ethiopian time is 7 a.m. and noon is 6 o'clock to an Ethiopian. Though both the Western and Ethiopian systems are used in larger cities, even Western-educated Ethiopians tend to think in traditional times of the day and it is good to verify appointments and be sure which time-reckoning system is meant. A dinner invitation for 2 o'clock is more likely to be for 8 in the evening than for 2 in the afternoon. In the countryside only the Ethiopian system of counting the hours of the day is used. Since Ethiopia is so near the Equator, the length of the day varies only slightly during the course of the year.

Trees and Flowers

The visitor arriving in Addis Ababa for the first time has the impression that the only tree that grows in Ethiopia is eucalyptus. It dominates the city and its environs, spicing the air with its clean, sharp odour. The tree has many uses in addition to providing shade and windbreak: lumber, poles for buildings and fences, fuel in many forms. Leaves and twigs are tied in bundles and sold for cooking-fires; they produce a quick, hot flame and light blue smoke. In the early stages of growth, eucalyptus puts out large powdery-looking blue leaves on juicy, resinous stalks. On older growth the leaves are smaller, more pointed, and have a deep, waxy-green colour. Crushed leaves of tender new shoots are used as a cold remedy; stuffed up the nose, they clear the sinuses; a natural form of Vapo-rub. Eucalyptus is such an established feature of the Ethiopian scene today that it comes as a shock to realize that only a hundred years ago the tree was unknown. It was introduced in the 1890s and spread rapidly. The area planted to it is still expanding. Though many kinds will grow in Ethiopia and CADU[2] has been experimenting with different varieties in controlled plantings in Arussi, almost all Ethiopian eucalyptus is of the *globulus* variety, also known as Tasmanian Blue Gum. In Amharic it is called *bahr zaf*. It grows everywhere above 1,500 m., forming forests around most of the older towns and villages, planted in rows along roads and along boundaries between fields in some parts of the country. Thanks to it, the process of denudation of the highlands which gained disastrous momentum in the eighteenth and nineteenth centuries has been largely reversed.

The older, native trees of the highlands were cut mostly for firewood. Most of them are naturally slow-growing and some, such as the native cedar (*juniperus procera*; Amh. *tid.*) and its relative, the pinnate-leaved *podocarpus gracilior* (Amh. *zigba*), which flourish in a sub-alpine environment, cannot restore themselves easily once an entire area has been cut over. Cedars still survive around churches and in large stands on some of the higher central and southern mountains. Isolated specimens in unexpected places attest to the fact that a large portion of the highlands was probably covered with thick cedar and podocarpus forests in prehistoric times.

The wild olive (*olea chrysophylla*; Amh. *weyra*) occurs all over the plateau, but is seldom found in large concentrations except around churches. It has the twisted branches, gnarled trunks, and shiny, grey-green leaves of its Mediterranean cousin, but bears only small inedible fruits. Its tough, oily wood was once widely used in Eritrea for beams and reinforcements in stone houses.

The fig (*ficus*) family is well represented in Ethiopia and several of its larger members reach enormous size, especially those called *warka* and *shola* in Amharic. Terminology in this family is confusing. *Warkas* are often called 'sycamore figs' by Europeans. They grow along rivers and lake-shores and often flourish as isolated trees in the countryside where they are left for shade for livestock and people in the midst of cultivated fields. By Ethiopian standards they are lowland trees, seldom occurring above 2,400 m.

The variety of figs in Ethiopia may be exceeded only by the kinds of acacias or thorn-trees. These form the principal component of savannah forests and seldom occur in large stands above 2,500 m. Some have a natural umbrella-like shape; some grow tall; some stretch their branches so far that the diameter of the tree may be two or three times its height. Their form seems to be determined by both inherent characteristics and their location. There are many kinds of leaves, seedpods, and bloom. Some bear legume-like clusters of pink or white flowers. The most striking bloom is bright, fuzzy balls of yellow and white. Some flower at the height of the dry season and others only after rains. Flowering acacias in the forests around the Rift Valley lakes (usually at their best in May) produce idyllic, perfumed scenes that recall European springtime among the lakes and valleys of the Alps. Acacia wood is close-grained and oily, excellent for both charcoal and firewood.

There are many other unusual native trees in Ethiopia, among them mimosas, which bear clusters of sweet-smelling yellow bloom near the end of the big rains, and the monumental *kosso* (*hagenia abyssinica*), preserved where all other trees have been felled because its reddish, medicinal-smelling bloom is believed to be effective as a vermifuge.

There are enough rare and unusual flowers to keep the professional student and collector continually busy, for habitats range from sea-coast mangrove swamps, desert islands, and lowland savannahs to temperate highlands and isolated alpine regions. The ordinary traveller will be impressed most with the spectacular displays of Maskal daisies (*coreopsis boraniana*) which burst into such intense orange-yellow bloom at the end of the rainy season that they seem to add light to the landscape. Aloes bloom orange in Lasta in October and November, crimson in the central highlands around *Timqat*-time, and golden yellow in Tigre in February. Rich-scented lilies spring up from highland fields as soon as the big rains soak the ground. True red ones are relatively rare, but a red-and-white striped variety is common around Lake Tana and white, pink and creamy yellow kinds occur in other parts of the plateau. The most splendid of all Ethiopian lilies is the fireball (*hemanthus multiflora*) called *yanbasa ababa*, 'lion's flower', in Amharic. Like many other flowers and trees it blooms at different times from one region to another. Its brilliant red globes, often 15 cm. across, burst forth in clusters along the steepest, rockiest slopes of the island of Tullu Guddo in Lake Zway in March and April. They come out in the mountains of Sidamo about the same time. In the north they can be found in September along the streams and gorges that lead down to the Blue Nile. Sorrel, ranging from pink to brick-red, blooms all over the highlands after the big rains stop. By the time it declines, globe thistles come into bloom and last in Arussi and Bale until February.

Hundreds of other flowers spring from the nooks and crannies of the Ethiopian landscape. Gorge-sides are among the most rewarding places to search for them because many that have been eliminated by ploughing and grazing survive there and sharp differences in altitude, soil, and exposure to sun and moisture give different varieties an opportunity to grow in close proximity. After one has become acclimatized to altitude, there is no pleasanter way to spend an afternoon than to drive out to the edge of one of the gorges or escarpments and hike for a few hours up and down the paths that centuries of movement by shepherd boys and their flocks have made. Not only will there be varied vegetation, there will also be dozens of kinds of birds, ranging from turquoise and purple starlings and jewel-like sunbirds to huge vultures and hawks soaring over the abysses. With luck one may also encounter animals – monkeys or baboons, perhaps klipspringer or dikdik, rarely wild cats, and sometimes, toward evening, hyenas. These natural scavengers are plentiful everywhere in Ethiopia. They sleep in burrows during the day and come out to roam and call during the night.

In the chapters which follow references to all these trees and flowers, and many others as well, will be frequent. I apologize for the inadequacy of many of the identifications, however, for I was never able to find an easy-to-use, comprehensive guide to Ethiopian vegetation. That apparently remains to be written.[3]

Eating and Drinking

Ethiopians have a complex cuisine and there is a great deal of sociability and sometimes ceremony connected with eating and drinking. Most foreigners find they have to educate their palates to Ethiopian food and drink. The traveller is offered drink more often than food, though offers of both are frequent. There are three traditional alcoholic drinks, in ascending order of strength: *talla*, *tej*, and *katikala*. *Talla* is home-brewed beer, normally made of toasted barley fermented with *gesho* (*rhamnus prinoides*), the green leaf of a shrub which is grown all over the country and sold in great piles at markets. *Talla* is usually cloudy and varies from light tan to dark brown, reflecting the degree of toasting of the grain. Its range of flavour extends from the light, yeasty, sour taste of newly brewed European beer to the deep, dark, bitter flavour of stout. Some housewives filter their *talla* to make it clear. In country houses it is kept in big earthen pots called *gan*. A good housewife keeps an ample supply of properly aged *talla* on hand at all times to provide for many refills of glasses when her husband brings in friends who sit around the hearth and exchange news. Traditionally *talla* was served out of horn beakers, clay goblets, or small gourd vessels and all these can still be found in use, though the visitor is usually served *talla* in a water-glass.

Tej may be served in a water-glass too and, if it is a strong *tej*, a water-glassful can generate a good deal of warmth and conviviality. *Tej* is mead, made of honey fermented with *gesho*. It can vary greatly in flavour, colour, bouquet, and potency. Some kinds, especially in the north, are thick and yellow and have a sourish taste. Some are pale amber and emit a bouquet of fresh honey. Elegant households in Addis Ababa and Asmara take pride in serving filtered *tej*. Sparklingly clear and dry on the tongue, it looks and tastes like a good sherry. Several brands of commercial *tej* are sold bottled in bars and grocery shops all over the country. They are much less interesting than the home-brewed kind. Traditionally *tej* is served from narrow-necked, bulbous pottery bottles that hold about half a pint. Clear glass bottles of the same shape are now widely used.

Katikala is a clear gin-like liquor distilled from grain. It can range from watery to fiery and local herbs are sometimes used to flavour it. The best *katikala* in Ethiopia is reputedly made in Gojjam. I have enjoyed it there as much as anywhere.

There are many other drinks. *Birz*, a mixture of honey and water, can be very refreshing, though for the guest it is sometimes made with so much honey that it resembles syrup more than a beverage. In the southern and south-eastern Galla country, the visitor is often presented with fresh milk. Coffee (*buna*) is popular everywhere. It is roasted over the hearth and pounded in a mortar by the housewife, then boiled in a clay pot (*jabana*) as the visitor chats with his host. Where European influence has not yet penetrated, it will be served with salt or cardamom and, among Galla, perhaps with butter! Tea (*shay*) is common only in the east and north, known nearly everywhere but seldom offered. In some areas coffee leaves (*quti*) and dried coffee husks (*jenfel*) are steeped like tea and served with salt and butter. 'Modern' drinks are now available wherever roads reach. These include Italian-style red and white wine from several domestic wineries, bottled beer, and carbonated drinks of world renown. Ethiopians seem to have come through their long history with very little natural craving for sweetness, but the present generation is changing fast. Sweet drinks are increasingly popular and along with modern beer will probably supplant nearly everything else in a generation or two. The wealth of available drink, plus the natural Ethiopian sense of hospitality, make for some of the most mixed drinking one can do anywhere in the world. I recall a visit with an Ethiopian friend to his home town in the country where we were entertained for eight hours by dozens of relatives and served, in various sequences, all the drinks that have been mentioned in the paragraphs above except tea, *birz*, and *jenfel*!

Injera and *wat* are the basic foods of Ethopia. *Injera* is flat bread baked on a griddle like a large pancake. It is most commonly made of *teff* (*eragrostis abyssinica*), a unique tiny grain which comes in white, black, and red varieties. White is considered best. *Injera* is also made of wheat (*sendey*) which in some areas is considered superior to *teff*. It can also be made with barley (*gebs*) and sorghum (*mashila*); the latter is felt to be inferior. *Wat* is stew.[4] It is ordinarily made of meat and vegetables with so much hot seasoning that the flavour of most of the other ingredients is overwhelmed. Ethiopians love herbs and spices, especially red pepper (*berbere*), and housewives pride themselves on home-ground mixtures of seasonings. *Doro wat*, made of chicken cut into pieces and steeped with small whole eggs in pepper sauce, is the favourite of all *wats*. Less popular but often very tasty are the meatless *wats* made for fast-days. Some are so well flavoured with spices that one hardly notices they are made only of vegetables. *Wat* is poured into the centre of a pile of several thicknesses of *injera*. It is scooped up with the fingers in small pieces of the flat bread. Several people eat around the same tray or *mesob*, the large eating-basket which rests on a conical understructure. Some *mesobs* are true monuments to the art of basket-weaving. An especially good Harar *mesob* may cost E\$300.

Many Ethiopian foods were developed so that they could be easily stored and carried and remain usable for days or weeks. Such foods are now popular snacks: parched barley (*qolo*); *chiko*, a concentrated pastry made of flour, butter, and spices and lightly baked; *quanta*, strips of dried beef. Children in the country pick chickpeas (*shimbera*) and fave beans (*bakela*), ripe but not yet hard, from the fields and present them to the traveller as a special delicacy. In the south and south-west, in the *ensete* country, a bread made of fermented *ensete* root, *kocho*, is more popular than *injera*. It is gelatinous and chewy and has a sourish taste, but I developed more of a liking for it than for raw *shimbera* and *bakela*.

Meat is the food Ethiopians love best. Since they have so much livestock, they consume more meat than most Africans, though many people cannot afford it as often as they would like. For days before holidays the roads into cities are crowded with herdsmen driving in sheep and goats to be sold for feasting. For major occasions a whole steer is slaughtered. It is a rare highlander, be he educated man or peasant, who does not enjoy raw beef (*brindo*). It is usually eaten in slices with red pepper.

In agricultural regions under 1,800 m., maize (*baqollo*) is a major element of the diet. Though the types grown are coarse, they have good flavour. Ears picked fresh from a field and roasted in the husk until they are lightly toasted make a fine camp-fire feast during travels in lower country.

What an Ethiopian does not eat is as important to him as what he does. For

Christians there are numerous fasting requirements – Wednesday and Friday of every week as well as many other periods prescribed by the church, 180 days in all during the year. Fasts are widely observed, even in the cities, and passionately honoured in rural areas. Fasting means no animal product – no milk, butter, eggs, or cheese – as well as no meat. Highlanders, both Christian and Muslim, are fastidious about game. Most birds are never eaten and only certain kinds of hoofed animals. Most traditional Ethiopians refuse all fish, but they are plentiful both along the coast and in many lakes and are now coming to be eaten by city people during fasts. Lower-caste lake-shore tribes have always eaten fish, of course, as well as animals such as hippopotamus.

There is almost nothing that does not grow in Ethiopia. Temperate fruits, vegetables, and grains as well as tropical ones have been introduced and most do well. But Ethiopians are conservative in their eating habits and rural people are quite content with the variety they already have. While many kinds of fruits and vegetables can be bought in the cities, they are often difficult to find in rural regions. The traveller intending to live mostly off the countryside will find the going a little rough in remote areas and will have to spend an inordinate amount of time seeking and preparing food. It is useful, therefore, to carry along a good supply of canned and dried items. Just about everything known internationally can be bought in the supermarkets of Addis Ababa and Asmara.

Names and Tongues

If conversation lags among a group of Ethiopians, a good subject to introduce is names and their meanings. An individual's name consists of his proper name plus his father's name, e.g., Yohannes Mikael (John, son of Michael), Hirut Belaineh (Ruth, daughter of Belaineh). Double names are common and many of them are religious: Wolde-Ab (Son of the Father), Tesfa-Tseyon (Hope of Zion), Gebre-Medhin (Slave of the Saviour), Haile Selassie (Power of the Trinity). When both the offspring and the father have double names, the full name consists of four elements: Amde-Mikael Gebre-Egzy (Pillar of Michael, son of Slave of God). Both civil and religious titles are often added before a name. The common courtesy titles are *Ato* (Mr), *Woizero* (Mrs), and *Woizerit* (Miss). A married woman keeps her own name. This makes it difficult on social occasions to keep couples straight until one gets to know them well. Foreigners who insist on calling wives by their husband's name provoke amusement among Ethiopians. Since they do not have them, Ethiopians have little feeling for foreign surnames and find them difficult to remember. They most readily address a foreigner by Mr + his first name. In several places I visited frequently, I became known as Ato Pawlos. Unless the foreigner exerts himself to become accustomed to the Ethiopian name system, he will constantly misaddress people and misunderstand names that are spoken to him.

There is an enormous variety of names for both men and women, for in addition to all the familiar Christian saints there are many Ethiopian ones and

• •

many religious terms used as names. Amharic, Tigrinya, and Ge'ez forms of the same name may be different. Many people baptized with a religious name seldom use it. Instead they use secular names consisting of common phrases, exclamations, or attributes. Some of these are cognates of European names; some are distinctly Ethiopian: Ababa (Flower), Alemayehu (I have seen the World), Berhanu (the Light), Dinkinesh (You (f.) are okay), Desta (Joy), Yigzaw (May he Rule), Melaku (the Angel), Fikre (My Love), Tsehay (Sun), Hailu (the Power) . . . There are hundreds and hundreds of them. Ethiopian Muslims are using more standard Islamic names, though many retain pre-Islamic tribal names. Galla often keep their own tribal names. All tribal groups have their own name traditions. Whatever the origin, religion, or tribal affiliation, the system of basic name plus father's name is now universal throughout Ethiopia.

Ethiopia has two official languages, Amharic and English. Knowledge of both is steadily expanding. Native speakers of Amharic constitute about a third of the population, but large numbers of people who speak other tribal languages also know Amharic. All elementary education is in Amharic. Students are also expected to learn enough English during their six years of elementary school to study most of their courses in English from the seventh year onward. Since many Indians, Ceylonese, and Filipinos have been employed as secondary-school teachers, the English used often has its own special flavour. In Eritrea English has replaced Italian as the second language of the younger generation. Amharic is well on its way to becoming firmly established as a true national language. The third language of Ethiopia, Gallinya, is probably spoken as mother tongue by as many people as Amharic. It is the rural *lingua franca* of most of southern and central Ethiopia. Its dialects are less divergent than the customs and manner of life of the numerous Galla tribes, some of whom have been completely absorbed into the highland Christian way of life while others still lead a semi-nomadic existence. Knowledge of Gallinya is of little use in Tigre and Eritrea, where Tigrinya is the basic language, though another related but distinct Semitic language called Tigre is also used in northern Eritrea. Amharic and Tigrinya both derive from the old church language, Ge'ez, and are as closely related as French and Italian. But their intonations are different. A foreigner with a good ear for Amharic may still have difficulty grasping meanings in Tigrinya.

Ethiopians are language-conscious. The Semitic languages as well as Gallinya are rich in forms and vocabulary. Men pride themselves on their oratorical ability which they exercise in local councils and courts. There is a great deal of time for talk. People entertain themselves with poetry, singing, proverbs, and tales. Puns are a favourite form of humour. Priests, schoolteachers, and village leaders often honour the visitor with a speech of welcome. The traveller who finds some appropriate words to speak in return will be doubly appreciated.

The Ethiopian Orthodox Church

The Ethiopian Orthodox Church is not simply a colourful adjunct to Ethiopian life, it is an essential part of it. In the countryside the church permeates all facets of human existence to an extent unknown in Europe since medieval times. In the cities, too, the church remains important. Urban Ethiopians are for the most part believers and churchgoers. Official life is closely linked to the festivals of the church. National holidays begin with religious services, which go on for hours and include singing, drumming, dancing, and elaborate processions. There is a delightful informality about the ceremonies of the Ethiopian Church which can be disconcerting to those accustomed to the efficiency of Catholic and Protestant services. But these and many other features of Ethiopian ritual will be familiar to those who know something of Eastern Orthodoxy.

The Ethiopian Church is very much within the Eastern Orthodox tradition, though it has unique characteristics which stem from Jewish practices older than Christianity itself.[5] The church is often called Coptic, but this is a misnomer disliked by educated Ethiopians and unknown in rural areas. Coptic means Egyptian. From the time of its conversion in the fourth century until 1959, the Ethiopian Church had been subordinate to the Patriarch of Alexandria, who sent a Coptic monk to serve as Patriarch of Ethiopia.[6] Looking back over all those centuries, it is hard to grasp how a people so tenaciously independent could have tolerated such an arrangement for so long. What appears actually to have happened during many periods of Ethiopian history is that the Egyptian-supplied Patriarch was a figurehead while true power in the Ethiopian Church rested in the hands of indigenous religious leaders.[7]

Ethiopia has produced a bevy of colourful saints of its own, such as Tekla-Haymanot, a Shoan patriot; Ewostatewos, a nationalist figure with a certain protestant coloration whose doctrines have been associated with the Monastery of Debra Bizen in Eritrea; and Abuna Gebre Manfas Qiddus, probably Egyptian in origin. He is said, like Methuselah, to have lived for several hundred years and eventually settled on top of Mt Zuqualla (2,989 m.), an extinct volcano south of Addis Ababa, which thousands of pilgrims still climb to celebrate his anniversary on 14 March each year. Ethiopians honour dozens of other familiar Christian saints, among whom the most popular are St George the Dragon-killer, St Michael the Archangel, and St Stephen. In keeping with the other branches of Eastern Orthodoxy, the Ethiopian Church also has a fondness for abstract concepts such as Selassie (the Trinity), Kidane Mehret (the Covenant of Mercy), and Senbet (the Sabbath). In the minds of the common people, these seem to have taken on a semi-corporeal status almost identical to that of the saints. Churches are given the names of both saints and concepts. A church is identified by the name of the district in which it is situated (or some natural feature) plus the name of the saint or concept to which it is dedicated: Weyname Kidane Mehret, Sendaba Yesus, Jingami Maryam, Narga Selassie, Amba Ras Medhane Alem. Young boys in the countryside enjoy entertaining and informing the traveller by standing on top of a hill or at the edge of a gorge and calling out the names of all the churches that can be seen in the landscape below.

Early Ethiopian churches were sometimes hewn from living rock. Hundreds of rock and cave churches are still in use in the northern part of the country. The most famous, of course, are those of Lalibela.[8] There is also an old northern tradition of rectangular-built churches which seem to derive from Near Eastern temple architecture. The oldest of them, known to have been in continual use since it was built, perhaps in the tenth century, is Enda Abunda Aregawi atop the *amba* of Debra Damo in Tigre.[9] Another old church, Betlehem Maryam in Gaynt, east of Lake Tana, illustrates the transition to the round church. Here a large circular thatched church was built over an earlier rectangular one which has many archaic Axumite features.[10] Rectangular village churches, many quite recently built, are common in Eritrea and Tigre, but in most of the country the standard Ethiopian Orthodox church is now a round structure.

In the Ethiopian context, the round church probably represents a reassertion of basic African, as opposed to Near Eastern, influence. Round, hut-type religious structures can be found throughout most of sub-Saharan Africa. Ethiopian round churches are frequently situated in groves which are known to have been sites of pagan worship. There is a good deal of architectural and ornamental variation in round churches. They are often located on top of knolls, on spurs along the sides of valleys and gorges, or on slopes which provide sweeping views. Some of the older round churches in Gojjam are enormous in size and have colonnades of wooden pillars. Churches built more recently make

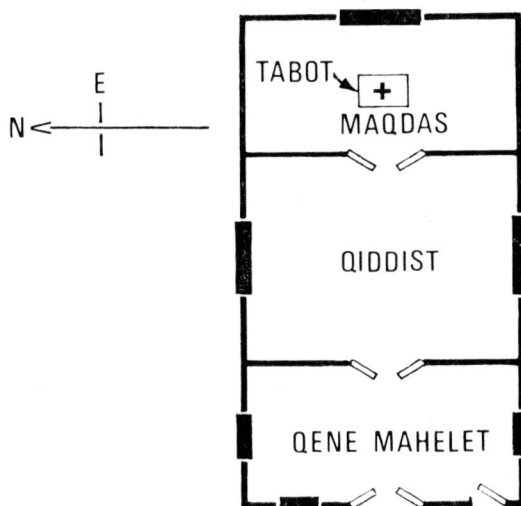

Fig. 2   Ground plan of rectangular church

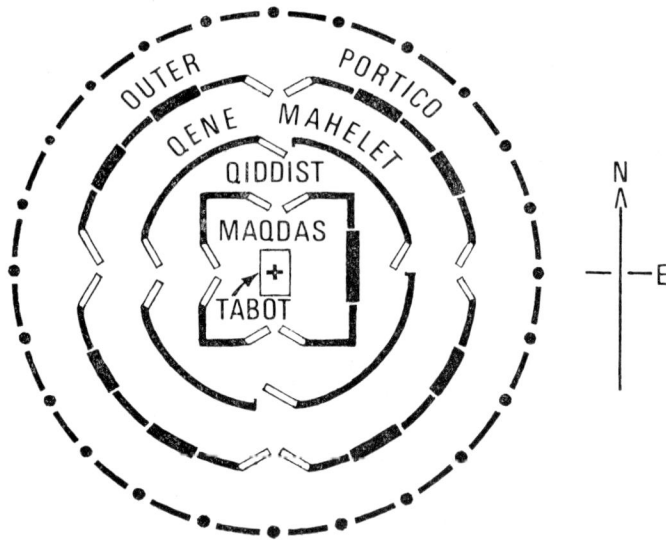

FIG. 3   Ground plan of round church

more extensive use of masonry. Parish churches in the central highlands, both old and new, are usually built of stones with mud-straw mortar. Thatched roofs are still the rule in remote areas, but over the next decade or two they are likely to become a rarity. Every congregation that cares about its church or its own prestige now collects money to finance a tin roof and the visitor is frequently given the opportunity to show his appreciation for the hospitality accorded him on a visit to a church by making a contribution to its *qorqoro* (tin) fund. Tin is much less picturesque than thatch, but it reduces the risk of fire and weather damage. A visit to a church whose paintings have been ruined by water seeping through poorly maintained thatch will convince the sentimentalist of the merits of tin.

Before entering a church the visitor must remove his shoes. A few churches have carpeted floors, but most have matting or straw. At certain seasons floors are strewn with hay, flowers, or sweet-smelling herbs. The round church is always divided into two concentric circles, the *qene mahelet* and the *qiddist*, around a central square structure, the *qiddus qiddusan*, the Holy of Holies, also called the *maqdas*. Rectangular churches are divided into the same sections from rear to front. Except in very simple small churches, at least one side of the Holy of Holies is always covered with paintings. In many churches all four sides, including the doors, are painted from floor to ceiling. There are many different styles of painting and the art still flourishes. The paintings are not merely ornamental and devotional. Paintings serve the very practical purpose of making it easier for the clergy to instruct their congregations in Biblical and church history. Individual icons are often displayed on a ledge around the Holy of Holies, though especially valuable ones, processional crosses, and hand-lettered parchment books and scrolls are usually kept inside this most sacred area, where none but priests may enter. The *tabot*, the altar tablet or sacred ark (it may be of stone or wood) in which the holiness of the church resides, is kept wrapped in expensive cloths in a wooden cabinet in the centre of the Holy of Holies. It is brought out and carried around the church on the head of a priest on ceremonial occasions. At *Timqat*, the Feast of the Baptism, it is taken to a stream or spring and kept beside it through the night. Ethiopians venerate many kinds of religious objects: icons, crosses, sacred books, saints' relics, but nothing ranks with the *tabot* in holiness or mystery. When its *tabot* is outside, the church loses its sanctity and then, only then, the layman or visitor may step into the *maqdas*. Unfortunately, as tourism has increased in recent years, wayward priests and gangs of thieves have sadly depleted the movable treasures of many remote churches and taken them to sell to dealers in Addis Ababa and Asmara, but I never heard of a *tabot* being stolen.

Rural Ethiopia has been called 'a haven of peace where priests are dancing before the ark and the courtesies of the ancient Orient continue to live'.[11] Churchyards are further havens of peace within the countryside itself. Churches are almost always enclosed in a walled compound with trees. After Sunday morning services, the people of the neighbourhood linger in the churchyard to drink coffee and exchange news. Priests, monks, nuns, and other people who serve the church and depend on its income sometimes live in huts along the walls or in stone gatehouses. Some church compounds shelter large numbers of mendicants. Churchyards are burial places. In older ones, open space is taken up by rock tombs and headstones. Many churches have sacred springs or pools (*tabal*) nearby. The water from these is used for sprinkling and drinking and is reputed to cure all sorts of illness from scrofula to infertility.

The principal service in an Ethiopian church is the Mass (*qeddasse*). It is normally celebrated on Sundays and patron saints' days, though in some churches Mass is said every day. It begins during the night and continues until after daybreak. Chanting, drumming, dancing, praying, marching with crosses and holy books, readings from the Gospels and saints' lives may all form parts of the service. Sermons may be delivered from the portico of the church to the congregation assembled in the yard. During a long service, people stand, sit, lie down, and even sleep. No special posture is required. No seats are provided except in a few modern churches and, now and then, in old churches where benches and supports made of tree limbs permit old monks and priests to rest during long services. Candles are held by worshippers. They are made of raw beeswax and exude a strong honey odour. Even more pronounced is the odour of incense which is burned in large amounts in all services. A frequently used church becomes permeated with its scent.

Some churches have vesper services. They are usually brief and consist mostly of singing. Funerals, weddings, and christenings are important occasions. Both in cities and in the country weddings involve not only religious services, but eating, drinking, music, and dancing. Children are christened during the first weeks of life and the parents give a feast for family, friends, and members of the congregation. A funeral usually attracts a long procession of mourners who accompany the deceased to the church and place of interment. Women wail, priests chant, riderless horses follow the coffin held high on the shoulders of pallbearers.

The high points of the church year are *Maskal* on 27 September, *Timqat* on 20 January, and Easter, which comes a week after European Easter. Christmas (*Genna*) has been receiving more attention in recent years, especially in the cities. The major saints' days are as important for particular churches dedicated to them as the great feasts. St Gabriel's Day (28 December) is celebrated at all Gabriel churches throughout the country, but the annual pilgrimage to Kulubi in Hararge on that day has become a major national event to which people come from all parts of Ethiopia.[12] All churches and monasteries have their special saints' and founders' anniversaries. In small country churches ceremonies are usually modest in size but impressive in the genuineness of the faith they reflect. Some remote churches associated with favourite saints or popular miracles attract enormous numbers of pilgrims. Piety is not confined to simple country folk. Well-dressed matrons and fashionable young ladies from Addis Ababa and Asmara, civil servants, and army officers will all be found at such observances. More exotic are the flocks of monks and nuns who travel around the country from one festival to another. Some who have taken vows of poverty or self-denial wear only leather or rags. Some walk with stones on their heads or chains on their legs. Some are passive and quiet, becoming exuberant only when the *tabot* comes out and the procession around the church begins. Other itinerant monks are revivalist preachers who harangue crowds of pilgrims to lead purer lives in endless sermons preached impromptu from steps or walls or from the top of tombs. The Ethiopian Church finds room to accommodate a wide spectrum of religious expression. Some holy men, in contrast to their ascetic brethren, dress in bright-coloured robes and flaunt their wellbeing. Beggars, lepers, and sellers of candles, sacred pictures, gilt parasols, and bags of holy earth add to the clutter and colour of major religious gatherings, both in the country and in the cities. Ceremonies get under way the evening before a feast-day. Travellers are almost always welcome on these occasions, but one learns not to wait until the appointed day to go. It is best to arrive the evening before and observe some of the night-time proceedings as well as the ceremonies which begin soon after sunrise and are usually completed well before noon.

The distinction between church and monastery in Ethiopia is often not readily apparent. Monasteries are not large buildings or highly organized complexes behind walls. The Ethiopian monastic tradition sprang from that of the Near East. Monastic communities began as small settlements of devout men or women in isolated places. The large Ethiopian monasteries now resemble sprawling villages with, sometimes, a few common facilities, such as kitchens and eating-halls. Most have several churches, some sacred caves and springs. Schools attached to monasteries are usually housed in simple huts and children are often instructed outside under trees. Many church sites attained the status of monastery (*gadam*) in earlier times, but have since declined to the point where only a few monks are attached to a single church. Some monastic communities are still populated almost entirely by hermits or semi-recluses (*bahtawi*) who dwell in caves in the side of gorges, living off wild foods or the charity of neighbouring peasants. Others, even though their style of life remains primitive, control great wealth in land and livestock. A monastery is headed by an abbot, *memhir*. The hierarchy of authority under the *memhir* may be loosely defined and varies from one place to another. In some monasteries, monks with autonomous status may have separate matters under their control, such as the manuscript library or relics of saints. Arranging to see such treasures may require diplomacy and more than one visit.

Ethiopian Orthodox priests, unlike monks, marry and produce large families. Enormous numbers of priests and monks are attached to some churches. There are also other categories of church personnel, non-ordained, who are as important as priests and monks in management of church affairs: *debteras*, who are lay specialists in song and dance, ritual, and tradition and sometimes also serve as scribes; and *diyakons* (deacons) who begin service as young boys, assist in all church activities, and eventually, if they remain committed to the church, become priests, monks, or *debteras*.

To observe Ethiopian life without some knowledge of the church is like trying to follow a conversation without knowledge of the language being spoken. How the Ethiopian Orthodox Church will eventually adapt to the processes of modernization that are steadily gaining momentum remains to be seen. For the present the church, though sometimes condemned as moribund by educated Ethiopians and foreigners alike, remains deeply embedded in the fabric of most Ethiopians' daily lives and patterns of thought. For the student of history and social evolution the Ethiopian Church has a broader significance as well. It is a survival of an aspect of human experience that has been superseded by evolution and change in most of the rest of what is still occasionally called the Christian world. Here one can go back in time a thousand years or more and experience something of what life must have been like in early Christian Ireland, medieval France, or Byzantium in its prime.[13]

On the Road

Most of the travel described in this book was done in a 6-cylinder, 10-seater 1969 landrover. It was equipped with full-length luggage rack and two jerricans for extra fuel. As I took longer trips to more distant points, I carried two spare tyres. Most 4-wheel drive vehicles will go anywhere the landrover will, but none is as comfortable. The landrover's aluminium body and its frame design give it a flexibility all the others lack. It is also the most widely used of all 4-wheel-drive vehicles in Ethiopia, so repairs and servicing are easier. To advocate a 4-wheel-drive vehicle for travel in Ethiopia is not to say that a good deal of travel cannot be done in any normal motor car. All the main roads and many of the tracks, in good weather, require no special power. One meets VWs and Fiats in very remote places.

Left to their own devices, rural Ethiopians seem content with rocky tracks which they seldom repair until they become totally impassable, but once a graded road is built or a highway paved, they flock to use it and seem oblivious to the fact that motor vehicles use it too. The main hazard of driving in Ethiopia is animal and human traffic on the roads – streams of people going to and from markets and herds of cattle and sheep, especially in the evening when they are being brought home by children from the day's grazing.

A car breakdown in the countryside can be costly in terms of time, but one seldom has to wait long for help, or at least company. There is an informal code of mutual assistance throughout the country. Motorists stop to aid vehicles in distress. The huge trucks that haul grain, cotton, hides, and timber are remarkably courteous and helpful to stranded vehicles. I have been pushed and pulled out of mudholes by them, taken to the nearest town to get a tyre repaired, offered gasoline. Carrying a reserve supply of gasoline is always a good idea, for in most parts of the country filling-stations are few and far between.

There are good hotels in Ethiopia, some of them in unlikely places. Some will be mentioned in the chapters which follow. Many places most worth visiting have no hotels worthy of the name. Camping is essential for travel in much of the country. Camp-sites[14] are easy to find and local people find nothing unusual about a group of *ferenjis*[15] setting up their tent in their fields, along their streams, or next to (but never in) their church grove. In fact, they usually enjoy the excitement the occasion provides. Now and then it is good to ask local advice about a camp-site, but not always wise to take it, for local officials may suggest a place in the middle of a village or in some other spot where hundreds of onlookers will gather and all pleasure of contact with nature will be spoiled. A good way to keep friendly but overly curious local people at a distance is to hire a local guard (*zabanya*) or two.

We had a roomy, lightweight tent and good sleeping-bags, but we always kept other gear lean: a simple cooking and eating kit, good lanterns, food-boxes. We always carried a jug of water because potable water is not always easy to find in Ethiopia. As we gained experience, we seldom used our gas camp-stove, but found it easier to get wood locally and add charcoal, which we carried in a box in the luggage-rack along with a few acacia logs to keep a camp-fire burning through the night. Insects, except for flies, are rare. Wild animals are seldom a danger if one takes a few sensible precautions. The delights of camping in Ethiopia far outweigh the discomforts or potential problems. There are the sunsets and the sunrises, the birds, the air, the sounds of the night, the occasions when local people come to sit around the fire and talk and one can learn about their way of life, their traditions, and daily problems and concerns ... But enough of generalities. *Ennehid! Wada guzoachin ennegeba!* Let us set about seeing Ethiopia!

NOTES

1 Seven years behind from September through December; eight years from January until September of any Gregorian year.
2 See below, pp. 112–14.
3 A useful book that is a bit too technical and too large in format to carry when travelling is W. E. Burger, *Families of Flowering Plants in Ethiopia*, Stillwater, Oklahoma, 1967.
4 In Eritrea and Tigre *wat* is called *zigani*.
5 Edward Ullendorff, *Ethiopia and the Bible*, London, 1968, 15–30.
6 The process of disengagement from the Egyptian Church was long and complex. It began during the Italian occupation, but was not fully consummated until Abuna Basileos was consecrated in 1959. It has been chronicled by Yolande Mara, *The Church of Ethiopia, a National Church in the Making*, Asmara, 1972.
7 The *Ichege*, head of the Monastery of Debra Libanos in Shoa, has since the fifteenth century been the pre-eminent native religious leader. Previously, the abbots of the Monastery of St Stephen in Lake Haik held this position. See below, pp. 48–51.
8 See below, pp. 51–8.
9 Cf. David Buxton, *The Abyssinians*, London/New York, 1970, 97–102; Georg Gerster, *Churches in Rock*, London, 1970, 71–8.
10 Gerster, *Churches*, 137–40.
11 Ullendorf, *Bible*, 2.
12 See below, pp. 204–12.
13 The best recent study of the Ethiopian Orthodox Church is Ephraim Isaac's 'Social Structure of the Ethiopian Church' in *EO*, no. 4, 1971, 240–88. The Ethiopian Orthodox Mission has recently broken new ground by issuing an English handbook, Aymro Wondmagegnehu and Joachim Motovu (eds), *The Ethiopian Orthodox Church*, Addis Ababa, 1970.
14 I use the word throughout this book in the elementary sense of a place to set up a tent, not the organized camp-ground with electricity and a dozen other amenities one finds throughout Europe and America.
15 The common Ethiopian word for foreigner derived, like so many similar words in Eastern languages, from Frank/French/Français. Its equivalent in Ethiopia in English is 'European' which as used in this book also encompasses all light *ferenjis* – Americans, Canadian, Latin American, Australian, Iranian, or Turkish, as well as inhabitants of continental Europe itself. Ethiopians are not agreed on whether other Africans should be called *ferenjis* and in popular usage, at least, they are not included in this category. What about Chinese, Japanese, and Koreans? They seem generally to be regarded as *ferenjis* and I have even heard them referred to as Europeans! The problem is even more difficult with American Negroes, for whom no entirely consistent terminology has developed.

2 North through Wollo

Along the Great Escarpment

Through Shoa to Wollo

Past the palatial grounds of the Russian and British embassies, the highway to Wollo – and to Assab and Asmara – leaves the capital's suburban fringes behind, crosses an eucalyptus-clad shoulder of Entoto, and proceeds north-eastward through pleasant plateau country towards Debra Berhan. This bustling country town has a wool factory, a teacher-training institute, and a large Saturday market. Beyond, the ascent of Mt Termaber provides a modest foretaste of the heights that have to be scaled farther north. During and after the rains, Termaber's high meadows display a wealth of alpine flowers. The ascent of Termaber is gradual; the descent to Debra Sina serpentine and precipitous. Three tunnels and an enormous switchback were built by the Italians who also set up a monument to commemorate their conquest of this mountain. Only the pedestal remains. It is a favourite gathering-point for the young boys of the area who sell for as little as E$1 apiece round, natural-colour goat-hair hats, which they weave as they watch their flocks.

Mt Termaber is a chunk of the Great Escarpment, the eastern edge of the main Ethiopian plateau. From here all the rest of the way to Dessie the road follows the lower edge of the escarpment, climbing up and down over several hilly ridges and descending to 1,500 m. as it passes through several tropical plains where large-scale agricultural development has begun in recent years and orchards of citrus, mangoes, and bananas thrive. Most of the low country is more desolate in appearance than the highlands, for much of the original acacia forest has been cut for wood and charcoal. The highway skirts several swampy areas close to the base of the escarpment with broad reed-beds and thick grass as well as some open water. These shelter large numbers of birds. To the west the escarpment is always visible and at times the road comes close in under it. Depending upon the time of day and the weather, the escarpment is blue, black, tan, or green, a jagged wall broken by chasms more than 1,000 m. deep with occasional peaks protruding well above the 2,800–3,000 m. average level.

The highlands above the escarpment include one of the most stubbornly traditional parts of the Amhara country, the Shoan sub-province of Manz, where cultivation and habitations extend up to 3,600 m. Manz is the homeland of the royal line which produced both Emperors Menelik II and Haile Selassie I.[1] The new road to Manz turns off the main highway on Mt Termaber before the first tunnel and the descent to Debra Sina. Only foot-trails lead up to the Manz plateau from the country farther north. North of Karakore the highway leaves Shoa and enters Wollo, remaining below the escarpment all the way to Kombolcha. The inhabitants of this lowland country include very few Amhara, who prefer to stay on their cool heights and leave the lowlands to Galla and Danakil. The hills along the edge of the lowlands all the way north through Wollo have always had a mixed population and many of the people who live here are still semi-nomadic. Most of them are Muslim. While the Amhara of Shoa are all Christian, there are Amhara in Wollo who have been Muslim for generations.

Kombolcha and Dessie

I developed a warm feeling for Kombolcha because it was always a special pleasure to arrive there after the long drive along the escarpment from either the north or the south and to know that the AGIP Motel would have good beds and good food. The motel is Italian-run and in all respects is a little bit of Italy. Noise is one of its most characteristic Italian features: loud music on the radio, trucks and cars arriving and departing all through the night at the service station outside, dogs barking, chickens cackling, people calling to each other. But in a jovial Italian atmosphere and after a good *brodo*, *francolino*, *salata di verdura*, *crema caramella*, good *vino rosso* and *espresso*, I always slept well and, on receiving the *conto* in the morning, there was the added comfort of finding that the stay had cost less than seemed likely. Kombolcha nestles in a wide, fertile valley between sharp mountains, outliers of the escarpment, on the west, and smaller hills to the east. The centre of the town is a three-way road junction marked by a three-sided obelisk in a traffic circle where the distances to Addis Ababa, Asmara, and Assab are inscribed: 377, 701, and 477 km. respectively. The Italians made serious efforts to develop industry in Kombolcha during their brief occupation and some of the buildings they put up still stand empty and half-destroyed. The airport which serves Dessie occupies part of the valley floor to the west of the town.

The 23 km. from Kombolcha to Dessie are indicated by a small, straight line on Ethiopian highway maps, a very schematic representation indeed. The first 3 km. are straight, it is true, but then the highway begins to climb the escarpment in a series of continual turns and switchbacks. Half-way up there is a ruined Italian fort. A brief stop here is rewarding for the views in all directions: over the valley back towards Kombolcha; along the edge of the escarpment towards the north; towards the first buildings of Dessie visible on the edge of the cliffs high above to the west. The Italians took great care to perfect this stretch of highway. Retaining walls were solidly built and the slopes above and below the road were carefully terraced. Ethiopian maintenance has capitalized on the Italian groundwork. The last few miles into Dessie are through one of those hanging valleys that occur in many places along the escarpment. After terrain that seemed to consist exclusively of chasms and precipices, the road winds along the edge of grassy meadows through thick groves of eucalyptus and, after a few more twists and curves, the southern portion of the capital of Wollo comes into view across a 300 m.-deep valley nearly filled with trees. This section of the

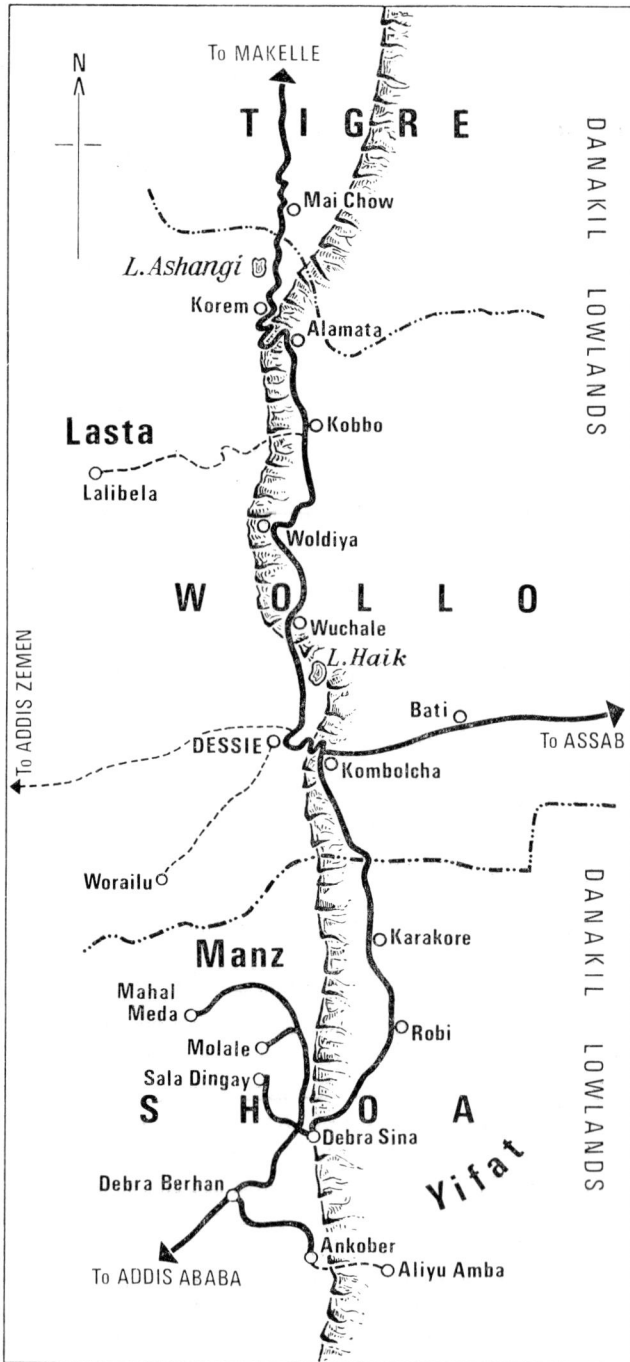

To MAKELLE

N

T I G R E

DANAKIL LOWLANDS

Mai Chow

L. Ashangi

Korem

Alamata

Kobbo

Lasta

Lalibela

Woldiya

W O L L O

Wuchale

L. Haik

Bati

To ADDIS ZEMEN

DESSIE

To ASSAB

Kombolcha

Worailu

DANAKIL LOWLANDS

Karakore

Manz

Mahal Meda

Robi

Molale

Sala Dingay

S H O A

Yifat

Debra Sina

Debra Berhan

Ankober

To ADDIS ABABA

Aliyu Amba

FIG. 4   The Imperial Road

city is built more vertically than horizontally. Houses cling to the western slope and look piled upon one another.

Dessie is a puzzling place. The name, which means 'My Joy' in Amharic, seems peculiarly inappropriate. I never learned who named it. Situated at 2,500 m. on top of the escarpment and clinging to the sides of several steep hills, the city consists of a jumble of buildings and rocky alleys that would seem to defy any effort to introduce order, for 50,000 people already live here and the population is said to be growing steadily. It is the fourth largest city in Ethiopia, but has none of the cosmopolitan flavour of Asmara and Diredawa and none of the international veneer of Addis Ababa. It is nevertheless bursting with life. I never passed through it when the streets were not crowded. Donkeys and horse-carts are more numerous than cars. Markets are busy most days of the week. The inhabitants include both Amhara and Galla. People point out the palace of Negus Mikael, last King of Wollo, on a prominent hilltop. There are several churches which are well attended on feast-days and whose precincts provide shelter for large complements of mendicants. Crown Prince Asfa Wossen was named Governor of Wollo, his mother's ancestral home, before the Italian invasion and retained that position after the Liberation. On our last trip there, in August 1972, Dessie was brightly decked out in bunting for the Crown Prince's annual summer visit and at the southern entrance to the city, where the Prince arrived after the drive up from the airport, a red ceremonial arch had been raised over the road with the inscription, '*Enquan dehna gebu, ye-Ityopya Berhan*' – '*Enter and Be Welcome, Light of Ethiopia*'.

The Market at Bati

Wollo is half highland and half lowland. Bati lies in the transition zone. The drive from Kombolcha takes less than an hour. It is best done in the rainy season when the air is humid but cool and the choppy hills are completely green. As the rainy season reaches its height, the fields of durra and maize, the major crops throughout this whole region below the escarpment, mature rapidly and their odour, especially if there has been rain the night before, perfumes the air. The cattle are sleek and water runs in all the streams. The great market at Bati assembles on Monday. People come to it from even greater distances than are customary in most of Ethiopia. On a Monday morning, parties on their way to market are seen 15–20 km. before Bati itself.

Bati is now a sizeable town, but it appears to have grown up only recently and probably owes its origin to its market which must antedate the town by at least 200 to 300 years. I have been unable to find references of very early travellers to Bati, which may have had a different name in earlier times, but in the eighteenth and nineteenth centuries it was famous, along with Aliyu Amba below Ankober, as one of the most important of the Ethiopian markets where products of the plateau were exchanged for goods brought in across the Danakil desert from the coast. In these markets highland Christians mingled freely with the Muslims and pagans of the lowlands, each respecting the other's status, though under most other circumstances they would have behaved as enemies towards each other. Market sites such as these were – and in many places in Ethiopia still are – completely deserted except on the particular day of the week when people come to trade. Little by little, permanent shops are erected, drinking-houses and inns are established, and a few people come to live permanently near the market area. Thus a village starts and a town develops. Bati must now have a normal population of perhaps 2,000. Having a main highway pass through it has assured its future. Aliyu Amba, in an analogous physical setting 250 km. to the south, has been less fortunate, for it can be reached only over animal- and foot-tracks. Its Friday market, still picturesque and worth a visit, attracts no more than a fifth of the people who come to Bati each week.

The Bati market gets under way relatively early. People from the low country want to be on their way home before the heat of the day reaches its height, so by 10 a.m. the greater share of those who come have already arrived. We reached Bati earlier, drove on through the town and down the steep curves of the highway to the east. Here from viewpoints commanding three switchbacks at a time we watched Danakil[2] come up the trails that parallel the highway in its straight stretches, but cut across the inner loop of the curves, climbing 45 degrees in places. They led both donkeys and camels in long lines. Men and women walked in separate groups. Danakil are all lean people.[3] They walk with grace and with an air of effortlessness. Men carried their rifles slung casually over their shoulders and each one had his broad, curve-bladed knife swinging from his belt. Some carried hides or other goods slung from yoke-sticks. Women had bundles on their backs containing goods or babies. It was difficult to tell which unless the bundles moved. Older Danakil children are usually left at home to tend the family flocks and seldom come to markets.

The market-place is on the south-eastern edge of Bati, though on Mondays the whole town is busy with market activity. A knoll rises above the market area on its south-eastern corner and provides a sweeping view of it. It is also, for some reason, the tethering area for camels. Hundreds can be seen there by mid-morning. Cattle are traded in this part of the market. They are often the great lyre-horned beasts popular in this region (Pl. 2a). Twelve to fifteen thousand people must come to Bati on market-day. By noon at least 10,000 can be seen in the market area at any one time. As at all Ethiopian markets, trading is a secondary activity for half the people who come. Relatives and friends meet and exchange news and everybody enjoys watching everybody else. For lowland Danakil and Galla who spend their days in the monotony of the semi-arid thornbush following their cattle and goats, sitting in the evening around their sparse camp-fires, sleeping at night in simple grass-and-twig huts, the weekly market represents the whole outer world. Women, most of them beautifully bare-breasted, display their elaborate silver necklaces and bracelets, their dangling, angling earrings, and their intricately braided hairdos (Pl. 3a). Equally striking are the hairdos of many of the Danakil men. They fluff out their hair and then trim it with great care and attention to symmetry to give it a helmet-like shape. Like their women, they butter it to make it glisten and hold its shape (Pl. 4).

Danakil catch the eye first at Bati, but all the other peoples of Wollo, which is one of the most ethnically mixed parts of Ethiopia, can be seen. There are highland Amhara in jodhpurs, their women in full flowing skirts with silver crosses around their necks and coloured headscarves. Amhara and Galla Muslim men often wear knitted skull-caps. Their women wear silver jewellery but, of course, no crosses. The jewellery of some of the Galla women is even more complex than that of the Danakil. Very black people are outnumbered at Bati by light, brown-skinned types. Many of the traders are Yemenis. Some are Tigreans.

Though every Monday market now attracts a few *ferenji* tourists, foreigners are rare at Bati and the local people are mostly indifferent to them. This is a tremendous advantage for the traveller compared to many Ethiopian markets where phalanxes of curious children and women follow his every turn and overly eager young men offer various kinds of help and advice that are not needed and even if needed can hardly be coped with in the turmoil and confusion that result from everyone trying to tell the visitor all at once what to see, buy, or photograph. At Bati we were able to wander unbothered. The prevailing mood of the people was friendliness tempered with shyness and reserve.

An enormous variety of things can be found for sale at Bati, with particular kinds of goods concentrated in separate areas of the market. Women bring in mats, men hides and saddlery. There is a section of salt-traders with piles of *amole* – rock-salt bars – stacked in front of them. Coffee and spices are sold in nearby sections and many small traders deal in both crushed rock salt and coffee. There are long rows of crude wooden stalls with roofs of branches at the western end of the market area. Soap, Chinese teacups, beads and trinkets, knives and pins and nails, flashlight batteries, small bottles of cheap cologne, all share display space with local products such as incense, wooden combs, and tooth-brushing sticks. The area is a kind of elementary Woolworth's. Cloth and simple, bright-coloured, ready-made clothing are now offered in quantity. Then there are alleys lined with sellers of spices, herbs, lentils, seeds, dried and fresh vegetables, medicinal items. Each trader has his wares set out around him. Onions, lemons, and peppers are sorted into small piles worth E10¢ or E25¢ each, though nothing is sold without haggling and bargaining over the quantity, quality, or price. The elaborate silver jewellery so much in evidence on the necks and arms of women at Bati can also be bought. Women who have ornaments to spare or who prefer a new dress to their extra jewellery sell to traders who, in turn, resell to others. One can get good buys by watching these dealings and striking a direct bargain with a lady who will not accept the price the dealer offers but is still eager to sell.

While my wife bargained for jewellery I bought several carved wooden stools and a grain-winnowing paddle made of tough hardwood and shaped like a well-designed shovel. It was difficult to leave this market, for the longer I wandered through it the more I found to engage my attention: great expanses of people and goods with panoramas of hill and valley stretching endlessly into the distance (Pl. 2b), donkeys braying, kites soaring overhead, the hum of ten thousand human beings chattering and moving about. While there was no feeling of prosperity about the Bati market, there was also no sense of poverty, by local standards, when I visited it in 1972. People looked well nourished and beggars were few.[4]

Haik Istifanos

At the northern edge of Dessie the old road past Magdala across the centre of the highlands to Debra Tabor and Lake Tana turns off to the left. During Italian times it was travellable by vehicle, but in the excitement of the Liberation the Ethiopians wrecked it and it has never been restored. One of these years it will have to be rebuilt, for there is no motorable route across the centre of the country between Addis Ababa and northern Tigre. The imperial highway leads on north along the edge of the escarpment through fertile, low-sided valleys with broad meadows and good stands of eucalyptus. At about 30 km., just beyond the small town of Haik,[5] the lake comes into view to the east. It is picturesquely situated, surrounded by distant mountains which descend as gentle hills to the large meadows along the shore. At first sight, because of the eucalyptus forests around Haik town, the countryside appears to be more lush than it is. This impression is enhanced in the rainy season when the landscape is clothed in new green growth. Actually this region, like most of the northern highlands, was deforested centuries ago and there are no stands of original forest near the lake. Views of the lake, as you approach it along the tracks that turn off at the village, are accented by twisted acacias and stands of candelabra euphorbia which bloom in both pink and yellow. Most of the land is cultivated and all that is not is grazed. In spite of centuries of use, the black volcanic soil is still thick and produces good harvests.

This is old Christian country. There are indications that Christian communities may have been established here by the ninth century.[6] The period between A.D. 600 and 1200 is the haziest in Ethiopian history and a formidable task for scholars to clarify. Much more may be learned about the early history of Haik as ancient manuscripts come to light and are studied. By the thirteenth century, Haik was a religious centre of importance. A monastic establishment on the mainland called Debra Egziabher (Mountain of God) was eventually overshadowed by the monastery dedicated to St Stephen (Istifanos) on the small island which lies off the northern shore of the lake. A fourteenth-century illustrated manuscript of the Gospels came to light here in the 1950s. It is now kept in the National Museum in Addis Ababa.[7]

Father Alvares visited Lake Haik in the early 1520s. Little has changed since that time:

> ... in the Kingdom of Amhara there is a great lake where we halted ... This lake has in the middle a small island on which is a monastery of St Stephen and many monks. This monastery has many lemons, oranges and citrons. They go to and from this monastery with a boat of reeds ... because they do not know how to build boats ... There are in the lake very large animals which they call in this country *gomaras*.[8] They say that they are sea horses. There is also a fish and it is very large. It has the ugliest head that could be described, formed like a large toad, and the skin on its head looks like the skin of a dogfish. The body is very smooth like the conger and it is the fattest and most savory fish that could be found in the world. This lake has large villages all around ... There are roundabout good lands of wheat and barley.[9]

On my first visit to Haik we had time only to drive down to the shore on the western side to a point where several old figs have survived among huge boulders. Local people water cattle and wash clothes here. The shore is reedy and there were large numbers of geese and ducks splashing in the water which is clear and fresh. A mile away we could see the monastery island and make out the roof of the round church among the trees at its highest point. It is as romantic a sight as any Ethiopia has to offer. When we came back with the express purpose of visiting the monastery, we found a landrover track which led to the crossing-point below a church of St George which sits on a small hillock a short distance up from the shore. A scattering of small trees stood in fields covered with wild marigold in bloom. This flower makes less of an impression on the eye than on the sense of smell. No one who crushes the flowers or leaves between his fingers could doubt that these quick-growing plants, which reach height of $1\frac{1}{2}$ m. in a few weeks once the rains set in, are original members of the marigold family.

The path to the lake-shore was well worn and there were many people about. Some were cleaning a catch of fish just brought in. They were black catfish, as ugly as Alvares described them, with a warty skin. The result of the cleaning process was to leave four long fillet strips of pinkish flesh dangling from the head, by which they were carried away, either on poles or by hand. Had we been camping at the lake-shore, instead of staying in the motel in Kombolcha, we would have bought some and grilled them over an open fire, for they looked as if they would make delicious eating. As we talked to the fishermen, two reed-rafts brought in passengers from the monastery island. The rafts, mere bundles of stiff reeds, were poled through the channel that leads 200 m. to the island. The passengers stood erect, as did the boatman who propelled the flimsy craft with a long pole (Pl. 5b).

When that pious missionary Krapf visited Lake Haik in 1842, he too crossed on one of these rafts and reported that the channel became very deep just before the landing on the island.[10] In those days rafts did not move on Saturdays or

Sundays. That has changed. Traffic on a Sunday afternoon was brisk. A wide stretch of reed-beds extends between the island and the shore. The crossing, an open channel about 6 m. wide, is protected by the reeds even if the lake is stormy. A stone track has been laid on the bottom of the channel which is no more than 1½ m. at its deepest, and we saw a couple of men walk through it carrying their clothes on their heads. Only males may set foot on the island, we were warned, and my two long-haired sons were scrutinized carefully before they were allowed to step on to a raft. They were poled, but the young fellow who took me jumped into the water and pushed the raft ahead of him. Stepping on to the island, I was greeted by a bald, white-bearded, spry old monk who chattered at great length in response to every question asked him. Soon a portly Amhara gentleman with almost Oriental features and a small retinue came strolling down the path from the centre of the island and introduced himself as Ato Gebre Hanna. He lived in Haik town, he said, and owned all the land around the lake. He had been paying a Sunday visit to the church. The old monk said there were about thirty of his brethren resident on the island. Except for a grassy area near the landing-site, strewn with large volcanic boulders, it was all cultivated, planted to maize, durra, *ensete*, grains, legumes, and garden crops. For terrain so well cultivated there was still a surprising number of trees, including two clusters of tall palms along the southern shore. Several trails lead from the landing-site. We took the one that went directly uphill to the church.

The present church is new and sturdily built of stone, roofed with tin. The windows even have screens, something I had seen nowhere else in the Ethiopian countryside. Sunday afternoon is not a good time to visit an Ethiopian church, however. After all-night sabbath services, priests are often sleeping. Here the priest who had the key had gone off somewhere visiting and there was no one who could let us in. There were not many paintings inside it anyway, we were told by the monk in charge of the *eqabet*, the church's treasure-house. This too was a new building, made of wattle and daub and roofed with tin. Inside there were drums and staffs and shelves held vestments, piles of coloured umbrellas, *sistra*, censers, and about three dozen manuscript volumes, most of them in leather cases. We did not have time to examine many, but few looked anything like as old as the monastery itself is reputed to be. The keeper was especially proud of two large canvas portraits of St Stephen and of a large, generously illustrated eighteenth- or nineteenth-century *Dawit* (Book of Psalms). He had deacons carry it under a fig-tree in the yard for us to photograph some of its paintings. He then took us to see the church's bells, a cast European type hanging on a wooden frame above a traditional stone bell, a metre length of columnar basalt.

After visiting the *bet-lehem*, where young men were building a fire under a big pottery griddle to bake *injera*, we walked through gardens and orchards and stopped for a while to watch a group of men putting new thatch on a house. Back at the shore, we had to wait for rafts to come over to take us back. Feeling more comfortable standing on the flimsy structure while being poled back, I could see that its primitive form had a logic of its own. Being loosely tied together, the reeds give way as the passenger shifts to maintain balance, but the rest of the raft is not affected at all. If it were more tightly bound together, it would be taut and the slightest movement on one end would be felt at the other.

Lalibela

South of Kobbo a bright yellow road-sign points to Lalibela and a track turns off the main highway to the left and leads straight towards the escarpment. The drive to the 'Eighth Wonder of the World' 120 km. away to the west in the sub-province of Lasta looks easy at the start. It is not. In fact, it was barely possible at all during the years I was in Ethiopia. The only reliable way of getting to Lalibela was by air. I regretted this because I like to approach a historic place overland to get a feel for its geographic context. Eight or nine months of the year, October to June, the dependable DC3s of EAL fly in every day. If you come in from the north, over the districts of Wag and Lasta, the plane flies in valleys below the level of the surrounding mountains on both sides! From the south the flight is only slightly less spectacular, for the usual route out of Addis is over Fiche and then up the main gorge of the Blue Nile where it forms the boundary between Gojjam and Amhara Saynt, the tenaciously Christian south-western corner of Wollo. The plane flies so low over some of the *ambas* that you can look right down into the farmyards and distinguish men and women on trails to their fields. So, in spite of the speed at which you swoop over it, you do get some feel for the landscape flying to Lalibela. The gravel airfield lies at 2,000 m. in the largest piece of flat valley bottom that appears to exist in this whole region. You travel by landrover to the town itself, 17 km. away, over a gravel track through raw, over-grazed, deforested hills, climbing most of the time. After the rains this landscape becomes a garden of orange and golden-yellow aloes. The town, at 2,600 m., seems low against the backdrop of Mt Abuna Yosef, nearly 4,500 m., but it has a commanding position, sprawling along the broken crest of a volcanic ridge which falls off into deep valleys on three sides.

Originally known by other names, Roha and Adefa, this town was one of the principal seats of the Zagwe dynasty which ruled much of the northern plateau in the twelfth and thirteenth centuries. The Zagwe rulers[11] were not Solomonic and appear to have been of Agau origin.[12] This may explain, by the dialectic process which often seems to operate in history, why they were so devout in their profession of Christian belief. According to tradition, the monolithic churches of Lalibela were carved at the order of King Lalibela, believed to have been the fifth Zagwe ruler, at the beginning of the thirteenth century. As a child, Lalibela, who was later made a saint of the Ethiopian Church and whose name was applied to the site in place of those previously used, was so pious and humble that prophecies were made that he would one day ascend the throne in place of his brother who had already become king. The jealous brother gave him a cup of poison which put him into a coma for three days. An angel appeared to Lalibela and commanded him, when he awoke, to cause to be built on earth churches such as had been revealed to him as existing in the Kingdom of Heaven. Later Lalibela lived in the wilderness and flew with an angel to Jerusalem where Christ showed him the Holy City. Thus his resolution to create new monuments to the Christian religion was reinforced. In time his piety triumphed. His brother was ordered by Christ in a vision to abdicate. Once on the throne, Lalibela carried out his order from God with the help of angels who laboured beside mortal workmen during the day, then continued by themselves through the night, finishing the monumental labour of hewing out all eleven churches in twenty-three years. Thus a new Jerusalem arose in the inaccessible mountains of Lasta beside the River Jordan, the name given to one of the streams in the valley below the town.

Some scholars have speculated that the creation of Lalibela was an attempt to establish a goal of pilgrimage in place of Palestine, which was no longer attainable by Ethiopians because it had been captured by the Saracens. There are many other theories about most aspects of this extraordinary site, but almost no hard facts. A tremendous amount of pious dedication was required as well as mobilization and management of a large labour force. The possibility that Indian stoneworkers may have been in part responsible for cutting the churches has been advanced. European craftsmen have also been suggested. Syrians or Greeks from Asia Minor seem more probable because of the old tradition of monolithic churches in that part of the world and churches and monasteries were still being excavated and decorated in Cappadocia about the time those in Lalibela are said to have been made. Whatever the degree of outside inspiration and assistance involved (and there need not have been much, for the tradition of rock sanctuaries in Ethiopia goes back to the earliest beginnings of Christianity and perhaps before), there is a great deal about the Lalibela churches that is distinctly Ethiopian in architectural style, ornamentation, and basic concept and almost nothing that seems outside of Ethiopian traditions.[13]

It has been estimated that the amount of stone removed in excavating the Lalibela churches equalled at least five times the quantity taken out in the carving of the great Egyptian temple at Abu Simbel. The symmetry of the churches is nearly perfect and there is no evidence of over-carving and compensation for errors in any part of the ornamentation, something that could not have been hidden when the medium was tough volcanic rock. But the most puzzling thing about these churches to me has always been the problem of light. The interiors are cleanly carved and some are ornamented, but they have only small doors and windows. How was such precise work done with only smoking torches or lamps? Something close to superhuman piety, devotion, and patience would seem to have been required.

Through the centuries, Lalibela's churches, even though carved out of living rock, suffered decay and makeshift repairs marred the overall architectural impression. In the mid-1960s an international group embarked on a serious project to restore damage and to forestall deterioration through protective measures.[14] This work was tastefully and efficiently done and, though the whole scheme has not yet been carried out, a large amount of clearing of rock-cut tunnels and drainage ditches has made the churches more accessible and shed new light on the original plan of the site and methods of construction used. This work has also given support to the belief that some of the structures may originally have been used as governing buildings and royal residences and later converted to churches.

Once started, one can go on writing about Lalibela almost endlessly. The uncertainties about the place inspire speculation. It may be better to follow the example of the first European visitor to describe these churches, Fr Alvares, who after compiling eight pages on them declared:

I weary of writing more about these buildings because it seems to me that I shall not be believed if I wrote more and because regarding what I have already written they may blame me for untruth; therefore I swear by God, in Whose power I am, that all that I have written is the truth to which nothing has been added, and there is much more than what I have written, and I have left it that they may not tax me with its being falsehood, so great was my desire to make known this splendour to the world and because no other Portuguese went to these buildings except myself, and I went twice to see and describe them because of what I had heard said about them.[15]

So I will speculate no more but will describe highlights of a single visit, my second, lasting a little more than 24 hours on a Saturday and Sunday in mid-October 1971.

Arriving by air in mid-morning, we were driven up to the Seven Olives Hotel, modest, expensive, and the only place to stay in Lalibela. We deposited our baggage and walked down through the busy village past colourful medieval scenes (Pl. 6b) to the market which takes place every Saturday at the south-western end of the town on a triangular-shaped, flat area that falls off on its two outer sides into deep valleys. This market is devoid of the influence of the modern economy. There is no way that traders who buy up produce wholesale could bring goods into or out of this region, with no practical roads connecting to main highways. The five thousand-odd people assembled here were of distinctly different facial type from the people one would see at a central or southern Ethiopian market – more longer, angular faces, more wavy hair, larger noses and more prominent ears, less dark skin. Some of the women had intricately braided hair, but most of them had practically all their hair cut off, an unattractive practice common in the northern Amhara highlands. Fewer women had bright headscarves and print dresses than at more southerly markets. Most were dressed in grey, weathered, smoke-permeated cotton homespun and some men wore locally woven material too, though many had manufactured trousers, shirts, and jackets. Men get 'modern' clothes first in a traditional area such as this, as do the teenage boys. Women and girls come later and the younger children get only shabby rags until they have survived long enough to be worth spending money on for clothes. There was a whole section of the market devoted to the salt trade, which is obviously very important here, and another section for honey, brought in in clay pots and leather buckets. We saw large quantities of grain, pulses, and small vegetables, but there was little trading going on in them. Unusual was the large amount of locally tanned leather for sale. Some hides were finished so as to have the quality of parchment. There was a brisk trade in animals, butter, and oil and scrappy firewood. There was no pottery of consequence. Much *gesho* was being offered, but there was no *talla* for sale at the market itself. *Tejbets* lining the route down to the market were doing good business.

We also had time during the morning for a first visit to the Second Group of churches: Bet Gabriel-Rafael, Bet Lehem, Bet Amanuel, Bet Marqorewos, and the Church of Abba Libanos. We approached them through the tunnel system which connects, drains, and in some ways isolates and protects these churches. There were no other visitors, hardly any priests; a few boys tagged along. The churches were all locked, but we had extraordinary views of them through openings in the tunnels. The morning sun was especially good on the regular, rose-coloured walls of Bet Amanuel, which stands in a deep pit. It is the best example of pure Axumite style at Lalibela (Pl. 6a). We admired it from below and then climbed through tunnels and past burial cells to the hillside above where we rested among the wild olives and enjoyed the panorama over the roof of Bet Amanuel and across hills covered with ripening grain to the blue-green slopes of Abuna Yosef.

After a meagre lunch at the Seven Olives, we retraced part of our earlier route through the village and turned down to the First Group of churches. Here we had confirmed what we already suspected: a little tourism can cause considerable confusion. Lalibela has been organized for visitors, up to a point. Shoes do not have to be taken off on entering the churches (absolutely required at practically all other churches in Ethiopia) and the churches are kept open in the afternoon for visitors. Purchase of a single *karne* entitles the visitor to see all of them. But none of the priests wanted to let only two of us in . . . They expected us to wait for the big afternoon tour group. It became a contest – we were determined to avoid tagging along with a large party and wanted to examine and enjoy the churches at our own pace. The priests found this difficult to understand, so at each church we had the same discussion over again. We succeeded in crossing paths with the big tour party only twice, but they overtook us at the First Group and we had to go back and start again at the Second. Nevertheless, it was a thoroughly enjoyable afternoon with bright sun, warm air, and the varied effects of light and shadow on the rich red stone. We found the inside of Bet Amanuel disappointing in comparison to its exterior and the inside of Abba Libanos likewise, but the outside of this smallish church, with its classic façade emerging from under an overhanging cliff, catches the afternoon sunlight beautifully. We liked its small cruciform windows, each in a perfect Axumite frame. Icons and books were on display at Bet Gabriel-Rafael, but the most exciting thing about this church, the highest in the Second Group, is the entrance to it across a shaky wooden bridge over a deep pit.

On the way between Abba Libanos and Gabriel-Rafael we stopped to visit a couple of local houses. Their mistresses were happy to have us enter and look around. These two-storey stone houses, perfectly round, are well designed inside. The stairway to the second floor goes up the outside wall, sheltered by the overhanging thatched, conical roof, and the lower story is often built into the slope of a hillside (Pl. 6b). The lower room in most seemed to be divided into two parts used for cooking and storage. The upper storey is the main living area. One upper storey which we visited had windows on three sides and a small alcove on the windowless side. A heavy crossbeam extended over the middle of the room above head level and the centrepole came down from the mid-point of the roof and rested on this beam, leaving the room free of the centre pillar common to most Ethiopian round houses. All the houses we visited (by the end of the day we had gone into at least half a dozen) were comparatively well furnished with wooden beds with crisscrossed leather strips, chairs, stools, many baskets, *mesobs*, pots, and all kinds of things hanging from wooden pegs on the walls. In many yards weaving was being done by men. The women do spinning and many twirled cotton spindles as they walked about, watched children, or gossiped with neighbours. Children ran after us in droves as we walked down alleyways from house to house, but the rest of the inhabitants seemed to take tourists for granted. Tourism seems to have almost no impact on the way of life that still prevails here.

It was past mid-afternoon by the time we got back to the First Group of churches again. It also consists of five churches: Bet Medhane Alem, Bet Maryam, Bet Maskal, Bet Dengel, and Bet Golgotha-Mikael. These churches form a more unified grouping than the Second Group. Bet Medhane Alem (Church of the Saviour of the World) is an immense structure resembling a Greek temple except that the solid columns which surround it are all square. Twenty-eight similar columns support the roof inside. A high living-rock wall with a narrow passage-way through it separates Bet Medhane Alem from Bet Maryam. This church has the most interesting interior of all those at Lalibela. Inside, ornamental stone carving is painted in rich earth colours. A central pillar is said to contain the history of the world, past and future – but it is always shrouded in cloth and no mortal is allowed to look beneath it (Pl. 8). In Bet Golgotha-Mikael we saw what was said to be the tomb of King Lalibela himself, draped in new, garish pink brocade. There was a well-preserved old manuscript on display there and I took time to examine the painted bas-reliefs of SS George and Quercus and five other unnamed companion saints. Outside we looked up at the silhouettes of old cedars on the edge of the pit in which the church rests. Nearby the tomb of Adam was pointed out to us – a short, thick, rectangular pillar of stone. The afternoon was wearing on. All the tourists from the big party had gone back to the hotel. Only a few individualists continued to wander through the churchyards and tunnels leading from one to another and down to the Jordan River where a thick cross standing in its bed signifies the holiness of the stream.

We saved the eleventh and most appealing of all the Lalibela churches until the end of the day. Shaped like a symmetrical Greek cross rising up from the bowels of the earth, Bet Giyorgis occupies a deep pit on a hillside with a small grove of old cedars and scattered wild olives forming a park-like setting. The double cross which is carved into the gently sloping roof is situated so that both the rising and setting sun accentuates its outlines (Pl. 7b). We descended into the pit through deep cuts in the rock, but found that the priests had already left for the day and the church was locked. But the whole setting was so attractive in the declining light that it mattered little that we could not go inside. We walked slowly around the edge of the pit and watched daylight fade on this unique architectural gem. I had arranged with local boys to bring down mules for the return trip to the hotel (uphill all the way) and we found them waiting for us as we crossed the narrow wooden bridge that leads out of the precincts of the church. On our mules we caused much amusement among the townspeople as we rode back through the main thoroughfare which leads up from the market-place where traders had just bundled up their remaining wares. Side-streets were crowded with merry fellows who had spent the afternoon drinking *talla* and *tej*. We stopped to bargain with boys selling old silver crosses. At the gate to the hotel compound local hawkers had a good supply of crosses as well as prayer scrolls and manuscript holy books. Gradually the ancient religious treasures of this whole northern highland region must be finding their way to Lalibela to be sold to tourists. The traffic is unregulated and, along with many mediocre items, some uniquely valuable ones are disappearing in this way. There is need for a handicraft industry here to cater to tourists.

Enjoying a drink on the hotel terrace in the rapidly cooling evening air, we watched the final tones of the sunset fade in the west. In the foreground the cooking-fires of the town, visible through open doors, dotted the landscape on all sides. The noises of people talking and shouting to each other, of children bringing in animals, of donkeys braying and dogs barking combined into a kind of evening symphony. After dinner, when we looked out over this same scene, we saw the light of a few fires, but the town was absolutely still. Dinner had been sparse, in keeping with the tradition of the Seven Olives, in spite of its French manageress. I knew it would be from a previous visit and came prepared with a bag of cheese, crackers, wine, and chocolate. After dinner a male *masenko* player and a woman who danced and sang entertained us in the hotel's round dining-room. The hotel's electricity is turned off at 10 (it is the only electricity in Lalibela and, for that matter, in all of western Wollo), so there was no alternative to going to bed in good time – and advisable besides because we had resolved to get up early and attend morning services in as many of the churches as possible. Hyenas were the only sound of the night.

The sky began to lighten about 5.30, though the sun did not appear from behind the high mountains east of Lalibela until nearly two hours later. We were on our way to the churches shortly after 6. They were in operation just as they have been since the thirteenth century. We were the only *ferenjis* present in any of them. Most had sizeable congregations in attendance with a large proportion of priests, monks, and nuns. We heard singing welling up from inside Medhane Alem as we came down the hill, so we went inside it first and were rewarded by an impressive service. Candles burned in tall candelabra at the front. There was good singing, some in parts, and attendants waved censers which poured out thick blue smoke. It filled the whole upper half of the church and flowed out of the windows. There was reading of scripture from large hand-written books and then a short sermon delivered with great persuasiveness by a young priest. A dozen or more priests were involved in the service in various ways. Three brought out a huge processional cross and marched through the congregation with it – the faithful bowed and crossed themselves on, beholding it. We stayed for more than half an hour. Worshippers kept coming in and many, especially women, gave evidence of great devotion and piety, kneeling to kiss the stone floor, walking over to embrace and kiss the great stone pillars which divide the interior of this huge rock structure into four aisles. Medhane Alem is over 30 m. long. As light of the day filtered down more strongly from the high windows, a curious combination of geometric patterns formed in the smoky air inside the church and the front wall was not visible from the entrance at the rear. When we had first entered this church, we had, in effect, descended back into the night. By the time we left, day had dawned inside Medhane Alem too.

Bet Maryam is said to be the favourite church of the clergy at Lalibela. It was the most crowded this Sunday morning and a great volume of sound poured out of it as we entered. Here, as everywhere we went later, priests, monks, and members of the congregation received us courteously, helped us find a good position from which to watch the service, and seemed genuinely honoured that we had joined them. We had only looked into the two smaller churches of the First Group the day before: Bet Maskal and Bet Dengel. Now they were filled with people and with candlelight and icons. Manuscripts were on display. Some of the best singing we heard at Lalibela echoed from their cavelike recesses. Golgotha-Mikael also had an energetic service in progress. But we did not want to miss services at the Second Group, so we hurried there and stopped at each church briefly.

Again we saved Giyorgis until last, arriving about 8.15. The service was still in full swing. The sun was up now, touching the uppermost portions of the church and gilding with its early light the rows of white-robed figures who stood along the rim of the pit, looking down at the church. All those people – and many others gathered in groups among the olives and standing around the frame which supports the church's stone bell – were clearly in attendance at the service just as if they had been inside the church The song emanating from the church was the best we heard this morning – strong, articulate, all in unison. It was magnified by reflecting against the walls of the pit as it rose. From the windows, located very high in the structure, the smoke of incense rose in steady streams, as if the church were on fire inside. We went down. The pit is so deep that the contrast of the shadow of its depths with the sunlight on the upper third of the church and on the figures on the rim above made it seem that we were again returning to night, even though it was now nearly 8.30. We had the opportunity we had missed the evening before to see the inside of this church. Because of the large doorway, and also because the ceiling is so high, Giyorgis gives the impression of being light and spacious, quite unlike the other Lalibela churches.

When we came back up again, the full light of the sun was bathing the landscape. The smoke of cooking-fires was rising from houses in the town. Ripening grain was swaying in the breeze in fields on the hills outside the built-up area. People walking on paths leading back to the town were throwing off their *shammas* as the air warmed. By the time we walked back to the hotel, the town was coming to life. The streets were filling with women and girls carrying water-pots, men were gathering in groups to talk, and dogs were scurrying around. Another day had begun at New Jerusalem with God glorified in all of His rock churches. It was the sixth of Teqemt of the Ethiopian year 1964 . . . and except for ourselves watching this lively medieval scene as the sounds of religious singing still floated up from the church area on the slopes below the town, the whole atmosphere was probably closer to the sixth of Teqemt 1264 than it was to the realities of the modern world of the seventeenth of October 1971 . . .

The Imperial Road

For those whose first consciousness of Ethiopia dates from the 1930s when the Italian invasion made the world aware of this isolated country, the route north through Wollo to Tigre evokes exciting memories. The names of the towns and other geographic features – Wuchale, Korem, Woldiya, Mai Chow, Amba Alagi, Lake Ashangi, Amba Aradam – recall correspondents' accounts of the fierce but futile resistance the proud Ethiopians put up against the unprincipled European invaders. As Haile Selassie's armies retreated, they gave the Italians more punishment than they expected and were routed only because their resolution to defend their homeland was broken by artillery, air bombardment, and the indiscriminate use of poison gas.[16] All these same places were back in the news dispatches again, though more briefly, in 1941 when the Italians retreated along this same route before British Commonwealth and Ethiopian forces who came up from the south as well as down from the north. The Italians made their last stand on Amba Alagi where they surrendered on 20 May 1941.[17]

To a greater extent then than now, this Imperial Road was the jugular vein of Ethiopia. It was not a very good road when the Italians invaded. They rebuilt much of it during their occupation and thus facilitated their defeat. The section from Dessie to Makelle remains one of the most spectacular highways in the world. Grades are reasonable and curves and switchbacks are well designed, but this road simply cannot be taken at great speed. Besides, the scenery is so breathtaking that only a mind blind to the thrill of monumental landscapes could want to travel quickly over it. No matter how early we departed from Kombolcha and Dessie to have plenty of time for this route, we found it impossible to get to Makelle before dark. The distance from Kombolcha to Makelle is 408 km.

After Haik the highway hugs the escarpment for nearly 100 km. to Woldiya. There are no extreme grades, only moderate curves, climbs, and descents, compared to what is to come later. The land is almost all cultivated. In the rainy season fields are green with maize and durra, *teff* and wheat in higher locations. In the dry season the predominant colours are tan, yellow, and brown. Wuchale is the most attractive town along this part of the route. It is the place where what is referred to in histories as the Treaty of Uccialli was signed between Menelik II and the Italians in 1889. The Italians later maintained that the treaty gave them a protectorate over Ethiopia until Menelik and his lieutenants corrected the illusion at Adowa in 1896.

Beyond Wuchale the road climbs up and down along the escarpment past several small villages almost obscured by stately old candelabra euphorbia. Urgessa and Mersa are busy roadside towns. Lowland Galla and Danakil begin to be seen here. Some of the men wear bushy shaped hairdos. Woldiya is a large town in a deep valley with a main street lined with hotels, bars, shops, and service stations. Beyond, the highway passes through a narrow defile and comes out on to the Kobbo Plain. Here the land is all cultivated and the soil is dark and thick. The people are mostly Raya Galla. The region is so warm that flimsy huts of reeds and stalks suffice for shelter. The villages look like temporary encampments and Kobbo itself, except for a few tin-roofed structures fronting the highway, looks even more like an overgrown village than most Ethiopian roadside towns. Large herds of broad-horned cattle are kept by the people of this area. At the end of the dry season, when the meandering stream in the centre of the plain offered the only convenient water, the road was blocked for miles as herds passed each other going to and from watering. There is a 20 km. stretch of absolutely straight highway before Alamata, which sits at the foot of the escarpment with gardens of citrus, banana, and papaya on its outskirts.

From the middle of Alamata, busy with trucks, buses, and boys selling fruit, it is difficult to guess where the highway is going to go next because ahead you see only the escarpment wall looming up 1,200–1,500 m. There is a cleft in it, you find, and the highway proceeds up its floor for 2–3 km. and then begins the single most spectacular road ascent that exists in Ethiopia. For nearly 10 km. the superbly constructed highway snakes and twists upward. The drive up is slow but not arduous because the curves are regular, well banked, and there is enough room to meet and pass easily vehicles coming from the opposite direction. What is most surprising as you rise higher and get a better view of the opposite side of the cleft is the realization that the mountain walls which fall off at angles as steep as 60 degrees are all cultivated. This must result from the fact that until a few decades ago the rich plain below was considered uninhabitable because of malaria and the hostility of the Galla, so the Semitic highlanders, under heavy population pressure, brought all the land on which they could physically stand under cultivation. A church perches in an inaccessible spot near the point where the rear of the cleft merges into the escarpment. When it begins to seem that the road will never stop rising, it emerges into a shelf valley and soon reaches Korem, a pleasant little town. A few kilometres farther it descends again and Lake Ashangi comes into view to the north-west.

Lake Ashangi is rather small, but the sight of any sizeable body of water after so many mountains and chasms, cliffs, gorges, and narrow river valleys is such a contrast that it seems large. The lake has a wild setting, unlike any other in Ethiopia, among mountains that look as if they had been formed vertically and then tipped over at a 45-degree angle. The mountains show little trace of vegetation at any time of the year, but during the rainy season the plain at the northern end of the lake is a smooth expanse of soft green lawn and a gathering-place for large herds of domestic animals. Near the shore on the eastern side, where the road passes through low hills with good views over the lake, Galla *tukuls* nestle among twisted acacias and clumps of candelabra euphorbia.

This region saw some of the most miserable fighting of the Italian invasion. In March 1936 Haile Selassie decided to rally his *rases* and make a last-ditch effort to halt the Italian advance in the country between Mai Chow and Korem. The Ethiopians had by this time been badly demoralized by bombing, gassing, and their own disorganization, but they made a brave effort to block the Italians. It was all over by early April and they fell back in disorder. Konovaloff, the White Russian colonel who fought with them, described the scenes of the retreat past Lake Ashangi:

The wide valley . . . lay level under the blazing African sun. To its side the blue surface of the lake was lightly ruffled by the breeze. Along the road the weary people dragged themselves, scattering for a moment in panic or massing together in groups. Four, six, eight bombs burst one after the other. They fell some distance from the road and hit nobody . . . Here is another aeroplane which seems to be choosing its victims as it flies just over their heads. One explosion . . . then another which raises a jet of earth clods, sand and stones. People are hit this time. Everything . . . disperses. I turn around and see someone dying on the ground. A form that slightly moves. Fear pushes the survivors upon their road without attending to the wretch that cannot follow them, for he has lost his legs. At the same moment our allies the Azebu Galla fire on us from the hilltops where their village lies. When they see stragglers, they kill them and strip the bleeding bodies of rifles, cartridges and clothes . . . Before us there is a corner of hell which none of us can avoid. On one side of the road is the lake, on the other are the mountains. The pass is narrow and the human flood finds it hard to press forward and through . . . At last we are near the caves of Korem which will shelter us from the Azebu bullets and the aeroplanes.[18]

Women carrying firewood in bundles on their backs, herds of cattle crossing the road to the lakeside meadows, or groups of loaded donkeys being switched along by men are the only challenges this peaceful route now offers to travellers.

Mai Chow[19] is the first town in Tigre. It sits in a broad, deep valley. The landscape is more gaunt now, more arid. It is a foretaste of the main Tigrean plateau. Beyond Mai Chow the road winds upwards again over Amba Alagi. This terrain must have reminded the Italians of their native Dolomites. There are two more high ridge-crests and two more deep valleys to cross before you finally come down to relatively flat plateau country. Bright red aloes make striking patches of vivid colour against the grey rocks and tan stubble-fields in January and February. Round churches are still frequent here, some of them in awesomely isolated locations. Most have groves of old cedars, some olives, and in a few steep and unreachable declivities in these mountains small forests of cedars survive.

After the final descent to the 2,400 m. plateau, several basic changes are apparent. Trees are almost absent. There are no more round, thatched houses. Villages are compact and of stone. The houses are square or rectangular and have flat roofs, usually of beaten earth. The language, though closely related to Amharic, has a completely different sound. Tigrinya is reminiscent of classical Arabic in its rhythms. The feel of the landscape and the effect of human beings upon it is that of the Middle East. But it is a pre-Islamic Middle Eastern atmosphere. There are Muslims in Tigre, but they have had little to do with the basic pattern of life in the province. Tigre is both the cradle of Ethiopian civilization and of Ethiopian Christianity, the old heartland.

NOTES

1 Life in Manz is described perceptively in Donald Levine, *Wax and Gold*, Chicago, 1965.
2 These people (sing. Dankali), also known as Afar or Adal, speak a Cushitic language and occupy the hottest, driest parts of the lowlands from southern Eritrea to the environs of Harar. They are noted for their fierceness and stubborn adherence to nomadic ways. No thorough study of them has ever been done and some idea of the amount of conflicting information even some of the better sources provide on them can be obtained by comparing, e.g., Ullendorff, *The Ethiopians*, London, 1965, 40–1, and the U.S. Department of Defense *Area Handbook for Ethiopia*, USGPO, Washington, 1971, 94–5.
3 With the exception of one of their highest-ranking traditional leaders, Ali-Mirah Hanfere, the Sultan of Aussa, who weighs nearly 150 kg.
4 Failure of rains the following year caused famine in this area which eventually attracted international attention and was alleviated in part by relief efforts in which many countries participated. It is to be hoped that better planning and organization will make it possible for the Ethiopian government to cope with such emergencies in the future.

5 In addition to being the name of this specific lake, *haik* in Amharic is the generic term for lake.

6 Taddesse Tamrat, 'The Abbots of Däbrä Hayq', *JES*, January 1970, 87–117.

7 Five illustrations from it are reproduced in *Ethiopia, Illuminated Manuscripts*, published by the New York Graphic Society by arrangement with UNESCO, 1961.

8 Amh. *gumare*, hippopotamus. There are no hippopotami in the lake now and it seems questionable if there would ever have been, for these animals occur in Ethiopia only in the Nile and Rift Valley river-lake systems. Alvares may have been inadvertently transferring information he had obtained on hippopotami in other Ethiopian lakes.

9 Alvares, *Prester John*, 249–50.

10 *Journals of the Rev. Messrs. Isenberg & Krapf*, London, 1843, 403–18.

11 Tadesse Tamrat, *Church and State in Ethiopia, 1270–1527*, Oxford, 1972, 53–68, offers as good a summary of the murky history of the Zagwe dynasty as has yet been put together.

12 See below, pp. 95, 181, 250 for more discussion of the Agau.

13 A good deal has already been written about Lalibela and a great deal more will undoubtedly appear as the site and the records and traditions pertaining to it are further studied. References to almost everything that had been published as of the time of its compilation in 1968 are included in Gerster, *Churches*.

14 *Lalibela, Phase I*, issued by the International Fund for Monuments, Inc., New York, 1967, reports accomplishments and plans as of that time. It has excellent illustrations and diagrams.

15 Alvares, *Prester John*, 226.

16 The best contemporary account of these events is that of the London *Times* correspondent, G. L. Steer, *Caesar in Abyssinia*, London, 1936. There are three excellent comprehensive histories of the Italian invasion: (1) the remarkably pro-Ethiopian work of Angelo del Boca, *The Ethiopian War, 1935–1941*, Chicago/London, 1969; (2) A. J. Barker, *The Civilizing Mission*, New York, 1968; (3) James Dugan and Laurence Lafore, *Days of Emperor and Clown*, New York, 1973.

17 The liberation of Ethiopia is succinctly described by Christine Sandford in *Ethiopia under Haile Selassie*, London, 1946, 106–18. Her husband, Brigadier Daniel A. Sandford, played a major role in it.

18 Cited in Steer, *Caesar*, 321–3.

19 This Chinese sounding name means Salt Water in Tigrinya and refers to springs in the neighbourhood. The Amharic-Tigrinya language boundary is crossed after the ascent of the escarpment between Alamata and Korem, but the boundary between Wollo and Tigre runs north of Lake Ashangi.

3 The Old Heartland

Tigre and Eritrea

Roads through Tigre

The province of Tigre and the neighbouring highland areas of Eritrea are historically and culturally a single entity. This region has witnessed an immense amount of history, much of it still only dimly understood. It is sprinkled with ancient monuments which reveal a successful blending of south Arabian and African elements with a seasoning of Hebrew, Greek, and Roman influences culminating in Axumite civilization. Many of these monuments are only now being excavated and studied. Others remain to be discovered. Axumite coins and metal objects, stone carvings, and inscriptions still come to light each year, but no thorough archaeological survey of this entire area has yet been undertaken. Tigre shows the effects of its history. The landscape looks worn, abused, and, in places, exhausted. The same stones have been used over and over again. Trails have been worn deep into the earth and the rock. The original natural vegetation has been so altered by the hand of man and the effects of domestic animals that one is surprised to find anything left at all. In Eritrea the Italians began erosion-control programmes and planted trees systematically, built dams and encouraged agricultural methods less destructive of what remains of the soil's fertility than age-old practices. In Tigre itself this kind of effort has only started in earnest during the past decade.

The most puzzling thing about Axumite civilization, when one reflects on it after seeing Tigre, is how a rich trading empire could have developed in such impoverished surroundings, how the surplus resources necessary for the erection of temples, palaces, reservoirs, and monuments could have been accumulated. And then one realizes . . . the landscape was not the same then. Thick forests provided wood as well as a home for wild animals who were hunted for ivory, horn, and hides. Forests retained moisture and, when they were cut only gradually, ensured a steady supply of fertile land for pasturage and crops. This was the kind of setting in which the most ancient agricultural societies developed in Asia Minor four or five thousand years before Axum at places such as Çatal Hüyük. There too forests were destroyed and environment slowly altered. Modern industrial man gets all the blame for debasing and polluting his environment. Much of Ethiopia, but Tigre more than most provinces, demonstrates how destructive traditional societies can be using tools no more sophisticated than the axe, the plough, and the hoe. It happened almost imperceptlbly. People took natural resources for granted. Their depletion was so slow that the causes were overlooked. Historically the progressive decline of the old heartland of Ethiopian civilization was not without its positive effects, for there was always the temptation, and usually the opportunity, to expand southward. Thus the whole highland region was settled by Semitic peoples, Christianized, and formed into the Ethiopian Empire. The area where it all began was left denuded.

Modern traffic passes through Tigre mostly in a north-south direction. Two main highways cross the province, one in the centre and one in the west. Traditional caravan traffic still moves along east-west routes (Fig. 5). The eastern half of Tigre is thinly populated lowland – the hot, dry inhospitable continuation of the Danakil Desert. There has been prospecting for minerals in this region for many years, but nothing exploitable on a large scale has been found but salt. Salt has been mined in the Tigrean lowlands from time immemorial and the salt trade is still a major activity in this part of the country. Salt is dug at several lakes where the water becomes so concentrated during the dry season that the whole surface hardens and the salt can simply be cut out in chunks and sawed into bars of transportable size. The quarrying is done by both Muslim Danakil and Christian Endertas. It is carried up to the highlands on camel-back, as it has been for thousands of years. The shortest salt-haul from Makelle requires an eight-day round trip, but many salt caravans spend two or three weeks on the trail. The human exertion which goes into the process of bringing salt to market seems out of proportion to the meagre return. Nevertheless, tens of thousands of people continue to make their livelihood from this trade and resent mechanization of it – which is gradually setting in as improved vehicle tracks make it profitable for trucks to bring up a whole caravan-load of salt bars in a few hours. Camel caravans cross the main eastern highway at Quiha and from there on to Makelle travel close to the side-road which links the provincial capital to the main north-south route.

Makelle is the main transfer point for the salt trade. Much salt is carried farther by caravans which follow old routes, many of them doubtlessly in use since Axumite times, into the western part of the province, to the Semyens, Begemder, and south to Sekota. Caravans carry other products too: hides, grain, coffee. Smaller traders ply these same routes, going from market to market, but usually put their wares on donkeys. Several decades of energetic country roadbuilding are going to be necessary before all this old caravan traffic is superseded by motor vehicles.[1]

The main motor highways through Tigre are well built and enjoyable to travel because there is less traffic than on roads farther south. The central Tigrean plateau around Makelle and through Quiha to Wokro is tan, rocky, rolling country. Villages are large and compact and always the colour of the landscape around them, for they are built of the same stone that clutters the fields. There is more stone than soil in many fields, but even the stoniest turn green after the rains and produce crops. Highland Tigre is thickly populated – three or four times as many people live here as in the whole huge province of Bale in the south-east. Tigre continues to be a source of people who emigrate to all other provinces in the country, where they settle in cities and roadside towns and are noted for their enterprise. An Amhara may characterize a fellow tribesman who displays unusual drive and industriousness as being 'a little bit Tigrean'. Depending on the circumstances, this may or may not be a compliment.

The route from Wokro to the Eritrean border is one of the most scenic in Tigre. Bulky, reddish sandstone mountains and deep canyons reveal millions of years of earth history in their stratification. The area recalls Arizona. I enjoyed travelling through it most in February when there had been light rains to heighten the colours and golden aloes were in bloom along the roadsides. The town of Adigrat, capital of the Tigrean sub-province of Agame, has an Italian air which comes in part from the tall red-brick church on its eastern edge. The highway from Adigrat to the Eritrean border is lined with intermittent old eucalyptus, stately survivors of battles in the 1930s and 1940s.

The most exciting road in Tigre is the one which climbs up from Adigrat into the red mountains to the west. It ascends for ten continuous kilometres, crosses a pass, and then begins a descent through gorges and eventually down to a valley edged by high *ambas* on both sides. There is cultivation at the bottom of all the gorges and terracing on the sides of some. At the 62 km. marker, a track turns off to the right and leads to Debra Damo, the oldest continually operating monastery in Ethiopia. It sits on a straight-sided *amba*, not the highest or largest but clearly the most inaccessible of all that are visible from the road (Pl. 10a). It is now possible to drive within half an hour's walk of the foot of the *amba*, but the ascent can be made only by foot and rope and only by males.

Farther on is the turn-off to Yeha, where the ruins of a large south Arabian-style temple still stand, and then the mountains of Adowa come into view. There are good views of them too from the westerly highway which comes out of Eritrea through Adi Ugri and Adi Quala, crosses the Mareb River, and comes into Adi Abun.[2] The most peculiar of the Adowa mountains stick up like fat fingers and thumbs of stone from an already rough landscape. In certain kinds of light, seen from Adowa itself or from the road to Axum, they take on a mystical quality and call to mind old stage backdrops that one thought were too exaggeratedly romantic to exist anywhere in reality. All the landscape around Adowa has a dramatic quality about it – a well-chosen setting for the famous battle fought in 1896 and celebrated as one of Ethiopia's most important national holidays every 2 March. Between Adowa and Axum boys pick geodes from the fields, crack them, and offer them to travellers along the roadside. They are also hawked on the streets of Axum. Some have lavender and blue crystals of unusual quality. Others are dazzling white inside.

We will return to Axum in due course, but let us first complete a rapid circuit of Tigre's main highways by moving on south over the western route into the sub-province of Shire, a lower region where a major effort at modern agricultural development is being made. Clumps of palms grow in lush meadows and the barrenness of the rest of the province is left behind. Beyond Enda Selassie, a nondescript town that will probably develop rapidly, the descent into the Takazze Gorge begins and beyond the gorge, on the south side, rise the

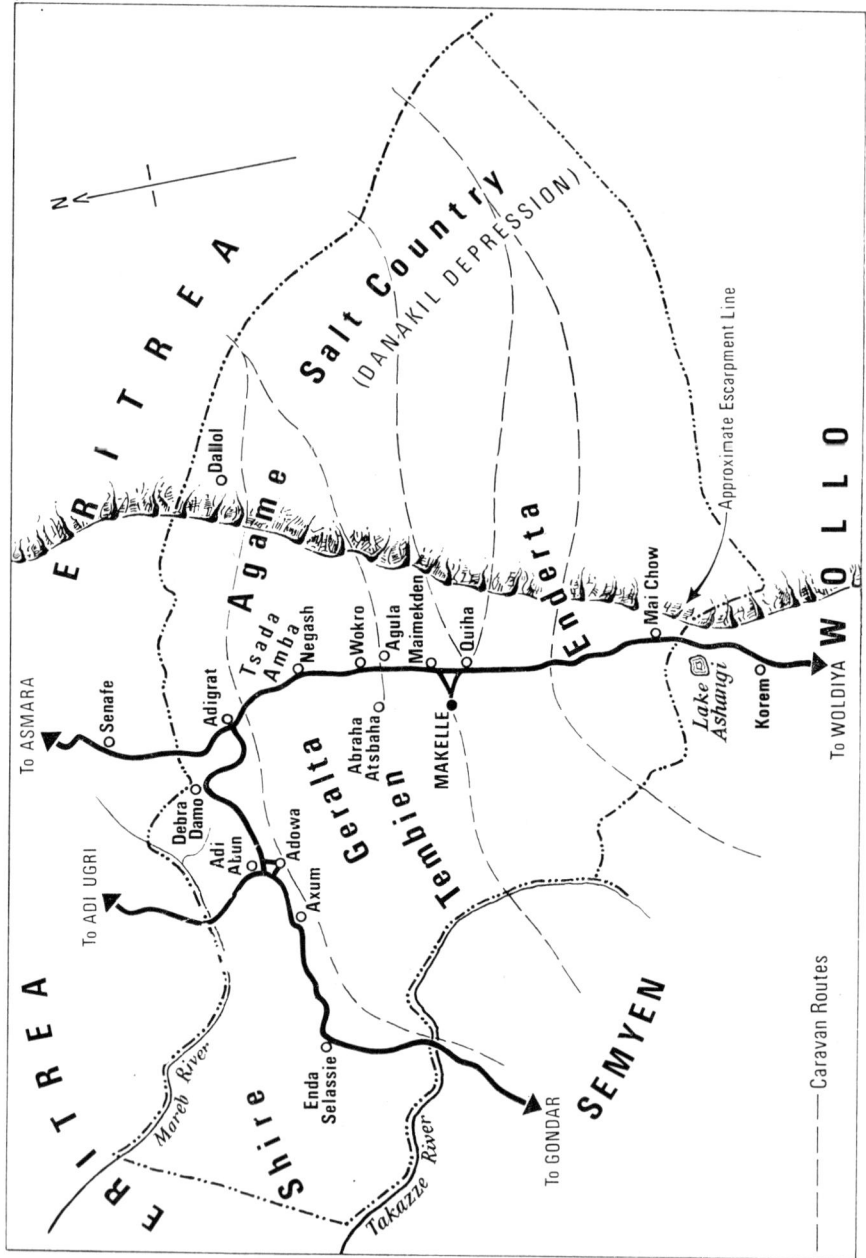

FIG. 5   The Province of Tigre

ramparts of the Semyens. The gorge of the Takazze seems newer geologically than many of the other great gorges of Ethiopia. There are good views of the river as the road twists downward. The area is almost unpopulated. The most exciting scenery comes on the Begemder side as you come closer and closer – though slowly, for the road climbs and winds endlessly – to the Great Northern Escarpment of the Semyen massif, the highest and most splendid landscape in Ethiopia (see below, pp. 157–79).

Makelle

Buxton wrote of the capital of Tigre in 1944:

> It is a dreary place set in a featureless landscape, dominated from on high by the fort of Enda Yesus. Fine sites were usually chosen by the Ethiopian kings, but I could never see the special advantage or attraction of this one.[3]

On first sight in 1970 I agreed with Buxton. But on closer acquaintance I concluded that Makelle had made a good deal of progress in a quarter-century. The town is still small, even in comparison with most Ethiopian provincial capitals, but it is lively and seems to be developing rapidly. As I became more familiar with it, drove along the roads and tracks that lead out in various directions, and climbed the low brown hills that surround it on three sides, I concluded that it does not have too bad a location. It may originally have been selected as a capital because the open space around it made it difficult for hostile armies to approach without warning. Tree-planting programmes during the past twenty years have begun to pay off and from the air, or from the escarpment to the east, the town now gives the appearance of an oasis of green in a tan desert.

The things I will always remember most vividly about Makelle are the sounds of the high winds blowing off the plateau in February, the night-time howling of hyenas at all times of the year, the bright lights of the town seen from the roof of the Castle Abraha at night, and the same view at sunrise when the smoke of dung and eucalyptus cooking-fires hangs like a light blue curtain over the whole built-up area until the warmth of the sun dissipates it. Two castles dominate Makelle: that of the Emperor Yohannes IV on the eastern side of the town and the Castle Abraha Hotel on the southern side. Both are of grey stone in essentially the same style which has become a hallmark of Tigre. Emperor Yohannes's castle had been long neglected, but is now being restored to serve as a provincial museum. The Castle Abraha is a restored residence which Dejazmach Abraha Araya had built for himself in the late nineteenth century (Pl. 11a). It crowns a small knoll with a full view of the town. It has a false air of great antiquity, but no matter; with comfortable rooms and a good kitchen, it was the most agreeable hotel I found in Ethiopia.

Ras Menegesha Seyum, great-grandson of Emperor Yohannes IV, was Governor-General of Tigre for many years. His wife, Princess Aida Desta, is daughter of Princess Tenagne-Worq, eldest daughter of Emperor Haile Selassie

I. This energetic young couple thus united two primary branches of the Ethiopian imperial line, the Tigrean and the Shoan. Both Ras Menegesha and Princess Aida took the business of governing very seriously and believed in close contact with their people. They took an active part in all the economic development schemes in the province, travelled frequently, and were always happy to meet visitors. They lived in a modest modern villa in the shadow of the Emperor's old castle. Princess Aida was also honoured by having one of Makelle's most colourful (yellow and pink) and prominent bars named after her. It occupied a choice location on the main square a short distance from the hot-pink Harambee Hotel.[4]

One of Ras Menegesha's favourite projects was TAIDL – Tigre Agricultural and Industrial Development, Ltd. It has been most successful in incense. The hardened sap of certain dry-country trees and bushes has been collected throughout the Horn of Africa and in south Arabia from well before the time of the Queen of Sheba. Ancient Egyptians sent traders to procure it. It is widely used in Ethiopia and in neighbouring countries for both religious and secular ceremonies. Coffee is traditionally served with incense burning in the room, adding its aroma to the spices used in preparing the beverage. In modern times incense, a natural resin, has been in demand among paint and varnish manufacturers in Europe and America. The TAIDL incense operation is headquartered in a large building along the highway which leads north-eastward out of Makelle. It is a practical combination of traditional work methods and modern managerial techniques. The incense is brought to rural collecting-points by gatherers and is trucked into Makelle. Women clean and sort it. It is then graded, bagged, labelled, and hauled to Massawa for export. Production was increasing slowly but steadily, we were told when we visited the TAIDL incense factory in 1970. Though wages are low, women compete to work as incense-sorters because there are few other opportunities for cash employment.

Another project, also an extension of traditional work methods, was developed by an American missionary family with support from the Ras and the Princess: the Makelle Garment Industry. Cotton is spun and woven by local methods into the rough but extremely attractive cloth which Ethiopians call *buluqo*. This is then made into bush-jackets, dresses, robes, and evening gowns artistically embroidered in native designs. The Makelle garment people have even exported quantities of their output to America, though initial demand among foreigners and Ethiopians in Addis Ababa and Asmara was greater than could easily be met.

Tigre has ancient traditions of high-quality handicrafts. Thousands of country people come each Monday to the Makelle market in the huge square off the main street and bring in leather, basketry, pottery, and cloth as well as many food products. Men offer large horn beakers and sometimes horn spoons and dippers and old women usually have a plentiful supply of large amber cakes of beeswax. In size they are identical to the local whole-wheat bread made in thick, flat loaves. Northern pottery is quite unlike that made in central and southern

Ethiopia. It has a very archaic look, reminiscent of old Egyptian shapes and colours. The basketry is also distinctive and recognizable both because of design features and the kinds of reeds and grasses used. A market in Tigre contrasts with more southerly Ethiopian markets because the people dress almost entirely in homespun garments which range in colour from tannish white to weathered grey and brown. Tigrean women braid their hair in tight strands which cover the whole head in neatly symmetrical rows. They seldom wear coloured scarves. Men, on the other hand, often wear turbans or headcloths. Baby-carriers are one of the most interesting sights in a Tigrean market. Carefully fashioned of soft brown goatskin, they are elaborately decorated with cowries, coloured beads, and dangling clusters of seeds and buttons to amuse the child who rides comfortably, bound in leather, on his mother's back. Christians usually advertise their faith by embroidering crosses of cowries on their baby-carriers (Pl. 13a).

During the morning at the Makelle market salt-trading is at its height. Camels keep arriving until 10 o'clock and hundreds gather at the western end of the market where alleys are lined with warehouses for storing salt bars (Pl. 13b). Some caravan leaders bargain with different purchasers before disposing of their loads; others appear to contract in advance. Wholesalers buy stacks of large salt bars. Retailers buy smaller quantities, saw them into standard *amole*, and usually get five of these, about 30 cm. long and 5 cm. square, from each large bar. Since the size and thickness of the large bars vary because of differences in the layers from which they are cut, there is a good deal of haggling about price and quality, for some of the salt is tan and obviously contains impurities. Most camels carry fourteen large bars, seven on each side. These weigh between 5 and 7 kg. Thus each animal carries around 90 kg. of salt. When we last visited the salt market in June 1971, the large bars were selling at E$1·35–1·75 each. The salt which a single camel has spent at least the better part of a week carrying up from the lowlands brings about E$20.[5] When the original cost of the salt plus the cost of the journey is taken into account, the net return is seen to be very small. Somewhat smaller *amole* were selling for E35–50c in Shoan markets during the same period.

Makelle is not only a government and market centre, it has become an educational centre in recent years. During our first visit the new and well-built local high school was paralysed by an extended student strike, a common phenomenon in Ethiopia during that period and a regrettable waste in a country where the thirst for learning is so great and the resources the government devotes to education represent, proportionately, such a large budgetary outlay. When we went back a few months later, the school was operating successfully again, packed with students from all over central Tigre. A large Orthodox seminary, which had been a building for several years, was opened in Makelle in early 1973.

Makelle is a scattered town which, in spite of its solid stone houses, has a chronically unfinished look. But it is well designed and little by little its streets are being kerbed and paved. New high-intensity streetlights give it an air of seriousness, as befits a provincial capital, at night. In another twenty-five years Buxton's characterization of it as a dreary place may no longer be debatable at all.

Seven Rock Churches

Nothing testifies to the ancientness of Christianity in Tigre more than the province's rock-hewn churches. And nothing demonstrates better how much there is still to be learned about Ethiopia than the fact that most of these churches have only become known to the outside world during the past ten years. Actually those known in the sense that they have been visited and recorded by educated Ethiopians or foreigners still probably represent less than half of those that remain to be 'discovered'. The first systematic effort to visit and gather information about these extraordinary churches was undertaken by a remarkable Ethiopian priest, Abba Tewolde Medhin Josef, who was born in Eritrea in 1916, received a traditional Ethiopian education, and then studied at the Ethiopian Vatican College in the 1930s and served in Adigrat from 1952 onward. In the early 1960s he became engrossed in work on rock churches. He astonished the Third International Conference of Ethiopian Studies in Addis Ababa in 1966 by reading a paper in which he listed a total of 126 rock churches in Tigre and formulated a set of hypotheses about their origin and significance.[6] Abba Tewolde-Medhin suffered an untimely death in 1967, but meanwhile several foreigners had developed a serious interest in the Tigre churches, among them Roger Sauter, Georg Gerster, David Buxton, and, above all, two intrepid English ladies, Miss Ivy Pearce and Mrs Ruth Plant. These last two have done the most to make available to other travellers what they have learned about the churches they have visited.[7]

Except for Wokro Cherqos the Tigrean rock churches are not for the casual tourist unless he has had the good luck to join companions who already know some of the churches and something about travel in Ethiopia. As secondary roads are built during the coming decade, access to other churches will be improved, but a large portion of these churches, because of their situations on mountain-sides, in gorges, and other out-of-the-way places, will always give the visitor the satisfaction of feeling that he has had to exert himself strenuously to reach them. In the course of two visits to Tigre I visited seven rock churches, though the last one, which we were unable to enter, should probably be counted as only half a visit. Let me describe the highlights of each of these visits as well as the principal features of each church itself (map, p. 71).

Wokro Cherqos

Makelle lies off the main north-south highway. To regain it, you take the road which leads north-west up a small escarpment. It leads through rough, rock-

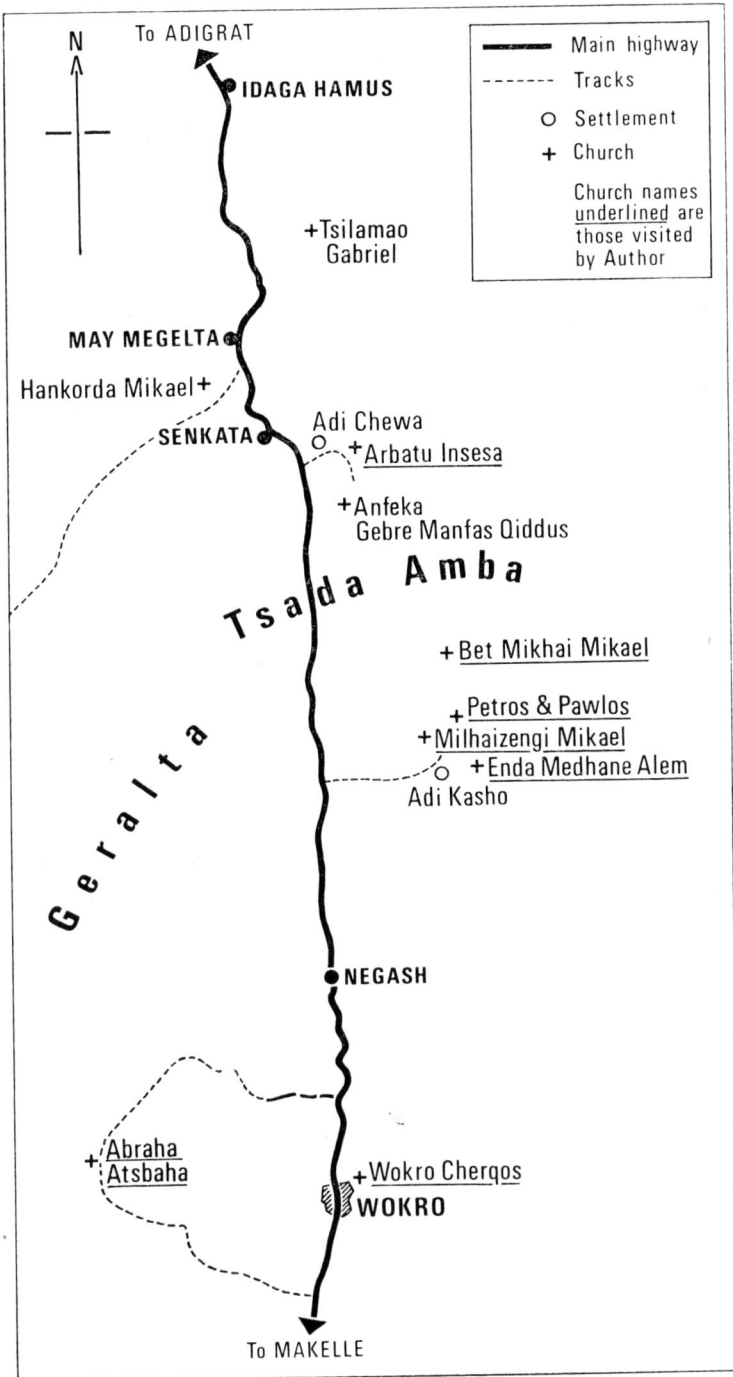

FIG. 6   Selected rock-hewn churches in Central Tigre

strewn country where small-scale quarrying is done to Maimekden. The people of this small town on the main highway weave carpets of coloured sisal fibres and hang them up along the roadside to sell. From a high point north of Maimekden the road commands a view of vast rolling hills with Wokro visible in the middle distance, directly to the north. Below to the east is the large agricultural village of Agula. Wokro is less than an hour's drive from Makelle and the church there is only a short distance from the highway and visible from it. For a long time it was the only Tigrean rock church known to the outer world. Napier's expedition passed by it and knowledge of it reached England in reports of this campaign.

We had no difficulty driving right up to the gate of Wokro Cherqos, for two secondary-school students immediately volunteered to lead us there when we turned off the highway, but we had trouble finding someone to let us inside. This church has a sheer front jutting out of a tannish-pink hillside and is surrounded by a stone wall (Pl. 11b). At the south-eastern corner of the wall a monk in black smock and round black cap was supervising the building of a new belfry. Workmen were fitting stones together with mud mortar and the square tower had already risen to a height of 4 m. The monk was proud of the progress that had been made. He told us the church dated from AD 246.[8] He took us to see his cell, built against the rock on the south side of the church. It was a simple square room with a sleeping-mat at the back and a few pots in a corner. The holy pictures on the wall were European prints. The walls were of dry-laid stone. The monk had sent for a priest who had the church key and he kept calling to him across the broad valley behind the church. He assured us the key would soon arrive.[9]

The churchyard had several trees, including good specimens of pink-blooming euphorbia, and a number of rather new tombs. The two-storeyed gate had recently been rebuilt and roofed with corrugated tin. Outside, below the gate, was a large area of graves and small round stone huts inhabited by nuns who begged in the town during the day and came back to sleep in the shadow of the church at night. Because this was a Muslim holiday (Wokro is half-Christian, half-Muslim), these tattered old ladies were at home sitting in front of their huts chattering animatedly. We peered into one of the old tombs in the rock wall beside the church where the masonry on top had come loose and saw piles of human bones, including several skulls, all mixed up together – nuns who had lived at the gate in centuries past? The monk called our attention to the church's bells. They hung from a tree below the new belfry. One was the transmission housing of an old motor vehicle and the other looked as if it had originally been the drive-wheel of an engine. He tapped them with a stone and both gave off clear tones. We forgot to ask whether he was going to install them in his new belfry, for he said he saw the priest coming across the valley and dashed off to meet him.

As we waited for the monk to return, we sat on the wall and listened to students droning out their lessons at a church school across the river. Our

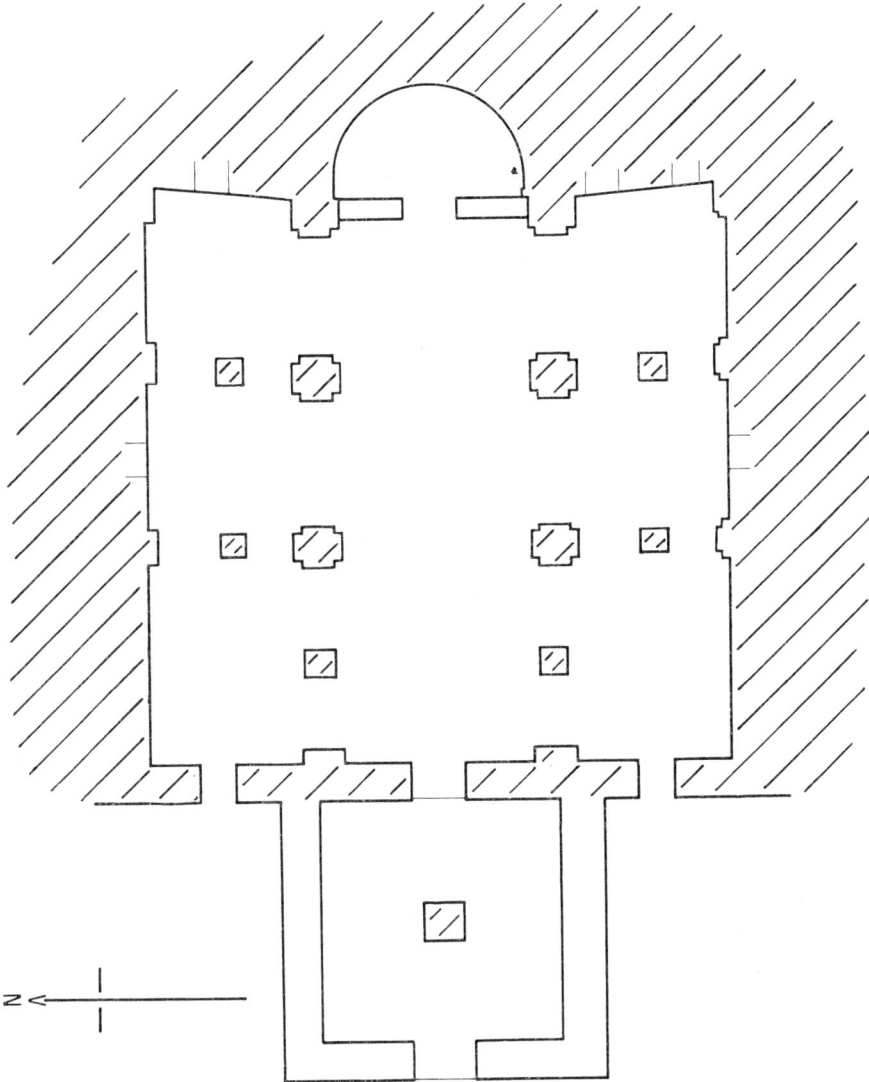

FIG. 7 Plan of Wokro Cherqos

student guides, who were not in the government school because of the strike that had persisted for several weeks, commented on their situation. They were bored, eager to return to classes, and fearful that if they did not do so soon, they would lose credit for the term. They were inclined to blame the strike on the sons of rich men who were doing badly in school and did not want to have to receive failing grades . . . so they kept making trouble. The monk returned and reported that it had been someone else – the priest had not yet been found. Since we had now spent nearly two hours, we decided to go on to Abraha Atsbaha and suggested that the monk arrange to have the priest return by 3 p.m. to let us in when we returned. In response to his plea for money, we promised a contribution towards completion of the belfry after we had seen the inside of the church.

Back in Wokro at 3, we found that a service had just concluded and the monk and priest were waiting for us at the church door. Having seen Abraha Atsbaha, we were at first disappointed in the interior of Wokro Cherqos (Fig. 7). The entrance has a curious feature – a column in the very centre of the entrance hall which blocks a direct view into the church from the door. The interior was dark, even with the afternoon sun streaming in the door. The ceilings looked smoke-covered. This, the priest said, was the result of one of the wicked Queen Yodit's fires.[10] The basic ground plan is the same as at Abraha Atsbaha, though on a smaller scale, with the *qiddus qiddusan* cut deep into the rock at the eastern side, a cupola in the ceiling above it, and a cross carved into the central ceiling panel with carved decoration around it. The architectural details were interesting, though as our eyes became accustomed to the dim light we could see that some of the ceiling carving was flaking off. There are good, clean Maltese crosses cut into the tops of the pillars that flank the door between the entry hall and the main body of the church. The door is framed in sturdy wood and has a double window above. Most of the pillars bear the marks of the sharp tools with which they were originally cut. The priest called our attention to several fragments of paintings on the north side of the entrance hall. These are believed to date from the fifteenth century and are painted on plaster which has flaked off in part, revealing more painting on lower layers. The best of these is of a saint in a yellow robe with a shaggy black beard.[11]

Abraha Atsbaha

At least two landrover tracks lead to this church from near Wokro. The best in the spring of 1971 was the one which turns off the main highway about 5 km. south of the town. We were sceptical when the students who led us there first pointed it out, but as we bumped down through a rocky field, we could see that a roadgrader at some time in the past year or two had pushed the larger rocks aside, leaving them to form a border for the track. We descended into a valley over rock ledges, circling a large village. At the bottom the road disappeared into a river-bed and followed it for several hundred metres. Fortunately the sand beneath the shallow water was so firm that our wheels barely made marks in it. The farther we went the more breathtaking the scenery became, recalling the American south-west in both form and colour. Great mesas and bastions loomed ahead in the distance. Close at hand rose sheer hillsides with masses of vivid red sandstone exposed in 45 degree waves and swirls. Vegetation became thicker. Large *warka* trees became frequent. We saw people everywhere. Children ran to the track to wave. Vehicles were obviously rare on this route. As we crossed a flat plain with clumps of doum palms, the students pointed to the east to the site of the church in a cliffside. As the track neared it, we drove under a clump of old fig-trees which formed an outdoor assembly area under their spreading branches. The portico of the church was now clearly visible, a white arched structure[12] protruding from a mottled red sandstone mountainside. We walked up to the main gate along a *warka*-shaded path worn deep into the sandstone. The whole area around the church, as at Wokro, was enclosed in a newly-laid wall of creamy orange stone. The impression of newness was heightened by the bright tin roofs of the wall-towers and gate. We were welcomed inside by a tall priest in white robes and turban and a group of two dozen other church dignitaries and novices. The church was open, they said, and they would soon be holding a noontime service. The tall priest made a speech in throaty Tigrinya welcoming us. Nearby a group of men were making a new *kabaro*, a large double-ended drum made of a hollowed treetrunk. They were tying the head and bottom skins together, lacing strips cut from a recently killed, foul-smelling cowskin. As they dried, the strips would pull the pounding surfaces taut across the calico-covered wood.

We went up to the portico, took off our shoes, and stepped inside. The entrance hall is only partly cut into the rock. It has a beamed wooden ceiling. As our eyes grew accustomed to the dim light, we became aware of the paintings. The walls are entirely covered and the colours are rich. They are recent, having been done in the nineteenth century. Priests and deacons carrying long beeswax tapers led us into the main body of the church, cut entirely from the rock (Fig. 8). There is a feeling of spaciousness with five aisles separated by thick columns that appear lighter than they are because they are so precisely cut and all the corners are fluted, giving the entire column the form of a thick Greek cross. An immense amount of rock had to be skilfully removed when this church was built. The ceiling is high with barrel-vaulting on both sides of the mid-section and good geometric ornamentation on all open ceiling surfaces. In the centre of the ceiling they pointed proudly to the cross carved up into the most elevated panel and held up the taper for us to see the designs cut into it. A cupola, also with incised patterns, occupies a section of the ceiling directly in front of the *qiddus qiddusan*, which is recessed deep into the back wall of the church. It has a barrel-vaulted ceiling, also with carving. The *tabot* stand was securely curtained from our view.[13] We noticed that the ceiling panels were nearly all blackened in the decorated areas. The head priest said that this was the result of a fire that had been set by Queen Yodit who had piled the church full of straw and lit it when she ravaged this region. He spoke of this event as if it had happened only yesterday and went on, in full seriousness, to relate how before this misfortune the Axumite square panels which form a frieze beneath the barrel-vaulting had shone with their own light, 'as if lighted by electricity'. There had then been no need for outside light in the church, the priest assured us, and pointed to the latticed windows on both sides. The light-giving properties of the ceiling had proved impossible to restore after Yodit's fire and the windows had had to be cut. We asked the priest the age of the church. He said it had been cut in the time of the twin emperors Abraha and Atsbaha, for whom it had been named.[14]

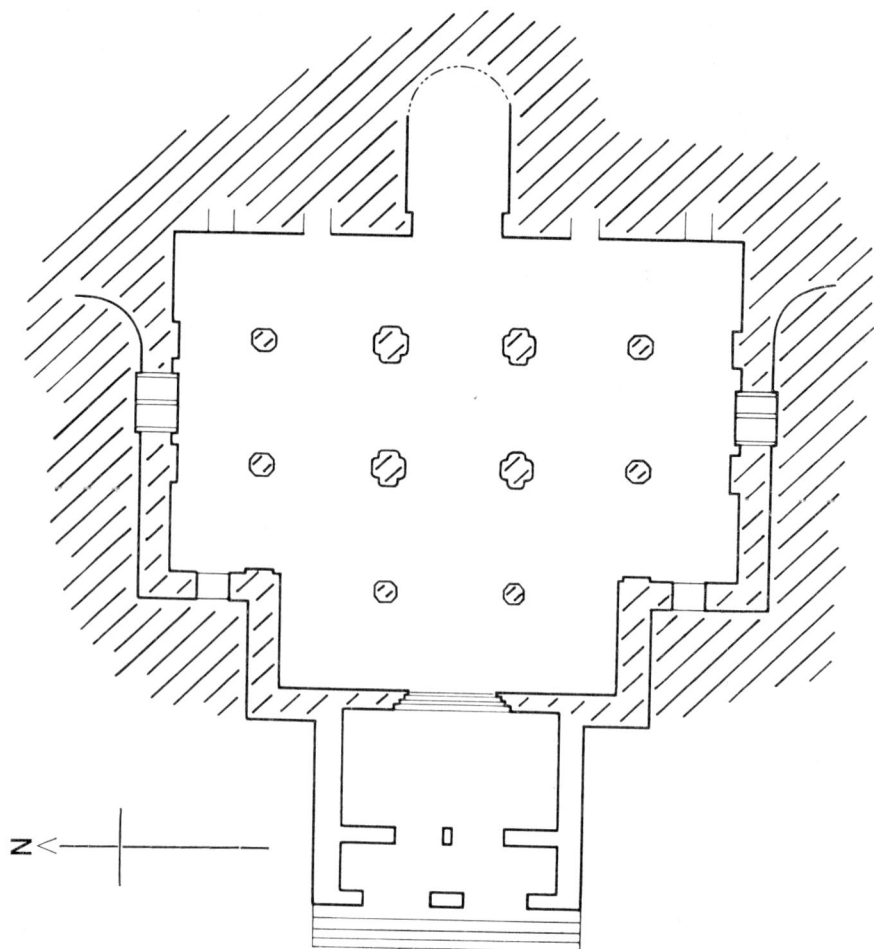

Fig. 8   Plan of Abraha Atsbaha

From the 2 m.-level upwards the walls are covered with paintings done on canvas glued to the stone. There seem to be several styles of painting, probably the result of work done at different times. Most look relatively recent, however, and are in good condition, though it appears that at some earlier period other paintings which covered the lower portions of the walls wore away. There is a huge secondary door made from a broad slab of gnarled wood set in a solid Axumite frame. It opens to the right of the main entrance and gives a good view of the broad valley to the north, ringed by red and purple mountains. We asked how many priests and monks were connected with the church and were told 'about a hundred'. More and more of them came to attend us as we walked through, holding tapers high to light the crosses cut at the tops of columns and the details of paintings, pointing out the place in the large cracked red sandstone column in the left centre where water drips – tears from Heaven – at certain periods when special holy days are observed. We asked and learned that these, fortunately, happen to coincide with the rainy season, so the tears can be relied upon to appear.

Outside again, the tall old priest who had originally welcomed us at the gate blessed us formally, chanting in Ge'ez. We gave him a donation for the church and a somewhat smaller one for himself and passed coins to others who had been especially helpful. A wizened old fellow pushed through the crowd around us and came up argumentatively. Our student guides translated his energetic Tigrinya: 'He says he is much more important than any of the others and you have not given him anything!' I gave him a whole handful of coins. A group of deacons led us out the back gate of the church compound and up over the rock into which the church is cut. Along the south wall we passed under the double windows with their thick wooden frames and latticing and noticed that a third window, farther to the rear, had been filled in with masonry. Perhaps someone had overestimated the amount of light needed from the outside after Queen Yodit's incendiary caper . . . The undulating sandstone slope above the church was all solid with no cracks. On the eastern edge of this slope we stopped at a wooden frame on which hung two slabs of stone – *dawals*, rock bells. They were situated so that their sound would rebound against the cliff behind and spread out over the valley to the north, summoning the faithful to worship or, at least, letting them know that they should not be working in their fields on holy days. Smaller striking-stones rested on top of each slab and they were struck lightly for us. One had a deep, metallic tone, the other a light tinkling sound. Our student guides told us that most of the land in the valley belonged to the church. It looked rich and fertile, some of the best land we saw in Tigre.

＊ ＊ ＊

The next five churches are all in an area called Tsada Amba about 75 km. north-east of Makelle. We managed to visit all of them in a single day in late June through a combination of fortunate circumstances. The afternoon before we had been invited to tea by Princess Aida, who offered to supply us with a guide. He appeared at our hotel at dawn the next morning, an unassuming but efficient young man with the classic Tigrean name, Abraha. We had risen before the last hyenas had stopped their howlings in the fields below the Castle Abraha and covered the route to Wokro and on through Negash as fast as we could. Negash is a smallish town with a few still-unoccupied Italian buildings and a large rectangular modern north Ethiopian-style church, a Maryam. Beyond Negash we passed another church perched spectacularly on a pinnacle east of the highway. Twisting through more hills, we gradually became aware of a long north-south escarpment in the distance on our right. It was in this escarpment that we were to spend the day. There were no signs of churches in it. Unlike round churches which are nearly always visible from a distance because of their natural situations or their encircling groves of trees, most rock churches are hardly discernible at all until you are upon them. This fact undoubtedly explains why so few of them were noticed by travellers until people went deliberately to seek them out.

Enda Medhane Alem, Adi Kasho

The early morning crispness in the air was disappearing when Abraha directed us off the highway onto field tracks which led towards an indentation in the escarpment. We drove for 2–3 km. over fallow and newly ploughed fields, turning now and then to avoid freshly planted areas. We passed several farmsteads and finally stopped below a steep rocky hillside where we left the landrover in the care of a *zabanya* chosen from among young men who came to greet us. A path led around a shoulder of the hill, over a large flow of volcanic rock which looked like petrified wood, and then across a small valley in front of the escarpment. There was a thick growth of trees from the base up over the top of the abutments – olive, cedar, and large acacias – and these continued back into the deep valley that cut into the escarpment at this point. The trail led upwards through the trees, then over a face of grey sandstone. Local people told us that the deep potholes in this 40 degree stone slope had been made by the feet of the horses of emperors Abraha and Atsbaha. We expected to see the church when we came over the top, but instead found that the trail continued through more trees.

We came to a tall stone gatehouse and passed through it into a compound shaded by old olives. Cut into the cliff wall to the south-east, barely visible at first, was Enda Medhane Alem, characterized by Mrs Plant as 'one of the truly great churches of Tigre' (Pl. 14a). In front was a burial area with small, crudely cut rectangular stones marking each grave. The church itself was apparent as a cut-out area, with whitewash, in the cliffside. Four large square columns 'support' the overhanging cliff roof. The space between them has been filled with masonry, thus forming a long entry hall which, we discovered as we stepped inside, shields the true front of the church. It has four columns with two doors and a window above each of them. The doors and windows with their heavy wooden frames in classic Axumite style were the most pleasing features of this church. The entry hall was covered with hay and along its outer side there were several old tree-branch benches, polished to a low sheen by centuries of leaning priests and monks. The main body of the church is essentially square, divided into nine sections by four thick columns, with a large niche in the rear for the *tabot* and a smaller niche on each side of it (Fig. 9).

We found the most remarkable feature of Enda Medhane Alem, in view of the hardness and dullness of the rock, the ceiling ornamentation both in the main body of the church and in the entry area. Each panel has different geometric patterns, many of which appear to be imitations of earlier wood

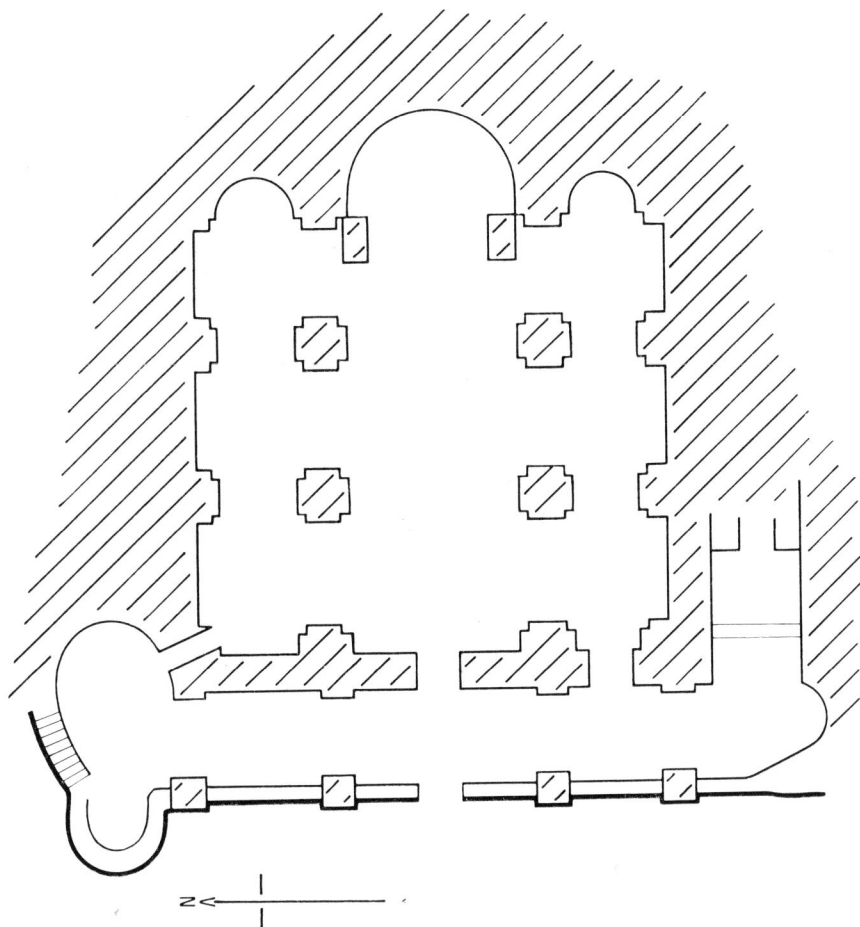

FIG. 9   Plan of Enda Medhane Alem

designs. Priests held up tapers for us to see this carving better and dripping wax lighted the hay on the floor. For a moment we had a great burst of light, but attendants rushed to stomp out the flames. We were shown a chest of parchment books sitting against the wall to the left of the *tabot* niche, but were given no time to examine them. Unlike the church of Abraha Atsbaha, which had smelled of incense, this one smelled of hay, a sign that services had not recently been held. It was nevertheless still in use and had a large clerical community connected with it. Several monks accompanied us on a visit to the *dawals* which hung from a tree and to the church's *tabal*, which flows into a tree-shaded pool at a point overlooking the deep valley that cuts the escarpment north of the church grounds. The water was cold and tasted good. The pool was edged by a good growth of bright green water-plants. It was said that it had never been known to cease flowing.

Milhaizengi Mikael

Coming back from the *tabal* of Medhane Alem, we had a good view of Milhaizengi across the deep valley. It is a precipitous outcropping, rounded at the top and bald, though trees and bushes cling to the lower slopes. To get there we had to return to the landrover and then drive across fields to a deep, dry stream-bed from which we had a short walk up the north side of the outcropping to the church. It is simply a primitive cave and contrasts markedly with the magnificence of the design of Medhane Alem and the other large churches. In this kind of church one can get some feel for the evolutionary process that probably led to the more elaborate churches. It is easy to believe that a cave site such as this might have been used for worship in pre-Christian times and then adapted to Christian use. The entrance door has an Axumite frame made of wood held by masonry in a large oval opening in the rock face (Pl. 14b). The door itself consists of two wooden slabs held together by strips of iron. Nearby there is a window opening and to the right of the principal door is a smaller door. To reach the entrance we had to crawl up a path in the smooth rock with deeply worn foot- and handholds. Inside the church consists merely of a long forehall and three separate niches carved into the back (Fig. 10). The centre niche contains the *tabot* whose painted cabinet we could see through a calico curtain and one of the side niches held two large *kabaros*. Artistically the most

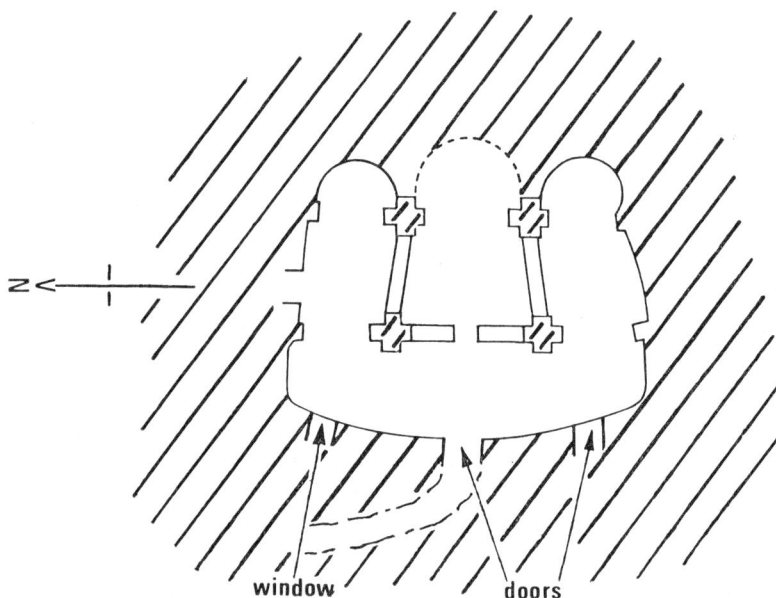

FIG. 10   Plan of Mihaizengi Mikael

noteworthy feature of Milhaizengi Mikael is the flattish cupola in the ceiling between the door and the *tabot* niche. It has been carefully carved with geometic patterns and has a cross at its centre. Even here, however, the ceiling is very low, no more than 3 m. from the floor, and I had to lie flat on the floor to photograph the cupola. There were paintings which the local priest pointed out with great pride. The recent ones were relatively well preserved; the older ones, said to date from the fifteenth century, were in poor condition.

Petros and Pawlos

Visible from far afield (when one knows where to look) because it is mainly a cliff church and only partly a rock-hewn one, Petros and Pawlos has a spectacular location half-way up the escarpment wall. It is also in the district of Milhaizengi. To reach it we had to drive through more fields to a deeply eroded stream-bed. A boy wearing a red blanket appeared to show us the trail onward. Our guide, Abraha, for reasons that never became entirely clear, kept trying to discourage us from going to this church – it would be too difficult to climb up to; we would not be able to get inside; besides, it was not really a rock church

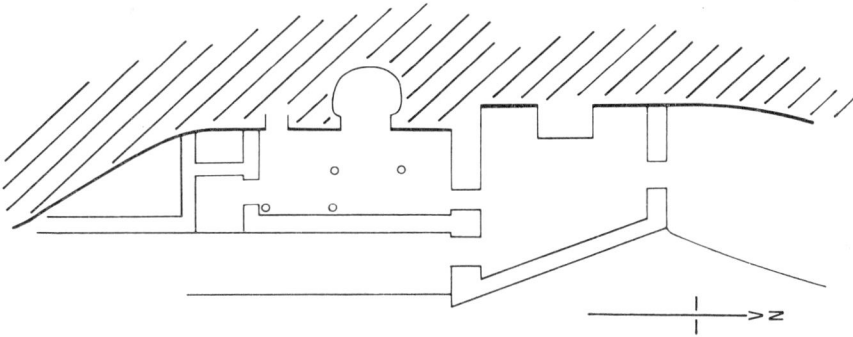

FIG. 11   Plan of Petros and Pawlos

anyway . . . We persisted. The way up was over a sandstone face with toe- and handholds that looked more difficult and precarious than they turned out to be – though Mrs Plant is right, this church 'should not be tackled by anyone prone to giddiness'. We pulled ourselves up in front of the church door without having suffered any real strain and soon a priest appeared to let us in.

This church, pressed into a narrow space on its ledge, must have one of the oddest ground plans in Tigre (Fig. 11). It consists of a series of stone walls, thickly whitewashed, which enclose a moderately roomy entry area and then a sequence of small, cramped chambers strung out one behind the other. The *tabot* niche has been carved into the cliff behind one of these. The back wall of all parts of the the structure is the cliff face. When we saw the paintings in the chamber in front of the *tabot*, we knew we had been right in insisting on coming up, for these are among the most interesting early paintings I saw anywhere in Ethiopia. All available wall space in this tiny room is covered with them. The paintings are small and all are done in rich earth colours – browns and brownish reds, tans, creamy yellows, and olive green. Though rather crudely executed with broad brush-strokes, they have an originality and liveliness often missing in Ethiopian painting of this early period (Pl. 15a). The wood-beam ceiling was also originally painted with geometric designs, though the painted surface of some of the beams has now peeled off. A monk brought out a couple of parchment books for us to examine. Both the style of the writing and the condition of the parchment – it was deeply browned on the edges – made it unnecessary for him to assure us that they were indeed very old. Beyond the central enclosed area, a door led out into a tiny courtyard with a view that penetrated 60 or 70 km. into the Geralta, the rugged heart of Tigre which is already known to contain at least three dozen rock churches and where more undoubtedly await discovery. Behind us was a small enclosed chamber and beyond that a walled but unroofed area which we discovered to be a charnel house, half filled with human bones. It was now mid-afternoon and, if we had not been eager to visit one or two more churches, we would have stayed longer to watch the light change over the Geralta where storm clouds were gathering. The descent down the cliff was less comfortable than the ascent had been. At the bottom, directly below the cliff church above, were the ruins of a round church which had been made of carefully laid fieldstone. All the wood used in it had rotted or been hauled away by local peasants.

Bet Mikhai Mikael

We drove again over fields and tracks to another eroded stream-bed to reach the approach to Bet Mikhai and then had a long hike up a wooded valley with a sizeable flowing stream. There was no sign of a church, just a sheer cliff of bright-tan sandstone looming continually larger before us. The area was much more populated than the surroundings of the other churches we visited this day. A stratum of soft stone and earth at the base of the cliff has eroded away, forming a massive overhang which makes a continuous rock shelter extending for 200 to 300 m. Large numbers of people, most of them monks and nuns, were living here. Clusters of women were cooking over fires. In between were tomb areas where walled enclosures had been built under the overhang. Some had collapsed and piles of human bones had spilled out on the ground. Once a holy person's bones reach this stage, it is apparently God's will that they be left to whatever natural fate befalls them.

We collected a large number of guides and followers who led us southward along the base of the cliff to the gate of the church compound. Here we were asked to remove our shoes – a most unusual procedure, since they are normally removed only at the church door. The requirement for removal of shoes revealed some special sensitivity about this place which foreshadowed further problems. Unfortunately there was no one among the people who had collected around us who had a key, so it had to be sent for. This took a long time and when a priest finally came with it, there had to be a further period of negotiation, for the keeper of the key and several other priests had evidently fallen into disagreement over permitting us to visit the church. Abraha proved his worth by arguing courteously but persistently for the opening of the church, citing Princess Aida's name and that of Ras Menegesha. Finally patience was rewarded and the huge key was placed in the lock and turned.

Bet Mikhai Mikael has a large forestructure, built of masonry, with a deeply excavated chamber behind. The interior was dusty and unkempt, the overall impression of the church one of roughness of design. A wooden screen separated the entry area from the main body of the church. The *tabot* niche was fully curtained and we were not permitted to look in. Walls and columns held several paintings. They looked early both because of style and method of execution, but many were difficult to see in their entirety because of fading. The best and most unusual of them is a rather dramatic Last Judgement. Christ holds up Adam and Eve, each by a single arm, while below two black phoenix-like creatures bare their teeth and extend their tongues. This painting is on a section of column that slopes backward 4 or 5 degrees from the vertical and has collected a thick coating of dust on its upper portions. The priest who had finally consented to let us in would not let me wipe the dust away before photographing (Pl. 15b). As with the skulls falling from tombs, it is apparently also God's will that dust should collect and it is not to be disturbed . . . We saw a large chest of books, but were permitted to take a quick glance at only a few. The friendliest part of our visit to Bet Mikhai Mikael was our departure. We put our shoes on again at the gate and the priest and his colleagues gave us a warm farewell. They were glad to have us gone – an attitude one seldom encounters at Ethiopian churches. We walked back past the women at their cooking-fires speculating that some inner tension must have unsettled the normal serenity of the life of this remote religious community.

Arbatu Insesa, Adi Chewa

None of the storms gathering over the Geralta had materialized in our direction and the light had improved during our visit to Bet Mikhai, so we decided to try one more church. We drove several kilometres north on the main road to Adi Chewa where the church of Arbatu Insesa (The Four Creatures) was said to have unusual paintings done with dark and light colours reversed, like photographic negatives, and a good collection of old manuscripts. If we were in luck, we might arrive for evening services . . .

Here again the church is carved into a sandstone cliff face which rises sharply from an almost completely flat valley, though Arbatu Insesa is situated comparatively much lower than Petros and Pawlos and the route up is a simple trail. Men appeared, but no priests or monks and there was no sign of evening

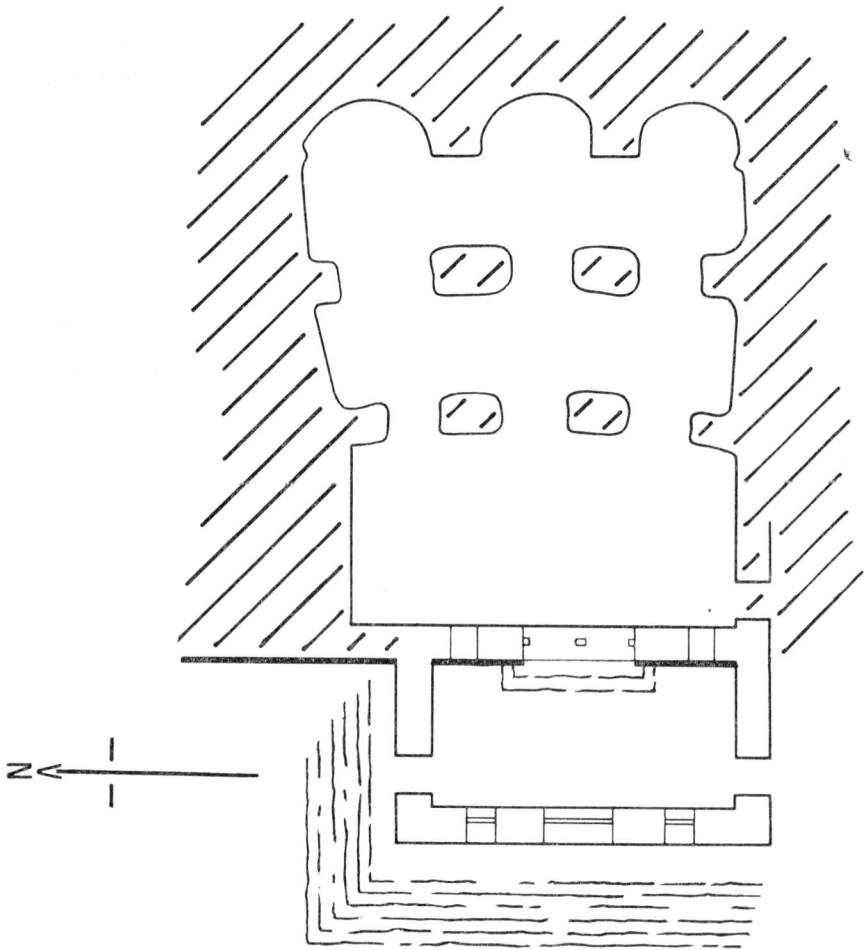

Fig. 12　Plan of Bet Mikhai Mikael

services. Someone went off to get the key from a man who lived – so they said – only ten minutes away. The only evidence of the church was a stout wooden door set snugly in an opening in the cliffside with a small window above it. The ledge in front of the door had been supplied with a low wall on its outward side. The sun emerged, casting long golden rays over the Geralta crags and bathing the cliffs around us in warm light. While we waited for the key to arrive, we explored the surroundings. There were two small empty stone buildings some distance back along a side-trail. Several cracks in the cliff were partly walled up and filled with human bones. Here too some had spilled out. People kept calling down below and the key was reported to be coming. But it did not. Two friendly local peasants came up and offered to pry the lock loose from the door, but we felt that this would be going much too far in spite of the fact that Abraha had mentioned Princess Aida as our sponsor. So we gave up and drove the 82 km. back to Makelle non-stop in an hour and twenty minutes through storms and spells of eery golden-brown evening light.

*   *   *

Each rock church is different and each visit an adventure in itself. For those who like to speculate on the past, the rock churches provide endless food for thought, because almost nothing can be said about them with certainty. No one can be sure when most of them were carved within a margin of less than several hundred years. What makes them especially appealing is the fact that they are still nearly all in use and play a part in the daily lives of the people around them. But though they are still alive, they are in no way of the modern world. Neither are they of the primitive world. They represent civilization in its early Christian form from a period so remote in time that we seldom have any opportunity to experience it first-hand. The commercialized Biblical sites in Israel and Jordan have lost practically all the feel of early Christian times which the Tigrean churches retain so well. A great deal of fervour, energy, and organization was necessary for the creation of these churches. Many of them call to mind the rock churches of the Cappadocian cone country in Turkey and it is interesting to compare the two, for I have visited the Cappadocian churches several times.[15]

The largest and finest of the Tigrean churches excel those of Cappadocia in architectural quality and refinement of ornamentation. The creators of the Cappadocian churches worked in tufa, which was easier to cut and shape than the sandstone and harder kinds of volcanic rock that prevails in Tigre. There are enough similarities in these two great groups of rock-hewn churches to make it impossible to believe that there are no links between them. But how direct and close are these links? Who were the people who developed them and by what routes did they communicate? Equally intriguing is the question of the relationship between the Tigrean churches and those of Lalibela. Geographically they are not entirely separate groups, for Tigre, though it has the greatest concentration and probably the oldest churches, is not the only Ethiopian province where they occur. There are rock churches all over northern Ethiopia, from Eritrea deep into Shoa.[16] The highlands south of Tigre which lead through Wag and Lasta to the region of Lalibela contain many rock churches.[17] The churches of Lalibela differ from those of Tigre, as well as almost all others in Ethiopia, in emphasis on the *exterior*. There is almost no interest in the exterior in Tigre, nor in the Cappadocian churches in Turkey, but the interiors of the larger Tigrean rock churches are superior to most of those of Lalibela in refinement of design and decoration.

Most of the Tigrean churches have collections of manuscripts and all have local traditions. Few of the manuscripts come close to being as old as many of the churches themselves must be. The traditions are often distorted into grotesque or merely entertaining tales. Nevertheless, they have never been

systematically collected and studied. After another generation or two they are
likely to have disappeared forever.

Eritrea

The Italian Red Sea Colony – *Colonia Eritrea* – lasted only a little more than
fifty years, but it left a deep imprint on the northernmost part of Ethiopia. The
Italians were the last of a long line of invaders who came into the highlands
from the Red Sea. The plateau here is separated from the coast by a narrow
strip of desert less than 80 km. wide called the Samhar. The earliest Semitic
immigrants from south Arabia had to cross this plain. The port of Adulis,
modern Zula, south of Massawa, was one of the major Red Sea harbours in
Axumite times. The coastal region has always had a mixed population. In the
late Middle Ages it slipped from Ethiopian control. Eventually the Turks
claimed suzerainty over the entire Horn of Africa from Massawa to Cape
Gardafui, calling the province *Al Habasha*. As the Ottoman Empire weakened,
the semi-independent Egyptians asserted themselves and dominated the coastal
region during the mid-nineteenth century.

The Ethiopians never gave up their claim to the coast, but were unable to do
much about it. During the Era of the Princes there was no central authority in
the highlands until Emperor Tewodros was crowned in 1855.[18] British interest
in this part of Africa increased steadily through the nineteenth century.
Tewodros was eventually ruined by his own impetuosity, which brought on the
famous Napier Expedition of 1868. This swift and for its day elaborately
planned and equipped punitive force set out from Zula and marched through
Senafe and Adigrat to Magdala where Tewodros committed suicide when he
recognized his situation as hopeless. General Napier's forces then turned around
and retraced their route to the Red Sea, leaving the Ethiopians to sort
themselves out.[19] Britain already had enough other colonial involvements to
keep her busy.

Italy, newly unified and a latecomer to the scramble for Africa, was more
difficult to discourage. A private Italian company bought the small trading
station of Assab in 1869. In 1882 the Italian government took over the port
from the company. Meanwhile Emperor Yohannes IV (1871–89) had established a large measure of control over northern Ethiopia, but he was given little
peace. The Sudanese Mahdists invaded the north-western lowlands. The
British occupied the Eritrean coast briefly again in 1884, removed the Egyptian
garrison from Massawa, and recognized the Emperor's claim to the coastal
region. He was unable to assert it before the Italians moved into Massawa in
1885. They proceeded to send 'scientific missions' into the nearby highlands.
Skirmishes with the Ethiopians ensued until a sizeable Italian contingent was
practically annihilated by the forces of Ras Alula, ruler of Hamasien, in January
1887 at Dogali, at the foot of the escarpment west of Massawa.

The victory proved ephemeral. Emperor Yohannes IV shifted troops from

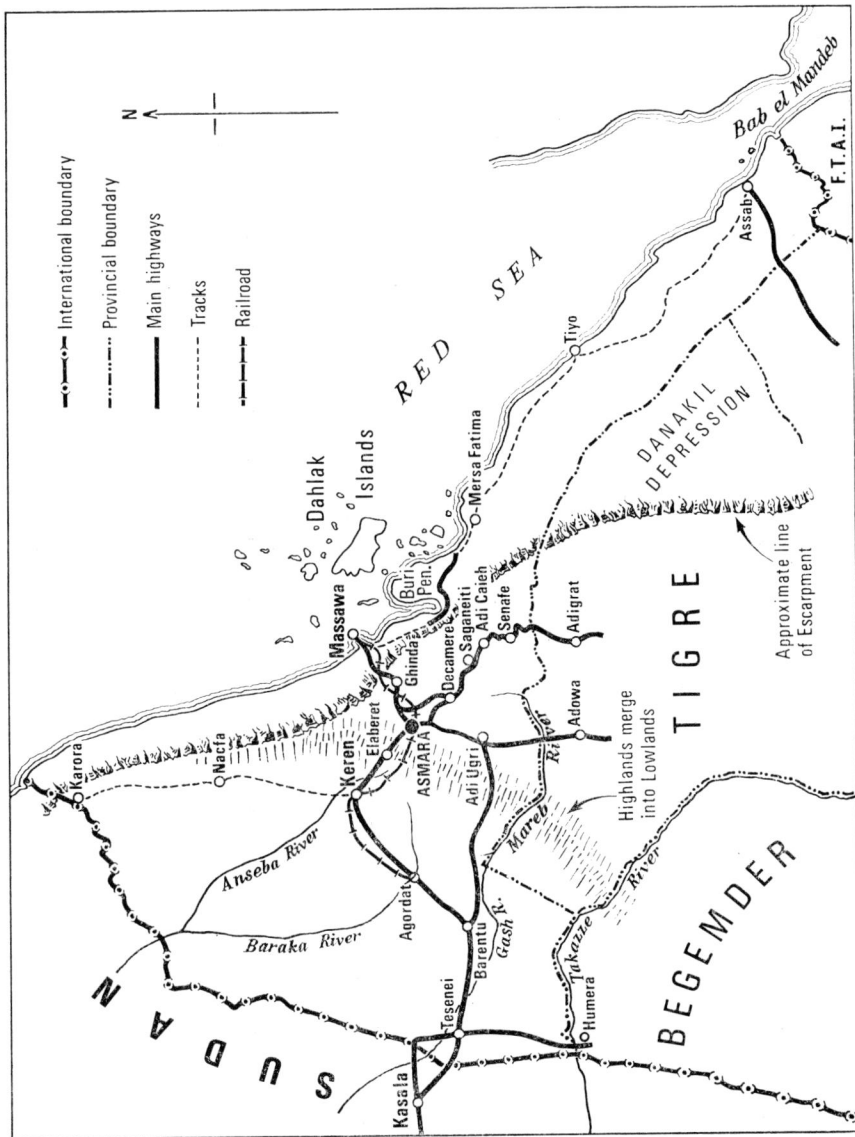

Legend:
- International boundary
- Provincial boundary
- Main highways
- Tracks
- Railroad

N

RED SEA

Bab el Mandeb

F.T.A.I.

Assab

Tiyo

DANAKIL DEPRESSION

Dahlak Islands

Mersa Fatima

Buri Pen.

Massawa

Saganeiti
Adi Caieh
Senafe

Adigrat

Ghinda

Decamere

Approximate line of Escarpment

TIGRE

Nacfa

Keren
Elaberet

ASMARA

Adi Ugri

Adowa

Karora

Highlands merge into Lowlands

Mareb River

Anseba River

Agordat

Baraka River

Barentu

Gash R.

Takazze River

BEGEMDER

SUDAN

Humera

Tesenei

Kasala

FIG. 13 Eritrea

the Sudan border to bolster defences against the Italians. The Sudanese
renewed their attacks. The Emperor led his forces back to the west, where they
defeated the Sudanese at Gallabat in March 1889, but at a terrible cost. The
Emperor was wounded in the final stages of the battle and died. Northern
Ethiopia fell into disarray. Taking advantage of rivalries among Tigrean nobles,
the Italians moved up on to the plateau and consolidated their control of the
whole region down to the valley of the Mareb in 1889–90. Asmara, which had
been Ras Alula's headquarters, became the principal Italian centre in the newly
conquered highland region. Site of a church, a market, and the houses of a few
hundred retainers of Ras Alula, the town expanded rapidly and was declared the
capital of Eritrea in 1897.

Hamasien, the sub-province of which Asmara is the natural centre, is the
northernmost section of the Christian Tigrean highland country. Though
gradually deforested through the centuries, it was still a thickly populated,
productive agricultural region until the 1860s. In the two decades before the
Italian conquest of Eritrea all of northern Ethiopia suffered epidemics of human
and cattle disease and famine resulted. A traveller in 1893 reported:

> ... Civil war, famine and an epidemic of cholera have, within the last decade,
> played fearful havoc in Abyssinia; villages are abandoned, the land is going
> out of cultivation and the wretched survivors betake themselves to the
> lowlands in the hope of finding employment and some means of subsistence.
> It is scarcely possible to realise, without visiting the country, the abject
> misery and wretchedness which has fallen upon the Ethiopian Empire during
> late years. Besides internal troubles, they have to contend with Dervish raids
> from the north, Galla raids from the south; bands of robbers haunt their
> mountains ...[20]

Thus the Italians took over a partly depopulated, war-ravaged country whose
inhabitants longed for peace and order. Italy was eager to gain as much territory
as possible. From the beginning substantial investments were made in Eritrea
and Italians were encouraged to come and settle, but until the defeat at Adowa
in 1896, Italy regarded Eritrea as a staging area for the conquest of the rest of
Ethiopia. After that humiliation, the emphasis was upon making Eritrea a model
colony by itself.

By whatever route you enter Eritrea, you notice Italian influence: well-
engineered roads, solid buildings in towns, waterworks, and plantings of trees in
the countryside. The sub-province of Serae, with large areas of flat, dark land, is
a rich agricultural region. So are the western lowlands. Akele Guzay, the more
easterly Christian sub-province between Asmara and the Tigrean border, is less
productive agriculturally but more spectacular scenically (Pl. 10b). The huge red
mountains that rise from the plateau around Senafe are among the most
splendid in Ethiopia. A good road leads through Adi Caieh to Saganeiti and
Decamere to Asmara. Saganeiti and all the towns around have tall Italian
Catholic churches – grander than most country churches in Italy – that rise on

prominent hills. All the buildings in Eritrea do not date from Italian times; some are more recent, including some well-designed schools. Decamere, which occupies an open valley south-east of Asmara and is 300 m. lower, was to be a large Italian city. It was practically abandoned during the period following the Italian defeat in 1941. Its development has not yet caught up with the master plan the Italians had for it and it still has aspects of a ghost town.

Italian influence did not penetrate everywhere in Eritrea. The Italians usually showed tolerance of local customs and religious attitudes, both Christian and Muslim. Only a few miles outside Asmara, visible from the highway that comes up from Decamere, is a classic, old-style north Ethiopian hilltop village close to the road. Built of tannish red stone, its single-storey rectangular houses cover the entire top of a small *amba*. Often on flights into Asmara the plane comes in low over such villages. They look ancient and show no modern influence.

Asmara, on the other hand, when seen from the air, looks like a model city on a drawing-board (Pl. 16a). The Italians laid it out well. With the escarpment to the east, it had open plateau to the north, south, and west to expand into, but it was not permitted to sprawl. The Italians designed the city as if land had been as scarce as in Italy itself. Streets were drawn in rectangular patterns. Houses, even large villas, were set in compact, walled gardens. Room was provided for monumental buildings, parks, and broad avenues too, but little space was wasted. Population pressure in Eritrea was not heavy, so the city never developed huge 'native quarters' that grew aimlessly. By 1930 Asmara had only 20,000 people. The conquest of Ethiopia and consolidation of Italy's East African Empire after 1936 brought a tremendous influx of colonists as well as local labourers. When Italian control ended in 1941 Asmara had about 100,000 people. Since then the population has increased to somewhat over 200,000 – very modest growth measured against the record of much of the developing world during the past three decades.

A Year's Visits to Asmara

I had to go to Asmara often, sometimes staying only a day, sometimes two or three. I never tired of this unique little city. It has charm and variety that many older and larger places lack. It deserves a book by itself, but no one who has lived there during the last thirty years seems to have written one. In the paragraphs which follow I set down impressions of visits throughout the course of an Ethiopian year.

*　　*　　*

September. Flying over Wollo and Tigre, we noted that the tops of all the mountains were yellow, as if someone had brushed paint across the higher parts of a relief map. Maskal daisies. As we descended over Eritrea there was a good deal of red visible in the landscape – cliffs and spots of bare earth – but all the fields and meadows were green, though red water flowed in most of the streams.

Patches of pinkish-purple cosmos were blooming along the edges of the Asmara airport. The city had a wet look, but bougainvillaea and other flowering shrubs and vines seemed brighter than ever, particularly around the Barattolo mansion on Andennet Avenue and in the streets of elegant old villas in the area around the American Consulate-General. I stayed at the Meneghetti and was awakened before daylight by the sounds of Christian chanting from a nearby church, great upwellings of sound, melodic but unearthly in the otherwise completely still night. Before the Christian sounds ended, the Muslim calls to prayer began, louder but less melodic, broadcasting over loudspeakers. The day began clear and sunny. Noon visit to the Queen of Sheba Market in the north-eastern part of the city. It is a walled area, built as a unit, a curious mixture of half bustle, half lethargy, with several long warehouse-like buildings separated by broad alleyways. Except for peppergrinders along the walls, all the other activity centred around wood- and metal-working, utilization of old tyres, tin cans, bottles. Beds were being made of angle-iron as well as round pipes, brightly painted trunks and duffelboxes were being made out of every imaginable kind of old lumber. Several groups of workers were fashioning simple oil lamps from Coca Cola and beer cans. Old scrap-metal was being turned into little cooking-stoves, cages, various kinds of containers. Blacksmiths were beating scrap-iron into digging tools, hooks, stakes, and rods. We stepped into several shops with large stocks of second-hand items: chandeliers and candlesticks, locks, handles, gears, coffee-mills, grinders, knives, small things of brass, tables, old furniture. There was probably nothing going on in this whole market that would be considered worth doing by the standards of profitability currently prevailing in Europe or America, almost nothing in the way of raw materials that would be worth exploiting in a modern industrial society, but it all still has value here and the simple handwork is obviously important to the economy of the city and the life of the people in it. – Evening drive out to the edge of the escarpment along the Massawa road, as far as we could go, to a checkpoint about 6 km. outside the city proper. Here the road winds through a pleasant park of eucalyptus and cactus with a carpet of daisies underneath. Everything green, soft evening sun casting long shadows. A reservoir along the road full to overflowing. A few donkeys. A few pedestrians. Old Italian signs still visible on some of the walls along the road, after thirty years. We stopped at the British War Cemetery, a serene park, well kept, with regular rows of light tan headstones and a scattering of shrubs and flowers in the light shade of eucalyptus (Pl. 16b). The names on the stones are a cross-section of the whole British Empire. Here in the thin, bright air of the plateau no moss gathers on the stones. Death seems not too depressing in this setting until one notes the ages. Most of them were in their early twenties when they were killed in 1941 or 1942 or 1943. – Back to the city for a *capuccino* at a sidewalk café along HSI Avenue. Fascinating mixture of faces, voices, tongues, and dress among the passers-by; the musical rhythms of Italian, the harsh fricatives and gutturals of Tigrinya. – Finally to Kagnew, the American communications station. The mood of World War II still seems near here. Everything about Kagnew reminds one of England and America in that now distant time: the PX with its clock-tower, the modest little chapel, the long, low barracks with their screen doors and windows and painted signs designating each unit; the old, well-polished fire-engines in their barn next to the APO, the orderly officers' bungalows with flower-beds in front, the trim hospital, the officers' and EM's clubs; the commissary, the well-paved street with stop and directional signs, young military men, those off-duty in sports clothes, young wives pushing baby-carriages; the main gate has rows of sheltered bicycle racks for local employees and a starched and polished MP who waves vehicles in and out . . .

December. Visits to olive-wood-working shops in the back reaches of the city. The first was a simple place on a side-street on the southern edge of the city, readily identifiable because of the large pile of gnarled trunks inside a walled compound. Behind, in open-walled sheds, were several lathes and half a dozen men working the oily, rich-smelling wood making bowls, plates, lamps, candle-sticks, drum bases. We ordered several bowls to be ready in five or six weeks and they took us to a shed to see their supply of porcupine quills and animal horns with which they make all sorts of garishly decorated items, much less attractive than those of olive-wood alone. A nearby shop had recently acquired large quantities of wood from abandoned houses in the countryside – mellow, well-aged pieces with golden shades inside and greyed and browned areas along the edges. I ordered a table-top cut from a single old beam. A larger workshop along the Keren road cuts its wood into blanks and allows them to age before they put them on lathes. Their prices were higher than at the other shops. – We dined in the evening at the Caravelle, a high-ceilinged Italian-style restaurant with a garden in front and a hall for dancing behind. Large numbers of stylishly dressed young people – Italians, Ethiopians, and mixtures of the two – were stomping and swaying to a loud band. At 10.30 the band stopped and everybody filed out to go home.

January. Warm, sunny days; misty, chill nights; heavy dew in the morning. The city conveys the impression of prosperity, activity, and orderliness. Many tourists have come: German, French, Italian, American, Scandinavian. There are more soldiers and policemen on the streets than a few months ago, but still fewer than in Addis. I walked from the Imperial Hotel into the centre of the city about 4 in the afternoon, strolled among the crowds under the palms on HSI Avenue, and then crossed over towards the Grand Mosque and the Orthodox church compound of St Mary on the north-eastern edge of the downtown area (Pl. 17a). By this time clouds had begun to boil up over the escarpment and billows of mist obscured the sun from time to time. Rains are still falling in the Red Sea lowlands. I wandered through the church compound for half an hour, watching the faithful praying, kissing the church doors, bowing, and waiting – large numbers of them. This huge rectangular church, built of grey stone with large framed mosaics dominating its façade, twin square towers on each side, and vivid old rose door and window frames, could look incongruous – but it doesn't. The buildings which edge the western side of the church compound are careful replicas of Axumite styles. This whole complex was built during the Italian period. From the church gate, I walked back to the Grand Mosque and then to the market area. Vegetable- and fruit-sellers were busy and their produce looked excellent. I spent a few minutes in the nearby junk market, wondering why sellers there would want to collect such huge rings of old keys and who would ever buy any of them. Like the piles of old gears, chains, broken tools, and locks, they looked as if they dated from well before World War II. The grain market – *Ehul Gebaya* – had many country types, mostly women, offering grain of many kinds as well as lentils and other legumes. I made my way back to HSI Avenue through narrow side-streets reminiscent of Bologna or Florence, except for the classic dark Tigrean faces and flowing robes of both men and women. Fog had enveloped this whole section of the city and the light was yellowish, but when I entered the small square dominated by the burgundy-and-ecru Banco di Roma, the sun broke through full force. At the Utet Bookstore I asked for a Tigrinya grammar. They had nothing. I bought a book in Italian on the Ethiopian economy published by the Asmara University Press. At another little bookstore I bought a couple of Tigrinya schoolbooks done by missionaries. – Dinner in the evening at Esposito's, a clean little restaurant run by an old Italian who started out in the inn business somewhere down along the Massawa road decades ago and only recently moved into his present location after a political assassination messed up his place near the railroad station. His wife is an Eritrean who took our pizzas out of the huge brick oven on a long wooden shovel. They were burned at the edges and tasted of charcoal; their dough was yeasty and chewy, their sauce rich with seasonings, peppers, and mushrooms. Then we had *scampi diabolo* and huge *fagioli*. Old Esposito hovers around the tables, enjoying vicariously every morsel his customers eat and always ready to bring more. Fresh Elaberet cheese for dessert and then *espresso*. A cold mist shrouded the city when we came out, like late fall in northern Europe. . . .

March. The flight now is over rocky outcroppings, barren valleys, and waterless streams with only a hint of green along their courses. The dry season is at its height and water is getting short in the city. Trees that line the avenues are being watered and everyone talks water shortage. – A late afternoon visit to the university. It would be hard to imagine an uglier building from the outside – a big, square box of light brown stone. But inside it is hollow. A big courtyard has a cheerful feel; it is ringed with balconies to a height of five storeys. On one side is a large church bell found by one of the sisters somewhere near Axum. It was apparently cast by Europeans, but it has an Amharic inscription. It rings on the hour to mark the change of class periods. The university has been brought into being by a small group of energetic Catholic nuns. The students, nearly all

Ethiopian but with a sprinkling of Italians, looked neat, clean, and serious. There was no long hair on males, no extremes of dress among the girls. We looked into classrooms and then visited the library. It occupies a huge hall which takes up one whole side of the building and has large bays of books classified according to subject. The Ethiopian history collection was rich in Italian works on Eritrea. The university must have fallen heir to a good collection assembled during the Italian period. The world history and American sections showed that USIS had been generous in its donations. – At dusk we visited several goldsmiths' shops – small, cramped places with rich assortments of jewellery in pure soft gold. No matter how intricate the workmanship of the item, everything is simply sold by weight.

June. Rain, vast torrents of it as we drove up the escarpment from Decamere to Asmara. We had to stop to wait out the worst of the storm and finally entered the city shortly after 4 o'clock through streets flowing with 15 cm. of water. The next day we had sun in the morning and heavy rain again in the afternoon. I took the landrover for servicing to the Mitchell Cotts garage in the morning and walked to the US Consulate through back streets on the eastern side of the city. This older residential section must have been developed originally for middle-class Italians; now its population is predominantly Ethiopian. There are many solid, well-kept houses. There was street-repair work in progress, after recent rain damage, and people were painting houses and walls. A large tiled mosque dominates a small hill with a park. Farther on streets were blocked with mud and rocks. People looked happy and a man told me the heavy rains were going to fill the newly completed city reservoir which is said to be large enough to supply the city's needs for the next fifty years. – An evening party at the US Consulate for departing officers: local orchestra in a tent in the garden; beer, Coca-Cola, and *tej* from a big basketry-covered bottle; hamburgers, hot dogs, and *zigani* with *injera*. Everyone danced Eritrean-style, to the delight of the orchestra. Another evening we drove to a high area on the north side of the city that appeared to have originally been a military encampment. It would now by fastidious standards perhaps be classified as a slum because most of the housing is in the form of stone-and-masonry round *tukuls* with thatched roofs, though in one section the thatch had all been replaced by corrugated tin. The whole area was orderly and clean and the people looked well dressed. Streets had fluorescent lights on metal poles and some of the houses had electric lines going into them. At the far end of the area a newer housing development had rectangular plastered houses around a large, barren square with a plaque on a pedestal in the centre indicating that HIM Haile Selassie I had officially dedicated the site a few years before. We took a new route back across the city, past the new central bus station and the Arab school, and down numerous streets alive with humanity: priests in black robes and white turbans, Muslims in skull-caps, women in all manner of dress from rags through full traditional gowns to miniskirts; boys playing soccer, workers lined up for buses, large numbers of people on bicycles. Everywhere are the monumental buildings the Italians built in colonial times, but the same style of architecture prevails in recent buildings too. Every few blocks a solid brick or stone church-tower looms over the skyline. The bells in the tall, square *campanile* of the Catholic Cathedral rang out as we came by. We drove on past the Governor-General's palace, set in a well-groomed small park, and out on to Queen Elizabeth II Avenue which leads past the new Nyala Hotel to the southern part of the city.

August. The EAL morning flight from Addis was packed with the usual motley mixture: tourists hung with cameras, Japanese businessmen, Muslim Ethiopians and Yemenis, clad in white robes, turbans, and skull-caps; local Italians on their way to Rome for summer visits; Tigrean women in traditional dress and hairstyle; stylish Amhara wives with well-dressed youngsters; Ethiopian students leaving for abroad, all trim, bright-eyed, and well groomed. Some will come back eventually with Afros and exaggerated ideas of their role in the world, but most will return and fit in and have less decisive influence on their society than they or the journalists who write about them predict . . . We came down to land over a totally green landscape. Asmara's streets were more spic-and-span than usual, for the Emperor had just completed his summer visit, during which he officiated at university graduation and visited public-works projects and factories. Even in this well-kept, well-administered city a visit by the Emperor serves the useful purpose of getting people to do little clean-up jobs they would otherwise not do so soon . . . – Aside from official business, this visit was mostly a gastrononic experience. The giant mushrooms are now in season. Some grow to a diameter of 20 cm. They are prepared for eating by grilling or frying, being first rubbed with garlic and olive oil. We had them at Esposito's one night after an introductory course of Red Sea oysters – pinkish and meaty, tender and with a good flavour. When we arrived at 7.30 the restaurant was empty; when we left at 9.30 it was full and most of the elite of Asmara were represented. The next night I dined in the Red Room of the Meneghetti and had an even more elegant meal: *prosciutto crudo con melone* followed by a fried mushroom and fresh steamed vegetables; a half-bottle of Vitalo *rosso* and another of Sabarguma; then a large slice of a torte constructed of blocks of meringue held together with whipped cream. I walked for nearly two hours through the city afterwards making a wide loop around the whole central area. The streets were filled with young people, usually in twos and threes, some older people, including both Italian and Ethiopian matrons. It was pleasant not to be besieged by crowds of streetboys begging, selling, offering some undesired service, as happens all too often in many Ethiopian cities. Boys do sell newspapers, candy and nuts, old coins and souvenirs on the streets, and hustlers on HSI Avenue whisper favourable rates for money exchange or female companionship. But if the visitor shows no interest, that is the end of it. Bars were busy with music and dancing. Some small shops were still open for business late in the evening. As always, I was struck by the normality of life in

Asmara. The insurgency that has plagued the Eritrean countryside for several years has almost no direct effect on the city. It is awesome to reflect on how many diverse groups of people, how many changes of economic direction, and how many different political orientations this city has experienced in its relatively brief history. But it is hard to take the aspirations of the insurgents too seriously. Asmara is not an Arab city or a Muslim city. It belongs to neither the Middle East nor to Africa, nor to Europe either. It has its own individuality and character and has already learned to avoid falling victim to passing pressures and fashions. Many colonial-built cities fit less well into their new countries than Asmara does into Ethiopia, which is, of course, not a new country at all, but a very old country which had its beginnings in these northern highlands of which Asmara is now the natural centre.

Keren and Massawa

Except for the darker skin of its inhabitants, Keren could easily be in Anatolia, Iran, or Afghanistan. The town is built of stone. Bougainvillaea twines around airy verandas and women in bright pantaloons stroll in the streets. A broad, sandy river-bed, dry except after heavy rain, winds through the town and provides a rest area for camels who bring in loads of charcoal and gnarled firewood each day. There is a Turkish-style mosque with a tall, thick minaret. In a military encampment at the edge of the town, soldier's families live in whitewashed *tukuls* with thatched roofs. The town has a large market area edged with lanes of small shops where craftsmen make shoes, clothing, ironware, and good silver and gold jewellery.

Keren has been a crossroads for centuries, perhaps for millennia. The surrounding region has a great variety of languages, tribes, and religions. Many of the people of this area are Tigre-speaking. There is also a large group of Bilen-speaking people in the Keren area. They are Agaus, remnants of the pre-Semitic population of northern Ethiopia. Many of these northern peoples were converted to Islam from Orthodox Christianity as recently as the nineteenth century. At the same time Western missionaries became active among them: Swedes, Americans, British, and Italians. As a result the region is religiously as complex as any in Ethiopia. Catholics, Lutherans, Baptists, Ethiopian Orthodox, and Muslims all brush shoulders in Keren. The Keren region saw the hardest fighting encountered by Commonwealth Forces as Eritrea was wrested from the Italians in 1941.[21] British and Italian war cemeteries are the only visible reminders of these battles. The area has been the scene of Eritrean insurgent activities in recent years.

Lying at 1,220 m., Keren has a warm, dry climate. The countryside around the town is dotted with isolated acacias and huge old baobabs. In this it is reminiscent not of the Middle East but of the savannah country of West Africa. The lanky, brown-skinned men driving their camels or donkeys across the landscape and the lithe women with their loose, bright-coloured garments blowing in the breeze create scenes identical to what can be seen outside the walls of Kano in northern Nigeria or as far west as Senegal.

The road from Keren back to Asmara climbs gradually to the park-and-garden country of Elaberet, where a large agricultural estate has been developed with private Italian money and management. Irrigation and modern machinery are used, along with a large quantity of local labour. Excellent butter, cheese, and sausage are produced and fruits and vegetables are supplied to consumers both in-country and abroad. During the European winter, several cargo planes can be seen at the Asmara airport every day loading produce from Elaberet and other Eritrean producers for the Middle East and Europe. Plans for greatly expanded winter fruit and vegetable production in Eritrea were dealt a bad blow by the closing of the Suez Canal in 1967, but a refinement of crop plans and emphasis on highest possible quality have enabled a sizeable export trade to develop on the basis of air transport. After Elaberet the route back to Asmara snakes its way up rocky valleys covered with goat-eaten scrub and spectacular stands of candelabra cuphorbia. As it enters Asmara, the highway passes the Queen of Sheba Stadium, scene of hard-fought football matches as well as displays of traditional dancing and jousting.

Asmara is connected with Massawa, as with Keren, by both road and rail. Both routes are marvels of engineering. They come very close together at times and cross over each other. During the cooler part of the year, the escarpment presents a relatively lush appearance, for there is a sharp divergence in climate between the highlands and the lowlands. When the plateau is having its heaviest rains, the lowlands along the Red Sea are at their hottest and driest. The rainy season in the lowlands comes during the period November–January, when there is no rain on the plateau. There is naturally some spill-over from both directions in the escarpment area. To help control erosion the Italians carried out terracing projects in many of the upper valleys along the escarpment – rocks were piled up into walls that follow the contours of the mountainsides. Eucalyptus trees were planted along roadsides and on wider terraces. The most common vegetation on steeper escarpment slopes is the prickly pear cactus. Great quantities of its fruit, golden orange inside, sweet and refreshing in flavour, are sold along the roadside and hauled up to highland markets during the long season that is at its height in November and December.

There is a good deal of agriculture along the mid-section of the escarpment, including a major irrigated development at Ghinda. A bit farther on, at Dongollo, are the springs which supply much of northern Ethiopia with table water under the labels of Dongollo and Sabarguma. On clear days the sea comes into view soon after the beginning of the descent, though during the lowland rainy season the escarpment is often thickly overhung with cloud. The foothills are rather narrow. A brief stretch of savannah vegetation leads on to the hot desert where the landscape is broken only by dry stream-beds and occasional clusters of doum palms. The view back towards the towering escarpment walls, here almost 2,000 m. of drop, is the finest sight from the coastal plain, though

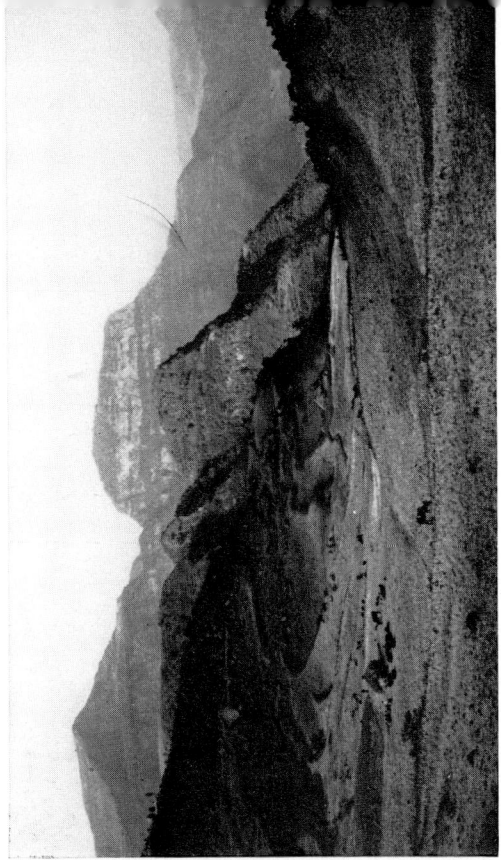

1 North through Wollo to Tigre. Scenes along Great Escarpment Highway

(a) Ascent between Alamata and Korem.   (b) Lake Ashangi.   (c) Valley near Mai Chow.   (d) Escarpment in southern Tigre

2 Wollo. Bati Market

(a) Great-horned cattle, common in foothills of Great Escarpment

(b) Panorama of Bati Market, where highlanders and lowlanders meet and trade every Monday

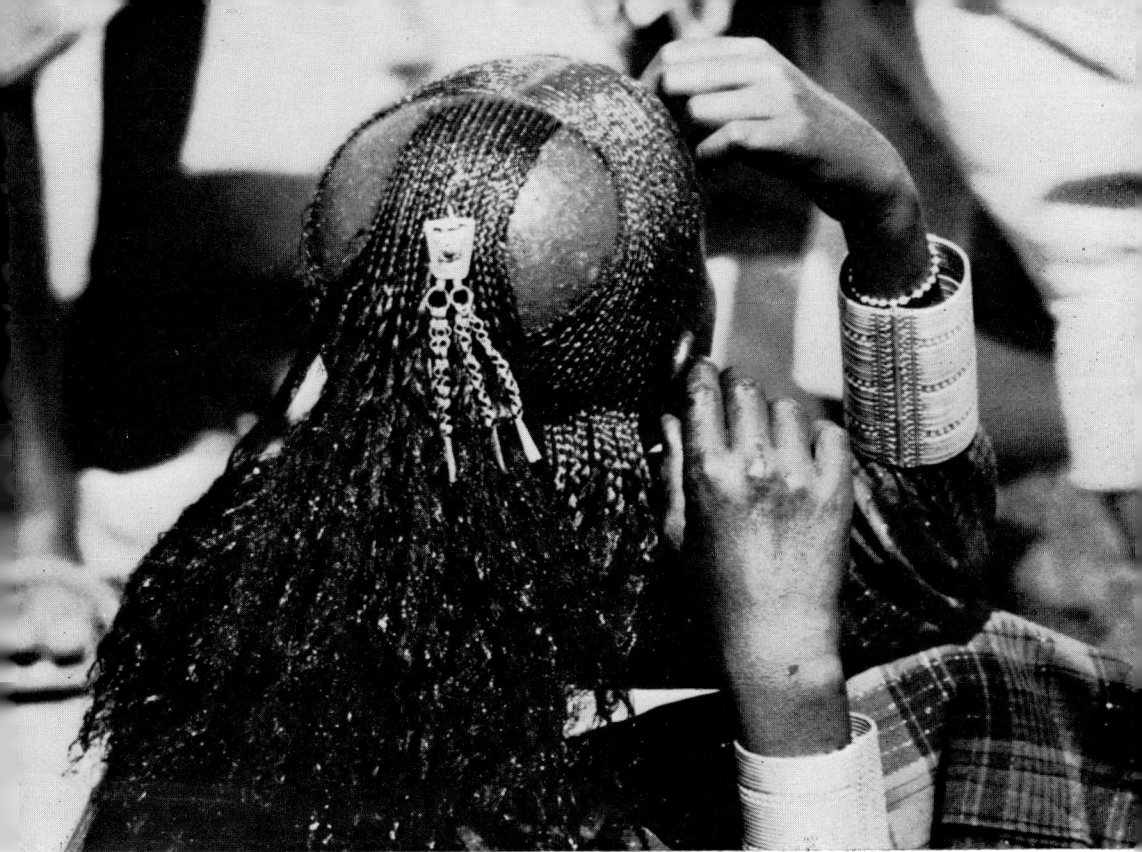

3 (a) Young girl at Bati Market displays silver jewellery and elaborate hair-do

(b) Wollo. Monk from the monastery of St Stephen in Lake Haik

4 Wollo

Men at Bati Market

5 Wollo

(a) The monastery of St Stephen, on a fertile island off northern shore of Lake Haik

(b) Lake Haik. Passengers are poled to monastery island on crude reed rafts

6 Lalibela

(a) Bet Amanuel. Splendid example of Axumite style, flawlessly carved from living rock

(b) The rock churches are part of a bustling medieval community, with characteristic two-storeyed thatched stone houses

7 (a) Church of Abba Libanos, nestled under a cliff facing south-east and catching morning sunlight

(b) First rays of morning sun warm worshippers gathered round edge of deep pit in which Bet Giyorgis is situated

8 Lalibela. Bet Maryam, most elaborately carved and painted of Lalibela churches. The large pillar, said to have past and future history of the world written on it, is kept covered and no human eye is allowed to rest upon it

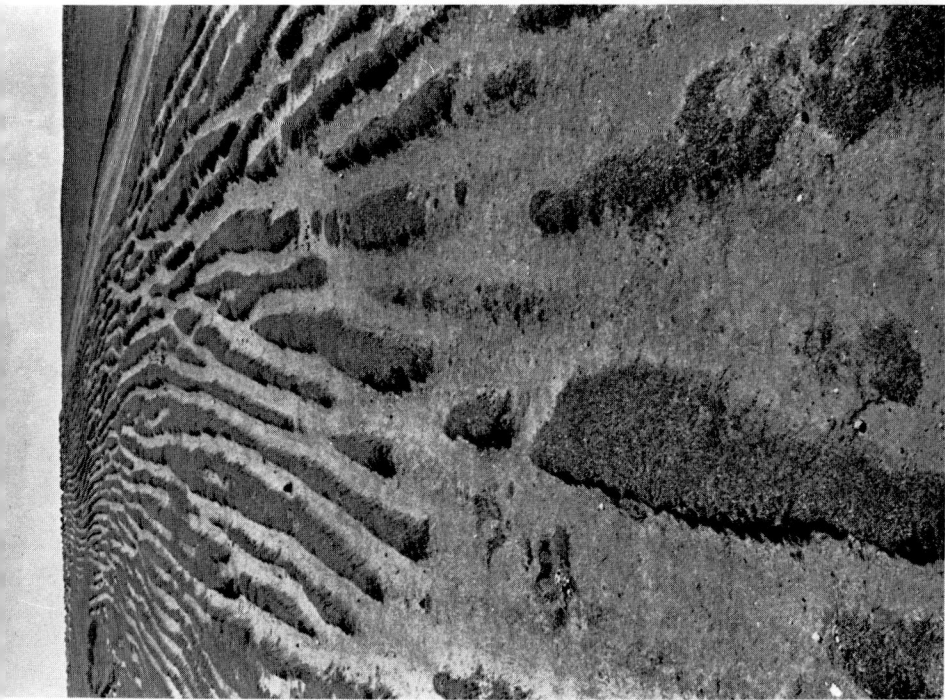

24 Arussi

(a) Age-old trails on flat southern plateau reflect centuries of wear. To right, smooth motor track

(b) Slender variety of lobelia rises to heights of 8–10 m. in valleys at about the 3000 m. level on Mount Chilalo

(a) Balambaras Biru, hereditary chief of the Zay

(b) Portraits of Father Daniel and King Honorius from the Tullu Guddo *Sinkesar*

(b) Women in southern Arussi wear handsome broad-brim hats and as much jewellery as they can afford

23 Arussi

(a) Galla couple sit astride horse

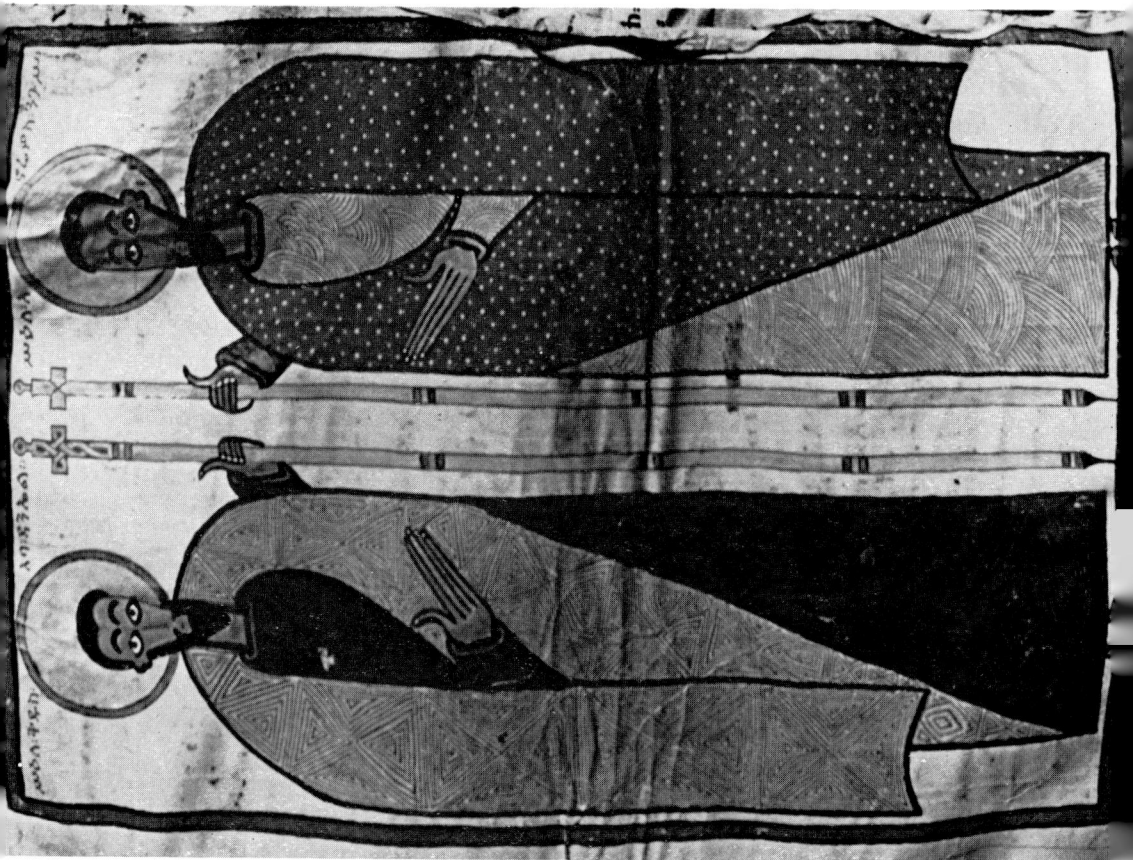

21 South-western bay area of Tullu Guddo has rich meadows backed by terraces on which cotton and finger millet are grown. In foreground, candelabra euphorbia

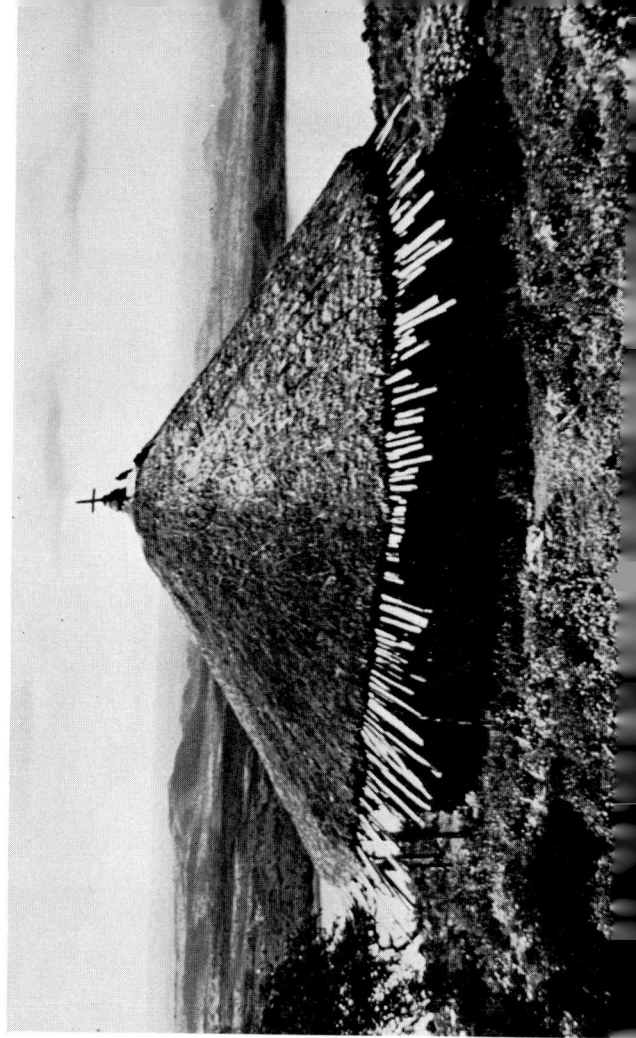

20 Lake Zway

(a) Enormous amounts of *tilapia nilotica* are taken by traditional means. A fisherman throws his net, edged with volcanic pebbles which cause it to settle firmly over shoals of fish which congregate in shallow reedbeds

(b) Old St Mary of Zion, classic round thatched church, commands view of Arussi plateau

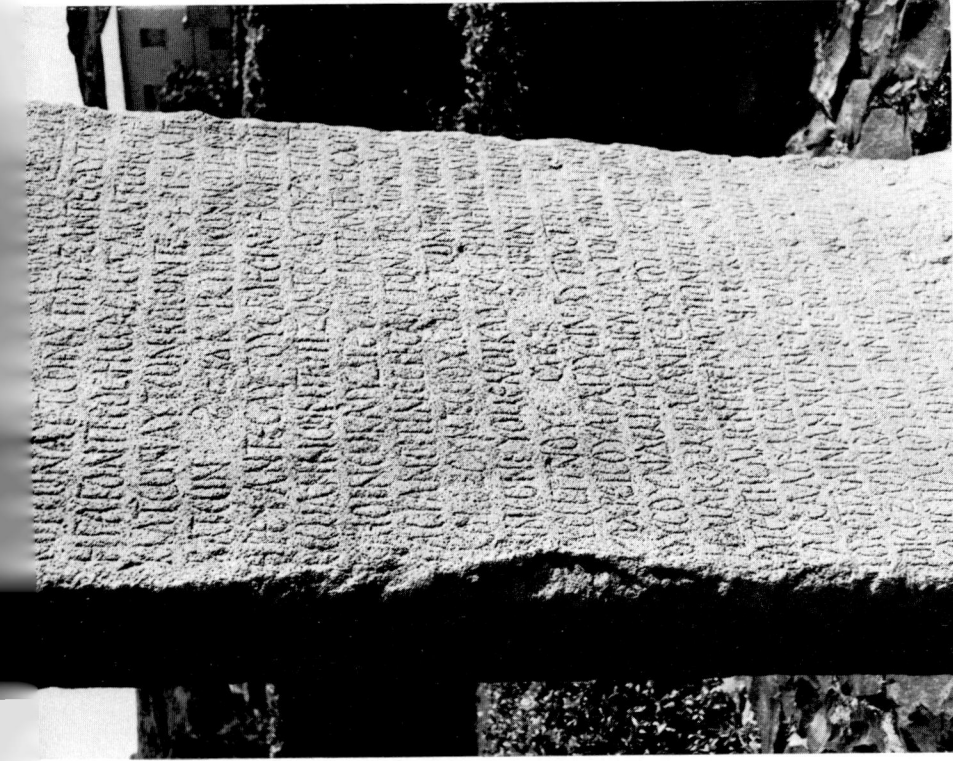

19 Tigre, Axum (a) One of King Ezana's inscriptions.

(b) Tallest standing obelisk rises 22 m.

18 Tigre, Axum

(a) Largest of Axum obelisks fell centuries ago and shattered into several pieces

(b) Large reservoir, Mai Shum, known as 'Queen of Sheba's Bath'

17 Eritrea

(a) Compound of Asmara Maryam, city's principal Orthodox church, contains interesting complex of buildings done in semi-modernized version of Axumite style

(b) Eritrean escarpment, vast jumble of mountains, valleys, gorges where land tumbles rapidly from over 2000 m. to sea level

16 Asmara

(a) Ethiopia's second city, compactly built with regular street patterns. With a more than doubled population in last twenty-five years, it still has room for expansion

(b) British war cemetery in sunny eucalyptus grove on edge of escarpment

15 Tigrean rock churches. Painting in many is primitive in style, but all the more attractive because of naïveté of expressions and earthy blends of colour

(a) Tiny cliff church of Petros and Pawlos in Tsada Amba

(b) Dramatic Last Judgment scene painted on column in Bet Mikhai Mikael near by

14 Tigrean rock churches

(a) Enda Medhane Alem, Adi Kasho has been cut deep into a tall cliff. The white walls are a later addition and form a long entry hall behind which the true front wall of the church has been hewn from the living rock

(b) Only two holes high on cliffside reveal existence of Mihaizengi Mikael

13 Tigre, Makelle

(a) Tigrean women carry their babies in leather carriers decorated with cowries and seeds

(b) Salt market. Salt bars unloaded off camels who have brought them up from the lowlands are a major item of trade. They are cut and trans-shipped to many other parts of northern Ethiopia

12 Tigre, Makelle. Sellers of clay coffee-pots at Monday market

11 Tigre

(a) Castle Abraha Hotel at Makelle

(b) Rock-hewn church of Wokro Cherqos, once thought to be unique

10 (a) Tigre, Debra Damo. Ethiopia's oldest monastery situated on top of isolated amba and reachable only by rope

(b) Eritrea. Some of northern Ethiopia's most spectacular scenery, found among the red sandstone mountains around Senafe

9 Tigre

(a) Volcanic peaks and knobs rising north and east of Adowa, dramatic features in landscape of old Ethiopian heartland

(b) Tigrean farmer uses primitive tree-trunk plough to break unbelievably rocky fields while naked son looks on

25 Arussi. Galla grave-sites are decorated in traditional style and with modern adaptations

26 (a) Arussi, Mount Chilalo. Ato Kebbede, Christian Galla farmer

(b) Kaffa. Coffee-drying floors on outskirts of Agaro

27 [opposite] Arussi Mountains

(a) Top of Mount Chilalo, dominated by rocks and springy stalks of burned heather, among which grow a rich variety of alpine flowers

(b) Mount Kakka looking westward from Meraro

(c) Saturday market at Asasa with Mount Enquolo in background

28 Illubabor

(a) Anuak women carrying fruit to Gambela market in calabash bowls

(b) Baro river at Gambela

29 [*opposite*] (a) Nuer beauties still wear more jewellery than clothes and smoke pipes from an early age

(b) Nuer tapestry from Itang

30 (a) Sidamo *tukul*, among the most beautiful types of traditional housing in Ethiopia

(b) Islands and promontories of southern end of Lake Abbaya, silhouetted against mountains of Sidamo

31 (a) Lake Abbaya. Graceful ambatch boat

(b) Lake Chamo. Galla herdsman brings his cattle to water at Uchule on eastern shore

32 People of south-west

    (a) Anuak mother with child, from Walinga

    (b) Gidicho woman of Lake Abbaya

MASSAWA

N

RED SEA

Beach

ABD-EL-KADER

PENINSULA

Salt Pans

Naval Hqs.

GERAR PEN.

Salt Works

Port

Old City

To ASMARA

Imperial Palace

MASSAWA I.

Grand Mosque

St.Mary's Church

Causeway

To ARKIKO

TAULUD I.

Red Sea Hotel

——— Highways/Principal Streets

+——+——+ Railway

0   ½ mile

0   1 kilometre

Green (Sheik Said) Island

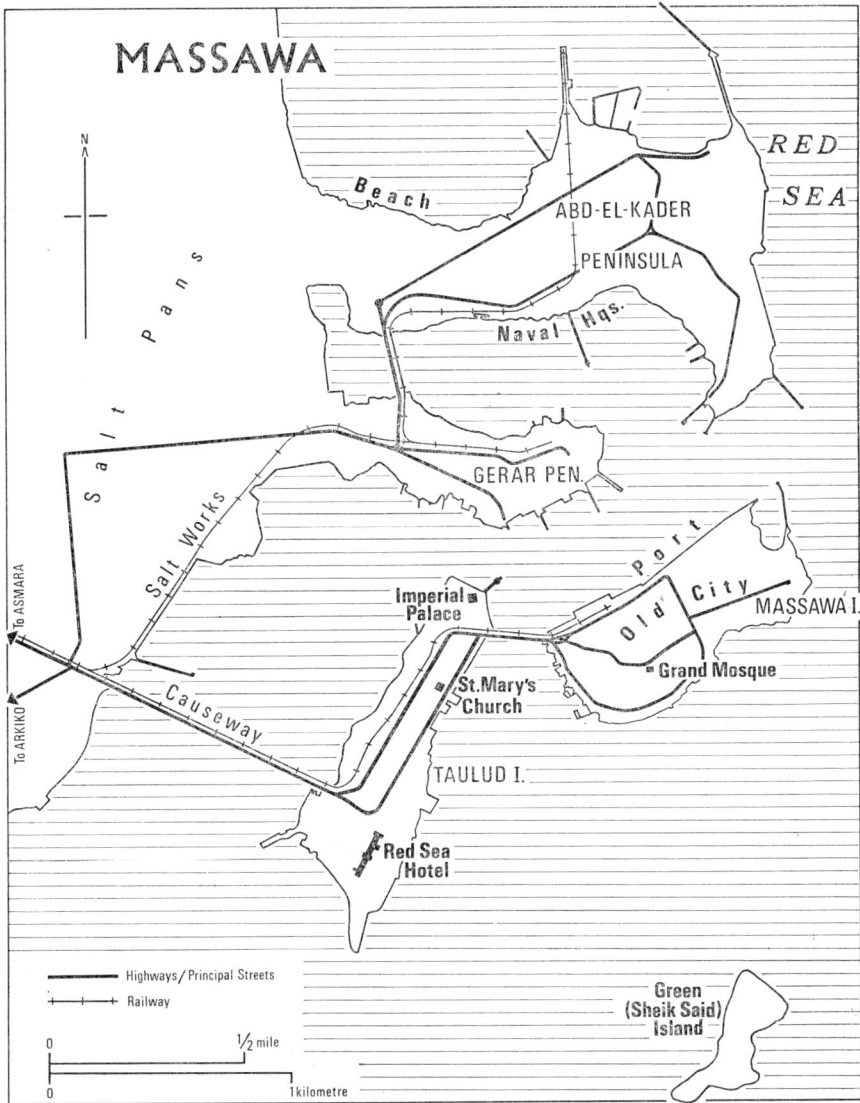

FIG. 14   Massawa

the rounded blue mountain that forms the backbone of the Buri Peninsula south of Massawa is also prominent. The old port of Adulis (Zula) lies on the bay that separates the peninsula from the mainland.

Massawa originally occupied only the outermost island of the group of two islands and two peninsulas that now constitute the city. Old Massawa – the outer island – is still a Turco-Arab style city. Buildings here are large, with high ceilings, double-tiered arcades, and enclosed balconies and porches,

4—EJ   *   *

many of them beautifully carved of wood, ornamented and painted. One of the most prominent features of the old town is the well-proportioned new mosque built with funds donated by the Emperor. It blends smoothly into the ageless Muslim atmosphere. The city's busy port occupies the north side of this island. A walk through the narrow streets of the old city any time from dusk to well after midnight corrects the impression one gets during the day that the island is occupied by far larger numbers of men than women, for at night the brightly lit bars that crowd in on each other are busy with music, dancing, and drinking. Friendly girls, representing every form of Ethiopian beauty, beckon passers-by. The area is full of small shops selling giant seashells, specimens of many kinds of coral, and the long, tooth-edged snouts of sawfish. Even in the coolest months of the year Massawa has a sultry feel about it. People sleep on bedsteads set up in gardens, on roofs, and in streets and alleyways as they do in the countries of the eastern Mediterranean.

Massawa island is connected to the island of Taulud by causeway and another causeway, which carries both road and railway, connects Taulud to the mainland. Taulud has several monumental buildings, including the Emperor's winter palace at its northern end. He used to come up every year to preside over Navy Days, the highpoint of Massawa's official year. Taulud also has an imposing Christian church, new St Mary's, donated by the Emperor to serve the still relatively small Christian population of the city. For hundreds of years Massawa had been almost exclusively Muslim.[22] The Italians permitted only one small Christian church to function – old St Mary's, an ugly square building constructed over the sea at the end of a narrow causeway. The new church, of cathedral-like proportions in Italo-Byzantine style, more than compensates for the low status Orthodox Christianity had to endure for so long here.

The southern end of Taulud is occupied by the Red Sea Hotel, Ethiopia's most impressive modern hotel until it was outdone by the Addis Ababa Hilton. The tall, ovoid arches of the wing which contains all the public rooms and which opens out on to a garden facing the sea are in Saharan style. A long jetty extends into the shallow bay, pointing directly at Green Island, mangrove covered, and other sandy islands that are the beginning of the Dahlak group, rich in history, legend, and marine life. The Red Sea off Massawa is clear as glass.

The bay along the south side of the Abd-el-Kader Peninsula is the headquarters of the Imperial Ethiopian Navy. The north side of this peninsula has a long stretch of unspoiled beach; the sand is dull brown in colour. Large areas of the mainland behind this peninsula and its smaller neighbour promontory to the south are occupied by salt flats where sea water is let into shallow depressions to evaporate. The salt which results is raked into piles that sparkle like new snow. Salt-making is one of Massawa's main industries and has been extensively mechanized in recent years.

It is good to come down to Massawa to get warmed up in the coolest season on the plateau, but during the height of the Red Sea summer, July through

September, when the temperature may stay above 35°C for weeks on end, the reluctance of anyone who has not been born and bred in the region to show much enthusiasm for the Eritrean coast is understandable. No mysterious historical laws need be postulated to explain why invaders were always tempted to push on up the escarpment where streams and springs, green forest, and cool air promised relief from the heat of the Samhar. It now takes only three hours to drive from Massawa back up to Asmara. Early travellers, facing the escarpment wall, had a far more arduous journey ahead of them. The first ascent of the Eritrean escarpment by a modern army was that of the Napier Expedition in 1867–68. They built a road which led directly into Tigre via Senafe. It went up considerably to the south of the present Massawa-Asmara route, passing close to the ancient city of Cohaito (Coloe). This route was probably the most important artery into the interior in Axumite times. It can be traversed, for the most part, only on foot or muleback now and then only when local security conditions permit. Thus we have to leap over this terrain to go back to the beginnings in the old heartland and have a more thorough look at the venerable old centre of civilization, the holy city of Axum.

Axum

No one knows how old Axum is. In Christian Ethiopia it has always been the holiest of all places, the seat of the foremost church, St Mary of Zion, and the location of the most revered *tabot* in the country, reputed to have been brought from Jerusalem by Emperor Menelik I, son of the Queen of Sheba and King Solomon. Axum became prominent as a Christian centre because it had already been important in past centuries. The first major archaeological work undertaken here was by the early twentieth-century expedition led by Dr Enno Littmann. It confirmed that the city had been a political and religious centre since well back into the first millennium BC. New archaeological work may push its history back even further, but it is unlikely that much of the uncertainty about its origins will ever be cleared up.

When Axum was first visited by European travellers, it was a dismal place. It is more attractive now because eucalyptus trees have grown up throughout the town, some streets have been paved, and several of the historical sites have benefited from clearing, landscaping, and planting of flowers and shrubbery.

I first saw Axum on a flying visit as escort for a small group in a private plane, coming in from Lalibela over the mountains of Lasta at 3 in the afternoon. Word had been sent to the Nebure-Id from the authorities in Addis Ababa that we were due and he met us at the dirt airstrip in his shiny black 10-seat landrover which he drove himself. The Nebure-Id of Axum is one of the most prestigious religious offices in Ethiopia. The responsibilities also include directing the civil government of the Axum sub-province. The Nebure-Id has ordinarily been an eminent old priest, but in 1968 the Emperor appointed one of the most energetic young men in the Ethiopian Church, Qes Ermiyas

Kebbede, to this position and encouraged him to start modernizing the sleepy old city and turn it into a historical site worthy of its great past. Qes Ermiyas set about his work with vigour. On this visit we developed a keen appreciation for his energy, for we never wasted a minute and learned a great deal about Axum, past and present.

We drove first to the famous churches: old St Mary of Zion with its paintings, then to its treasury behind with imperial crowns and manuscripts, emperors' robes and crosses, and large tablets with inscriptions of Axumite kings. From here we walked past the square chapel which houses the Ark of the Covenant, the first *tabot* of Ethiopia. Its fine-featured old keeper came out to greet us, smile, bow, and be photographed. No one dare step inside, not even the Nebure-Id. Then on into the new cathedral of St Mary of Zion – a vast, austere, flat-domed building completed in 1965.[23] It must be impressive when filled with worshippers at festivals. From there we drove the short distance to the Garden of the Stelae and admired the great standing pillar and the even taller fallen one (Pl. 18a). A good beginning has been made at turning this area into a park, but we were also struck by the thought of how much work there still is here and elsewhere in Axum for archaeologists and restorers. From the garden we went to the Queen of Sheba's bath, Mai Shum, an ancient reservoir still in use, and then on to the tombs of the emperors Caleb and Gebre-Maskal. The tomb site, with a view towards the mountains of Adowa, is in itself worth the visit. The tombs are well constructed of cut stone fitted without mortar. We descended into them by candlelight. Three sarcophagi remain in Gebre-Maskal's tomb; otherwise both are empty. On the way back into town we stopped to see the site of a new tourist hotel, one of the Nebure-Id's proudest projects, for which foundations had just been started. It has an excellent location, about 30 m. above the level of the town with a view of all the principal large monuments and a picturesque old twisted fig-tree clinging to a rocky spur behind. We finished our tour at the Nebure-Id's newly opened tourist centre in the middle of the town where we were served a strong, creamy yellow local *tej* and shown the handicraft shop where locally made crosses, jewellery, and good-quality replicas of Axumite statues, stelae, and clay heads were offered at reasonable fixed prices. By 4.45 the Nebure-Id was driving us back to the airstrip so we could reach Asmara before sundown. We bade him a breathless goodbye and took off. It had been a good visit, but I was glad to be able to return again for another look at the old city.

My next visit was leisurely. It was late June and we had a sunny afternoon for an initial stroll among the stelae, time to admire the precision of the carving on the one still standing (about 22 m. high), time to examine the detail on the huge broken one (over 30 m. in length) and to contemplate several smaller standing stelae (Pl. 19a), some simple monoliths with no refined carving. At the east end of the Garden of the Stelae we walked over to the rectangular stone church of Enda Yesus, shaded by trees. We found a good example of a smaller carved stela lying against the church wall. Beyond are still more smallish stelae, many still standing but some at odd angles. Farther on, *en route* to Mai Shum, we came upon a badly broken but well-cut stela lying in a gully. It is hard to envision what the complete complex of stelae must have looked like when they were newly erected. Little is known about their origin and the time of their erection except that they seem to date from late pre-Christian times. They are thought to have been grave-markers and sacrificial sites. The multi-storeyed form must have some relationship to south Arabian 'skyscraper' architecture.[24]

We soon attracted a bevy of bothersome boys, some offering Axumite coins, stone icons, and clay heads for sale, all clamouring to show us additional points of interest such as the dubious tombs of the Queen of Sheba and Menelik I in a field outside the town. To escape the commotion we drove off to the other end of the town to the ruins of the large palace which straddles the main highway to the south-west. This must have been a magnificent building in its heyday, as large as any structure erected in Ethiopia until very recent times. It may be the Axumite kings' palace described by the Greek trader Cosmas Indicopleustes in the sixth century A.D. when Christianity was already well established. Before we had a chance to tire of the palace ruins, a thunderstorm overtook us. We returned in its wake to the cathedral compound, now totally empty except for a couple of priests who were pleased to have visitors during the waning hours of the day. We looked at the stone thrones and into the wall towers, where several monks were sleeping, and then spent more than an hour in the cathedral itself, photographing the paintings, and in the treasury, examining the crowns, manuscripts, and inscriptions. In the gloomy, chill atmosphere with a light drizzle falling outside, the old church was more attractive than I had found it on the first visit. One could sense the timelessness of Ethiopian Orthodoxy and get a little feel for the special holiness of this place. The paintings are not extraordinary and are not especially old, but some have an unusual freshness about them, especially that of St Yared, founder of Ethiopian church music, and the panel with the nine Syrian saints. The priests, spurred by our interest in their treasures, competed to show us as much as possible and explain their understanding of the history behind it. Eventually we rejoined the women of our party (women cannot enter the old cathedral grounds) at the Nebure-Id's handicraft centre and then returned to the Touring Hotel for dinner in the round dining-room. Here students from the high school in Adowa were selling tickets to a play they were presenting that evening at the Nebure-Id's new community hall. We took along a retired American couple from California on their first day of a flying tour of Ethiopia. The play was a high melodrama in Amharic about an army lieutenant whose wife fails him while he is off in a border region enduring hardships. Between acts there were humorous musical interludes in Tigrinya. A serious young teacher showed us around the community centre which was so recently completed that it smelled of wet plaster and fresh paint. In addition to a large hall it had rooms for smaller gatherings and space for a substantial library which the Nebure-Id was hoping to build up with donations from foreign embassies.

I awoke as the last hyena calls heralded the clear dawn and hurried over to the cathedral area. A multitude of white-robed figures had already gathered at old St Mary's and sounds of chanting poured out from inside. Women, many of them wearing nuns' caps, hovered outside the cathedral precincts. Inside, hundreds of monks, priests, and young deacons were scattered through the grounds, reading prayer-books under trees, praying against walls, strolling among the graves that fill much of the churchyard. The sun began to rise. Across the open area to the north the big standing stela shone golden and soon its smaller neighbours were bathed in the same glow. I walked through the small streets behind the Garden of the Stelae, watching people going about their early morning chores, and then on past Enda Mikael and Enda Simeon. The streets were quickly filling with people and boys looking for tourists spotted me. From one I bought a segment of sparkling lavender geode for E$1. After a visit to the park at the east end of the town to examine King Ezana's inscription (Pl. 19b), I devoted the remainder of the morning to the present-day side of Axum, making a presentation of books to the library of the local high school and calling on the Nebure-Id in his office. Hundreds of people were gathered at the municipal centre waiting to transact some sort of business; many of them seemed to be waiting to see the Nebure-Id himself. He obviously put into practice his belief that both church and civil officials should be close to the population.[25]

One leaves Axum with a sense of curiosity whetted but not satisfied. The French who are doing the most important digging in this area now are bound to make discoveries which will shed new light on both Axum and on the rest of northern Ethiopia's past. The most comprehensive book on Axum which has yet appeared is the work, surprisingly, of a Russian. It is remarkable for the diligence with which information from more than 400 sources, practically the entire body of scholarly and travel writing on north Ethiopian antiquities, has been worked into its 275 pages.[26] But like so many Soviet works the book is marred by the fact that it had to fit the political line current at the time it was written. Its conclusions stress the 'Africanness' of Axumite civilization. No one would want to denigrate the African aspects of Axumite, and for that matter Ethiopian, civilization, but the fact of close ties between Axum and south Arabia is incontrovertible. The religious symbolism, the style of architecture, the written traditions themselves as recorded in the inscriptions all attest to close south Arabian connections, as do of course the script and the languages themselves. In the period immediately before the rise of Islam, in fact, parts of south Arabia were under Axumite Christian rule. It is not only to future archaeological work in northern Ethiopia itself that we must look, therefore, for new light on the history of Axum, but also to the Yemens:

> Among the ancient high cultures of the Near East none is so little known as the one that flourished in southern Arabia – the 'Arabia Felix' of classical times – in the first millennium BC.[27]

Political conditions in the Yemens have been so unsettled in recent years, in part because of Soviet-Chinese rivalry for the allegiance of local radical movements, that no serious archaeological or historical work has been done. It is to be hoped that conditions will change for the better before many more years have passed.

NOTES

1 There is a considerable literature on the Tigrean salt trade. Recent accounts include Haile Michael Mesghinna, 'Salt Mining in Enderta', *JES*, July 1966, 127–35, and Kevin O'Mahoney, 'The Salt Trail', *JES*, July 1970, 147–54.

2 'The Village of the Abuna', where the Egyptian-born Patriarch of the Ethiopian Orthodox Church used to reside.

3 *Travels*, 119.

4 A distinctly Ethiopian way of showing affection for a prominent personality is to name a bar after him. There are John F. Kennedy bars all over the country.

5 £4·00 or US$10·00 at 1973 rates.

6 *Proceedings of the Third International Conference of Ethiopian Studies*, Haile Selassie I University, Addis Ababa, 1969, I, 83–98. The same paper with additional data, photographs, and drawings was published separately as *The Monolithic Churches of Tigray*, Central Printing Press, Addis Ababa, 1970.

7 Mrs Plant's discoveries are summed up in an issue of *EO*, XIII, 3, devoted exclusively to the Tigre churches. It appeared in early 1971. David Buxton also contributed to it. Seventy-two individual churches are described in this issue with plans, sketches, and photographs. There is nothing else even remotely comparable in usefulness for the traveller who wishes to visit any of these churches. She published notes on additional churches in *EO*, XVI, 1, in 1973.

8 Unlikely, since King Ezana of Axum is believed to have adopted Christianity only in the fourth decade of the fourth century.

9 Ethiopians usually speak of the church key as they do of the *tabot* in a personified way: *Qolfew yimattal* – 'The key will come'; *Tabotu matta* – 'The tabot has come'.

10 Just who this hateful, energetically destructive queen was has not yet been firmly established. She has been variously identified as a Falasha, a renegade Tigrean noblewoman and a member of a tribe from the Sahel region along the Red Sea. Some of the legends surrounding her have been summarized by Dr Sergew Hable-Selassie in 'The Problem of Gudit', *JES*, January 1972, 113–24.

11 Illustrated in Gerster, *Churches*, Pl. 180.

12 It is said to have been built during the Italian occupation.

13 The floor-to-ceiling height of the cross at the centre is 7·3 m., that of the cupola in front of the *qiddus qiddusan* 6·7 m. according to Mrs Plant's measurements.

14 These legendary figures are said to have ruled in the mid-fourth century. In popular tradition they have replaced King Ezana, who was converted to Christianity at that time. It seems unlikely that this church could be so old, though the site may have been used at that time. The church of Abraha Atsbaha is so skilfully executed that it appears to rank relatively late among Tigrean rock churches.

15 Ivy Pearce has made a brief comparison of some of the features of the two groups in *EO*, XIII, no. 1, 57–78.

16 There is an unfinished rock church on the slopes of Mt Entoto north-east of Addis Ababa – Yekka Mikael; cf. A. F. Matthew, 'The Monolithic Church on Yekka', *JES*, July 1969, 89–98. Another still in use – Adadi Maryam – is situated south of the Awash, 60 km. south-west of Addis Ababa; cf. Buxton, *Travels*, 66–8. Many abandoned cave churches have been recorded recently by the Pankhursts in valleys south of the capital; cf. Richard Pankhurst, 'Caves in Ethiopian History . . .', *EO*, XVI, no. 1, 15–35.

17 Several are described by Ivy Pearce, '. . . Cave and Rock Churches of Lasta', *EO*, XII, no. 3, 142–63.

18 The complex history of this period is well summarized by Mordechai Abir, *Ethiopia, the Era of the Princes*, London, 1968.

19 The expedition is well described by Frederick Myatt, *The March to Magdala*, London, 1970; the events which led up to it are objectively summarized by Donald Crummey, *Priests and Politicians*, Oxford, 1972.

20 J. Theodore Bent, *The Sacred City of the Ethiopians*, London, 1893, 11–12.

21 Well recounted in A. J. Barker, *Eritrea 1941*, London, 1966.

22 When the Portuguese landed here in 1520, the city was still in Ethiopian possession, but the population was entirely Muslim. Masawa became Turkish in 1557.

23 Dedicated during the visit of H.M. Queen Elizabeth II to Ethiopia that year.

24 Plates 12 and 13 in Hans Helfritz, *Aethiopien, Kunst im Verborgenen*, Cologne, 1972, provide a striking comparison.

25 Six months later he was called back to Addis Ababa and appointed General Manager of the Ethiopian Orthodox Church.

26 Yuri Mikhailovich Kobishchanov, *Aksum*, Moscow, 1966.

27 G. W. Van Beek, 'The Rise and Fall of Arabia Felix', *Scientific American*, December 1969, 36–46.

4 Arussi

Mountains and Plains

Now the smallest of Ethiopia's fourteen provinces, Arussi bears the name of the large Galla tribe that forms the major component of its population.[1] Traditionally the entire area across the Awash River to the south and east of Addis Ababa was called Arussi and older Ethiopians still apply this name to the northern Rift Valley lake region. Until the 1950s, in fact, the four northern lakes (Zway, Langano, Abiata, and Shala) were included in Arussi province along with the town of Shashemane and the Kambatta region to the west of it. When the dusty track leading southward past the lakes was transformed into a modern highway, it became more practical to join the area to Shoa. The inhabitants of the lake region are still predominantly Arussi Galla, though many Amhara, Tigreans, and Gurage have moved in among them.

Arussi province in its present form is primarily a highland region – an undulating, grass-covered plateau averaging 2,400 to 2,800 m. with several mountain masses rising above 3,650 m. The western boundary of the province passes through Lakes Zway and Langano and the northern boundary is the Awash River. Thus along its western and northern edges Arussi includes a fringe of lowland country. This lowland region marks the northernmost extent of Arussi tribal penetration. Until very recent times it was wild thornscrub country with plentiful game but no agriculture of any consequence.[2] In the Awash valley south of Nazareth (formerly Adama), Arussi tribal territory gives way to that of the Karayu Galla and, farther east, the Danakil.

The Lowland Fringes

Since 1950 the Awash valley has undergone a remarkable transformation. It is now one of the fastest developing regions of Ethiopia. The Koka Dam was built with Italian reparations money and inaugurated in 1960. The dam has added a whole new lake to the Rift Valley group. Being new and having drowned, or half-drowned, farmland and acacia forest, Koka Lake is still as much of a scar on the landscape as a thing of beauty. Nevertheless, seen from different points at different seasons and times of day, it has its attractiveness in spite of the expanses of dead tree trunks and mud flats. The highway to the south passes along its western shore and a good road leads off the Nazareth highway to the dam itself. Many birds have been attracted to the lake. The level of the lake rises 3 m. or more during an average summer rainy season and the dam has sometimes not been able to contain the entire summer accumulation of water. It has, nevertheless, made possible a dependable flow for irrigation of sugar-cane

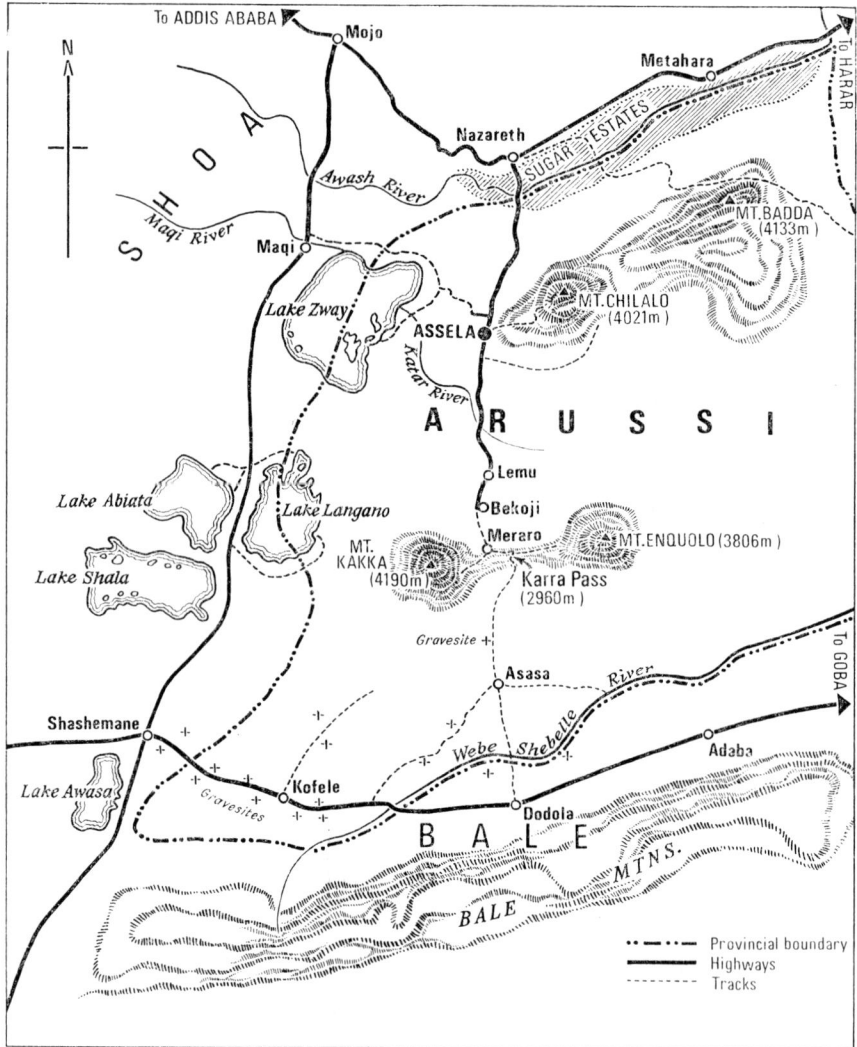

FIG. 15 Arussi

plantations along both sides of the river for more than a hundred kilometres to the east.

Seen from the hills above Nazareth these vivid green bottomlands are a beautiful sight at all times of the year, but especially during the dry season when the surrounding landscape turns tan and brown. The sugar estates have been developed by Dutch capital and Dutch specialists, many from Indonesia. The area is so well suited to growing sugar-cane that by the early 1970s Ethiopia was satisfying its own steadily growing needs for sugar and developing a surplus for export.[3] Not only sugar, but many other tropical crops – cotton, bananas, citrus, rice – can be grown here. There has been a great deal of agricultural development in the Awash valley and there is more to come. Enterprising individuals, groups of government officials pooling their resources to form corporate farms, and some foreign investors are involved – and there has been room for all. There is only one common denominator: all the initiative has been from outside the area, for the local inhabitants have been reluctant to abandon their nomadic habits. Their lives are still centred on their cattle, goats, and camels. They practise only the most marginal agriculture and are usually reluctant to go to work on the new agricultural undertakings. These depend on tractors and modern machinery. For work in the sugar-fields which cannot be performed by machinery, the sugar corporations bring in industrious Kambatta from the south-west.

There are still immense expanses of primeval thorn forest in the Awash valley, but they are being cut, bulldozed, uprooted, and burned at an increasingly rapid rate. Only in the relatively small area set aside as Awash National Park is the natural forest secure from destruction. The area immediately west of the park boundaries was still untouched when we visited it in 1971 and settled for a pleasant morning along the river bank to watch crocodiles sunning themselves on the opposite shore. In the steep clay banks on our side of the river, thousands of carmine bee-eaters, the most beautiful of all African small birds, had dug out nests. They were flying relays to a nearby termite mound, catching the insects as they emerged to swarm and bringing them back to feed their insistently twittering nestlings. Just a year later we set out to take a visitor to witness this same spectacle. Driving along the river we stopped to watch Danakil watering their cattle and bathing along a rocky stretch of river-bank. This scene cannot have changed for centuries. We then cut across thorn forest, passing a herd of lesser kudu, several waterbuck, and a troop of baboons, and headed towards the river again. We had a rude shock when we found ourselves up against a tall heap of earth that extended in a straight line off to the north as far as we could see – a new irrigation ditch and dike. Beyond was an expanse of flat, bare ground with all trees removed. The sugar company was preparing a new area for planting. We found an earth ramp over the ditch and then drove for 5–6 km. along another dike on the side of the plantation nearest the river. But the way to the river was blocked by more ditches and dikes. Without a long and problematic hike, there was no way to retrace our way to the place where the carmine bee-eaters nested in the river-bank.

We gave up, drove on westward to the main road leading south from Metahara, across the Awash bridge, and into the established sugar plantations. It was a changed world – vast expanses of green cane in rectangular fields with roadways and canals dividing each sector at regular intervals. The air felt moist and the odours were the contrasting ones of fresh, green cane and of molasses, which is spread on the roads like tar and makes a smooth, dustless surface. Young flame-trees coming into bloom along the roadsides were mirrored in the irrigation channels. It was a civilized, prosperous-looking sight. We reminded ourselves that this terrain too, not so many years ago, had been thorn forest where wild animals wandered. Attractive as it can be, the primeval African savannah is a raw, harsh environment which provides a living for only a sparse population. Transformed into sugar-fields, the same ground becomes the source of dependable income which feeds the whole economic development process. In the Awash valley there is room both for preserving some natural areas and developing others.

During the rainy season the molasses-tempered roads of the sugar estates are still easily drivable. The other tracks of the region turn into tangles of muddy ruts, chains of puddles, and, in places, broad shallow lakes. I went once in August to visit an Ethiopian friend who was developing a new farm south of the Awash beyond Sodere. When we finally reached it, the farm with its modern barn and new brick house, galvanized grain storage silos, and other trim outbuildings, was like an oasis in the wilderness. The grounds were landscaped with paths and garden plots and shrubbery had been planted everywhere. Rows of pumps were ready to bring water to fields during the dry season, operating off current brought from Koka over a new electric line. We inspected the fields, driving over tracks that were just barely passable after heavy rains the night before. The soil was thick, black, and deep, easily cultivable with tractors. The family proudly showed me their sprouting fields of *teff*, corn, and legumes and we stopped to look at experimental plantings of citrus. Over cool drinks back at the house we talked of the good return an orange-juice freezing plant would bring. A vision of the Ethiopia of the future . . .

Several modern farms are also being developed in the lowlands east and north of Lake Zway. A trip through this area, from Assela to Maqi, is a good single-day outing from Addis Ababa. The track turns off north of the bridge at Kulumsa, 8 km. before Assela, but it is not easy to find and we stopped passers-by several times during our first few kilometres to be sure we were actually heading towards Maqi. At 34 km. from Kulumsa we passed through a sprawling town called Oglacha Ketema. From this area there were good views of Lake Zway, with its islands, deltas, and bays. Coming closer to the north shore of the lake we entered a cultivated region with extensive grainfields in the thorn forest and villages of beehive-style round houses with thick layers of papyrus as thatch on the roofs. These belong to Watta, a lower-caste tribe of hippopotamus-hunters who, like similar peoples in other parts of Ethiopia, probably represent a remnant of earlier inhabitants. On this trip I passed through the territory of the Watta and went on to the main Rift Valley highway at Maqi, completing the 65 km. traverse from Assela in about three hours.

I later went back to see more of the Watta, exploring their villages, walking trails with them along the papyrus-lined Zway shores, and penetrating into the delta of the Maqi River which brings the waters of the Gurage highlands into the lake. The Watta appear now to be assimilating rapidly into standard Amhara-Galla culture patterns. They devote most of their energy to agriculture, cattle-raising, and cutting of wood for charcoal burning. They said they no longer hunted hippopotamus.

More interesting because of their richer culture and unusual history are the people who live on the Zway islands. I made eight voyages on the lake to visit them and several more trips to various points along the shore where they have also settled during the last few decades. They deserve separate description (map, p. 111).

The Islands of Lake Zway

The inhabitants of the five Zway islands are Semitic Christians who have flourished here since late medieval times. They call themselves Zay, but are now more commonly known as Laqi, a name given them by the Galla, which means 'paddlers' or 'rowers'. They are related to the Gurage who are now concentrated in an area well to the west of Zway around the towns of Butajira and Endeber. Their language, which they still use among themselves, is a Gurage dialect, but it has close affinities with Harari, the unique Semitic language now spoken only within the walls of the old city of Harar. Their houses and some of their handicrafts also suggest old links with Harar.

Lake Zway is rich in fish, especially the *tilapia nilotica*, a flat fish with excellent white meat. The islanders learned, perhaps from the Watta, to make swift, manoeuvrable boats from bundles of papyrus which grows in many places around the lake-shore and on the islands (Pl. 20a). As Muslims pressed into the highlands from the east, the people who took refuge on the islands were increasingly cut off from kinsmen on the mainland who either fled westward or were absorbed by the invaders. The islanders' isolation was intensified during the period of Galla expansion in the sixteenth and seventeenth centuries. Meanwhile they had developed a viable, self-contained way of life and were able to satisfy all their needs by fishing and intensive agriculture. The islands were eventually terraced from top to bottom; no cultivable soil went unused. Shore walls were constructed to contain and extend lakeside meadows as cattle pastures. The Zay remained fervently Christian.

Churches had been built on the islands in the earliest period of Christian settlement, probably in the thirteen or fourteenth century. That on the largest island, now called Tullu Guddo,[4] but then called Debra Tseyon – Mount Zion – attained the status of monastery, supported a sizeable monastic community, and accumulated a library of manuscripts. Like the holiest Ethiopian church in Axum, this principal Zway church was dedicated to St Mary of Zion (Pl. 20b). Ties to the Christian north were maintained and from time to time monks and emissaries from Tigre and northern Shoa came to visit the islands. Surrounded by Muslims and Galla, however, the islanders became more and more cut off. The Galla taste for cloth woven by island men from cotton grown in their terraced fields resulted in the growth of trade between the islands and the mainland during the eighteenth and nineteenth centuries.

Legends about the Zway islands had proliferated during their long period of isolation. Portuguese travellers reported some of them in the sixteenth century, but no Portuguese, as far as is known, visited the islands. In the middle of the nineteenth century, King Sahle Selassie of Shoa (1813–47) declared:

> It is my intention shortly to undertake an expedition to the great lake in Gurague. In it be many islands which contain the treasure of my ancestors. There are jars filled with bracelets of solid gold. There are 40 drums of elephants' ears and many holy arks pertaining unto ancient churches, beside 700 choice Æthiopic volumes . . . Elephants abound on the borders. In the trees are found black leopards of a most ferocious nature, multiplying always among the branches and never descending upon the earth . . . The waters of the lake . . . teem with monstrous *gumare* and with fish of brilliant colours . . . Moreover, there are specifics against smallpox and other diseases. No resistance is to be anticipated from the inhabitants, who are chiefly Christian monks who have often invited me . . . I must no longer delay to recover the lost wealth of my forefathers.[5]

Though Sahle Selassie invited visiting British officers to accompany him, help construct boats, and share the glory of the reunification of the Zay with the Ethiopian Christian Empire, his expedition never materialized. It remained for his grandson, the Emperor Menelik II, to reconquer the Zway region in 1886. Menelik, too, was moved by a conscious desire to bring old southern Ethiopian lands into his rejuvenated Ethiopian Empire and he felt a special obligation to the people of Zway who had maintained their Christian faith and Ethiopian loyalties through the centuries. He granted them lands on the mainland, guaranteed them freedom from molestation by the Galla, and reaffirmed their traditional status as an independent tribal entity under their own ruler, to whom he gave the title of *balambaras*. The official chronicler of Menelik II's reign, his faithful Gurage retainer Gebre Selassie, summarizes these developments:

> . . . a week was spent going around the lake. There was a Galla area called Katar whose inhabitants kept the Zway people from going to and from their islands. Emperor Menelik laid it waste . . . The Emperor forbade his soldiers to disturb the Zway people or their possessions . . . Emperor Menelik then proclaimed: 'The Zway people will have freedom to come and go wherever they wish; they will be able to trade; whoever disturbs the inhabitants of Zway will be my enemy'.[6]

The Zway islanders are still recognized by the Ethiopian government as a separate tribal group and their traditional chief, now Balambaras Biru (Pl. 22a), functions as their political and administrative leader. During visits to Tullu Guddo, I had the pleasure of being invited to his house below the church near the top of the island's eastern peak, drinking coffee and *talla* and meeting other Zay elders. The Zay are hard-working, hospitable, intelligent people who have

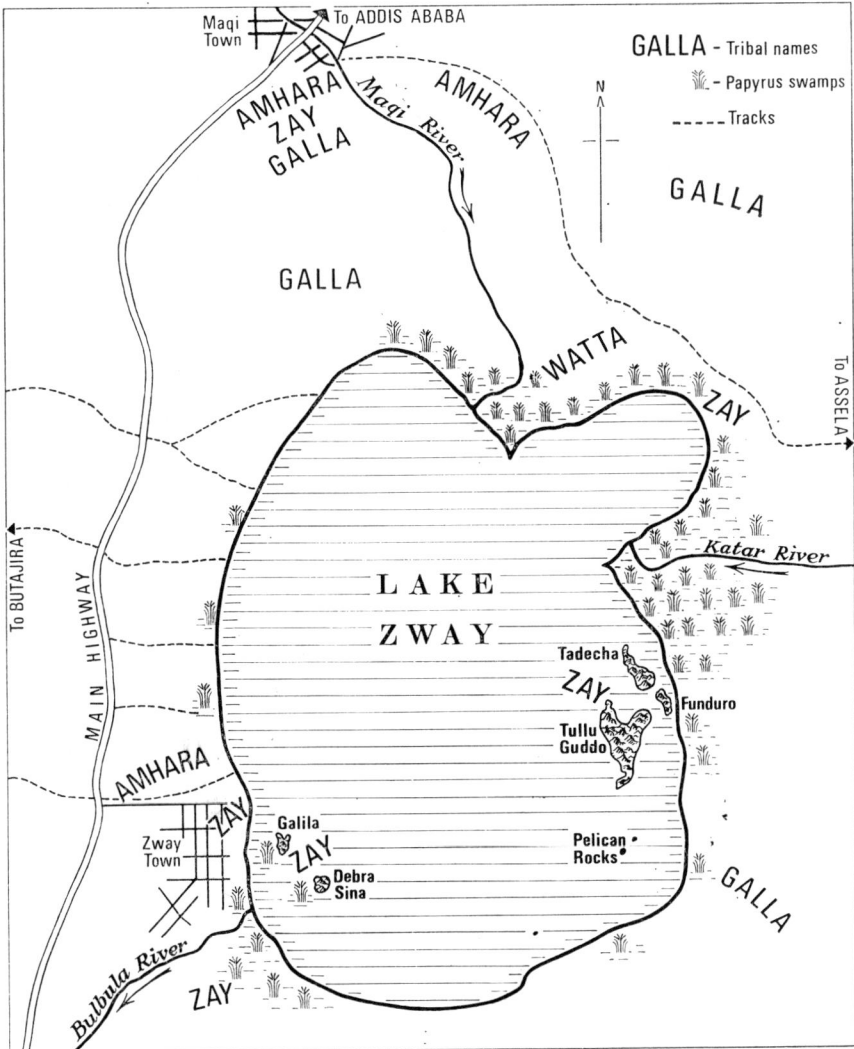

FIG. 16   Lake Zway

been slow to abandon their traditional way of life because it satisfies their needs
so well.

Only the three islands along the eastern shore of the lake – Tullu Guddo,
Funduro, and Tadecha – are still inhabited and cultivated. Little by little,
since their liberation by Emperor Menelik II, the Zay who lived on the two
smaller islands in the south-western corner of the lake – Galila (Galilee) and
Debra Sina (Mt Sinai) – have moved to shore lands. They still maintain their
old way of life, but pressures for assimilation into the mainstream of modern
Ethiopian life are mounting. On the eastern islands ancient patterns persist.

Terraces are cultivated, cattle are pastured in lakeside meadows, a pungent golden beer is brewed from finger millet (*eleusine tocussa*), and cotton cloth is woven and taken to mainland market towns such as Maqi and Alemtena to be sold. A great deal of fishing is still done from papyrus boats and increasing quantities of fish are sold commercially on the shore. Fish still form a principal component of the islanders' diet. A delicious fish *wat*, reminiscent of bouillabaisse, is served at christenings and other special feasts. Activities connected with fishing – net-making and repair and cutting and drying of papyrus for boats – are important tasks in the ever-recurring annual work-cycle.[7]

Church festivals are important too, observed as major holidays by all the islanders. The Patriarch of Arussi, Abuna Lucas, who has his residence in Assela, maintains a modest house on the south-west bay of Tullu Guddo and visits it several times a year. Until the spring of 1972, when a new elementary school was built by the government on Tullu Guddo, the *abuna*'s house was the only modern building on the islands. Thanks to Abuna Lucas, I was able to examine and photograph some of the rare manuscripts which are kept in the church treasury at Debra Tseyon Maryam. One of them, a richly illustrated *Sinkesar*, is one of the oldest and finest of its kind in Ethiopia and probably dates from the fourteenth century (Pl. 22b).

To Assela

Soon after the highway crosses the Awash bridge south of Nazareth, it begins to ascend the Arussi plateau. Much of the acacia forest has been cut for charcoal and firewood, even where the land was unsuitable for cultivation. This ravaged landscape provides only poor pasturage for livestock, but good range-management could produce much richer grazing. Perhaps the Swedish aid scheme, the Chilalo Agricultural Development Unit (CADU), will eventually tackle this problem. For the present CADU's priorities are better grain, better marketing, and improved livestock-breeding in more fertile parts of Arussi. No one can travel across the Arussi plateau and remain unaware of CADU's activities and the profound impact they are having on the life of the area. This large-scale Swedish development project got under way in the late 1960s. The Swedes wished to make a major effort and concentrate on a single area. Arussi was a good choice.[8]

Once the road comes up onto the main plateau, the character of the countryside changes – broad, rolling uplands, immense cultivated expanses with good soil. In June the whole landscape is green. In December it is yellow-tan with ripe grain and stubble. In March it is grey-black – ploughed fields. In the villages tractors stand beside houses along with other brightly painted farm machinery. Corrugated tin roofs are almost universal in the villages, but farmsteads in the countryside are still mostly of the traditional kind – small clusters of round *tukuls* with their storage huts. These are huge baskets which sometimes sit on the ground, but more often stand on legs or on a platform and always have thatched tops which can be taken off for access to the grain underneath. Piles of dried dung – the family's fuel for the rainy season – are thatched in similar manner. Occasionally unusually large *tukuls* have an air of prosperity about them, but most of the farmhouses, in contrast to the fields that surround them, give an impression of poorness.

An attractive new motel opened in Assela in 1970, the Assela Abay. During my stops there in the following year, I found it well maintained with excellent first-class rooms at E$10 per night and clean, austere third-class rooms at only E$4 for a double bed. It was then managed by a Swiss who had spent many years at the Ras Hotel in Addis Ababa. He found the quieter atmosphere of Assela agreeable, but complained of the cold. Though Assela is nearly 300 m. lower than Addis Ababa, he said it was much chillier most of the year.

Assela has little history, as far as I could determine. It is a large village in the process of turning into a country town. The broad main street has low buildings on both sides, some brightly painted (orange is a favourite colour here), and modern streetlights. The town has been planned on a grand scale with straight side-streets running at right-angles to the main north-south road through the centre. Some of the side-streets are paved with rock; many are earth. The market area lies west of the main street in the north-western section of the town. Market-day is Saturday. Assela's principal church, a Maryam, is situated in a park-like compound in the south-western part of the town next to the rambling residence of Abuna Lucas, Patriarch of Arussi.

Both entering and leaving Assela one is reminded of the Swedish presence in Arussi. On the northern end of the town there is a large secondary school consisting of several long separate buildings of concrete and glass with tin roofs, the standard model of the Ethio-Swedish School Building Unit (ESBU). On the southern end of the town, along an asphalt road which branches off to the west, is CADU Headquarters and the Swedish residential area. Long, low ramblers built of red brick line curving streets. No walls or fences separate the grounds of the houses. All have green lawns and flower-beds, many vegetable gardens as well. Lawn furniture, children's swings, and various items of equipment for outdoor living prevalent in Europe and America catch the eye: charcoal grills, badminton nets, bright umbrellas, lawn-sprinklers . . . The Swedish suburb includes a school and community centre.

During our first visit we drove on to other parts of the CADU domains through experimental plantings of eucalyptus and conifers, past repair and maintenance buildings, and onto range land where various forms of pasture management were being tried out. Water-pipes led to wood and concrete watering-troughs for cattle. Each water outlet had a bright green plastic bucket and a length of green plastic hose. In Ethiopia, where plastic is still almost unknown, seeing this sort of thing in the countryside comes as a shock. There were experiments in erosion control with eucalyptus stakes and stone walls in gullies and across watercourses. At a machinery maintenance station men (all Ethiopians) were doing their evening chores.

On a later visit I was a guest in one of the Swedes' houses and heard about CADU activities from one of the oldest members of the Swedish team. Relations between Swedes and Ethiopians are easy and the Swedish effort to train local people to do all jobs as fast as they are capable of taking them over seemed to be working well. Like all such development efforts, however, the changes that CADU is bringing to Arussi are forcing social and political issues that can easily become contentious: questions of landownership and sharing of gains from better yields and better marketing practices. Politicians in Sweden have demanded land-reform measures and social adjustments which Ethiopians have resented. Swedes on the scene are more mindful of local sensitivities, more inclined to concentrate on economic development than to worry about social and political consequences – or, at any rate, there is less emotional discussion of such things among them. One thing seems to be certain, no matter how CADU develops during the next few years: the Swedes have already made a lasting impact on Arussi and more than their rows of brick ramblers will remain in future years as a monument to their presence here.

Over the High Plateau

The distances never came out the same on trips to southern Arussi, for there were always different turns and detours, but it takes more or less 150 km. of travelling from Assela to reach the Webe Shebelle. The distance seems greater because of the boundlessness of the landscape and the fact that the roads themselves are always an adventure. All available maps, I found, were wrong in some particulars[9] and some of them were very misleading. But this was not all due to the carelessness of the compilers of the maps, for different tracks are used at different times of the year. Fords and valley crossings which present no problem in the dry season have to be given wide berth during rains. In years to come the main north-south route through Arussi will undoubtedly be graded and paved and it will not be a difficult job, compared to most roadbuilding undertakings in Ethiopia, for the terrain is for the most part smooth and open and not many bridges will be required. Perhaps this is one of the reasons improvement of this route has so far had no priority. IHA is concentrating on more difficult tasks and knows it can turn to this one at any time and complete it easily.

I travelled this route from north to south three times in 1971, first at the height of the dry season at the end of February, again in May when the big rains had already begun, and finally in December when the rains were past but the streams not yet completely dry. On one trip we had an altimeter and made a record of the altitudes along the way. Soon after we left Assela we climbed up to 2,500 m. and remained above that height all the way to the Webe Shebelle except for a brief dip to 2,447 m. as we crossed the Katar River 30 km. out. The highest point we reached was the Karra Pass between Mounts Kakka and Enquolo, south of Meraro, where the altimeter registered over 2,960 m. At the

Webe Shebelle ford south of Asasa, we were down to 2,317 m., almost the exact
height of Assela again. The road was fair gravel to Bekoji, less than fair gravel
on to Meraro, and from there onward just a track, at times a whole series of
roughly parallel tracks . . .

The first part of this route passes over the lower south-western slopes of
Mt Chilalo, with excellent views of the dome-like upper portion of this
mountain back towards the north-east. The region is mostly cultivated and the
fields are dotted with old trees, some of them imposing giants, remnants of the
much thicker sub-alpine forest which covered the region not too many decades
ago. Some stream-beds still have clumps of young trees. The most spectacular
plants in this area are the giant thistles which grow in clumps rising to 3 m.
along the roadside and along the upper sides of small valleys. They bear huge
balls of burgundy red bloom, often 12–15 cm. across. These are at their best in
December and January. They turn brown by the end of February. Small black
and white birds of canary size and habits favour thistle clumps as perches, often
sitting comfortably atop the big balls themselves, for the flowers are not prickly
even when dry. Every other part of these plants is covered with sharp spines.
Since they are not hurt by the light frost that may occur here and since they are
very drought-resistant, they grow on from year to year forming stiff, woody stems
which only a heavy bush-fire can kill. Thistles similar to these can be found in
many parts of Ethiopia, but nowhere have I encountered specimens as vigorous
as those that flourish in central and southern Arussi.

The Katar, which drains the central portion of the Arussi plateau into Lake
Zway, is a well-developed stream with a modest flow of clear water even at the
height of the dry season when a good number of birds congregate along its
banks. We saw grey geese and black ibis there in February. The bridge over the
Katar is an iron frame one with a plank surface. It is the only bridge of its kind
on this route. After Bekoji there are no bridges at all, only fords.

In an area called Lemu, shortly before Bekoji, an American Baptist mission
nestles among thick groves of eucalyptus. It is typical of mission stations in many
parts of Ethiopia, less affluent than some. When we drove in one morning in
May, we were warmly welcomed by two typically American ladies, one a
schoolmistress and the other a nurse. Three male missionaries were off on
horseback in the countryside, visiting other parts of the plateau country in the
mission's territory. The mission compound with its smooth green lawns, fenced
gardens, simple neat buildings was like a small settlement in Nebraska or South
Dakota and the wooden houses in which the missionaries live were of a typically
old-fashioned American mid-western style. The ladies showed us through the
schoolrooms, which were being given a Saturday scrubbing-down. Their school
is a six-year Amharic-language one which meets Ethiopian Ministry of
Education standards. Children come great distances to it. Their clinic – a crude
but effective hospital – attracts large numbers of people from even greater
distances. It was busy with morning sick-call as we walked through. I found it a
striking example of what can be accomplished with dedication, good sense, and

limited resources. We walked through the small village that has grown up next to the mission station and the market-place that has become the economic centre of the area. After our tour the missionary ladies invited us back to one of their houses for coffee and cinnamon rolls.

On both sides of Bekoji the terrain is flat and open – huge grainfields extend as far as the eye can see. Some are separated by rows of recently planted eucalyptus. Farm compounds are often enclosed in thick sod walls. Bekoji, a large market town, nestles in a thick grove. There was a town of sorts here during the Italian occupation and perhaps some military action, for several pieces of broken roadbuilding equipment and old vehicles lie in the meadows along the roadside partly covered with sod and vines.

Bekoji's Saturday market attracts thousands of rural Galla. They trade grain and food, animals, skins, and cloth. Beaded and cowried women, many still wearing the traditional Arussi leather dresses, sell *talla* from big red clay pots. Crowds of curious teenage boys who followed us around here were continually chided by their elders for their forward behaviour. I found some outstanding basketry here for very low prices and was led by a lady from whom I had bought a *mesob* to a man who had a huge wooden bowl to sell. It had been carved from a single piece of good light wood and measured 71 cm. across. He asked E$5 for it. I examined it carefully and found no fractures that would dry into cracks, so I offered E$3.50 and got the usual first response of the bargaining process – a look of dismay from the man, 'Much too little!' I found a minor flaw which had been smoothed over with a mixture of clay and dung and pointed it out. By this time a crowd had gathered and were enjoying the whole proceeding. I interrupted bargaining to enquire what the bowl was for. Onlookers explained that it could be used for mixing dough for *injera* or for pounding *ensete* root for *kocho*. I offered E$4 and turned to walk away. The owner called me back. He felt E$4 was a good price. So I gave him four green dollar notes, we shook hands, and the crowd cheered a good bargain.

All the way to Bekoji there had been evidence of CADU in the countryside. Milk collection stations had signs in Amharic and English and posters showing better ways of caring for cattle. At other points new buildings, the simple 'modern' pole-and-*chiqa* type with tin roof, were labelled 'multi-purpose co-operative'. None of these had been opened, so we were unable to see what purposes they were to serve, but they appear to be countryside general stores. Beyond Meraro we were out of CADU's major area of activity. In February fields and grasslands had been thoroughly burnt over and for miles on end the main colour in the landscape was a deep, matt black. The air smelled strongly of smoke and ash. Great pillars of smoke rose from Mt Kakka (4,190 m.) a thousand metres into the air. When I next travelled this route, at the end of May, all signs of fire had disappeared and Kakka's slopes were bright green with new vegetation.

There are few churches in the Arussi countryside, but north of Meraro a church caps a small knoll and has a group of trees around it. As we circled the knoll, we met a large crowd of people and a long line of horses in bright saddle-cloths, all without riders. We soon saw why. A coffin was being carried high on the shoulders of pallbearers from a stream to the west back up to the church and the people had come to watch the procession. They all spoke Gallinya. Meraro is a very stretched-out town and always, when I passed through it, had a rather deserted look. Sod walls can be seen in most of Arussi, but here every compound is marked off by them and far out on the edges of the town they enclose fields and gardens. Meraro offers a good view of Mt Kakka, directly to the west, and would be a good place from which to strike out to climb this mountain by mule and foot. Though its lower slopes are cultivated, its upper slopes appear to retain a good deal of alpine vegetation. I was told by Swedes in Assela that nyala can still be found on Kakka as well as on Enquolo (3,806 m.), whose striking peak rises south-east of Meraro.

After Meraro, as the track climbs over the Karra Pass, come the best southern Arussi landscapes: rolling grasslands with hills and mountains always in the distance, fewer farmsteads and fewer people, but immense herds of cattle and horses and riders dashing across the plains. Men and women usually ride separately, but one also sees couples astride a single horse. We stopped to photograph one friendly pair who were shyly pleased to be the centre of attention (Pl. 23a). All the other people who gathered to watch us wanted, of course, to be photographed as well. The Karra Pass is a wide saddle between Mts Kakka and Enquolo, but this plateau fits together on such a grand scale that we did not realize it when crossing it. Only after we had crossed the Webe Shebelle and looked back from the Bale side could we see the central plateau region as an entity. On the south side of the Karra Pass the country is almost totally treeless and there is less cultivation. Nevertheless, the shapes of the barren hills, the changing outlines of the distant mountains, the twisting courses of the minor stream-beds, the isolated farmsteads with their haystack-style houses, provide an endless variety of simple, lean, often gaunt, views. A bit farther on old lava flows and stretches of loose rock make for rough driving. Curiously enough, some of these rocky areas are cultivated when other smoother places are not.

Eventually Enquolo recedes into the distance on the north-east and a long ridge of forested mountains becomes visible on the southern horizon – the great ranges of Bale. In between flows the Webe Shebelle, southern Ethiopia's largest river. A large walled pagan Galla cemetery marks the point where the road begins a very gradual descent towards the river, which is still 20–25 km. away. This cemetery is enclosed in a 75 cm.-high wall made of rough reddish stones held together with mud. An entrance in the wall faces directly west. Inside are several grave-sites, the largest marked by thin rectangular stone slabs inserted into the ground, some lying lengthwise, others standing upright. The tall upright ones have carving which seems to resemble a picture-language and in proper light a few human figures can also be discerned. The other graves are more modest, but some also have stones with inscriptions. Several smaller burial sites are marked by small upright slabs or simple piles of rocks. The land around this cemetery is all open and barren. There is no cultivation, no signs of human habitation, hardly any signs of animals. The wind always blows, the sun strikes down without shade from early morning until late in the afternoon. Directly to the south there is an unimpeded view 60–70 km. into the forested mountains of Bale. The largest component of the view from this lonely cemetery remains the sky – a high, wide, endless canopy of blue. In Gallinya the words for sky and God are the same: *Waqa*. We always stopped at this cemetery and rested a while, lunching or having a mid-afternoon snack, stretching landrover-weary legs with a brisk walk over the stony terrain. When the sun is right, you catch its reflection on the tin roofs of a town far to the south-west. It is Asasa, market for the southern end of the plateau north of the river. There is good farmland around Asasa and modern farms are being developed on a large scale. Carefully marked rectangular fields, wells for irrigation, sheds for tractors catch your eye as you cross the 16 km. between the cemetery and the town. Just north of Asasa several springs pour out fresh water and form pools which attract large numbers of birds, cattle, and people. The area around the pools is green even at the height of the dry season when the largest numbers of birds congregate. Asasa's Saturday market is smaller than Bekoji's but even more colourful. It is a good place to bargain for the bright striped cotton cloth that is woven and sold all over southern Ethiopia. Red, black, and gold was the colour combination favoured here when I stopped, the patterns all simple stripes or geometrical variations.

On market-day, both entering and leaving Asasa, you meet parties of horse-men and groups of braided, beaded, chattering Galla women along the trail. Market-day or otherwise, you must stop here to have the tracks towards the south and west pointed out and to get information on their condition. The local people know when the Webe is fordable and can usually give some information about the condition of the fords on the track that leads west south-west and connects up with the Shashemane–Goba road. The track which crosses the Webe Shebelle and goes on to Dodola in Bale leaves Asasa in an easterly direction, but soon turns directly south. A few kilometres through grainfields and you catch sight of the river flowing at the bottom of a well-defined trough, 50–60 m. below the level of the surrounding countryside. The ford was easy to cross (only ½ m. deep) in December and is probably even shallower in February. By the end of May, when there had been generous spring rains, it was already impassable.

The route west out of Asasa meanders as it crosses half a dozen small tributaries of the Webe Shebelle and winds up and down the grassy slopes between them. This appears to be an older and more heavily used caravan trail than the one which goes directly across the Webe ford. Deep ruts between ridges of sod formed by countless animals' hooves over the centuries have left beautifully regular patterns on many of the hillsides above the fords (Pl. 24a). When the rains begin, sudden thunderstorms fill the stream-beds and wash down the previous season's accumulation of sand, silt, and broken stubble. Spread over a ford, even a good solid, rock-bottomed one, such a mass of flash flood debris can cause a 4-wheel-drive vehicle to slither as if it were standing in a pool of grease. We were glad we had friends in a second vehicle when this happened to us so that each could help the other through.

According to figures from one trip, it takes 28 km. to travel from Asasa to the main Shashemane–Goba highway. The point where the track joins the main road is 24 km. from Kofele and 49 km. from Shashemane.

Parkland, Plains and Tombs

Like the route from Assela southward, the road across the south-western corner of Arussi seems longer than it is, but for different reasons. Each few kilometres bring change of landscape. It was September when I first travelled this route and the big rains had not yet come to an end. The bright yellow Wonji sugar road sign at the turn-off point north of Shashemane gives the distance to Adaba as 107 km. That promised to be an easy afternoon round trip, but we covered less than half the distance, for we were plagued by flat tyres. These had nothing to do with the road, which was in good condition, but resulted from the fact that our landrover had at this point travelled for nearly a year over all kinds of Ethiopian roads and tracks with no flat tyres at all. They all started to go at once.

Proceeding eastward from Shashemane, we passed for several kilometres through low-lying country, warm and semi-tropical in look and feel. It was well farmed with houses in several styles, an indication that the area had been settled by people of different origins. There were smooth, fully thatched Sidamo-type houses, more conventional *tukuls* of modified Gurage style, rectangular houses of several kinds with both thatch and tin roofs. The fields looked fertile. Some were being cultivated by tractor and vehicle tracks led off the main road on both sides to other areas of agricultural development. Then we began to climb and entered a very different countryside – rolling hills with occasional deep valleys and parklike alternation of forests of towering old trees and open fields of grain and hay. Thatched round houses predominate in this area. Most farmsteads have large round corrals constructed of bamboo basketry. In glades beneath the old trees brilliant blue salvia bloom. Many trees are festooned with vines and some have heavy accumulations of bromeliads. The area is like a huge botanical garden. Animals in the fields looked well nourished. The people too have a relatively prosperous appearance. Embroidered skull-caps were frequent among the men. We saw no church compounds. At the sprawling, formless town of Kofele, there had been a market (it was Monday) and, as we drove on eastward, we passed large numbers of people going home from it. Many were riding good horses. Others drove donkeys dragging bundles of bamboo poles. We saw no bamboo growing in the region through which we passed, but a great deal must grow somewhere nearby, for it is an essential ingredient of the local way of life.

Soon we had completely left behind the large trees and pleasant glades and entered a gaunt landscape of immense barren valleys with long views of grassy plains both to the north and south. Here most of the farmsteads occurred in clusters of three to six houses and were surrounded by patches of *ensete*, as in the Gurage/Hadiya country of the south-west. But in this same area, at other points, there were huge round rough-looking *tukuls*, among the largest I had seen in Ethiopia, with one or two smaller *tukuls* and a corral adjoining. This kind of homestead is typical of highland Arussi and Bale. The yards around these big round houses were barren except for a storage basket or two, a thatched pile of dung, a few dogs. No trees, no bushes, no gardens. Highland Galla seem to feel no need for vegetables.

Flat tyres and rain overtook us and we had to return. On the way back we noticed one of the most interesting features of this region – groups of Galla tombs, often visible from the roadside, sometimes occupying heights in more distant fields, often on the edge of a patch of forest.

Not far east of Kofele, where the road comes out on to the high open plateau, an especially striking grave monument stands about a hundred yards north of the road. It is a slab of stone, 2 m. high, in an open field (Pl. 25a). Animal and human figures decorate its south side and the north side has more rudimentary figures and designs which appear unfinished. When I last passed by here in May 1972, a new elementary school had been built in the fields beyond this monument and had already attracted a tremendous student body. It was difficult to see how all the children playing outside could ever be fitted into the smallish *chiqa* building with tin roof and bright new Ethiopian tricolour fluttering in the wind.

In early December 1971 I devoted the best part of a cool, sunny day to visiting all the graves visible from the main road through a 30 km. stretch on both sides of Kofele. At many sites boys and young men offered to lead me to others away from the road, so on this day alone I estimate that I saw at least one hundred individual graves. The Arussi, even now, do not date their gravestones, though they decorate them in other ways, and there has been confusion about how old some of these tomb-sites are. Earlier travellers used to consider them ancient, characteristic only of pure pagan times, and they have often been termed 'prehistoric'.[10] I was able to satisfy myself by direct enquiries that many of them are not ancient at all. In some, burials had taken place only a few days before. All of the people declared themselves Muslims, but the tombs and grave monuments are obviously of the same type the Arussi constructed before they made any pretence of adherence to Islam.

We were told that the large slabs of softish volcanic rock, a smooth tufa, on which geometric designs are cut, are brought from a location off towards Mt Kakka and other hills directly to the north. There is no rock of this kind near the road. For square tombs built with mud mortar, however, local harder volcanic stones and boulders are used. These do not lend themselves to carving. Only important men rate large tombs which consist of a built-up, usually squarish, central portion, often with a protruding device capping off the centre and with one or two openings in the sides, near the bottom. These openings are to let the spirit enter and leave and for presentation of offerings. Around the central structure stand upright slabs. Usually they form a complete circle, though occasionally only a semi-circle is erected. Smaller graves consist of simple piles of sod and rock. We saw some of these that were also very new and were told that they held children who had recently died. The occupant of one elaborate large grave was an honoured old man who had been buried just five days before. The people of the area spoke of him with great solemnity. His tomb was still in the process of being plastered and decorated.

Older grave-sites were sometimes firmly identifiable because of the fact that they had trees growing out from between their stones. On some older upright stones we noticed Arabic inscriptions. This, of course, in itself indicates some tie with Islam. The protruding centre ornaments had no Islamic symbolism, however. They appear to be linked with other forms of phallic imagery which occur among many Ethiopian peoples who have never, or only recently, been Christianized. One recent monument on the south side of the road in a wooded area has a portrait of the deceased, lightly carved and then painted in black, white, and tan. He is riding a horse and has a leopard skin around his shoulders (Pl. 25b). On his head he wears the tropical helmet popularized by Haile Selassie I and now essentially a symbol of the older generation. On its reverse side this large square slab features a rampant lion painted in similar style. Galla tomb art is obviously proving adaptable to modernization. But such modern monuments are rare.

In the well-wooded country nearer Shashemane a rather extensive cemetery stands in a grove of euphorbia on the south side of the road. The largest of several monumental tombs here is quite new but adheres to the traditional style. The central portion is plastered over with concrete and the protruding top ornament is also made of concrete. It is surrounded by several elaborately incised slabs which have all of the traditional geometric designs carefully cut into them and outlined in rose red and bright blue paint. On the second occasion I stopped to visit this cemetery, I had along an Ethiopian friend who was also interested in learning more about Arussi grave monuments. As we were examining the slabs around the biggest tomb a local man appeared and informed us that he was a professional tombstone carver. This tomb, he said, belonged to his own father! His father, he explained, had been a local man of high status and had also been a tombstone carver in his own day. Carrying on his father's profession, he had carved the upright slabs with curving lines and geometrical patterns that attested to his father's importance. A group of wavy lines on one slab indicated that his father had killed three leopards in his lifetime. Other designs indicated the number of his children. Three of the man's grandchildren came up and played among the graves as we examined them. The little girls had their heads completely shaved except for an inch-wide border around the front. They were very light-skinned and had grey eyes. The tombstone carver invited us to his house nearby for fresh milk. It was a classic highland Arussi *tukul* built with sides of split cedar and a well-aged thatch roof. Inside it smelled of many years' accumulation of smoke. Our host said it was nearly twenty years old.

Since the highway across the south-western corner of Arussi is part of the main east-west route across southern Ethiopia from Bale to Sidamo, Wollamo and Gamu Gofa, all regions with large numbers of Muslims, one often meets wandering Muslim holy men. They usually claim to be – and sometimes undoubtedly are – coming or going from Sheik Hussein, the great Islamic pilgrimage site along the Webe Shebelle in the northernmost part of Bale. They dress in dirty but often colourful rags, wear their hair long, often matted in braids or tied up in a red turban, and carry an extraordinary amount of paraphernalia hung about themselves – strings of wood and amber beads, drums, amulets, knives. All of them carry one or more peeled, rubbed, forked wooden sticks, a sign that they have participated in ceremonies at Sheik Hussein. I remember an especially dark-skinned but Caucasian-featured fellow whom we met west of Kofele, who, among other things, had a yellowed human thighbone slung over his shoulder. He begged for *caramelle* as compensation for being photographed. He had two women accompanying him. They had beads and carried forked sticks, but carried the cooking-pots and bundles of baggage as well.

From Kofele all the way across the Webe Shebelle to the region around Adaba in Bale many of the Arussi women wear a peculiar kind of finely woven straw hat with a large full crown which is sometimes almost egg-shaped. These women are naturally of an open and friendly nature and many of them are very attractive. The hats add to their charm and give a few an air of elegance (Pl. 23b). Women in this area usually wear dresses of factory-made cloth and wrap a white *shamma* around their shoulders. On special occasions they bring out their traditional beaded leather capes. Late one afternoon we drove past a group of a hundred and fifty or more who had gathered in a clearing in the forest. They were celebrating some local feast which involved picking mulberries. They all had baskets full of the fruit and most of them had smeared patches of its juice on their foreheads. Each one carried a knobbed staff and all wore, in addition to their capes, great quantities of beads, bracelets, earrings, and head decorations. By stopping to watch them we interrupted their singing and dancing and they all came running across the meadow to the road to greet us. Clamouring for *caramelle* and *shilingi* and trying to sell us mulberries, they completely enveloped the landrover and we had to drive on to escape them.

Up Chilalo

From almost any direction Chilalo (4,021 m.) appears to be a gentle mountain. It is seldom climbed, even by the Swedes who work in the development projects around Assela. I wished I had had the opportunity to go up it two or three times to see the effect of changes of season and to get a better idea of what wildlife still exists there. One visit convinced me that Busk was wrong when he dismissed Chilalo, which he apparently did not climb, as being of no mountaineering interest.[11] The great gash on top which separates Chilalo from the ridge that leads eastward to the Badda summit (4,133 m.) offers excellent opportunities for rock-climbing and all manner of ascents and descents over precipitous cliffs and steep slopes. A traverse of the entire Chilalo–Badda ridge from west to east would take three or four days.

I climbed Chilalo on the last day of April 1972. There were three of us on this outing, just right for an easy overnight trip necessitating a minimum of gear and preparation. We stopped three or four times *en route* to Assela to examine the outlines of Chilalo through field-glasses. The Chilalo–Badda mass changes shape as you move around the north-western side of it. When you first emerge from the Awash valley, the Badda sector is most prominent with the summit of the whole range appearing (which is correct) to be well back to the east of Chilalo. The closer you come to Assela, the larger Chilalo looms while Badda recedes into the background.

The best track up Chilalo leads directly east from the centre of Assela. We had to ask directions several times to be sure we stayed on it. We passed through groves of eucalyptus, climbed very gradually, and saw scattered houses, meadows, and fields. The soil where newly ploughed was a rich reddish brown. There had been recent rain. The ground was damp and the air was pungent with wet eucalyptus and cedar. We reached a small settlement and found our way blocked by a row of trees growing right across the track. They permitted only animals to pass. We looked around to find someone to ask where we were. A rustic-looking fellow with a sheepskin thrown over his shoulders told us we were at Grazmach Dasiso's estate. '*Bamakina yellem, kezzih baigir yihedal*'. It was not possible to go further by vehicle. From here we could go only on foot.

This man, Ato Kebbede, a local farmer, was eager to be helpful. He spoke simple, easy-to-understand Amharic, but was a Christian Galla. His Gallinya, we noticed when he spoke with neighbours, had a curious guttural sound, as did that of all the Galla on this mountain. He led us across a newly ploughed field to a recently used threshing-floor which he suggested as camp-site. Its outer edge was covered with a thick growth of new grass, its centre with fresh straw. A huge cedar stump on one edge made a good fireplace. After Kebbede helped us set up camp, he returned a short distance down the slope where he was hacking a cedar log to pieces. We could see rainclouds in the west, but our camp-site was in sun. A steady parade of big white clouds kept passing over the summit of Chilalo. From time to time between them we could see the mountain's barren top, our goal. When Kebbede came to bring us firewood, I asked him what the top of the mountain was like. There was only heather, he said, no trees. He offered to guide us up the next morning. How long would it take? Three hours. That seemed scant to me. But then Ethiopians are all great walkers and climbers and Kebbede was obviously thinking of the process of climbing the mountain as a single sustained effort – no allowance for stops to examine the vegetation, look at the views, observe animals and birds. His estimate was encouraging, for it meant that we could allow for all the things we would want to do on the way and still reach the top in four hours or a little more. I agreed with Kebbede that we would start at 7.30 sharp the next morning – *and saat takul* Ethiopian time.

We still had ample daylight to explore our immediate surroundings. Our camp-site was at about the 3,000 m. level. The area was like a park – patches of ploughland and pasture among scattered large cedars and podocarpus. The soil was black. As I set out along the trail up the mountain, a troop of about twenty hamadryas baboons ambled away from me. A little farther on I came to thick clumps of St John's Wort, wild raspberry, and rhododendroid. The St John's Wort was past its blooming prime, but there were still a few flowers and many dry and open seedpods. All the rhododendroids were fresh with new leaf growth, but there were no buds or evidence of bloom. The raspberries were in all stages of development at the same time – lavender bunches of bloom, thick clusters of reddish orange fruit, old knoblets where the fruit had been eaten by birds.

I looked back towards the west and there was Lake Zway (1,637 m.) far, far below, glistening in the silvery light of the lowering sun. Crossing an open area I came in sight of a rectangular, thatched house with walls made of new reddish cedar stakes. Four yapping dogs came out. To avoid them I turned down a side-trail that led into a steep valley where I could hear a stream flowing. This valley was a deep vein extending down the side of the mountain. There are many of them, but they are so filled with growth that they are indiscernible from afar. Here the basic vegetation of the mountain survives in its original form – cedar, podocarpus, and *kosso*, wild olive and various members of the fig family, bushes of many kinds but no heather until the forest itself stops. On Chilalo heather and St John's Wort seem to occur only separately, while in the Semyens the two are intermingled. Neither seems to reach the height on Chilalo that both do in the Semyens or in Bale, but this may be the effect of burning, cutting, and cultivation.

I crossed the stream, clear and cold, above an 8 m.-high waterfall. Trees in this part of the valley, very steep-sided, were hung with thick growths of lichen and many bromeliads. A steep path led up to open country on the other side of the valley. Here a large flat area was being cleared of its natural forest cover and some ploughing had already been done between stumps and clumps of bushes. To get back to camp I had to cross the stream again much lower down its deep valley. A slippery trail led down to another waterfall and I crossed on a ford above it. The slopes were dotted with slender lobelias, some of them with bloom stalks 8 m. high. Silhouetted against the darkening sky and the still glistening surface of Lake Zway, their stalks and spiky leaves made a splendid sight (Pl. 24b). I got back to camp a little after 6. My companions had a brisk cedar fire ready for the soup-pot and a small group of men and boys had gathered to keep us company during the early evening.

This evening, night, and morning were filled with experiences that make camping out in Ethiopia a joy: the sharp smell of cedar smoke in the brisk night air, the good-natured questions of the local people about everything that occurred to them. How long had it taken to drive from Addis Ababa? What was our work? What did our landrover cost? What was our tent made of? What kind of meat were the sausages we grilled over the fire? Then, shortly after 7 when darkness was complete, they all rose and left, wishing us a good night. The sky was almost entirely clear, but dark. At 8 o'clock, light began to increase behind Chilalo until its outlines glowed. There were a few wisps of cloud. Then the disc of the full orange moon appeared and soon the whole immense circle was resting on the crest of the mountain. As it rose higher its light caused all the undulations of the upper slopes to become visible and soon the area around our camp-site was bathed in the same cool light. We heard a hyena howl loudly nearby. There were no other night sounds except the rush of the stream in the deep valley. We put thick acacia logs on the fire to last through the night and retired. We were awake again at 5.45 as dawn began to break. The moon was now half high in the south-west and the sky was dotted with big puffy, silvery, swiftly-moving clouds, though the air around us had no movement. It was cool and it felt good to hunch over the fire which had held well through the night. Chilalo's outlines soon glowed again with an apricot and then a golden light behind them. As the face of the sun became visible over the mountain's northern shoulders, we noticed that the straw on the threshing-floor had sprouted a rich growth of mushrooms during the night. They were tall, delicate, and translucent with glassy grey tops that melted as the sun hit them. Exactly at 7.30 Kebbede arrived. (How had he known, without a watch?) A young fellow, also called Kebbede, came up and volunteered to go along, so we made him camera-bag bearer. There was good sunlight and the top of Chilalo was clear.

Kebbede set a cruel pace at the start. We raced up through the same terrain where I had taken a leisurely walk the evening before and went on up the deep valley I had crossed twice. We slowed a bit as we passed through grassy glades, clumps of bushes, clusters of tall trees of many kinds. Kebbede told us their Gallinya and Amharic names. During the first half-hour we passed scattered groups of thatched *tukuls*. Most of them seemed to be newly established homesteads. The high middle slopes of Chilalo appear to have been permanently settled by cultivators for only a decade or two. People looked at us with great curiosity. We were greeted as old friends by two men who had been at our camp the evening before. There were occasional medium-sized herds of cattle, but the Galla here seem to keep far fewer of them than their lowland cousins do. Many of the larger trees supported an apparently parasitic vine with waxy leaves with five petals coming out from the stem at the same point. Orange, bell-shaped flowers dangled from some of these vines.

As we came higher, we found more and more purple *erika* growing in places where the original vegetation had not been too disturbed. Then came meadows with purple iris and another small member of the lily family with a delicate pinkish bloom hanging from a slender grass-like stem. A well-defined trail led on through a thickly overgrown draw with a scattering of huge old *kosso* trees, some of the finest I had seen in Ethiopia, and we emerged onto a flat area covered with low heather, most of which had been burned three or four years ago. The springy stalks had deteriorated very little, though many of them showed charred edges. From the roots lush new growth had sprouted. When the charred heather was rather low, up to $1\frac{1}{2}$ m., it was not too difficult to walk through. When, farther on, it lengthened to $2\frac{1}{2}$ m., it was misery to keep beating the slashing stalks aside and we became covered with black dust from them. The air became continually cooler. We proceeded up a slope between two deep draws filled with thick brush and old *kossos*, and heard baboons among them. When we had passed the upper end of these draws, we were past the tree-line at about 3,400 m. There was no evidence that trees had ever grown on the upper slopes (Pl. 27a).

With a sure sense of where he was going, Kebbede led us from one little rocky outcropping to another along the main ridge that forms the western side of the mountain. To our right there were other undulating ridges that also led to the main crest. To the left the slopes of the mountain dropped away a bit more steeply and there were several veined valleys. A large stream formed in the nearest and deepest of them, gathering in smaller streams that came down from the top. We could hear the roar of two small waterfalls. Numerous clumps of white *helichrysum* had just passed their blooming peak in this area. A flat, brilliant yellow, daisy-like flower became more frequent. When we first encountered them, these flowers were fairly small. They became continually larger as we went higher. Their leaves, shiny and rich green like spinach, lie flat on the ground and the flowers have almost no stem at all. The plant is well adapted to flourish in high, cold, windy places and can probably do well under intermittent snow. Snow must fall occasionally on top of Chilalo in December and January and ice must form in streams and pools of water. In April there was no sign of either, but even at this time of the year, the warmest season in the Ethiopian highlands, the temperature must fall close to freezing at night.

We encouraged Kebbede to look for signs of wildlife. He said he had seen nyala and other *agaza* on earlier ascents. One of our party, when he was a good distance from everyone else, saw a large brown animal with big horns. It sounded like a nyala, but he was not sure and none of the rest of us saw it. There were frequent piles of animal droppings, some resembling those of rabbit and dikdik, some much larger. From the point where we had started up the heather slopes, hawks, kites, and Lammergeier soared above us. A few patches of heather had escaped the fires. These were a pleasure to walk through after the slashing and slapping of the burned stalks, but it was harder to see and we got separated from each other. After 3,700 m. we began to feel the brisk east wind which came whipping over the top of the mountain and racing down the folds of the western slope. We could see its gusts as they pushed down the vegetation before them. The soil was soft, damp, and moss-covered. Some of the large patches of moss were unusually beautiful with bluish and greenish shades of turquoise and malachite highlighted by the contrast of the reddish-brown earth around them. These moss concentrations, we soon learned, tended to collect over humus-laden earth in slight depressions where running water had piled up silt. If we stepped directly on to the moss, we sank into it to the knee and came out with shoes and socks coated with mud. Rocks, plentiful all the way up, were mostly of a light, pinkish-grey tufa. Many had heavy growths of lichen which became brighter and thicker nearer the summit.

Three or four times we quickened our pace to surmount what appeared to be the final ridge only to discover that there was still another slope leading upward. Heather clumps were more widely scattered. Open spaces had tall tan grass with delicate seed-heads. It was dry and seemed out of place on the cold, damp soil with alpine vegetation around it, for it resembled the grasses of savannah country. Finally a line of boulders and piles of rocks marked the highest part of the western side of the mountain. The wind nearly swept us off our feet as we came up against its full force. It was carrying huge white clouds over the top and we were so close that we had to turn our heads quickly to follow them individually as they sped by. There was almost no heather on Chilalo's summit, but there was a heavy growth of low vegetation – yellow and white daisies, several small legumes, a good deal of moss, several succulent crawling plants, and a brilliant silvery plant with leaves somewhat like a white-edged geranium which had become more and more common after 3,400 m. On top, it grew in large beds. Kebbede said its Gallinya name was *mida* (Pl. 80a). On a cairn of small rocks, capped with a larger one, someone had painted his initials in white: 'RPS – 1960'. We had reached the top at exactly 11.45. It had taken 4 hours and 15 minutes from our camp-site and we had easily dawdled for an hour and a quarter along the way, so Kebbede had been right when he had said the climb took three hours.

We remained on top for half an hour, walking around a good deal. Just where Chilalo ends and the next mountain begins is difficult to say. We could not be absolutely sure that the point we reached was the highest, either, for the main ridge (onto which we had emerged at the northern end) extends for $1\frac{1}{2}$–2 km. at almost exactly the same height all the way, bending slightly to the south-west at its southern end. Beyond it, to the east, the rock falls away sharply into a deep gorge which bisects the top of the mountain from north to south. It would be quite a task to get a quantity of supplies and equipment over it. The chasm opens up spectacularly along the north face of the mountain (Pl. 27b). Through this opening we had views over the Awash valley and the hilly country of Minjar north of it. The clouds were being blown by so fast that details of the landscape, in whatever direction we looked, were continually being obliterated and then revealed again.

We began the descent at 12.15, taking a more northerly route at first, passing through tall unburned heather down small draws filled with red-hot pokers and lesser flowers. We slipped up quietly behind rock outcroppings to look for animals and were rewarded with a good view of a pair of klipspringer, but saw no nyala. The evening before, some of the men who gathered around our camp-fire assured us that there were many nyala farther east in this range, but said that the best way to get to them was to go up to Arba Gugu from Metahara. They said kudu were plentiful there too.

During the first hour of the descent we got separated again. Starting a short distance apart at the top, we could have ended up miles, and chasms, apart at the bottom. We eventually joined up again and retraced the route of our ascent from 500 m. below the top on down. We were diverted from the annoyance of the slashing heather stalks by the magnificent views to the south, west, and north-west. Storms had begun to form in the western distance as we left the top. During the next two hours two massive storm centres moved directly down the broad valley in which Assela is located, obscuring Lake Zway and drenching the plateau to the south. Mt Kakka was enveloped in a blue-grey thunderstorm. For a while we could see Zuqualla off to the north-west, but it was also soon shrouded in stormclouds. Chilalo's summit remained entirely clear and we made our way down in brilliant sun, removing jackets and rolling up sleeves again as the air warmed. We stopped to photograph flowers in meadows near the tree-line and listened to the roll of thunder from the storms. On the cultivated slopes many people were out and greeted us warmly, enquiring of Kebbede whether we had got to the top. We found that heavy rain had reached up as far as our camp-site and we were glad we had packed everything into the landrover before setting out, always a good rule during the rains in Ethiopia no matter how good the weather looks at the start of the day. The descent had taken less than three hours. The landrover slipped and slid down the wet track at Assela, which we left at 4 p.m. We stopped several times along the road back to Nazareth to examine Chilalo (still in full sun) and retrace our route. By 7.30 we were back in Addis Ababa.

NOTES

1 The best modern description of the Arussi is in Eike Haberland, *Galla Süd-Äthiopiens*, Stuttgart, 1963, 406–516.
2 James E. Baum, *Unknown Ethiopia – New Light on Darkest Abyssinia*, New York, 1927, includes good descriptions of this area in the 1920s.
3 'The Wonji Sugar Estate', *EO*, V, June 1957, 147–50.
4 This Gallinya name means 'Big Mountain'.
5 W. C. Harris, *The Highlands of Ethiopia*, London, 1844, II, 31–4.
6 Guebre Selassie, *Chronique du Règne de Menelik II*, Paris, 1930–32, I, 335–8.
7 I have described the Zway islands at greater length in an article in *EO*, XVI, no. 2, 1973, 76–88. Haberland, *Galla*, 647–77 provides the only other published description of the Zway islanders and their way of life.
8 Workaferahu Kebede, 'The Chilalo Project', *Addis Reporter*, 24 October 1969, 6–9.
9 The sketch map (p. 106) shows the actual relationship of the main landmarks and towns to each other and the tracks which connect them.
10 Haberland, *Galla*, and A. E. Jensen, *Im Lande der Gada*, Stuttgart, 1936, contain numerous references to Galla burial practices and many photographs, plans, and drawings of tomb-sites.
11 Douglas Busk, *The Fountain of the Sun*, London, 1957, 225.

5　Contrasts in the South-west

A Museum of Peoples

Kaffa

We crossed the Omo from Shoa into Kaffa about noon and stopped to watch crocodile-hunters from the bridge. They were camped on a sand-bar beside the rushing water, confident at this season (it was early January) that no sudden rains would cause the river to rise. The guard on the bridge told us that both crocodiles and hippos were plentiful in the river. The Omo has carved a deep gorge.[1] On the Shoan side we had descended through recently burnt-over slopes. On the Kaffan side there had been no fires yet. Clumps of thistle, *garawa*, and tall tan grass with graceful seed-heads lined the road which wound through broken landscape with several prominent volcanic cores visible to the south. Farther on, the valleys became more open and the road was edged with vivid lavender acanthus and *hypericum quartinianum* in full, deep yellow bloom. Nearer Jimma the country became flatter and less wooded. Between grainfields there were patches of *ensete* and bananas. Cultivation was in irregular fields interspersed with homesteads, occasional small villages, and clusters of habitations around churches and mosques. The population here is mainly Muslim.

There would be no point in going into the city at dusk, so we looked for a camp-site east of Jimma. Grassy slopes with scattered fields and thickets extended from the road down to a long lake in a flat valley. We drove down and found a threshing-floor with a 15-cm. underlay of chaff as a tent-site and rushed to gather firewood before darkness set in. As we walked nearer the lake, we discovered that it was full of hippos and alive with waterbirds coming home for the night. Night came, dark and quiet. We went to bed about 9 and slept soundly until the moon rose after midnight. The lake glistened in its light and we could hear hippos and birds grunting and splashing. We went back to sleep, but the hippos became more and more active. Most of them left the lake and came to graze in the shore meadows. Some seemed to be right outside the tent, though we were 300 m. from the lake. At the first light we gave up trying to sleep. I looked outside for hippos, but none had actually come near.

We walked towards the shore, but by the time we reached it all the hippos had returned to the water where they were obscured by puffs of fog rising up like smoke, hiding and then revealing old tree-stumps and clumps of vegetation. It was an eerily primeval scene. As I made my way through the marsh grass, I raised up a flock of noisy Egyptian geese who caused the hippos along the opposite shore, invisible in the fog, to splash and grunt. Sounds carried far in the damp air. I found hippo tracks and paths at several points along the shore; the footprints were enormous. The sun rose warm and golden at 7 o'clock and more birds came to life. The lake was too big to walk around – about 5 km. long, though only 300–400 m. wide. In the strip of lush vegetation above the meadows, jasmine vines climbed over acacias and other trees and perfumed the now warming but still damp morning air. Back at camp for breakfast, we found the light good enough to examine the lake with field-glasses. We spotted a large cluster of hippos directly below our camp-site. During the next hour this group never contained less than ten and sometimes as many as fifteen or sixteen. Animals came and went from it, but the group remained a constant feature. They were standing on a mud-bar with their bodies half out of the water and their dirty backs looking like boulders. We saw several good displays of movement in the water – splashings, divings, cows with calves apparently giving them swimming and manoeuvring practice. We set out for Jimma about 10 a.m.

The highway passes through extensively built-up areas, most of them having a certain tropical lushness, before it reaches the centre of Jimma. The city is still in the process of being built, but the streets are broad, some of the buildings are well designed, and there is plenty of room for air and traffic and people. A pleasant park is being developed near an imposing government building with a clock-tower at the town centre and towards the northern end of the city is the governor's palace in parklike grounds. There are hotels and blocks of arcaded shops, some unoccupied in spite of the continual commercial activity which pervades the town. Every day is market-day and the market spreads over a large area much like the Addis Ababa *mercato*. We stopped at the Ras Mesfin Hotel for lunch. It has a high-ceilinged bar/dining-room with a wall behind the bar rising over 6 m., painted deep red, with a medallion portrait of HIM Haile Selassie I in the middle and small shelves with bottles of liquor extending upwards on both sides in a V-shaped design. The omelettes were excellent and the bread outstanding. Only the coffee was disappointing – here in the heart of the Ethiopian coffee country, where the name itself originated![2]

Jimma, with 40,000 people as of 1970, is growing rapidly. What is now the province of Kaffa was a group of fiercely independent kingdoms until the time of Menelik II. The Kingdom of Kaffa[3] itself was located to the south-west of the present capital which takes its name from another kingdom, Jimma Abba Jifar. The capital of this latter kingdom was Jiren, north of present-day Jimma. Jimma was originally the principal market of Jimma Abba Jifar and was then known as Hirmata.[4] The area has an intricate history, having been subjected to some Christian influence in the late Middle Ages and then invaded by Galla who took control of large parts of the country, but never completely replaced the earlier Kafficho and related Sidama peoples who still predominate in the central and south-western parts of the present province.[5]

We drove from Jimma to Agaro on new asphalt into the heart of the coffee country. Coffee-trees need shade. Larger trees have to be kept to shelter them. Country where coffee is grown looks lush with old acacias, figs, and many other tall trees, including some palms, towering over the undergrowth of shiny-leaved coffee shrubs. All this forest provides a home for large numbers of birds and colobus monkeys. In addition to coffee we saw plantations of bananas, a few of citrus, many plantings of *ensete*. The houses were not impressive. In this lowish country (1,800–2,100 m.) there is little need to build solidly. We saw several coffee-drying centres with coffee berries spread out on drying-floors. We also passed several wood-burning coffee-washing mills, their machinery grinding and clanking. At Yabo, the first town we reached, there was a large market in progress. All the people here spoke Gallinya. Pavement turned into gravel and then there was a long detour over red clay country tracks where the highway was still being bulldozed through a hilly region. On the edge of Agaro coffee-drying floors occupied several acres on a hillside above a stream (Pl. 26b). The different patches ranged in colour from red to deep brown, depending on the stage of drying reached. Agaro is said to be the richest town in Ethiopia, because of coffee income, but it does not look opulent. A walk through its crowded market was revealing, however, for there were almost no handicraft items for sale but large amounts of manufactured goods – a sign of plentiful money. The market had its traditional aspects too – salt shops piled high with *amole* selling at E40¢ and a group of six *garriba*, itinerant entertainers, beating drums, singing, and telling stories in the middle of one of the busiest inter-sections in the market area. Agaro's streets were crammed with trucks, landrovers, and VWs as well as horses, donkeys, and people on foot. We called at the governor's house and were presented by his wife, Woizero Aster, with a bottle of her own best *tej*.

Beyond Agaro the coffee country was soon behind us. We entered Illubabor and began a long descent into the deep valley of the Didessa River, a rather modest stream when we finally crossed it. We had some of the best views of the journey as we climbed up the north side of the Didessa valley. The landscape was a huge park – endless variations of open space and patches of forest, small groves of bananas, hedges of low-growing bushes covered with vines, magnificent single fig- and thorn-trees standing out like ornaments on the landscape. We saw several large ground hornbills as well as many smaller arboreal ones. Houses and people looked poor, though the region seemed thickly inhabited and much of the land was under cultivation. At Bedele a busy market was still in progress in the late afternoon. Many of the women had bushy Afros. Bedele was less prosperous than Agaro, but there were new buildings and a water and drainage system was being installed. The highway on to Metu, the new capital of Illubabor, tempted us, even though it was still under construction, but there was already a feel of evening in the air, so we turned back to Kaffa, stopping several times to watch colobus monkeys. We also stopped to watch a weaver work on white cotton *buluqo* at his loom set up in the yard beside his rectangular thatched house while his two wives and a small child watched us. We also visited a Muslim cemetery. The graves were marked with upright pieces of columnar basalt. Some of the larger graves had enclosures of wooden pillars with rounded tops, like a big bedstead.

Up on the plateau again about 10 km. north of Agaro we found an appealing camp-site in tall grass under spreading thorn-trees above a small river on the edge of a grassy plain. The site was far enough from the road to be free of dust raised by passing vehicles which hung in a low cloud beside the road. In the morning we discovered that a small coffee plantation occupied the slopes that led down to the stream. During the long, slow dusk while the western sky turned vivid pink, we gathered wood and built a good fire and then drank Woizero Aster's *tej* before dinner. It had the smoothness of a good sherry. Having been up well before sunrise, we were ready for sleep as soon as we had eaten.

The countryside was totally quiet except for an occasional birdcall or insect chirp. An hour after midnight the moon rose. It was waning, already half-spent, but it shed a brilliant light and the overhanging thorn-trees cast sharp shadows on the tent roof. It also woke most of the wildlife in the area. I heard a hyena in the distance and then several birdcalls. Strangest of all was a loud squawking which came from the trees close to our tent, just above the river. The squawks echoed up and down the valley as other squawkers replied. After each outburst came whimpering noises that seemed to be connected with the original burst of sound. We thought first that some large bird must be killing prey. But as we were awakened again and again by these raucous blasts and their more distant echoes, we concluded that they could not come from a beast or bird finishing off its kill. They had to come from an animal that felt quite safe in making such a furious burst of sound and then was answered in turn, and in kind, by other kindred souls up and down the whole valley . . . It was only at the first light of day that we discovered the cause of the sound: colobus monkeys, large males, magnificent black-and-white caped creatures with long tufted tails. There were three not far from our tent, sitting in a giant thorn-tree, calling to each other and to others nearby and enjoying themselves thoroughly. Around them females and young frisked in the first rays of the sun. As we stalked these monkeys around the camp-site, we discovered that when they were really alarmed they became completely quiet. So the night calls are, as we had deduced, evidence that they feel safe and confident and are letting others know. When we moved directly under their tree, they began chattering to each other in low, excited tones and then the males all took off with great swings and leaps and headed upstream, settling for a few moments in one tree and then moving on to another. Meanwhile the females and young very quietly retired to the inner branches of the original tree and sat motionless, hoping that the spectacular display of the males would divert us from them. We gave the males a chase. They kept moving farther, but made no sounds until they were sure that we were no longer pursuing intently. Eventually they settled on a high tree about 300 m. away and resumed their cackling and trumpeting.

Leaving the monkeys to return to their own normal pattern, we set out to explore the coffee plantation below camp. Fully half the trees had not yet been picked, though the grass and bushy undergrowth had been cut to make access easier for pickers. The air was clean and cool and the only odour was of the newly cut grass. The coffee-trees were all about 3 m. tall and some of them were very thick. Berries were in all stages of ripening from light green only tinged with pink through cherry red to chocolate brown. A few birds darted about, but there were no insects. We discovered later in the day that coffee-flowers have a wonderfully tangy smell, a compound of the odours of orange blossom and jasmine, but the berries and leaves seem to be without any scent at all.

Heading back to Jimma we took longer on the detour south of Agaro. We had enjoyed this narrow, deep red road the afternoon before, but it was even more pleasant at mid-morning with a good deal of foot and animal traffic, good views of fields, homesteads, and coffee-groves, lavender and brilliant yellow morning glories climbing over the vegetation along the roadside. We stopped to wash the dust off ourselves at a clear, swift-flowing stream and chatted with people passing by. Their world was small, but they seemed well adjusted to it.

There is an especially serene quality to life in south-western Ethiopia. Left on their own, the peoples of this region were content to follow the same pattern of life unchanged for centuries, perhaps millennia. There is evidence of possible very early migration into this region from areas far to the north-west where the old civilizations of Kush, Meroe, and Nubia developed and there are traditions of ancient Egyptian connections.[6] In time archaeology and study of local oral history may provide the basis for more informed speculation on these intriguing possibilities. Through whatever channels influence flowed, the peoples who settled in these regions soon attained a level of social and political stability that was self-sustaining. Their basic needs were all provided by favourable natural surroundings. Weather posed no challenges. Disease kept population in balance most of the time, but if it did not and pressure of excess people required new land for settlement, it could always be found over the next range of hills. It is not surprising that such a fertile and happy region became a primary goal of raiders as the slave trade burgeoned in the eighteenth and nineteenth centuries. The tranquillity of south-western Ethiopia had already been disrupted by Galla invasions. By the beginning of the twentieth century, severe depopulation had occurred and once settled regions had become wasteland. A few of the local kingdoms nevertheless remained havens of order and social stability. During recent decades, in spite of local upheavals, there has been a steady restoration of peaceful conditions, continual population increase, and now accelerated economic growth. Though modern roads are being bulldozed through these lush hills and valleys and evidence of change is visible both in towns and countryside, the region as a whole retains a sense of life in balance with nature which must have been characteristic here centuries ago.

In Jimma again we spent a couple of hours in the market, buying several of the large cylindrical 'hat-box' covered baskets made here from *ensete* leaves and also some decorated calabashes. I found that good Maria Teresa dollars[7] could be bought for E$3.50 compared to E$4–5 in Addis Ababa and I also bought two good Menelik dollars for E$6 each. Our final and major purchases in Kaffa were made on the way back to the Omo Gorge. Through the last 50 km. before the descent, woodcarvers were displaying stools and chairs every few kilometres along the road. Excellent three-legged 'Jimma' stools were selling for E$3.50 each. I bought an ornately carved, finely shaped high-backed chair for E$11. While I was strapping it to the top of the landrover, two men came rushing up with a monumental throne. Carved of a single piece of wood, it was smoothly finished and stained deep brown. The seat was 80 cm. across and the high back was cut out in an intricate lattice pattern. '*Wagaw sint-a naw?*', I asked, looking down at it eagerly. '*Silsa bir*', they replied – E$60. I offered E$40 and they immediately accepted it. We tied it on and then began the long, twisty descent to the Omo.

Illubabor

Illubabor is synonymous with remoteness in Ethiopia.[8] Smallish among Ethiopian provinces, it includes very different kinds of terrain. Its westernmost and lowest part sticks out like a thumb into the Sudan, which it resembles (map, p. 136). Having penetrated into the eastern highlands of the province, I was eager to see the low country, especially the old river port of Gambela and some of the mission stations along the Sudan border, but reports of others who had made the trip by landrover left me with little desire to drive it. The roads are rutted tracks and streams have to be crossed on rafts – picturesque and exciting and without hardship if one organizes well, but it consumes a great deal of time. I was happy when the opportunity came to join a group flying to Gambela in a small plane. From Addis we flew over the beautiful crater lake on top of Mt Wonchi, south of Ambo, then crossed the northern tip of Kaffa and the full length of Illubabor. We had high mountains beneath us, then mixed field and forest, finally thickly forested hills.[9] It was March, the height of the dry season, and the haze in the air became thicker as we came down into the lowlands around Gambela. Here only a few choppy hills rise above the flat landscape and a short distance beyond there is only savannah cut by meandering rivers. The local inhabitants burn the elephant grass at the end of the dry season and the smoke from these fires hangs in the hot, still air until the rains come to clear it.

Gambela has the feel of a sleepy, run-down tropical European settlement that has seen better days. At the turn of the century it was a busy river port oriented towards the Sudan. British, Greek, and Arab trading firms built warehouses. Much of the Kaffa coffee crop was shipped out on river steamers that came up during the rainy season. The warehouses still stand along the river-bank, locked and empty. Some are built of tin, some of stone, many of red brick. They are raised a metre above-ground to protect their goods during high water. Monumental old mango-trees shade the warehouses and the road along the river-front. They were hanging thick with fruit in March, but it was not yet ripe.

Low as it feels when you come in from the highlands, Gambela is still 520 m. high. The river here is the Baro and the town is at the head of navigation on it.

It is built entirely on the north bank of the river which rises about 7 m. above the low-water level. In better days frangipani were planted along the long main street. Some have died, many look neglected, but a few have flourished and bloom well. Gambela is a strange mixture of old buildings which recall those restored colonial villages in so many parts of America, but much less neat – much more like what the original American colonial villages must have been in reality. Alex's general store, the commercial centre of the town, was packed with goods and customers. Near the municipality, a ramshackle old building, work had been proceeding slowly on a new gasoline station, the first with pumps in western Illubabor. We stopped to watch a procession of local women carrying bananas and papayas in big calabash bowls on their heads and then walked past the Sudanese consulate, a Pennsylvania colonial-style building, with broad porches around a plain central two-storey structure set in a large open area with a few small outbuildings around it. Its electric generator was making a loud clatter. The market area includes many small shops and permanent stands and is shaded by large trees. It operates every day of the week, but business did not appear brisk. Lines of shoeshine boys were doing nothing at all. Hawkers came up to impress us with the details of the decorated calabashes that are a speciality of this area in all sizes and shapes. Stands had a good assortment of the dark grey clay pipes in the shape of heads of men and animals that the local Anuak make. There was more fruit than is common elsewhere in Ethiopia. What looked like small bundles of kindling proved to be dried fish.

During the dry season, the Baro River spreads so thinly over the shallow sections of its bed that people walk across it. It still carries heavy traffic in long dug-out boats which are paddled in deeper water and poled or pulled through shallows (Pl. 28a). They range from 3 to 10 m. in length but are always narrow. The trunks from which they are made lend themselves to being hollowed out to leave only thin sides. Two or three boatmen can move one of the larger dugouts along at great speed. By the time the rains reach their height (late June), the water overflows the highest part of the river-banks and spreads out over the countryside across the river to the south of the town. Large sections of savannah become shallow lakes and travel over roads ceases. High or low, the Baro is a very used river. Even at low water, there was a good current and the water was clear. It is free of bilharzia. People bathe in it, fish in it, wash clothes in it, simply sit in it. The indigenous population of Gambela is nearly all Anuak, though there is a sprinkling of other Sudanese Nilotic tribes, such as Nuer, Dinka, and Shilluk, many of them refugees from the other side of the border.[10]

We walked down-river a kilometre or two and watched a group of women and children bathe and fish. The children were all completely naked. Most of them had smooth, suede-black skins, not as dark as some West Africans, but very dark compared to highland Ethiopians. Many wore small earrings and some had beads around their necks, wrists, or ankles. Their tightly kinked hair was cut short on both girls and boys, so the only way of telling the sexes apart was to look at their anatomy. Since most of the women also wear their hair very

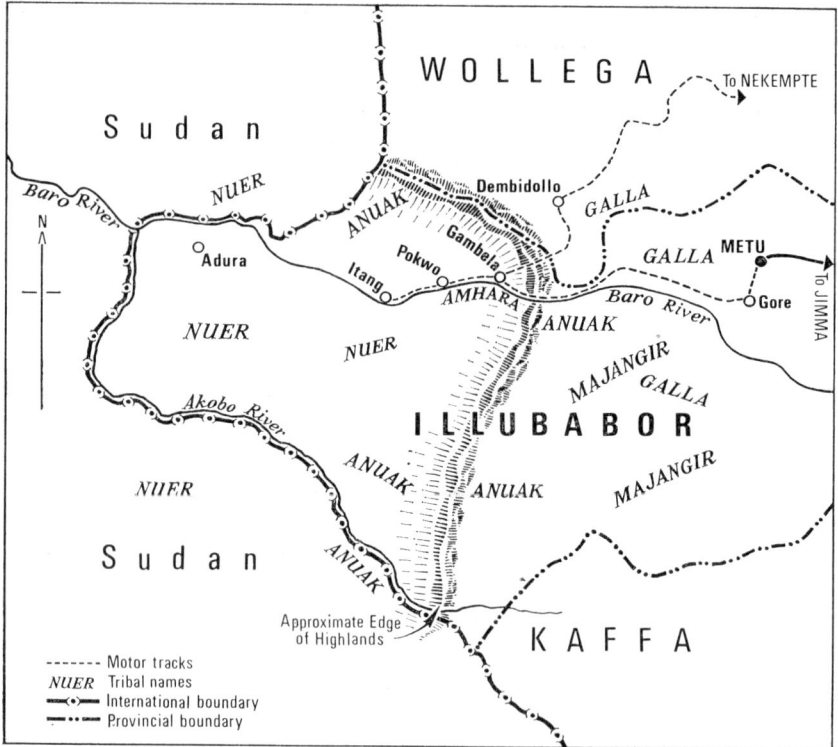

FIG. 17   Western Illubabor

close-cropped, sometimes cut, sometimes tightly braided in rows along the scalp, they would also have been difficult to tell from men if they had worn much. Very few did. As we came around a bend of the shore, a completely naked, highly pregnant Anuak matron gave a mighty tug on her fishing line and jerked back a 4-kg. Nile perch which landed at our feet.[11] She was as surprised to see us as we were to see the fish and we all laughed. We raised our cameras for a picture of the lady with her catch. She began to wave and shout, '*Dollaru, dollaru!*' There seemed to be no modesty involved, simply a desire to make some money. We gathered a large following of excited children who were chased away by boatmen when we stopped to watch dug-outs land to unload their piles of bright ears of golden maize which had been brought up from Pokwo for sale in Gambela where it was now in short supply. Farther on a group of Anuak men were whiling away the morning bathing in a lagoon. In physique they ranged from lanky to gangly, but they stood straight and the muscles of their arms and legs looked taut and tough.

We stayed at the NAMRU[12] house, a bungalow of indeterminate age with screened-in porches and cross ventilation in all rooms. It must be one of the most exotic outposts maintained by the US Navy anywhere in the world, and one of the farthest from the sea. NAMRU specializes in research on tropical diseases. This part of Africa offers a generous selection. Skinworm is a particularly prevalent and debilitating affliction. This microscopic worm, the NAMRU men told us, is transmitted by biting insects. Once lodged in an individual, it spreads to the entire skin, causes it to dry, lose some of its pigmentation, and atrophy. Eventually the worms begin to affect the eyes and by middle age, if untreated, cause clouding of the lens and blindness. The treatment is not too costly or difficult, but as they are killed the worms set off allergic reactions in the body, people feel nauseous and have pain and conclude that they are much worse off from the cure than they were with the worms, so many avoid treatment or begin it and stop. NAMRU's major project at the time of our visit was a study of all local fevers. For this purpose they had selected two Anuak villages and were keeping complete medical histories of a large portion of their inhabitants.

By midday the temperature was well over 40°C and we found ourselves more interested in cold drink at lunchtime than in food. After lunch we walked across newly burned grassfields to the cemetery at the western edge of the main part of the town. This cemetery is basically Belgian, but adjoining the Belgian area we read gravestones of British, Greeks, Arabs, and Italians. More than a hundred Belgian and Congolese soldiers were buried here according to an inscribed memorial which commemorates these casualties of the liberation of Gambela in 1941, a sub-chapter in the history of World War II of which I had been unaware. Care had been taken after the Belgians were first buried, but the cemetery was now in a dismal state of neglect: tall grass and weeds were growing around graves, pieces of rusty machinery were lying on the ground, the flagpole in front of the collapsing gate had been bent over. It was now the hottest part of the day and we walked back to the NAMRU house reflecting on how decay and neglect in the tropics seem more depressing than in temperate climates.[13] A siesta was welcome.

When we had passed the peak of the heat of the day, we drove upriver along a track paralleling the bank. People lived in simple grass huts. Each corn- or durra-field had a platform from which children scare away birds. We skirted a wooden area where trees had been uprooted by elephants during the last rainy season, but there were said to be none in the vicinity now. Our destination was a group of small islands, mere outcroppings of rock piled with pink sand, below a roaring cataract. Half our party had already come up by boat and we joined them in fishing the deeper river channels from the islands. During the next hour we caught two small Nile perch and a vicious-looking, bright-coloured tigerfish. Several perch gave good fights and got away. Downstream we heard hippos surfacing. Thick vegetation across the river contained many birds. The sun slipped slowly into the haze while still quite high and became a fuzzy-edged pale peach-coloured ball floating above the western horizon. I went back by boat. The river was smooth and still. Every detail of the shore was mirrored in it. In places the boat had to be poled over the bottom, scraping on sand and rocks. We saw crocodiles lying on sandbanks, people bathing in the water, others washing clothes, filling water-pots, walking across the river with possessions on their heads. For the most part crocodiles and people seem to respect each other along the Baro, though we were told about a PCV who had been killed by a crocodile the year before. The most striking sight of the 10-km. voyage back to Gambela was the puppet-like profiles of the long-legged children on their bird platforms in the fields waving to us. We saw many herons. As the light began to fade, we rounded a bend and pulled up below the high bank at Gambela. The town, now relatively cool, was bustling with people.

As dusk gave way to night, we drove to the UN compound to have drinks with the Austrian head of the Sudanese refugee programme. He and his hospitable wife were comfortably established in newly completed concrete-block *tukuls* interconnected by thatched walkways. The living-room was a single *tukul*, the bedroom and bathroom another; others served as offices and kitchen. We had scotch and soda and generous hors d'oeuvres and heard a great deal about the refugee problem which was complicated by the fact that there has always been movement of people across borders in this area.

Later in the evening we took a long walk through the town, past local families roasting corn over open fires beside their houses, past small bars where young people were dancing to rock music. We finally settled on the terrace adjoining the general store and ordered cold yoghourt, one of Alex the Greek's many contributions to Gambela. A German volunteer came up and joined us. He was a serious young man, covered with dust which clung to his sweat-soaked workclothes. He had wavy, shoulder-length blond hair, bright blue eyes, and very fair skin. Muscle-sore from a strenuous day, he was totally absorbed in his roadbuilding project south of the town. He described each step of his day's work, most of which had consisted of cutting and hauling away trees. He had two beers and two glasses of yoghourt and then excused himself to go off to bed, saying he was too tired to talk more.

We walked along the main street through the warm darkness, looking in doorways to see faces in the light of cooking-fires and now and then a family group in a room lit by a gas lantern. The only electricity in Gambela is supplied by generators at a few individual buildings. As we came out along the riverbank, we saw a wide orange glow on the southern horizon far out in the bush on the opposite side of the river – a massive brush-fire. Smoke was billowing up to meet the clouds with the light of the flames reflecting off it. We walked down to the sandbars to spot crocodiles, their eyes glowing like fire when caught in the beam of a flashlight. By the time we got to bed the warm air was oppressive. Time and again I dozed off only to be startled awake by a violet bang – mangoes dropping from the overhanging trees onto the house's tin roof. When the mangoes stopped dropping, cats began to fight. In between bangs and yowls the night was deathly still. The grey dawn was welcome.

After a quick breakfast we joined two NAMRU men on a regular visit to one of their 'fever villages', Walinga, near Gambela (Pl. 32a). They brought along their registry books and a medical chest. The village chief welcomed us. Our visit was a combination of tourism and medical service, a good way of seeing this picturesque place at the start of a new day. The sky was still yellowish grey when we arrived; by the time we left, the sun was beginning to penetrate the haze. The NAMRU men said that compared to those in more distant areas this village was relatively dirty, the influence of the town. We were nevertheless impressed by its orderliness, and especially by the cleanness of the house compounds with their packed-earth floors where everyone lives and works most of the time. A few women, dressed only in wraparound skirts, were already at their daily chore of pounding maize with 2-m. pestles in sunken wooden mortars. Others were sorting pounded corn by rhythmically shaking it in long boat-shaped baskets until the coarse grains come to the top to be scooped off with a pink mussel-shell into a calabash bowl. The fine meal is then mixed with water in spherical pots. The pottery of the lowlands is very different from that of the rest of Ethiopia – black and tough, it seems to imitate the calabashes. It is moulded from coiled clay and decorated with geometric and animal designs like the calabashes. Well-made walls of reeds and durra-stalks separated compounds and groups of houses. The houses themselves varied greatly in quality. The best had smoothly plastered and decorated doorways and were well arranged inside. Many had small verandas around their full circumference, sheltered by the overhang of the thick thatch roofs.

The main event of the day was a flight to Adura, a Presbyterian mission station far to the west, only a few kilometres from the Sudan border, and then back to another mission station at Pokwo, closer to Gambela on the Baro River. By the time we were strapped into the small plane coasting down the stony runway of the airport, the sun was out full force and we felt as if we were going to be cooked. It was a relief to become airborne and feel the cool air of 1,500 m. flowing in through the vents. We flew over flat tan country with grassland, swamp, and broad, slow-flowing rivers. Directions were to fly a specified number of minutes on a compass bearing and then expect to see an airstrip and a native village beside a river. If we flew a minute longer, we would be over the border and were to turn back to Gambela and make another try. Conditions were tense along the border and straying into the Sudan might result, as it had with a group of Ethiopian officials a few weeks before, in being interned for weeks. But there it was – just in time! A large group of long-legged Nuers constituted our welcoming party at Adura. An American couple emerged from among them as we came out of the plane and greeted us heartily. They and their little mission station recalled the American high plains in late summer. But the Nuers resembled nothing seen in America and we could not take our eyes off them – legs so long and thin they seemed to lack muscles, even more spindly arms, brown-black skin, long faces with fine features, hair so close-cropped and kinky that it looked glued on. All those at the airstrip wore clothes. A short distance away across the flat plain was a traditional Nuer village, its houses and woven-reed compound walls were so beautifully built that we immediately understood what the NAMRU men had meant about Walinga (Pl. 29a). Here fewer clothes were worn, and some of the women had none at all. In the wearing of clothes, the influence of the mission did not seem to extend very far.

The missionaries, the Jordans, were eager to show us their own little bit of frontier Africa. Their house, built on a slight rise above the Adura River, was a one-storey, red-brick rambler furnished with a motley mixture of simple furniture, bookcases filled with religious books, walls covered with family photographs including several of their children who had been born and raised in the Sudan. These missionaries, like many in western Illubabor, had spent most of their lives in the southern Sudan until they had been expelled several years ago because they were considered too friendly to the non-Arab Sudanese southerners by the Khartoum government of that time. Here, along this Sudanese edge of Ethiopia, they were still entirely devoted to the Nuers and other Nilotic peoples. Mrs Jordan served us home-grown cantaloupe filled with home-made ice-cream. Electricity from their own generator powered a good many appliances as well as their radio, part of the Ethiopian missionary network which links remote mission stations whose staffs may see each other only once or twice a year, if that frequently, but are in almost daily radio contact. They depended on the Missionary Air Service for supplies and mail. We strolled around the fenced lawn overlooking the river now choked with water hyacinth which they said would all be washed away as soon as the water rose with the rains. The countryside around, they told us, was full of game: elephants, buffalo, and large antelopes such as the white-eared kob and the Nile lechwe. The local Nuer do little hunting, however; their lives revolve entirely around their cattle and their cornfields.[14]

No longer having to worry about straying over the border, we flew low from Adura to Pokwo and spotted a herd of buffalo and another of wildebeest with at least 150 animals in each herd. As we came in to land on Pokwo's grass-and-gravel airstrip, we saw more vegetation: thorn-tree and brush country interspersed with swampy areas and expanses of burned grassland. Pokwo, established in 1952, is a metropolis among western Ethiopian mission stations with a complement of ten Presbyterian missionaries, a clinic which serves the population of a large area and not infrequently has patients walking in from deep inside the Sudan and even a few from the other side of the White Nile. It has a school, an agricultural experiment station, and a handicraft centre. The missionaries' houses have a well-established feel about them, shaded by mango-trees and covered with bougainvillaea. Some were in modified local style, made of round sections with steep thatched roofs with walls of reeds and poles. At lunch in one of these houses, a portly lady evangelist with the accent of the southern Virginia mountains recounted her adventures in remote Anuak villages, where she went for weeks at a time to bring the women to Christianity while teaching them sanitation, homemaking, and family management. She always carried her fishing-rod along and described some of the giant Nile perch she had landed on her journeys. We learned that the missionaries' ultimate plan for Pokwo was to turn it over to converted local people who, with some IEG assistance, would keep the mission going themselves. During the afternoon we visited the hospital and the handicraft centre where local women were making necklaces of fish vertebrae and glass beads. Nuer woodcarvers had recently brought in a small stock of graceful curved dipper-like spoons made of a fine-grained white wood. There were piles of the long cornmeal-sorting baskets used throughout this whole region. They are tightly woven of tough reeds and a springy vine fibre with stripes of rust and black. The ornamentation is never the same, but the quality of all the baskets we saw was uniformly excellent. In between each segment of our visit to the various parts of the Pokwo mission, we were served iced lemonade from the fruit of local trees. Our last stop was at the church, round and thatched like an Ethiopian highland church, but with the entire interior a single open space. There were panels of texts in large Amharic and Latin Anuak lettering and a set of local drums used for beating rhythms during services. Open spaces along the sides provided good ventilation.

A more leisurely trip by landrover provided another opportunity to revisit Pokwo and go on to the Swedish mission station at Itang. The track is never far from the Baro River, though it is sometimes separated from it by small stockaded villages with fields of corn and calabash. These little settlements are frequent near Gambela, fewer farther on. Enormous drainage channels intersect the track from time to time, swallowing the landrover as it descends into them. We saw frequent sausage-trees (*kigelia africana*). Around one a group of boys was practising throwing spears at the 'sausages'. Farther on another group of boys had devised another game. One in the centre of a circle was swinging a 'sausage' around his head on its long, rope-like stem while the others were bending to avoid being hit as it sped by. We had our own excitement watching for new birds, very different from those we knew in the highlands: woolly-necked storks, Hadada ibis, and Abdim's storks. In brushy areas a bit away from the river we saw flashes of the black-headed crimson gonolek. One area swarmed with the tiny azure cordon-bleu waxbill. Later in the day, at twilight, we suddenly had to stop to avoid running over what looked like a flock of black birds fluttering near the ground squarely in the roadway. They turned out to be merely two male standard wing nightjars whose long feather-tipped wing standards trailing behind gave the appearance of several birds together. This may, of course, be just the impression this defence mechanism has evolved to give.

We stopped briefly at Pokwo and went on to Itang, 20 km. further down the Baro River. Itang is an old Nuer village in rather barren countryside. While the NAMRU men went to check on recent occurrences of fever among the villagers, we admired a captive serval cat tied on the veranda and then went inside the Swedish mission hospital for a cold Carlsberg in the doctor's attractively furnished quarters. The doctor's wife, a professional textile-designer, had undertaken a project to encourage artistic expression among Nuer women. Noting that their only form of traditional art was decoration of calabashes and pots, she first taught a few women to transfer their designs to paper and then to watercolour them. These were used as patterns for weaving on locally made looms with wool from Debra Berhan. The women enjoyed their newly learned skill and produced lengths of tapestry decorated with representations of cattle being milked, giraffes, crocodiles, snakes, lines of trees, and rivers – beautiful examples of primitive art (Pl. 29b). The colours used had no relation to reality. The doctor's wife had already sent shipments for sale in Addis Ababa and had exported some to Sweden. The project was intended to bring cash income to a group of people otherwise living marginally. It remains to be seen whether it can survive the departure of the Swedish couple. Unlike the highland peoples of Ethiopia, the Nuer and other western lowland tribes have no tradition of textile-weaving, having until recent times felt no need for cloth.

A new village had been built near the hospital at Itang some distance from the older one. Friendly people surrounded us as we came into it, eager to show us around. Most of the men were smoking chunks of local tobacco in pipes of various designs. The most impressive were nearly a metre long, made of wood in two sections joined with leather and ending in a clay bowl with its own lid to press a hot coal down on the tobacco. Many were decorated with beads and all were made to rest on the ground when the smoker preferred to sit. The new houses were remarkable examples of the creative possibilities of mud and grass. The roofs were thick layers of thatch cut in steps. Both men and women wore thick ivory bracelets, usually high on the arm. Some were horizontal cross-cuts from a tusk. Others were oval-shaped and had been carved from vertical tusk sections. The men all had the classic Nuer forehead scarring. It was apparent that these were proud and independent-minded people, deeply attached to their traditional ways. Schools at both Itang and Pokwo are bringing the benefits of modern education, whatever they may turn out to be, to the next generation of these people.

Sidamo

Mention Sidamo in Addis Ababa among either Ethiopians or *ferenjis* and chances are good that the conversation will first turn to Sidamo *tukuls* and next perhaps to the fact that the roads to Kenya pass through this southern province. Great road-improvement projects are now under way. German aid money was used to hire an Israeli construction firm to complete the first phase of the work from Dilla to Yavello. By the 1980s tourist buses will probably pass regularly through Sidamo on their way from Addis Ababa to Nairobi. For the next few years, nevertheless, the trip from Ethiopia to Kenya will continue to be a fairly major endeavour. New highways through Sidamo will result in improved secondary roads and eventually inaccessible sections of this fascinating province will be opened up. Like most modern Ethiopian provinces, Sidamo is an amalgam of several traditional tribal areas and old principalities and kingdoms. Wollamo, the region directly north of Lake Abbaya,[15] is a thickly populated sub-province that has a long history as a separate kingdom with traditions of medieval links with the Christian North.[16]

Sidamo is part of the eastern plateau. The Great Rift Valley is the western boundary of the province. Several systems of mountains and valleys cross the northern and central parts of Sidamo. Altitude declines gradually towards the south. The whole southern part of the province, which forms almost the entire Ethiopian boundary with Kenya, is known as Borana. It is the traditional homeland of one of the most important sub-groups of Galla who still lead a semi-nomadic existence.

Sidamo *tukuls* deserve to be famous, for they are one of the most unusual Ethiopian native house styles (Pl. 30a). They are really inverted baskets, pointed at the top and narrow below the peak, then curving gracefully outward until they encompass a large round space with straight side-walls up to a height of 2 m. It is a style best suited to country that is moderately warm, though they can be thickly thatched from peak to ground and are then nearly as snug as a highland house with stone or mud-plastered wooden-stake walls. You see Sidamo *tukuls* along the roads that lead east, south, and west from Shashemane and they become even more common once you cross the borders of Sidamo itself. The same basic pattern is used for small houses as well as large ones. In northern Sidamo most of the people live in the midst of fields with *ensete* gardens around clusters of three to six houses. Here too, as in so much of Ethiopia, even modest prosperity brings tin roofing. Since tin cannot be adapted to the round peaked style, rectangular pole and mud-plaster houses are becoming more common.

The capital of Sidamo has recently become Awasa, situated beside the lake of the same name, smallest of the seven Rift Valley lakes. The lake has light fresh water and provides good fishing. It enjoyed some popularity with week-enders from Addis Ababa in the 1960s, but has recently declined as a resort. A decade or two ago sisal plantations were established around Awasa. Sisal-fields with their rows of spiky plants are at their most impressive when they send up new-bloom stalks which rise to 6 m. Unfortunately sisal seems to have been superseded for almost all commercial purposes by artificial fibres. Try as they will to find uses for it, governments which encouraged its cultivation now find themselves trying to make the best of an anachronism that is very difficult to dig up and replace once it has become established. Sidamo has to rely on other crops for its agricultural development: coffee, grains, oil-seeds, and cotton.

I would like to have visited some of the higher Sidamo mountains, especially the Amaro range to the east of Lake Chamo. The greatest heights are between 3,000 and 3,600 m. and the mountains look inviting when seen from either across the lake or beyond their foothills from the east. The central portion of the range is inhabited by people called Amaro who have traditions of a kingdom going back to the sixteenth century. They are related to the inhabitants of the islands of Lake Chamo, the southern islands of Lake Abbaya, and a few other small tribes along the shore who, all together, make up the Ometo

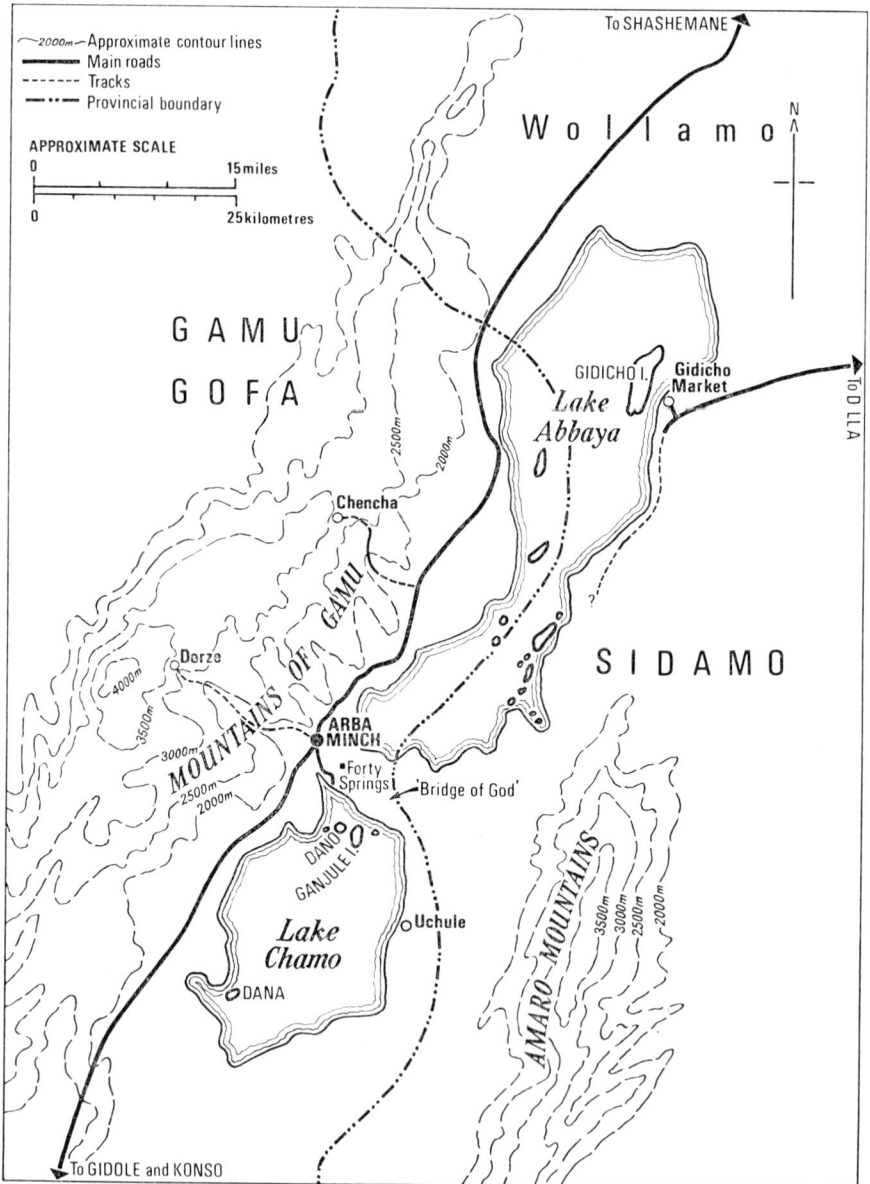

FIG. 18   The Southern (Rift Valley) Lakes

language-group. The Ometo peoples appear to represent an older population which once occupied a much larger territory, but were pushed back into mountains and onto islands when the Galla and Galla-related groups expanded into this region.[17] Since I had made a study of other island peoples in Ethiopia, I made a special effort to visit those of the southern Rift Valley lakes (map, p. 144.)

I went to Lake Abbaya first. Branching westward at Wondo, we took the gravel road to Dilla and had our first view of the lake when it was still 75 km. away to the south-west, a broad, whitish sea. It is by far the largest of the Rift Valley lakes, over 75 km. long and nearly 30 km. across in its northern basin. Dilla, a busy town with brightly painted tin-roofed buildings, is a slightly reduced version of Shashemane. Stopping there to have a *gommista* fix a hissing tyre, we were told that the track to the lake was quite travellable, but there was still construction and unfinished bridges. During the first 25 km. we descended through thorn forest, pasture, and cultivation dotted with Galla farmsteads. Farther down two large 'modern' farms were being developed with machinery. When we reached the broad plain that extends the full length of the eastern side of the lake, averaging 15–20 km. in width, the road crossed long stretches of black cotton soil that would turn into black glue after rain. No rock or gravel had been spread on it. Fortunately it was now dry, but we realized we might be stranded if heavy rains came while we were at the lake-shore. We hoped we might have the alternative of driving down the eastern side of the lake and around its southern end into Gamu Gofa, but no one in Dilla was sure of this route, marked only as a broken line on the IHA map.

The plain showed no sign of population or cultivation. It was covered with thick scrub and looked like first-class game country. During the heat of mid-afternoon no large animals were out. We scared up a 2-m. monitor lizard when we crossed a small stream-bed. At 52 km. from Dilla we reached the shore. Seen close up the lake water is a coffee-with-cream colour with no transparency. The shore was lined with tall cat-tail reeds. Tracks led both north and south. The most used went north towards a table mountain, the most prominent landmark along the eastern side of the lake. We followed it to the Gidicho market, situated where the strait which separates the large island of Gidicho[18] from the mainland is at its narrowest, about 1,100 m. The people who live on this island are also called Gidicho and, along with the Gatami, an Ometo people who live on several of the other Abbaya islands, represent the most interesting cultural survivals of the southern lakes.[19]

The Gidicho market is evolving into a village, with two dozen rectangular, thatched reed houses situated around the boulder-strewn market-place. What caught our eye first on arriving there, however, was something far more unique. Two of the high-prowed *ambatch* boats that are the glory of this lake (Pl. 31a) were tied up at the shore. They are made by both the Gidicho and the Gatami and are probably the most handsome still in use anywhere in Africa. Resembling boats depicted in ancient Egyptian tomb murals, 7 m. and more in length with prows rising 1½ m. above the water, they are built of peeled logs of *ambatch,* the balsa-like member of the acacia family that grows along most Rift Valley lakes and rivers. The boats are not watertight but float on the surface like rafts. Waves slosh up through the logs which are lashed together with bark. Passengers and goods rest upon piles of brush spread over the bottom. They are propelled by two or three men who stand at the back and punt with long poles tipped with chunks of the thick lower trunk of the *ambatch* (Pl. 31a). They look heavy, but when we lifted them, they were as light as foam plastic. These two boats had come over to take grass and green reeds back to the island to feed cattle. Their owners explained that *ambatch* was called *soke* locally. A boat had a life of about a year, they said, before the wood became waterlogged. This accounts for their fresh light colour. By the time the wood has begun to weather, the boat is discarded and replaced by a new one. Another man came up and said that next day there would be great numbers of boats, for it would be market-day and most of the people from the island would come to shore. We were delighted at this good luck, for we had not been able to find out before when market-day was held here. It is Sunday.

On the side of a small promontory south of the market site was a ruined concrete dock and a little farther on a new one, rising high above the shore. This is the landing for the ferry that plies the lake, crossing from the south-western corner, where there is a similar dock. The guard told us the ferry could carry up to six vehicles and large numbers of people and animals and that it came twice a month. Several men were fishing near this dock, pulling big ugly catfish out of the milky water and placing them in a pool which had been formed by blocking off a section of the shore with volcanic boulders. They are eventually carried up to Dilla for sale. On the track down we had met several porters carrying two catfish each on shoulder-yokes.

Returning to the market site, we were approached by two young men who rather surreptitiously asked whether we would be interested in buying hippopotamus teeth. They motioned us behind a bush and from a burlap bag drew out several enormous specimens, some matched pairs. They resembled fine ivory. A bit of bargaining and we had the best of their lot for E\$2–4 apiece. The men were Gatami, the traditional hippo-hunters of the lake who have a village on Gidicho island but live mostly on the more southerly islands (of which there are nine in all, some now uninhabited) and along the eastern shore. Only a third or less of a hippo tooth extends beyond the gum. Most of it rests in the jawbone and since hippos are browsers whose teeth must grind enormous quantities of vegetation each day, their teeth grow during their entire life-span. In older animals the largest incisors may reach a curve length of 45 cm. and weigh up to 2 kg. I asked the Gatami whether they ate hippo and they admitted somewhat embarrassedly that they did.

Gidicho would start arriving for market by 8 the following morning, the Gatami told us, so we decided to find a camp-site and settle in so we could be up early in the morning to witness the whole sequence of boat arrivals and market activity. The track southward along the shore, though it bore no evidence of recent vehicular travel, was in good condition. We drove to a slope dotted with thorn-scrub and candelabra euphorbia across from the southern end of Gidicho island. The 4-m. tall reeds along the shore were interrupted every 300 to 400 m. by breaks used both by hippos as grazing exits at night and by cattle as watering-points during the day. We could find very little wood, so we gathered dry dung to cook our evening meal, stowing a bag of it under the landrover for use in the morning in case rain fell during the night. The haze of the afternoon had dissipated and we could see across the full width of the lake to the mountains of Gamu. The sun appeared briefly and coloured the mountains orange. Then everything turned deep grey and the waves of the lake lapped ominously against the reeds as the wind rose. A rain-squall forced us to retreat into the tent to finish dinner, but by 9 o'clock all the storms in the area had disappeared. On Gidicho fires were visible. The night air was so warm and humid we hardly needed our sleeping-bags. Lake Abbaya is 1,285 m. above sea-level. We expected to hear hippos during the night, but instead were awakened by the frantic yapping of a jackal who kept circling our tent. We concluded that we had placed our camp in the middle of his regular path to the shore and he was offended at finding our tent looming up in front of him as he made his night-time rounds. I drove him away by concentrating the high beam of our flashlight directly on him.

At daybreak we were aroused by two Guji boys bringing us a gourd of fresh milk. They stayed to help us get our dung fire going for coffee. It is surprising how much heat, how quickly, a good dung fire will give. Rain had highlighted the fact that the slope on which we were camped was sprinkled with broken jasper geodes, mostly of a bluish-white colour, with good crystals. We collected a basket full of them. By 7 o'clock people began to pass along the lakeside trail, early market-goers. Men carried little, but all the women had containers of milk and bundles on their backs. These were Guji Galla going to sell to the island Gidicho.

An armada of high-prowed boats was already plying the channel between island and mainland when we arrived at the market site shortly after 8. They made a beautiful sight far out on the open water, their muscular punters lifting their long *ambatch*-tipped poles and then pushing them in unison down deep into the water again, maintaining steady speed (Pl. 31a). Among the passengers older gentlemen and well-dressed ladies sat under umbrellas, a symbol of status as well as sunshield. As they came into the shore-channels through the reeds, the punters broke rhythm and guided their craft more delicately with poles, slowing as they approached the landing area and finally leaping ashore to tie up to boulders. As many as twelve people alighted from some of the boats. Some had piles of bags and skin sacks filled with grain and cotton; others brought bundles of bananas. Some boats did taxi service, returning for more people and goods as soon as they had unloaded. There were perhaps as many as fifty boats involved in this mass movement.

The first phase of market activity was devoted to selling fresh milk, most of which was consumed on the spot by purchasers. I had never seen a greater variety of milk-containers, some of them works of art. Some were gourds. Many were wood. Others combined gourd or wood with upper sections of basketry. Most of them, whatever they were made of, had beads, leather thongs, cowries, carving, metal strips, and braided copper wire as ornamentation. Some of the wood was so smoothed and polished by long use that it glistened like burnished pottery. A few women brought their milk in tall-necked decanter-style containers made entirely of fine grass, woven so tightly that it must have been practically watertight even before it was given a coating of wax. Each kind of milk-container had its own name. The decanter was called a *guji*, indicating that it was typical of the local Galla.

I asked several of the women if they would sell containers. They wanted to sell the milk, but considered the containers valuable possessions – as well they might. A lady who sold her milk-container would have to go to considerable effort to replace it. Just the same, a spirited matron with an outstanding *guji* was tempted to offer it to me and encouraged to do so by her husband, so I began bargaining in earnest for it. But it was the reverse of the usual Ethiopian bargaining process – she kept raising her asking price. In the course of half an hour I had to go up from a first offer of E$6 to E$11 to close a deal. Gallinya was the common language. Only the men spoke a little Amharic. The Gidicho spoke their own language among themselves. Though related to Somali, it did not sound as harsh as Somali usually does.

Most of the women, whether Galla or Gidicho, wore the Gidicho hair-style. Some of these hairdos, especially on the young Gidicho wives, were a spectacle to behold. The hair is braided around the crown of the head, but puffed out over the ears and off the back of the head like a thick hat-brim (Pl. 32b). It is decorated with clusters of jewellery consisting mostly of red, white, and blue glass beads. All the Gidicho had light skins, fine noses, thin lips, and large, sparkling brown eyes. Faces were lean and regular. Few Gidicho were very tall and all were slender. There were very few children. They had been left home on the island.

Butter was being sold in balls wrapped in dried *ensete* leaves which kept the sun from melting it. White sweet potatoes were selling at E10c for four or five. Heaps of light-brown leaf tobacco were much in evidence. There was *ensete* dough for sale, but from the quantities of lentils, maize, and other grains being offered it appeared that local eating habits do not centre on *kocho*. Like many island peoples, the Gidicho have a tradition of weaving. Cotton was being traded in quantity. Towards mid-morning a large section of cloth-sellers got ready for business and Galla women who had sold their milk and vegetables came to spend their earnings.

Two Gatami came up and whispered that they had a new batch of hippo teeth to show us. They led us to a house in an area well removed from the market, closed the door after seating us on wooden stools, and poured a burlap bag that contained 19 pairs of teeth on to the earthen floor. Some were superb specimens with well-polished grinding surfaces, but we had no interest in buying so many. The Gatami insisted we make an offer. We did; they considered it too low and we left and went down to the shore to talk to boatmen in hopes of arranging a visit to the island. We found several willing to take us but only later in the afternoon. The Gatami appeared again with a counter-offer. After two more bouts of bargaining with them we ended up buying the entire bag-full of teeth . . .

It was now noon and the market area was emptying fast, as the sun became hotter, but the boats remained tied up at shore. No one was departing. Instead they were all moving into the *tejbets*, the rectangular thatched structures around the market area, to relax over *talla* and *tej*. Women joined the men in drinking. We realized that even if we did persuade a boatman to take us to the island, it would be practically depopulated until late afternoon and most of the population would return tipsy. So we drove back up to Dilla. I had no opportunity to return to Lake Abbaya's eastern shore, but I did manage a visit to the islands of Lake Chamo.

Gamu Gofa

Leaving Addis Ababa early, for we were towing our boat, we filled up on gas at Shashemane 2½ hours later, then crossed northern Sidamo and stopped at Wollamo Soddo to visit the huge, colourful market. By late afternoon we were driving through the half-cultivated, half-wild country along the western shore of Lake Abbaya. We reached Arba Minch well before sunset. This town, Gamu Gofa's new capital, sits on a sloping plateau at the western end of 'The Bridge of God', the strip of land which separates Lake Abbaya from Lake Chamo. We had a good night at the Bekele Molla motel and next morning descended the 300-m. escarpment to Chamo's shore.

We passed the turn-off to the government dock as we neared the lake and continued along the Gidole road. Friends who had been here before had drawn us a map showing the way to the only practical launching-site on the western side of the lake, but we missed the turn and soon found ourselves in a village. The villagers confirmed we had come too far. As we turned around, another landrover which had followed us from Arba Minch came alongside. It belonged to a short young man with a wispy beard, green uniform, and great consciousness of his official status, accompanied as he was by several attendants. He introduced himself as the government fishguard and asked to see our fishing licences. 'But we are not going to fish'. 'What are you going to do then?' 'Just explore the lake, go to the other shore, and visit the islands'. 'You are sure you are *not* going to fish?' 'You can see we have no fishing gear with us; we are not interested in fishing.' He drew himself up stiffly, 'I will still have to inspect you when you come back to see that you do not have any fish'. Since Lake Chamo now attracted a small number of *ferenji* fishermen, the conscientious young fishguard found it difficult to grasp that other *ferenjis* could be bringing a boat to the lake without wanting to fish. It did not fit the pattern he had come to take for granted, since in Ethiopia, as in so many developing countries, foreigners are all expected to want to do exactly the same thing. Still sceptical of our intentions, he guided us back to a point where a cattle trail led into the bush, past tangles of vines and clumps of wild hollyhock and over a small ridge to the launching-site.

Chamo's western shore consists of continuous reed-beds, 15–50 m. wide. The reeds stand 3–4 m. high. Launching at this place was possible because there was a 7-m.-wide meadow behind the reeds, just enough room for the landrover and boat-trailer to manoeuvre. The channel into the lake was easy to find, but it had not been used for several weeks and was partially blocked by an old reed raft which we had to break apart to remove. We had heard that the Chamo shore teemed with crocodiles, but encountered none here.[20] It was 11.30 when we finally poled the boat out through the reeds, leaving Zeneba, the *zabanya* we had brought from Arba Minch, to spend the day guarding the landrover and trailer. He claimed to be a 10th-grade student when we engaged him at the motel, but from talking to him on the way down to the lake we had already deduced that he had had no more than two or three years of schooling and was probably not going to school now. He was old enough to be a 10th-grader, however, and had a flair for English. Like so many young Ethiopians, he lied about his school status because he feared *ferenjis*, who are usually partial to students, would think badly of him if he were honest about his station in life.

Open water with a cool breeze was most welcome after the heat of the reed-beds. Lake Chamo is only 1,233 m. above sea-level. The lake has risen greatly in recent decades. Hulks of old trees, some of them very large, protrude far out from shore, slowly rotting in what now must be 5 m. of water. They make for difficult navigation until you are well out, but they also make good perches for fish-eagles and other water-birds, though birdlife on these southern lakes tends to be rather sparse compared to the more northerly ones. We headed straight across the lake towards the eastern shore, 20–25 km. away. The land rose up steeply from the lake and the Amaro mountains loomed beyond. When we looked back, we were equally impressed by the mountains behind the western shore. Though not quite so high as the Amaro range, they were covered with green vegetation all the way to their summits.

An hour and 15 minutes of steady running on two motors brought us to a small inlet about a third of the way down the eastern shore where a stream had built up a black-sand beach. It was a cattle watering-point, well used, with a rocky, eroded trail leading up the steep hillside. Several hundred cattle were arriving, watering, and returning up the trail. They were attended by half a dozen Galla who spoke no Amharic. They said the place was called Uchule and they lived on the plains above (Pl. 31b). We had been told in Arba Minch that there were large herds of zebra on these plains and many other kinds of game; the area is scheduled to become a game reserve. We were tempted to hike up, but the heat and dust discouraged us and our goal of the day was to visit the islands on the lake. So back in the boat, we cruised along the steep eastern shore for 2 or 3 miles. We then turned towards the north-west and passed a small acacia-forested island which is not indicated on maps.[21] As we neared the highest and largest island, we could see that it consists of an agglomeration of volcanic upthrusts. Blocks of red aggregate overlie grey and black lava flows. The sides are very steep, in places sheer cliffs. We saw no signs of life or cultivation until we rounded the northern end. There were terrace walls on a high slope and a little farther on a village came into view. A red-sand beach had two of the same high-prowed *ambatch*-boats we had seen on Lake Abbaya drawn up on it. It was not immediately apparent that the village was still inhabited. The houses were tall beehive-type completely covered with thatch (Pl. 34a).

Soon people began to come out as word of a motor-boat coming in to their shore passed from house to house. By the time we slipped up on to the beach half a dozen women and children had already reached the shore. Only one of the women spoke a little Amharic. What did we want? We wanted to see their village. She pointed to a man racing towards us over the terraces which extended up to the village. He introduced himself as the island's *balabat* – speaking good basic Amharic – and said his name was Sawiyeto, Chief of the Ganjule.[22] Like the Gidicho of Lake Abbaya, the island and people have the same name. We asked about the other islands. The one to the west was called Dano. It was large, low, and thickly forested. Sawiyeto said there were no people on it and it looked as if it had not been inhabited for a long time. The large headland across the 150-m. strait to the north was called Zeti-Zuma. Ganjule lived there and on the mainland beyond in an area called Maddo. Were there hippos? None in this area . . . They were off to the south-west around another island called Dana. Did Dana have people? No people. Sawiyeto was a rather small man, wiry, with large eyes and light skin. Fortyish, he was bald (Pl. 33a). By the time we started up the trail to the village behind him, we were followed by twenty-five people. They were mostly women, a couple of older men, and a good many children – girls wearing dresses, boys completely naked.[23] There were no young men. They were all on Zeti-Zuma and Maddo, Sawiyeto said.

The houses – there were about twenty of them in the village – looked like poorly made haystacks from the outside, but inside they proved to be well constructed and intelligently arranged. Sawiyeto took us into the largest one first which he said belonged to him. We passed through a door carefully woven into the thick thatch of the wall. Inside a sturdy centre pole rose 6 m. Around it, covered with smoke varnish, was a cluster of some sort of dried plant, each branch of which contained a wasps' nest. A fire was burning on a hearth on the left side of the entrance. The house was divided into two unequal parts (the front section being larger) by a long clay-plastered wall which rose a little over 2 m. The front was a cooking/sitting/sleeping area. The rear was a store room. We sat in this house only briefly – being welcomed to it seemed to have a ritual significance – and then went out to walk up the hillside above the village. Walls and terraces built of red volcanic rocks extended far up the slope, but none of the terraces was now cultivated and there appeared to be no agriculture anywhere on the island except for a few pumpkin vines planted around houses. The soil looked poor. The Ganjule now cultivate much land in Maddo, Sawiyeto said. Descending again, he invited us into another house which he said also belonged to him. To my question as to how many wives he had, he answered one, but it was never clear which of the several women we met in his houses filled this role and I suspect he had several. There were also a good many children, some of whom Sawiyeto identified as his, some as his grandchildren. To my question about the religion of the Ganjule, he said they practised Islam, but they seemed not far from their original pagan state, for none of them had Islamic names and there was nothing about their way of life which gave the impression of even perfunctory adherence to Islam.

Seated in Sawiyeto's second house, we were asked if we wanted coffee and we accepted. I was given the seat of honour next to the centre pillar. The women busied themselves preparing the coffee in a well-smoked *jabana*. They offered us parched maize meanwhile which they had been roasting when we entered. In this house the hearth was on the right side of the door and towards the back. The coffee, served out of Chinese teacups, was heavily flavoured with salt and cardamom and tasted as if powdered marigold had also been added. After the first shock of the unexpected combination of flavourings, I found I liked it, for the coffee itself was mellow, almost like chocolate. I had a second cup. Sawiyeto took down a big bolt of cloth from rafters above the bed on which he sat. It was an unusually fine-quality thick, creamy-white *buluqo* with broad red borders. Did I want to buy it? If the price was right – what did he ask? Sixty. I gasped. Expensive! What would I offer him? Twenty-five. He raised his hands in mock horror and thrust the bolt aside. Further bargaining over the next ten minutes concluded with my agreeing to pay E$50 for the entire bolt containing eight lengths of cloth totalling about 30 m. I might have got the price down another 5 or 10 dollars, but I felt Sawiyeto deserved some consideration for his hospitality and we had both had our amusement out of the bargaining process.

When the money had been exchanged and the cloth placed beside my seat, Sawiyeto offered us *katikala*. One of the women brought a bottle of clear liquid from the storeroom and another set to work washing small glasses in a pan of water. The *katikala* had been distilled from raw maize and had a sharp odour and a harsh, unpleasant taste. While we dawdled over it to avoid being offered a second round, Sawiyeto took a *masenko* off the wall and began to play. The children lined up and began a shuffling dance, monotonous movements over and over again to the same melody punctuated at the end of each round by a change of tune and leaps by the dancers. I suggested that we move outside so that I could photograph the playing and dancing (Pl. 33b). This went off well, but they soon complained of the heat of the sun and suggested we go back inside.

On the wall near the door hung several bundles of dried fish taking a final cure in the sun. They liked fish, Sawiyeto said, and they also liked hippo meat which they ate as often as they could. On the rafter above the bed, where the cloth had been, I noticed a long spear with an ambatch float in the middle. Sawiyeto proudly reached up to show it to us and said it was for hunting hippo. It was 3½ m. long and had a formidable iron head. With enough gestures that we could clearly grasp what he was saying though I could not understand all the words, Sawiyeto illustrated the process of hippo-hunting. The beast is first speared from a boat and let go. The float shows where he settles down. He is pursued and speared again and again until he becomes exhausted and can be pulled to shore, where he is finished off.

As we were making our way back to the beach – it was past 4 o'clock by this time – Sawiyeto said hippo teeth 'were coming' for us and urged us not to hurry away. As we stood on the beach, a large *ambatch* boat brought a group of people over from Zeti-Zuma. Several of them asked for medicine and we passed out all the aspirin, chloroquin, and vitamin tablets we had with us. Then the hippo teeth came – they were still in the head of the hippo! A man laid the big jaw on a rock and began hacking at it with an axe to dislodge the teeth. Ten metres away we still got a heavy dose of the odour of the rotting flesh.[24] In a few minutes he extracted six teeth which the women washed in the lake and then presented to us. We pushed off from Ganjule amid cheering and waving from the whole island population as well as the dozen additional people who had come in from Zeti-Zuma.

It is easy to believe that the Ganjule of Lake Chamo and the Gatami of Lake Abbaya are the same people. They use identical *ambatch* boats, build the same kind of houses, eat fish, and hunt hippopotamus. Their languages are said to be very similar. During earlier periods, when the hostility of shore tribes kept them concentrated on their islands, they kept their cultural traditions intact. Since the Ethiopian conquest at the turn of the century, pressures that kept them a group apart have eased and they are now well on their way to abandoning their islands entirely. This seems more true of the Ganjule than of the Gatami. For all the warmth of our welcome there, it was apparent that the island culture of the Ganjule was in the final stages of decline. Keeping to tradition, the chief still maintains his residence and the island serves as a base for fishing and hippo-hunting. But there is no cultivation and young men do not remain. In another generation, if not sooner, the Ganjule will have moved entirely to the mainland and will gradually become absorbed into the mainstream of Ethiopian life. They do not appear likely to maintain their identity as long as the Gidicho or the Zay.

We crossed close in to the neighbouring island of Dano, thickly forested, with many birds. We then passed another small, high island and turned south-westward to return to the western shore. We had to twist constantly to avoid the long lines of sunken trees that extend far out into the lake in this section. When the lake-level rose, it must have occurred suddenly and since that time the shore appears to have remained quite stable, for there is no indication of fluctuation of the reed-beds. If we had not hung an orange life-preserver on a snag to mark our exit point, we would have had great difficulty finding it. We cruised in smoothly and moored the boat with the intention of returning the next morning to go down to the island of Dana and observe the hippo herds before driving on down to Gidole and the Konso country. As we drove back towards Arba Minch, we met the fishguard, who inspected the landrover to satisfy himself that we had no fish. Under his officious manner, he had a sense of humour and we parted with jovial handshakes.

In Arba Minch we resumed our explorations of the day before. The town is called Shercha by local people. Unpaved but kerbed, divided, four-lane avenues form the main streets. These have modern streetlights which make it seem like a small metropolis after dark. In daylight they look incongruous along these broad avenues through empty fields. Arba Minch has more future ahead of it than it has past behind it. The name means 'Forty Springs' and comes from a group of clear, cool, swift-flowing springs in a thickly forested glen 300 m. below the town site. We drove down in the early evening and visited a new pumping-station which would soon go into operation to supply water to the town. Young men offered us spring water from cups made of huge leaves of a plant that grew along edges of pools. We got back up to the motel just at sunset and had incomparable views over both of the great southern lakes with range upon range of mountains beyond (Pl. 30b). As we enjoyed drinks on the motel terrace, a young ostrich ambled by and snatched snacks from the table with lightning speed. There were several others, less bold, in the compound.

Rain began to tinkle on the roof of the motel after midnight. Increasing in intensity, it woke us again and again and continued until 10 in the morning. When we attempted to drive over the clay track out of the motel, the landrover spun its wheels as if on butter and we had to be pushed by a group of bystanders. When we finally got on to one of the grand avenues, we could still hardly move. Our *zabanya* of the previous day, Zeneba, joined us, as he had promised, but any effort to reach the lake-shore again, let alone to go on to Gidole and the Konso country, was out of the question. The police had put up a barrier on the road to the lake. Zeneba suggested we go up to Dorze, in the mountains to the north-west, where there was a big Monday market. Markets in Gamu Gofa do not get under way until noon. But when we reached the rocky track down from Dorze it was simply a stream-bed. Even if we managed to drive up it, a further bout of rain could leave us marooned.[25] We slithered back through the mud to the Arba Minch police station and found a helpful lieutenant who promised to arrange a guard for our stranded boat on the lake-shore until we or friends could return to retrieve it.

We had to be back in Addis Ababa the next evening, so we headed north again, apprehensive that new rain might make the fords along the west shore of Lake Abbaya impassable. Some were pools of mud where trucks had got stuck, but with chains we managed to get through. After crossing one, as the sun came out, we took half an hour to stalk a small group of saddle-bill storks in roadside meadows with telephoto gear. It was good sport, for these beautiful, tall birds with red, yellow, and black bills were wary and clever. I had to crawl low from one clump of bushes to another to outwit them. There were great white egrets in this region too, not far from the south-western shore of Lake Abbaya. They were less shy. Thunderheads were gathering all around us, so we hurried on. Driving steadily, we reached Lake Shala at sunset as a heavy rainstorm swept across it, churning its dark waters into grey-black waves. It was late June and weather such as this has to be expected in most parts of Ethiopia at this season. The discomfort it causes is compensated for by the spectacular skies and clouds and frequent rainbows and by the fresh, cool nights when the storms are past. We had a quiet night at Shala and awoke to a cloudless sky the next morning.

NOTES

1 This large river flows south-west into Lake Rudolf. In its lower valley, under alternating sedimentary and volcanic layers, rich fossil-beds have been discovered in recent years. They contain many animals as well as hominid remains over 3 million years old. Henri Baldet, 'Some Aspects of the Prehistory of Ethiopia', *EO*, XV, no. 1 (1972) summarizes recent discoveries.

2 The names apparently developed in the same way that other place names such as Mocha and Java became applied in less generalized fashion to the beverage. In Ethiopian languages the word for coffee is *buna*, which obviously has no connection with Kaffa.

3 Much of what is known about this traditional kingdom is summarized in G. W. B. Huntingford, *The Galla of Ethiopia, the Kingdoms of Kafa and Janjero*, London, 1955.

4 A history of this kingdom has been reconstructed by Herbert S. Lewis, *A Galla Monarchy, Jimma Abba Jifar, Ethiopia, 1830–1932*, Madison, Wisconsin, 1965.

5 Much light is shed on this little-known history by works reproduced in C. F. Beckingham and G. W. B. Huntingford (eds.), *Some Records of Ethiopia, 1593–1646*, London, Hakluyt Society, 1954.

6 Otto Bieber, *Geheimnisvolles Kaffa, im Reiche der Kaisergötter*, Vienna, 1948, includes speculation based upon traditions of Egyptian connections collected by the author's father, Friedrich Bieber, at the turn of the century just after Menelik II's conquest of the old Kingdom of Kaffa.

7 This beautiful coin ceased to be legal tender in Ethiopia after 1945. Its long and colourful history is recounted by Dr J. Hans, *Maria-Teresien-Taler*, Leiden, 1961.

8 There are relatively few earlier travellers' accounts of this region. One of the best is Arnold W. Hodson, *Where Lion Reign*, London, 1929, which describes his extensive travels in both Kaffa and Illubabor in the 1920s when he was British Consul in Maji. His equally extensive travels in other parts of southern and south-western Ethiopia are covered in an earlier book, *Seven Years in Southern Abyssinia*, London, 1927, which relates his experiences as British Consul at Mega during the period 1914–21.

9 A relatively primitive people who inhabit these hills are described in detail in a recent anthropological study, Jack Stauder, *The Majangir*, Cambridge, 1971.

10 Most of these returned to the Sudan after the north-south political reconciliation during the summer of 1972.

11 Very small for this species which commonly reaches more than 50 kg., with record specimens up to 200 kg. in the southern Rift Valley lakes.

12 Naval Auxiliary Medical Research Unit.

13 On returning to Addis Ababa, we reported the condition of this cemetery to the Belgian ambassador who took steps to provide regular care of it.

14 The Nuer of this region have recently been described, somewhat melodramatically, in B. H. MacDermot, *Cult of the Sacred Spear*, London, 1972. A classic account of the

Nuer, based on observations in the Sudan, is Ray Huffman, *Nuer Customs and Folklore*, Oxford, 1931, reissued by Cass, London, 1970. A Harvard University group produced an outstanding documentary film on Nuer life in the Gambela region in 1970.

15 This lake is generally called Margarita by foreigners, but the official Ethiopian designation is Abbaya. It has more than half a dozen local names: Beke, Gumaraki, Bato, Abba, Bagade, Dambala and is still referred to by older Amhara names, Yigidicho Bahr (Lake of the Gidicho) and Qay Bahr (Red Lake). The bewildering variety of names of most natural features, as well as peoples, in this region is discussed in Haberland, *Galla*, 681 ff.

16 Authoritatively discussed in Haberland, *Untersuchungen zum Äthiopischen Königtum*, Wiesbaden, 1965, 255–80.

17 Helmut Straube, *Westkuschitische Völker Süd-Aethiopiens*, Stuttgart, 1963, 72–140, describes the Amaro region from an ethnographic and historical viewpoint.

18 Nothing in southern Ethiopia has only one name. The island can also be found on maps as Ano, Hano, Oddola, and Haruro.

19 Haberland, *Galla*, 678–717, has a comprehensive description of the Gidicho. See also my 'Patterns of Cultural Survival on Islands in Ethiopian Highland Lakes', *EO*, XVI, no. 2, 1973, 89–96.

20 The northern Rift Valley lakes have no crocodiles. Lakes Abbaya and Chamo are plentifully supplied with them.

21 Most maps show Chamo as having three islands. I observed five.

22 Practically nothing has been written about these people and they seem never to have been studied by ethnologists. Haberland's *Galla* has brief references to them on 716–17.

23 Male nakedness, contrasting with a feeling that females ought to be clothed, occurs among other peoples of Gamu Gofa. Cf. C. R. Hallpike, *The Konso of Ethiopia*, Oxford, 1972, 152–3.

24 It is a rather distinctive odour and, after smelling it here, I was sure that I had noticed it in Watta villages on the north shore of Lake Zway a few weeks before. The animals are plentiful in Lake Zway, but the Watta insisted that they no longer hunted them because it had been forbidden by the government.

25 The Dorze, one of the dozens of small peoples who make up the population of Gamu Gofa, live in tall bamboo-basket houses and are famous throughout Ethiopia as weavers. Cf. Judith Olmstead, 'The Dorze House', *JES*, July 1972, and the same author's 'Ethiopia's Artful Weavers', *National Geographic Magazine*, January 1973.

6 Into the Semyens

The Roof of Africa

One day in early December 1971 on the regular EAL flight to Asmara we flew closer than usual past Ras Dashan. The air was crystal clear and the view of the huge Semyen[1] massif the best I had seen in a dozen such flights. The great ramparts, deep gorges, high tablelands were all visible from 11,000 m., 6–8,000 m. below. Why not go into these mountains during the Christmas season, I thought. Why not climb Ras Dashan?

When I returned to Addis Ababa, I found many people interested in joining a Semyen excursion. But it turned out to be difficult to get accurate, recent information on what a trip into the mountains would involve. The best published description of the whole region, by far, remained Leslie Brown's account of his 1963 explorations[2] and his sketch maps were as good as any we could find until we discovered in a cupboard in the embassy a copy of a beautifully done large-scale map issued by the Bayerische Landesvermessungsamt in Munich in 1968.[3] But this map covered only the area from Emetgogo eastward, omitting the entire region between Debarak and Geech. We also managed to get a copy of an out-of-print ETO pamphlet, *The High Semyen*, which was useful.

The notion of climbing Ras Dashan receded into the background. From Brown's book it was clear that the ascent of Ethiopia's highest mountain was one of the less exciting things to be done in the Semyens and if we concentrated on that, there would be little time for anything else. We settled down to a party of five, assembled light camping gear, warm sleeping-bags, and a good supply of canned food and made sure that everything would fit into duffel-bags that could be strapped to the backs of mules. One thing was quite clear, published reports of a landrover track notwithstanding: the only way of getting from Debarak into the high mountains was on foot, horse, or mule.

We set out two days after Christmas. The road journey across Gojjam and past Lake Tana in this dry, cool season was a delight, but it belongs in another chapter (see Chapter 9). One member of the party, surfeited with Christmas cheer and the after-effects of an Armenian wedding, flew to Gondar to join the rest there on our second day out. Our Semyen journey really began at that point.

Gondar to Debarak

The warden of the Semyen National Park had recently had a car accident. He was in hospital in Gondar, but we were able to get some practical advice from him. We also met a party of three Swedes on their way into the mountains. They had flown up from Addis Ababa that morning. One was a Swedish soldier

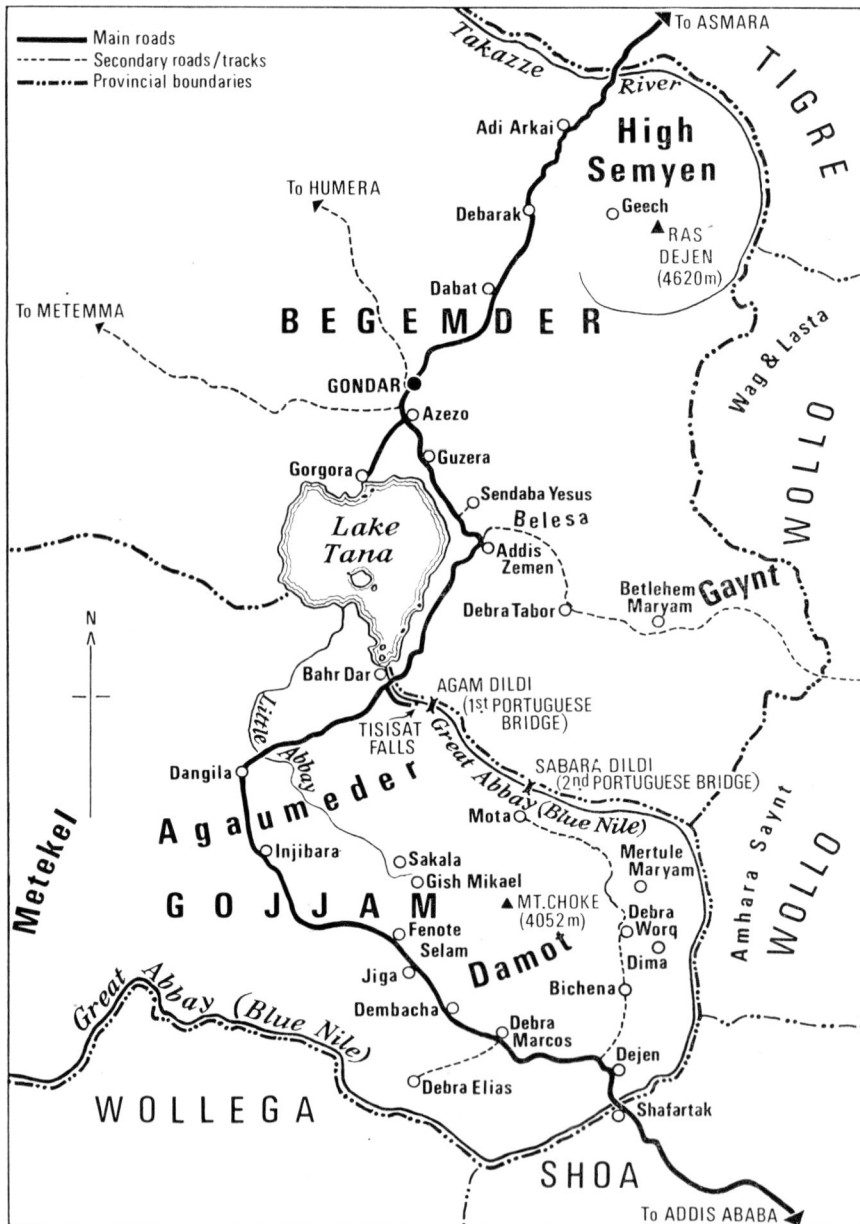

FIG. 19 Begemder and Gojjam

on Christmas leave who had come to join friends in this venture for which they were allowing only five days. We were going to take nine. They raced off in a taxi while we were still eating lunch in the circular dining-room of the Itege Menen Hotel. They wanted to hire animals and get on into the mountains before nightfall. We set off in our landrover at 2 p.m. confident of being able to cover the 106 km. to Debarak by 4.

The road north begins to climb as soon as it leaves Gondar, but levels off at about 2,600 m. and winds over gently rolling, cultivated plateau country reminiscent of the Shoan highlands. We looked in vain towards the north-east, where we knew the centre of the Semyen massif lay, for views of distant heights. They never came into view. Unlike mountains which result from the folding of distinct ridges, the Semyens are a bulky volcanic mass, probably formed at a much lower altitude and raised to its present height in the early stages of the great movements, still continuing, which will eventually break off the Horn of Africa from the rest of the continent.[4] This mass is slightly tilted, with its highest part at the north, where it has split off from the terrain below and the Great Northern Escarpment has resulted. Ridges which occur in the Semyens have been formed by erosion. Drainage is from the escarpment back towards the south and east, but all the Semyen rivers flow into the Takkaze, which forms on the south-western side of the mountains, circles the whole massif, and then flows off to join the Blue Nile system in the Sudan (map, p. 158). Thus the approach to the Semyens from the south is like climbing a low, sloping roof with the crest-line too close to the horizon to be visible. The feature of the landscape which remains most vividly in mind from this mid-afternoon drive to Debarak is a lone volcanic peak which rises high above the undulating plateau – Mt Wogen. There is cultivation to the mid-level on its slopes and scrubby vegetation, indicative of grazing, above. During our subsequent days on the trail in the Semyens, we often saw Mt Wogen far off on the south-western horizon (Pl. 34b).

Debarak was abustle with people, animals, and vehicles. The manager of the Semyen Mountain Hotel, a two-storey wood structure gaily painted in yellow and blue, came out to invite us in as we slowed down to ask the way to the police station to make our presence known and find out where to find Ato Eneyu, organizer of mules. A period of happy confusion ensued, with greater and greater numbers of local people gathering around the landrover. We had sent a telephone message to Ato Eneyu from Gondar. When a boy led us to his house, we found that the message had got through, but Eneyu had done nothing about our mules; he had been too busy with the Swedes. They had left Debarak shortly before we arrived. Eneyu gave us his word of honour that mules would be ready the following morning. We said we wanted to set out at dawn. He looked sceptical and said he would come by shortly to discuss details. The police chief urged us to camp in a meadow behind a building which housed the Semyen district police headquarters as well as the local prison. This helpful man, Major Tamre Bellehu, remembered with pleasure a training trip he had made to the States a few years before. A group of Malaria Eradication Service workers (all young Ethiopians) had already pitched their tents nearby.

As soon as we had our tent set up, Eneyu appeared. A couple of dozen other men joined the conversation. How far did we want to go? How much baggage did we have? Would we be buying local food? How many days could we travel? Arrangements for pack travel cannot be made rapidly in Ethiopia. Everyone wants to enjoy the process and there are always disagreements among local residents as to what it is best to do. We did not hurry the discussion but began sorting our baggage into tentative animal-loads while asking questions about trails and distances. Could we get to Geech in a day? Some said yes, some no. Eneyu said it was unwise; it would tire the animals. Better to overnight at Senkaber. We deferred a decision. I asked about Teshager, the dependable camera-bearer Leslie Brown had praised. A boy ran to find him. He came and introduced himself (Pl. 35a). He was a rough-looking man with a broad, open, friendly face and the largest and widest feet I have ever seen on a human being. He would be delighted to join us, he said. He had already made 35 trips into the mountains and had climbed Ras Dashan 16 times. Only he called it Ras Dejen, as did everyone in this area. By the time we were ready to start cooking dinner, we had settled on four men, six pack-animals, and three riding-animals (some horses, some mules). For this group Eneyu wanted E$24 per day, with half the total sum to be paid before we departed and the remainder on return. Teshager would be E$2.50 per day extra. Major Tamre was happy to keep the landrover beside the police station and promised to have it guarded. Setting a departure time was more difficult. I knew Ethiopians dislike getting up early. Eneyu said that setting off at dawn was impossible. As the sun slipped low and the smoke from nearby houses began rising into the still, chill air, we began to have doubts ourselves. We settled on departure at sunrise, *anda saat* Ethiopian time, i.e., 7 a.m.

Major Tamre ordered the crowd away and we sat down to dinner. The temperature dropped rapidly here at 2,750 m. As we were finishing coffee, Eneyu and several friends returned, bringing two bottles of tart, milky-yellow *tej*. This was a very full-bodied kind, with a high alcoholic content. For an hour or so we toasted Ethiopia, America, and a good journey into the mountains, emptied both bottles, and then slept well.

We were up as soon as we sensed daylight. The morning was clear, but it was 7 before the sun's rays began to be apparent behind the screen of eucalyptus that shielded our meadow on the east. The town lay under a thick blanket of smoke from the fires of the night. There was no sign of Eneyu's animals or men. The Malaria Eradication people were already striking camp. As we heated water and scrambled eggs, scraggly-looking horses began to drift in by ones and twos; several sleepy, *shamma*-wrapped men accompanied them. When Eneyu finally arrived, about 8, loads were put onto the animals, but the whole business seemed interminable. This group of animals and men had never functioned as a team before. Teshager arrived and proudly shouldered our 500 mm. lens and

33 Lake Chamo

    (a) Sawiyeto, traditional chief of the Ganjule

    (b) Ganjule children perform traditional dance

34 (a) Lake Chamo. Ganjule haystack house

(b) Begemder. Two country boys before Mount Wogen

35 High Semyen

(a) Ato Teshager Gared after completing his thirty-sixth trek into the mountains

(b) Giant heather tree, more than 8 m. in breadth, stands on edge of escarpment at Senkaber

36 High Semyen

(a) Approaching Serekaka Gorge, with slopes of Mount Buahit hidden in clouds to left

(b) Camp site at Senkaber, with view down full length of Gorge

37 High Semyen. The 'Abyss' with the falls of the Sinbar river, a thin line of water in the dry season, falling 500 m. down escarpment wall

38 High Semyen

(a) Approach to village of Geech, through wheatfields growing luxuriantly at 3400 m.

(b) Geech farmstead surrounded by walls of stone and heather and sparse eucalyptus growth

39 High Semyen

    (a) Lobelias flourish in the meadows above Geech

    (b) Campsite at Geech among clumps of tree heather

40 High Semyen. East peak of Sederek rising from very edge of escarpment north-east of Geech

41 High Semyen. Looking down into the country below Great Northern Escarpment near Sederek

42 High Semyen. Head of Amba Ras from Emetgogo. Here the escarpment turns almost directly south. Slope in farthest background is Ras Dejen, Ethiopia's highest mountain

43 (a) Gondar. Castles in imperial compound. Square building (r.) with round corner towers was built by Emperor Fasil (1632–67); that on *l.* belonged to Emperor Iyasu I (1682–1706)

(b) Begemder. Empress Mentuab's castle at Qusquam, outside Gondar

44 [*opposite*] High Semyen

(a) Looking down the 'Key', only passage from top to bottom in escarpment's main sector

(b) The 'Tongue' as seen from east peak of Sederek; the immense chunk of rock hangs as if suspended from escarpment's main wall

(b) Gatehouse at church of Debra Tsehay, next to Qusquam castle

45 Gondar. (a) Falasha woman at Wolleqa pottery market

46 Awash National Park

(a) Graceful Beisa Oryx, still plentiful on plains along Middle Awash

(b) *Chat* grows on neat terraces in valley which leads from Harar down to Diredawa

47 Harar

(a) From south, seen from Jigiga road

(b) Outside walls, near Erer Gate, shortly after sunrise

48 Harari maidens are famous for the grace of their carriage

49 Harar

(a) Servant pounding coffee in front courtyard of classic Harari house with monumental doorway   (b) Baskets for sale in house near Muslim market

50 Diredawa. Somali quarter

51 [*opposite*] Hararge

(a) Chercher hills. Cedar and podocarpus stand among fields of durra and maize

(b) Fording stream-bed near Diredawa after September flash flood

(c) Modern Somali-type house in Diredawa

52 Kulubi

(a) Great December pilgrimage

(b) Emperor Haile Selassie with Patriarch Tewoflos

53 Webe Shebelle

(a) When it first descends from Bale mountains, it flows over high barren plateau

(b) Grove of acacias near Adaba

54 Middle Earth. Bale Mountains above tree line as seen looking southward from highway between Adaba and Goba

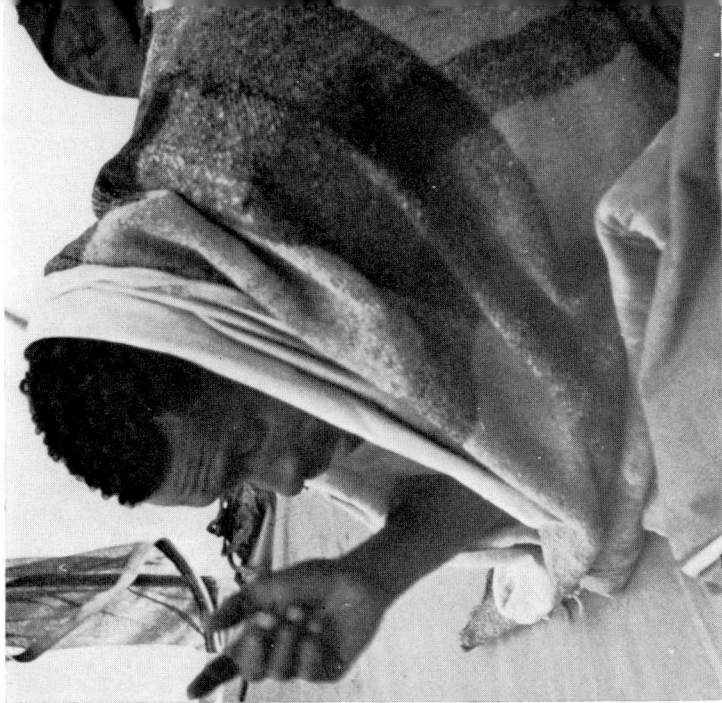

(b) Sendabo in our tent on slopes of Tinnish Batu

(a) Cattle water at pool in high mountains west of Dincho

55 Bale

56 [*opposite*] and 57 Women of Bale. All photographed at Tuesday market in Dincho, except girl (57c) photographed at Senana village

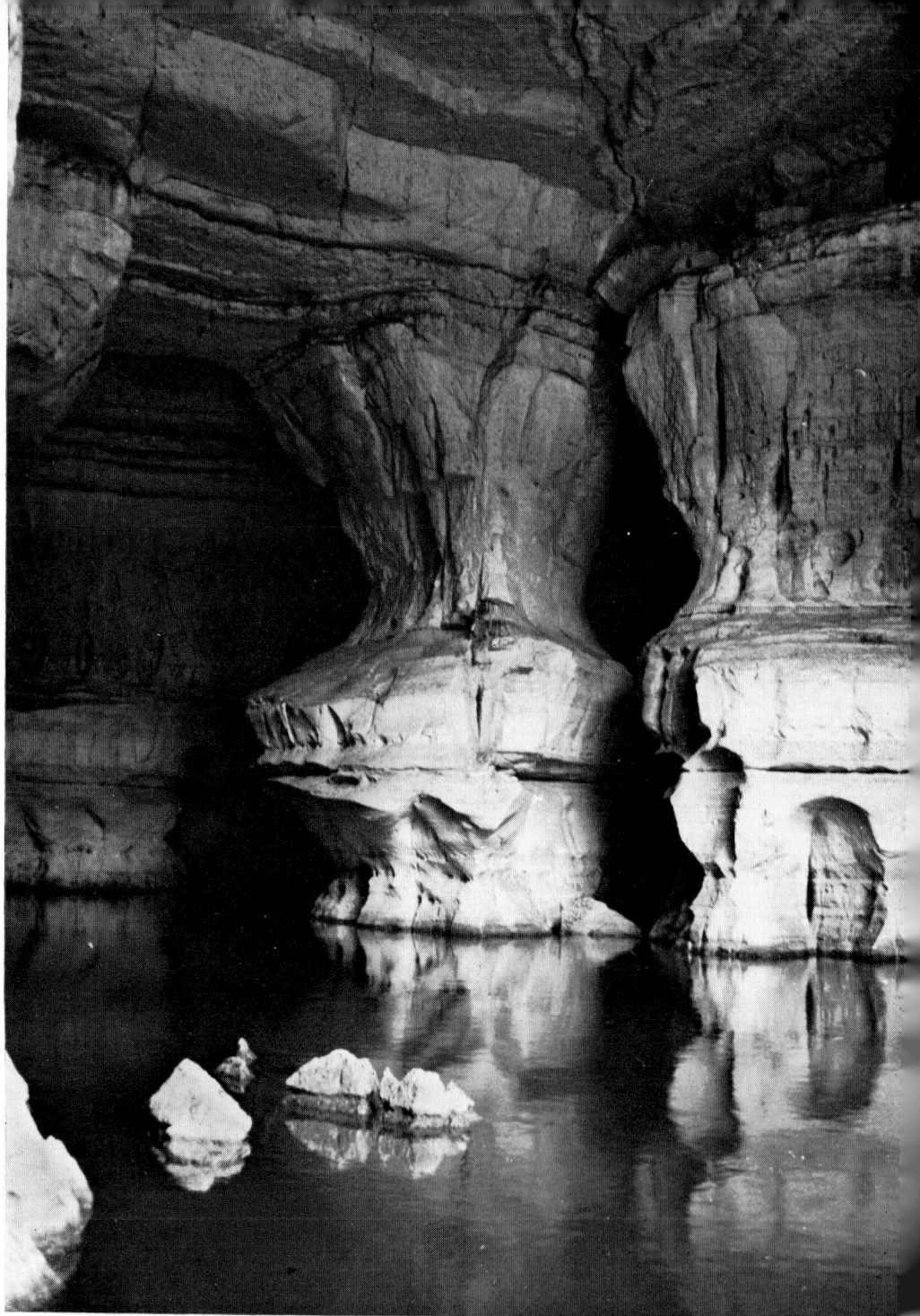

58 Bale. Caves at Sof Omar, age-old Muslim pilgrimage site

59 Bale

(a) Jagged peak near centre is Tinnish (Little) Batu, but said by locals to be highest; two peaks on *r*. are segments of Batu massif

(b) Euphorbia stockade pasture used as camp-ground

60 Bale basketry

(a) Small storage basket woven in vari-coloured natural straw

(b) Milk drunk from large *tunto*

61 [*opposite*] Bale

(a) Ato Girma bargaining for basketry with members of Haji's family

(b) Evening storm gathers over village east of Adaba at foot of Bale mountains

62 The Great Abbay looking upstream (December, a time of low water) from Shafartak Bridge; Shoa on right, Gojjam on left

63 Gojam churches

(a) Lake Tana. Ura Kidane Mehret has angels and other decorations painted on underside of beautifully thatched roof

(b) Gojam. Typical country church grove approached through fields of flowering *nug*

64 Gojjam

Boy at church school at Dima reads scripture from parchment book

everybody's camera-bags. It was exactly five minutes after 9 when we finally set out. We let out a cheer as we crossed the main road, entered the broad market-place to the east of it, and moved out through rutted, narrow streets of the eastern half of the town. We found some unexpected members in our party. A young man with a little education, some English, and a fair degree of bluster had offered his services as guide the previous evening. It soon became apparent that he had probably never actually made a trek into the mountains and would be more of an encumbrance than a help. Besides, he wanted E$10 per day. We turned him down. He turned up just the same as we marched across the market-place, hoping we might have changed our minds. Another young fellow identified himself as a game-guard assigned to Senkaber and, after first trying to persuade us to hire him, said he would go along with us anyway because he was expected to report back to duty. He had been attached to a *Life* photographic team a few weeks before. This explained his relative affluence – new boots, new clothes, shiny rifle. The would-be guide dropped off as we reached the edge of Debarak, but the game-guard, Shifferaw, stayed with us and proved a good addition. He came from a village beyond Amba Ras, knew the area well, and made a conscientious effort to tell us all he knew about the terrain, people, and wildlife.

As we emerged into the meadows at the eastern edge of Debarak, we realized this would have been a much better place to camp, for we could have saved the half-hour march through town before getting on to the trail. By this time our party was strung out for nearly a kilometre and there were so many extra people and animals tagging along that we had no idea who belonged to our caravan. We feared half of Debarak was going to accompany us into the mountains, but gradually the extras dropped off. Eneyu bade us goodbye and we were on our own. It was 9.35.

Debarak to Senkaber

The first hour was confused and scenically dull. The landscape was like that we had driven through on the way to Debarak: rolling hills and gentle valleys, all covered with grass, streams, occasional habitations visible on distant hillsides, no trees but eucalyptus around farmsteads. The animals seemed unfamiliar with the trail and when we came to the first ford, over the Zengwa River, they wandered off in several directions. It appeared that we would never make Senkaber, let alone Geech, that first day. The horse with tent and sleeping-bags did not like the way his load was strapped on and did his best to shake it off, twice almost succeeding. Our men – two of them were actually teenage boys – shouted and dashed back and forth. It was a good show of energy, but there seemed to be little rationale in their actions. Something had to be done to give the party a bit of basic organization, so when all the animals had been reassembled, we assigned each man responsibility for certain animals and gave them positions in line.

We had descended a bit during the first 3 km. out of Debarak; now we began a steep ascent. The trail was deeply rutted into a dusty hillside. There were boulders and loose rocks, bushes which had been chopped and bent back but were still firmly rooted into the slope, adding snags and twisted branches to other obstacles on the track, It was like thousands and thousands of country trails all over Ethiopia. No one takes responsibility for maintaining or improving them and they continually deteriorate. The ruts grow deeper until new paths and ruts are made beside the old ones. Rocks accumulate. Rains gouge the ruts deeper and pile up pebbles on flat sections. A little care, work that could be done easily with the simplest of tools, could turn these trails into safer paths that would permit much more rapid travel. But it never seems to occur to rural people that this would be a possible, or even a desirable, thing to do.

After the first ascent, we travelled for several miles through a cultivated area called Mindigebsa. There were clusters of sturdy houses and a church compound shaded by *kossos* and cedars. The thatched church in its centre was a Maryam, our men, all Christian, told us. When we stopped beside the trail for lunch, women from nearby houses carried up big clay pots filled with *korefe*, a thick brown beer. The men, Shifferaw and Teshager, all drank it from horn beakers at E5¢ a fill and pronounced it excellent.

We had had some cloud during the morning. The afternoon was clear. Beyond Mindigebsa we climbed higher and from a broad pasture had a splendid panorama towards the east with the Serekaka Gorge in the middle distance and the slopes of Mt Buahit rising beyond to the south-east (Pl. 36a). Getting the animals up and down the sides of small, steep valleys was an ordeal. Baggage tore loose and had to be restrapped. But nothing was lost or seriously damaged. These deep valleys gave us our first real taste of the fascinating alpine vegetation of the Semyens: giant heather-trees and tree-size St John's Wort (*hypericum*) laden with brilliant yellow waxy-petalled flowers resembling wild roses in shape but not in odour (Pl. 8ob). The odour is vaguely reminiscent of skunk. Shifferaw pointed out the boundaries of the national park, recently proclaimed legally, as we crossed them. There were stands of giant thistle now and many more flowers: purple scabiosa, end-of-season Maskal daisies, and clumps of sorrel in full bloom. The sorrel in the Semyens was more vividly red than anywhere else in Ethiopia.

About 4 p.m. we reached the side of the Serekaka Gorge. It starts a few hundred feet behind the edge of the Great Northern Escarpment and extends southwards for 25–30 km. We were astonished to note, as we examined its walls, that there were patches of cultivation and several farmsteads deep down along its sides and everywhere, except in the most inaccessible declivities, regular cutting of firewood has kept the natural vegetation down to brush size. Left to return to something resembling its original natural state, which may happen if the Semyen National Park becomes well established, this gorge would provide shelter for large numbers of wild animals. We saw a few Lammergeier and buzzards hovering over the gorge, no animal life. Shifferaw said there were

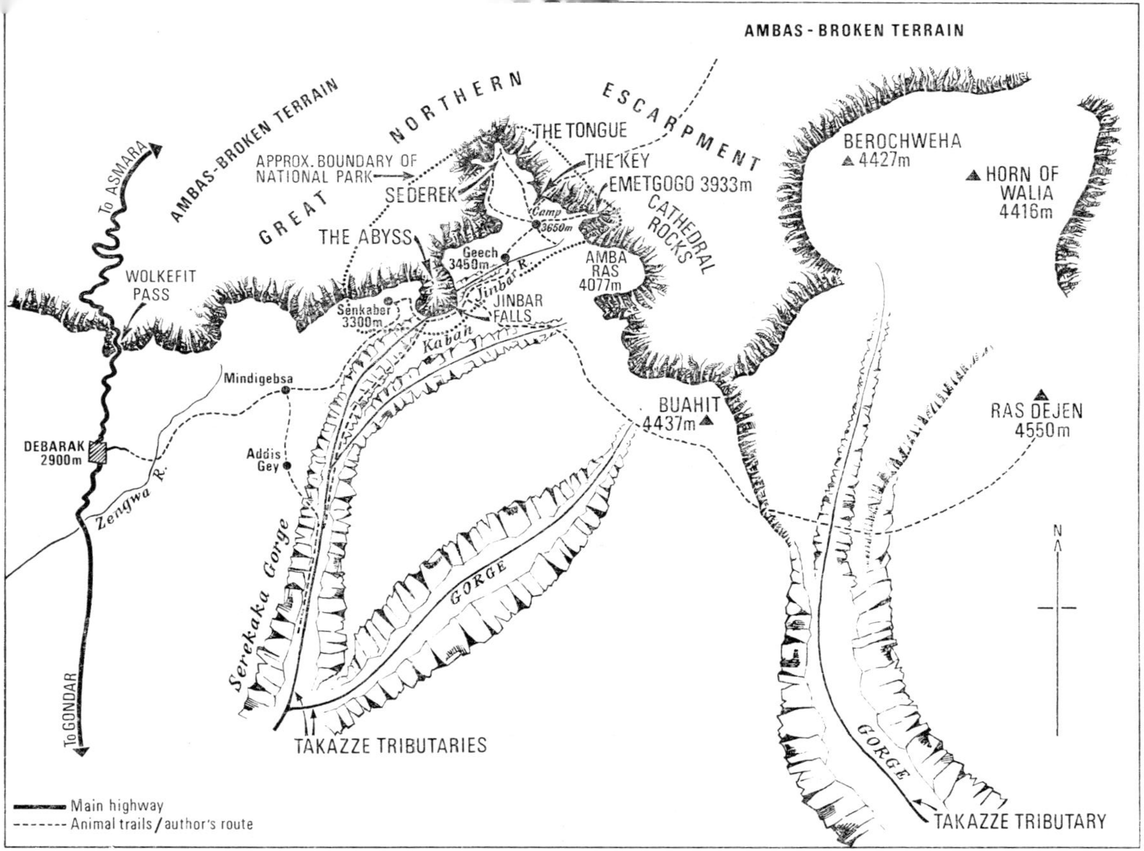

FIG. 20 The High Semyen. Heights shown on this map differ from others given in the text. These are taken from Bernhard Nievergelt, 'Simien: Ethiopia's threatened mountain area', *The Mountain World 1968/69*, London, 1970, 132–7. The results of the joint US-Ethiopian surveys of the late 1960s have unfortunately not yet been published; when they are available, they will be the most accurate measurements available.

agaza – a general Ethiopian term for most small and medium-sized members of the deer/antelope family. Here they would be reedbuck or bushbuck. There were also many baboons, he said, and wild pig. No walia ibex. The gorge is too accessible to man for them. We went on towards Senkaber along the north-west side of the gorge. The trail climbed gradually, crossing small watercourses with only a trickle of water. The vegetation became much thicker and we found ourselves walking through a lane of wild roses, then an avenue of giant thistle followed by patches of medium-sized St John's Wort interspersed with lace vines that climbed thickly over everything on which they could gain a hold. Shifferaw and Teshager pointed to the Senkaber camp high up on the edge of the gorge to the north-east. We had by now decided to stay there for the night, for we did not wish to miss any Semyen scenery by travelling after dark.

Shortly before Senkaber, Shifferaw led us off the trail to the left to the edge of the Great Northern Escarpment. This great wall is deservedly the most famous feature of the Semyens. The grass was thick, the ground damp, and the air already cool in the glade through which we passed. Teshager signalled us to be absolutely still. The sun, slipping low and leaving parts of the escarpment to our left in deep shade, still glowed on the thick cluster of giant heather-trees on our right. The heather clung to a rounded shoulder of black earth which suddenly ceased and the cliff below dropped down, down, down to other cliffs and piles of rocks and still more cliffs and rocks for a thousand metres and more. Teshager and Shifferaw climbed out on to a promontory overhanging a sheer rock wall and scanned the cliffsides to the west for walia. They found one grazing in a shaded 30 degree meadow 600 m. below. We watched it for 15 minutes through binoculars. The stillness was broken now and then by a whistling sound like a bullet. Semyen pigeons were diving almost straight down the face of the escarpment seeking warmer surroundings for the night after spending the day on the sunny heights. Behind us, 2–3 m. lobelias grew in a small opening in the heather. There were large, healthy-looking rhododendroids and many smaller wild flowers in the grass. There must be precipitation on the face of the escarpment at all times of the year. Shade enveloped us, the air became frosty, and we were glad to return to the trail, which was still in full sunlight, and go on to Senkaber, where our animals had already arrived and been unloaded.

The ridge between the escarpment and the head of the Serekaka Gorge is the top of a thin wall where the gorge has almost eroded through the escarpment. We found a fine camp-site on good grass among 3-m. blooming St John's Wort with a view down the full length of the Serekaka Gorge (Pl. 36b). Senkaber consists of a group of round campers' huts, with tin roofs, lightly camouflaged with thatch, and another small group of buildings, also round and with similar roofs, in which the people connected with the management of the park live. All of these buildings are built of stone with cement mortar, the inspiration of foreign advisers who have helped set up the park.[5] A game-guard, Ato Amare, in khaki uniform and smart bush hat with walia insignia and with a polished rifle, came out to welcome us and all the women and children at the place, about a dozen, gathered about. Camp went up quickly. Our men found a natural shelter among the St John's Wort in which to build their fire. They had bought two goats along the trail during the day and set about preparing to slaughter one for dinner. It protested its demise energetically and its companion protested long afterwards with penetrating bleats and wails.

A bottle of Duff Gordon *amontillado* had come through the battering the duffel-bags had taken on the trail, so we toasted a successful day with sherry as the sun began to set. As we ate dinner, we reflected on how little we had ridden, and how much we had walked, during the course of the day. Three riding-animals for five people had worked out well. Local saddles were not comfortable for long and on steep and rutted sections of the trail stirrups brushed against bushes, banks, and rocks and made riding miserable. Teshager, Shifferaw, and our men joined us for tea after dinner and we reviewed local words we had learned during the day. *Koricha*, meaning saddle, is used for any riding-animal, horse or mule, in this region. To urge an animal on, however, different words are used depending on whether it is a horse, mule, or donkey. To a horse you say *cheh*! To a mule you say *muchh*! To a donkey, *wush*! or *zurr*! During the day we had caused much amusement by getting our *cheh*'s and our *muchh*'s mixed up. Fortunately we had no donkeys. We liked another word we heard Teshager using all the time: *dink*. Alone-Stokes[6] lists it as meaning 'wonderful', but Teshager used it over and over again as meaning simply 'Okay' or 'Alright'. He was a naturally cheerful fellow and everything was *dink* with him.

It had taken us $8\frac{1}{2}$ hours to get to Senkaber from Debarak. Allowing for time we had taken to eat, readjust baggage, photograph, and look at vegetation, birds, and walia, we had spent about 6 hours covering this stretch. Shifferaw and Teshager said it would take another 4 to 5 hours to reach Geech the next day, so we knew we could take as much time as we wished for exploring the area and watching walia in the morning. The sun rose quickly with no cloud to obscure it. Gradually its rays penetrated down into the depths of the gorge, dissipating a light mist and changing the purples and greys of the dawn into lighter blues. There was no discernible movement of air. Buzzards, eagles, and Lammergeier appeared over the gorge and we had many large, thick-billed ravens around camp. We breakfasted quickly and set out for the escarpment edge, 5 minutes north of our camp-site. Teshager and Shifferaw proved their skill as keen-eyed walia-spotters. They chose separate perches on rocks that projected over the escarpment and pointed out where we should look with binoculars, occasionally taking a look through the glasses themselves to verify what they saw with bare eye.

The walia ibex (*Capra ibex waliae*) is a goat, one of the rarest in the world. Still relatively plentiful during the early part of this century, though seen by few foreign travellers,[7] it suffered during the Italian occupation when it was intensively hunted for meat by Ethiopians taking refuge in the high mountains, though it had always been hunted to a limited degree by local people. Hunting was only one cause of its decline, however. Its habitat has for centuries been progressively restricted by the cutting of forest and the spread of cultivation. In centuries past its range probably extended over the entire Semyen massif. Now it appears to be confined to the escarpment area between Senkaber and Emetgogo. Leslie Brown estimated the entire remaining walia population at 150–200 when he made his survey in 1963. The walia inhabits ledges along the escarpment, but occasionally also ventures into the grassy meadows above. Considering its agility, the walia looks stocky. Males have huge horns and become darker on their forequarters as they grow older and their beards grow thick and long. Females and young, as well as males, have thick, warm brown hair on their backs. During the main part of the day walia retreat into caves or take shelter under rock-ledges. They come out to feed on grass and brush in the early morning and again in the evening. This morning at Senkaber our party together sighted perhaps ten individuals in all.

I found the morning too exhilarating to sit still for long and spent a couple of hours wandering along the edge of the escarpment, taking in the views both to the west and to the east as the outlines of the landscape emerged in the light of the rising sun. The giant heather at Senkaber was especially impressive. Individual trees were more than 6 m. tall and some were that broad as well with thick trunks and twisting limbs that had taken decades, perhaps centuries, to grow (Pl. 35b). Much of this heather was in bloom. Small, thick clusters of flowers covered most of the outer surface of the tree. The colour ranged from creamy white to yellowish purple and varied greatly from tree to tree. Wherever there was steady dampness, the heather was thickly hung with long streamers of grey-green lichen. Sheltered locations had groves of St John's Wort, clusters of giant-leaved, heavy-thorned nightshade, and huge tangles of wild roses, always with delicate cream-coloured flowers but with the same fresh scent as the pink wild roses of America and Europe.

The landscape immediately below the escarpment was still in twilight when we first reached the edge, but there too day soon dawned. We had beneath us an immense panorama of valleys, small mountains, isolated *ambas*, deep gorges, 1,000, 1,500, 2,000 m. down. We examined this terrain closely through binoculars and realized that the whole region has been cut over and ploughed, grazed, interlaced with paths, settled by human beings. One wonders how long? Probably longer than most people would think likely and much longer than the people living there themselves know. This seems to be the pattern everywhere in the world. Man has been around longer than he has given himself credit for in most parts of the world. Everywhere archaeology is pushing back the beginnings of agriculture farther and farther in time. This tumbled, tangled, fragmented landscape must originally have provided a home for an immense quantity and variety of wildlife, but most of it is long since gone. It cannot compete with man, even in regions such as this where modern technology has not really penetrated at all.

Gradually the air warmed as the sun rose higher and I returned to camp

through small valleys which drain back from the escarpment. Somehow one has
the impression here that the escarpment itself must still be rising. A cluster of
round stone huts, three of them interconnected, made a pretty sight in a
clearing. They had newly painted red shutters and tin-thatch roofs. They were
locked and looked not recently used. I learned later that they were the residence
Park Warden Nicol had built for himself and his family in 1968.

Senkaber to Geech

By 11 we were on the trail out of Senkaber. It rose gradually along the upper
edge of the Serekaka Gorge, leading through sheltered stands of heather and St
John's Wort, affording excellent views down and across the gorge. The gorge in
its upper reaches levels out and forms several expanses of meadow. On one we
spied a bushbuck. A little farther on we met men driving a few cattle down the
trail. They said they had just seen a walia dashing into the heather from the
head of the meadow. This grassy saddle is called Kabah.[8] It is ideal terrain for
wild animals and in future years, as the park is developed and protected, one
hopes wildlife will become plentiful enough that it may be easily viewed in
places such as this. We rested briefly at Kabah, then the men and animals went
on along the main trail up the slope to the south while Teshager and Shifferaw
led us on foot along a faint path into the heather forest. We thought they were
looking for the walia that had been reported here. We climbed a little, then
began to descend. We could hear our horses and mules on the trail high above
us, their noise becoming ever dimmer as we pushed deeper into the low forest,
crawling on hands and knees over the moss to avoid the springy heather
branches.

We came out on a spur of ground that overlooked a deep basin on our left (to
the north) across which rose a high wall of cliff. A few yards farther on we
climbed up on to a narrow lava dike, with the grain of the rock running
crossways. Like a solid wall it formed the inner (southern) edge of the spur. We
were totally unprepared for the view that opened up before and below us as we
reached the highest point on the lava dike: a vast basin, over a thousand metres
deep. We could see very little of its floor. Off to the right (south-east) was an
almost sheer wall of unbroken rock and down it tumbled the highest waterfall I
have ever seen. It was the Jinbar River which flows in a broad and even upland
valley from the edge of the escarpment above Geech (Pl. 37). There was not a
great deal of water flowing over these falls now, but enough to make a good line
all the way to the bottom, though half the flow turned into mist in the course of
the drop. The volume which flows here in the rainy season must be immense.
We stood breathless and speechless admiring this fantastic sight. This basin is
what Maydon, and Leslie Brown after him, called 'The Abyss'. The Jinbar falls
have attracted no attention from travellers and could easily be missed, for from
the main trail they are completely invisible. I found that it took two full frames
of my 40 mm. lens to take in the visible extent of the falls which I estimated at

nearly 500 m. in height. Two hundred metres from what appears to be the bottom of the basin the water breaks on rocks and tumbles on down a series of cataracts.

The view from the other side of the spur was exciting too. Teshager spotted a walia on the outer edge of the chunk of escarpment that forms the north-western corner of the basin and lies directly across from the tip of the spur, 600 m. away. It was a fine old male with huge horns. Teshager said they were among the largest he had ever seen. The old male had a totally inaccessible ledge to himself and was enjoying the sun and morning air, grazing beside the edge of the cliff. We watched him for a long time and set up the 500 mm. lens to photograph him, but even through it he looked small. Somewhat closer, directly across from us, was another spectacle of wildlife. A group of young Gelada baboons were playing on a dirt slide on the side of the mountain. Five youngsters had two sliding-areas well worn and were having an exciting time pushing each other down and then scampering back up for another try. They were easier to photograph with the big lens than the walia. Mixed cloud caused the sun to come and go and the variations of light in this immense basin added to the grandeur of the scene. What had happened here, geologically speaking, was that a huge chunk of the Great Northern Escarpment had worn away. The Jinbar River, millennia ago, must have flowed down smoothly from its head behind Emetgogo, into the plain of Kabah and then down the Serekaka Gorge. When the Abyss was formed, the river was diverted over the edge of the escarpment. The Abyss is a deep indentation in the otherwise regular east-west line of the escarpment in this area.

We climbed steeply back through the heather forest to regain the main trail. We began to puff from the altitude for the first time and cursed the men who had gone on ahead with the animals, for it would have been a welcome relief to ride up part of this stretch. Eventually we overtook them, far up on the mountainside overlooking the Jinbar valley. We looked back now over the small, gently flowing river below us. Had we not just seen its great waterfall, we would never have suspected its existence.

Ahead of us the upper Jinbar valley formed an almost straight trench between the gradual rise of land on the left (northern) side – the Geech plateau – and the equally gradual rise on the south side which forms Amba Ras. In this area we saw what has so angered other visitors to the park – new cultivation on slopes that should never be disturbed. Grass had been newly ploughed on several stretches of slope that lay between angles of 40 degrees and 60 degrees. The freshly turned soil was black and will no doubt produce a good crop of grain for several years. Farther on, along both sides of the Jinbar valley, people were harvesting grain from older fields. Whole families were out cutting and tying up sheaves of heavy-headed wheat and barley. Our men stopped to pick bundles of chickpeas. They regarded them as a delicacy, like country people all over Ethiopia. We took turns riding. The sun was out full force again and felt hot on the skin. But we were at about 3,400 m. and the air was cool – cold when the clouds hid the sun for a few minutes. The trail became deeply rutted when it began to go down to the river. We had to dismount and the animals had to be watched closely to keep them from tearing the baggage loose. If an animal left the trail, one or two of the men would immediately pursue it, block it, and lead it back. It was a great contrast to the disarray of the start of our first day.

We crossed the river over a log bridge built by Nicol in 1968, the first in the Semyens. The river flowed clean and fast beneath it. Considering the dryness of the terrain and the fact that the river had only 7 or 8 km. of watershed to drain up to the edge of the escarpment, the flow was remarkable. We ate lunch in a meadow below the bridge, above a small waterfall, and shook our lunch down on the steep climb up to the Geech plateau. The last few kilometres before Geech were a complete contrast to everything we had seen in the Semyens so far: great rolling fields of wheat and barley undulating in a light breeze (Pl. 38a). The grain was nearly ripe. The heads were extraordinarily thick. The trail was rocky and badly eroded in places, but the fields were well maintained and the grain contained almost no weeds. Though this area must originally have had some growth of heather and St John's Wort, lobelia perhaps as well, there was little trace of it now. It must have been cut over and ploughed long ago. Some visitors have maintained that all the cultivation has occured in this area only in the past 20–25 years, but I am sceptical. Geech is a Muslim settlement said to have been converted during the invasions of Ahmed Grañ in the sixteenth century. People must have been doing some farming here at that time, though cultivation has undoubtedly expanded in recent decades.

Geech is a series of hamlets and house clusters scattered around the higher edge of the cultivated area. The houses are of stone with mud and straw mortar and their curved walls (most of them are oval in shape) look thick enough to keep out the icy breezes that prevail here much of the year. The compounds are neatly fenced with pickets interwoven with branches of heather. The roofs are all of thatch. Most of it looked very well weathered. There were eucalyptus growing around some of the compounds – not very many and not very impressive specimens; they looked as if they had been planted five or six years ago and were probably doing as well as could be expected at 3,450 m. Not many people came out of their houses at Geech and there was no excitement about our arrival. We were told that people were staying inside during the day because it was Ramadan. A woman sold us eggs and our men bought *injera*. Eggs were E2¢ apiece, the lowest price I found in Ethiopia. They were small, but good.

Beyond Geech we crossed an area of tuft grass and lobelias. There was no more cultivation and very little evidence of grazing of cattle or sheep. If these high grassy expanses can be kept intact, there is hope that as a park the area can be effectively preserved for an expanding population of wildlife. The high grasslands must be the original vegetation of this part of the mountains for, except in sheltered places – behind outcroppings, in valleys – the weather is probably too rugged most of the year to permit heather or St John's Wort to flourish. Lobelia, however, appears to thrive on cold and wind and not only in the valleys; farther ahead and on higher ground the open meadows were dotted with it (Pl. 39a). There were lobelias in all stages of development, a good sign that it is not declining. It takes several years for a lobelia plant to grow to maturity. Soon after it blooms, it withers and dies. As the stalk decays, layers of tough fibre overlying each other are exposed. They are like ornamental screens rolled one within the other, with different designs.

It was past 4 o'clock when we passed through the last deep rutted valley beyond Geech and nearly 5 when we reached our camp-site. It lay about 3 km. beyond and above the Geech settlement on a spur of land which juts out over the Jinbar valley, with a good view of Amba Ras across the river to the south. A camp much like that at Senkaber has been built here as a beginning of elementary tourist facilities. There are two groups of round stone huts with tin roofs. On the hill above the camp-site there were even latrines in a small log stockade, and poles for a radio antenna too. Across a small valley to the east stood the house of the park warden and the unfinished house begun by the PCV recently assigned here. The stone campers' huts looked cold and uninviting. We were glad we had a good tent.

Geech Camp, Sederek, and Emetgogo

It was not easy to find a tent-site in the thick grass. We finally settled in a good spot with a clump of blooming heather-trees on one side and a short distance away a sheltered dip in the terrain where our men could build their fire (Pl. 39b). They soon had a good one going, made of heather twigs, lobelia stalks, and dried dung. The animals were set loose to graze. We wandered around the area too and tried to orient ourselves in relation to our inadequate maps. The most enjoyable part of our first evening at Geech was the sunset. It lasted a full half-hour. First the whole landscape was bathed in warm light which was so all-pervading that it kept us from realizing that the air was swiftly cooling. Heather and lobelias turned from silver to gold to copper as the sun sank. The few clouds in the western sky reddened. The sun set as a fiery ball near Mt Wogen, whose peak was clearly visible. Long after the sun had disappeared the sky was splashed with pink, orange, and purple streaks. As daylight faded away, the new moon and many sharp stars became apparent. We delayed dinner to enjoy the spectacle. But the temperature had dropped close to freezing. We heated all the cans making up our dinner, including fruit for dessert, in a big pot of boiling water and drank red wine and tea with the meal for further warmth. It was a fast-day, so the Ethiopians ate only *injera* with tea around their dung fire and kept their remaining goat tethered to a heather trunk. Zipped up in our sleeping-bags, we heard no night sounds except occasional movements of our horses and mules.

At 7.15 we emerged into brilliant sun. The grass was coated with frost. Great puffs of blue smoke were rising from the men's fire, following a new application of dried dung. Water left in our wash-pan in front of the tent had become ice and there was ice around the spring on the slope below where we scooped up water to heat for coffee and tea. Teshager and Shifferaw urged us to waste no time getting over to the escarpment to watch for walia who would be coming out of their caves and rock shelters to graze and warm themselves in the early sunlight.

The last day of the year 1970 was our finest day in the Semyens. It was, in fact, an endless feast of scenic magnificence: high meadows covered with thick tuft grass, jagged peaks, sharp cliffs, great drops down the escarpment for a full 2,000 m. in places, fine vistas of distant heights, outcroppings, crags, great veins of volcanic rock, and expanses of boulders; thousands upon thousands of tall lobelia, giant heather twisted into a hundred different shapes on all slopes leading down to the lowlands . . . Our party of five *ferenjis* and six Ethiopians divided into smaller groups, but we all spent the day in the area north and east of Geech, on the high meadows and along the escarpment, taking along food so that we would not have to return to camp to eat until evening.[9] Teshager earned his pay many times over as camera-bearer, walia-tracker, guide, and source of information on landscape, animals, and vegetation.

We first walked directly north towards Kadadit. There were lobelias in the lower areas (swampy in places) between the low rocky ridges which rise ever higher towards the edge of the escarpment, but for the most part the terrain was open grassland. In many places the ground was honeycombed with ratholes. We saw hundreds of these energetic Semyen rats, but they were difficult to photograph, they move so swiftly. We looked for Semyen foxes, but saw only two. They are believed to live off the rats. At Kadadit, Lammergeier were soaring over the lowlands. From there we moved eastward to a point which gave a full view of Sederek (Pl. 40). Sederek forms a corner of the escarpment. To this point its main direction is almost true east-west. From Sederek the line of the break turns towards the south-east as far as Emetgogo and there, as we observed the following day, the escarpment turns directly towards the south. Sederek's most prominent features are two pieces of mountain that have nearly broken off the main section of the escarpment wall and seem to hang out over the lowlands. Both appear to drop off sheer from their north side, but it is impossible to get a full view of that side because both peaks extend farther out than any point from which they can be viewed. Both curve upward at their outermost end. You have to descend 350 m. or so to reach their bases before climbing back up to their high points. The western promontory rises to a sharp point. Behind this peak it is partially covered with heather, but there are also meadows forming good pastures for walia. The eastern promontory has a rather rounded top, but it is even more striking than its companion because it is forested with heather to its summit and is connected to the main body of the escarpment by a long causeway. The causeway has expanses of bare lava, but in its mid-section it is grassy and thickly dotted with lobelias. When you have crossed it towards the peak and begin to climb, you look back and see the most unusual feature of this whole complex of extraordinary formations – a great rounded tongue of land (Pl. 44a). Smooth, almost flat on top, from below it must appear to be a giant column of rock. The southern end of the Tongue rises slightly and there is a moderate growth of heather on its jagged tip. Otherwise it is a lobelia garden with a few other low bushes.

As we stood on a rocky ledge taking all this in, Teshager identified other features. We could see the main bulk of the Semyen massif behind the shoulder of land above us, slightly off to the south-east. In the farthest distance was the triangular peak, *Yewalia Kund*, Horn of Walia. It was dusted with new snow and the light sparked off it when we looked through binoculars. (It was a little after 10 at the time; by noon the snow had melted.) Directly in front of us to the east, in the far distance, rose a striking *amba* called Addi Selam. It takes seven days to reach it from Debarak, Teshager said. There is a monastery on top and a large market at the foot of the *amba* on Saturdays. From where we stood it appeared that Addi Selam would be at least 30 km. away in a straight line, but to reach it one would probably have to cover three or four times that distance with continual ups and downs. Farther to the north there were several other *ambas* and many outcroppings in the middle distance, no more than 15–25 km. from where we stood, but in all likelihood two or three days' travel-time away, for one would have to descend 2,000 m. to reach a trail that would lead to them.

We decided to move on down to the causeway that links the east peak of Sederek to the tongue. It was easier said than done. The grass along these northern slopes was high, thick, and tough. The slope was steep enough for us to work up a good deal of downward momentum, but it was often difficult to find open spaces between grass tufts to set the feet, so we slipped and tumbled and cursed the small rocky watercourses that we had to cross because they could seldom be seen until we had stepped down into them. The sparse grass and bare lava of the causeway were a relief. While the rest of the group stayed below, two of us climbed the peak. It was steep, but there was well-anchored grass and shrubbery to hold on to. By this time it was 11.30 and the sun was hot. The breeze at the top was welcome. The views were incredible. To the west we looked out over the western Sederek peak rising in a neat curve to its final point. It was a terrestrial representation of a musical crescendo. Behind it layer upon layer of sharp cliffs in various shades of lighter and lighter blue marked the line of the Great Northern Escarpment, visible 40 km. or more as it receded towards the west. To the south were the jagged edges of the main and highest part of the escarpment and all the outliers of it, isolated ages ago from the main cliffs. Beyond and behind this escarpment line was the solid body of the massif, from *Yewalia Kund* past the *Berochweha* ('Water Gates') peaks to Ras Dejen. A light mixture of cloud had gathered over all the higher elevations, probably moisture from snow and frost melted by the sunlight. From the Sederek eastern peak we had to look *up* at the entire panorama to the south.

On the way down we heard commotion among our colleagues below. Had someone fallen? We sped down the steep mountainside. No one was harmed.

One of our group, crawling along among the heather-trees at the edge of the sheer eastern side of the base of the peak to get into a better position for photographing, had heard rustling in the nearby heather. Suddenly a large walia emerged, crashed past him, nearly pushing him off the edge, dashed down the slope, and raced on across the causeway to the same slope we had descended to reach the promontory. It had all happened in a minute or two. The two of us who had climbed the peak realized that we must have passed only a few feet from this magnificent beast as he watched us, standing motionless in the shadow of the heather. Teshager was delighted because he had assured us we would encounter walia here.

We hiked over to the tip of the Tongue and settled down for lunch. Below us was a Shangri-La landscape close in under the escarpment wall. There were groups of vivid green fields among minor mountains with homesteads perched on top. We could see that some of the streams carried a good flow of water, but we were too far above to hear them. Only silence, the soft sounds of the breeze in the heather, and the intermittent calls of birds – but mostly silence. In front of us a huge bay was walled in by the main escarpment face extending eastward towards Emetgogo. This immense wall gets almost no direct sun. Several frozen waterfalls were visible along it. At this time of year the air never warms enough to thaw them. Ice gradually accumulates and falls of its own weight.

We decided to make our way back up the ridge along the main north-south line of the escarpment and move over the high meadows towards Emetgogo. We had to make a wide circuit to get around a deep, rocky gorge that separates the Tongue from the slope beyond and then we had a hard climb through tall grass. Half-way up this slope Teshager's sharp eyes caught sight of a fresh pile of dung on the path. 'Walia', he smiled, as he juggled a handful of shiny brown pellets. He was sure it was from the same walia that had come crashing past us at the foot of the Sederek peak. On the top of the ridge we met our horses again, in the care of Asfaw and Sinishaw, but the terrain was too choppy and rocky for much riding. Besides, we wanted to stay as close to the edge of the escarpment as we could. In this way we intersected most of the gashes that provide views out into the great bay beyond. There is something especially dramatic about coming upon a view of isolated peaks and pinnacles through a narrow break. The most memorable break along this route was called the Key by Maydon because it is said to provide the only footpath from the top of the escarpment to the lowlands in a distance of 40 km. Westward, the Wolkefit Pass north of Debarak is the next regular descent route. Teshager knew no local name for this trail, but said it was regularly used and that it took a full day to get to the bottom of it (Pl. 44b). As we stood there, a man and a boy climbed out carrying bundles of reeds and confirmed that they had gone down the day before and had started back this morning. When we got back to camp that evening, we learned that two others of our party had watched a group of walia here in the Key for nearly an hour in the morning. There were none to be seen in mid-afternoon, but as we crossed to the south side of the opening, a mountain reedbuck jumped out of the grass below us and bounded gracefully in a wide semicircle down the slope, disappearing in a small draw. About 25 m. away we discovered a group of Gelada baboons (*Theropithecus Gelada*). The males' flowing brown manes were only a little darker than the deep tan grass in which they sat. They can be – and have been – mistaken for lions.[10]

It had been about 2 p.m. when we left the tip of the Tongue. It was now 4 and clouds were blocking the sun. At 3,900 m. the temperature dropped with startling suddenness as soon as shadow enveloped us. Climbing on towards Emetgogo was not an appealing prospect in the cold, so we turned back towards the south-west, towards camp, and concentrated on the finer features of the landscape: lobelia in all stages of growth and decline, rocks and their mosses and lichens (some brilliantly coloured), flat areas laced with rat warrens, clumps of white *helichrysum* (Pl. 79b). A few wind-blown heather-trees stood beside rock outcroppings and in sheltered basins. Hawks soared overhead and there were many small birds, chirping and darting about in sheltered folds of the landscape. Teshager, Asfaw, and Sinishaw picked up armloads of lobelia stalks – *jibara*, they called them. They are light and do not burn long, but they make a hot, bright fire for a brief period. When we reached the crest of the ridge above the Jinbar valley, we caught sight of two *ferenjis* on the near slope below us. They were lightly dressed and without headgear. We trotted down and crossed their path. They were two of the Swedes who had preceded us out of Gondar and Debarak. They had crossed Amba Ras and were now heading out to Emetgogo. Their third compatriot was setting up camp near ours at Geech. We tried to dissuade them from continuing on to Emetgogo at this hour, but they had dashed off into the cold dusk determined to reach it. We still had a good distance back to camp. Taking turns riding the horses, we had to dismount every ten minutes and walk at a brisk pace to warm up.

The senior Swede was putting the finishing touches on their camp when we arrived back at ours. We were able to gain very little warmth from the sun's final rays as they burst through the now rather heavy cloud. We anticipated a chillier night than before. With our Coleman stove turned high, we boiled a big pot of soup. Then *lasagna* and vegetables, all heated in their cans in the pot, along with a big can of stewed peaches. All this provided enough warmth so that we could enjoy a bottle of naturally chilled rose wine. As we were finishing dinner, the two Swedes returned from Emetgogo. They were blue from the cold but happy that they had penetrated to the farthest point they had hoped to reach in their Semyen venture. A bit later we compared notes with them as we all drank tea with our Ethiopian companions around their bright lobelia-stalk fire. They had started the same afternoon we had arrived in Debarak and had already covered half again as much ground as we had – going all the way up the Buahit Pass to have a view of Ras Dejen before crossing Amba Ras to Geech. We admired their energy and drive, but concluded that their perseverance had cost them much of the pleasure we had had from our more leisurely approach to the Semyens. The warmth of the tea and fire livened up everybody and the

Ethiopians, having been told that this was the eve of a big *ferenji* holiday, began singing and dancing. Their spirits rose as they sang and they were soon plastering dollar notes on their foreheads and raucously shouting out bawdy songs with much gesturing, laughter, and clapping of rhythm from everyone. The youngest of our men, Ibabu ('Snake'), outdid the others and the Swedes' men joined in too. The sky became clear and a thin sliver of new moon sent its cold bluish rays down on us. At 8.30 we brought out a bottle of champagne I had kept packed in a duffel-bag and we all toasted the New Year. One bottle of chilled champagne, divided among eight of us, was all the cold liquid we could absorb this crisp evening. More lobelia brought the fire to a final burst of light and warmth. No one cared to remain up to welcome 1971 personally.

When we crawled out of the tent a little after 7 the next morning, it was a wintry world that greeted us. The sun had risen, but was hidden by a thick bank of cloud which hovered over the eastern end of the Jinbar valley. The ground was thick with frost and the air was grey. Water left out in pans and jugs was solid. We prepared breakfast in this cold gloom, but as we finished eating, the sun escaped from the cloudbank and the landscape changed completely. The frost sparkled and crackled, then quickly melted as the temperature rose 5–8°C in as many minutes. The temperature climbed over 20°C and the sun stayed out for three full hours. We set out in a straight line across the high meadows for Emetgogo, taking two horses but riding little. We had to surmount a small ridge before we came in sight of the causeway that leads out to the promontory of Emetgogo. Here too the land rises right up to the edge of the escarpment and the promontory, protruding well beyond the main escarpment line, is highest at its outward end, nearly 4,000 m. This was the highest point we reached during the entire Semyen trip.

The first part of the Emetgogo causeway is as smooth as a paved street, but it becomes rough midway and narrows to a jagged ridge. It is impossible to make the whole traverse along the top of the ridge. A barely discernible trail leads through tall grass a short distance below it on the south side and we had to do a little rock-climbing to regain the ridge a few hundred metres farther on where it is again relatively flat on top and 4–8 m. wide. On both sides we had superb views. To the north we looked out over a sea of pinnacles that have been called the Cathedral Rocks back towards the Key and Sederek and could clearly see all the gashes in the escarpment we had passed the previous afternoon. To the south rose the highest section of the escarpment. First there was the head of Amba Ras and then several other great projections beyond it looming like huge capes from a misty blue sea, their upper reaches bathed in sun, their foundations lost in deep shadow and mist. The sheer drop here must have been 1,500 m. or more in most places, as it was from the sides of the Emetgogo promontory itself. The escarpment line led in the middle distance to Buahit and beyond to Ras Dejen, glistening in frost and snow.

We roused a troupe of Gelada baboons who were browsing along the south side of the causeway. They disappeared over the side with indignant barking from the males. There were many small birds. Hawks, buzzards, and Lammergeier soared over the great basin. We looked intently for walia, especially on the isolated outcroppings north of the causeway where there were good 40 degree slopes covered with grass and moderate-to-heavy heather, but we saw none. It took 20 minutes to reach the end of the promontory. As we sat at the tip, clouds began to form, very high, and cast shadows over the landscape. The effect of the light changes on the entire scene was extraordinary. The huge head of Amba Ras and the cliffs beyond alternated between looking like dark hulks and then suddenly glowing with light that seemed to come from inside them. The grassy surface of Amba Ras changed from tan to purple to grey as the shade moved across it. When we started back to camp, we had good views all the way down the Jinbar valley, over Debarak, and out to Mt Wogen, but not for long. By the time we were back at our tent, clouds had piled up in the west and the air had turned chilly again. We lost no time breaking camp and loading animals. The Swedes, who had spent the morning north of Geech, had already left.

Return to Debarak

We departed from the Geech camp-site at 1.30 p.m. in a hailstorm, facing dark clouds in the west. The trail was slippery and the horses and mules kept meandering off into ploughed fields as we descended through the Jinbar valley. The sun finally came out above the Jinbar Falls, squadrons of fast-moving pigeons flew past us there, and we began to meet more and more local people on the trail. We learned that an official of the Wildlife Department in Debarak had died and people were going down for his funeral the next day. A group which included a *masenko*-player was resting under the trees at the side of the trail just before Kabah. The views over the Serekaka Gorge were different from what they had been during our upward trip, for the light rain had left a blue mist in the air, like autumn smoke, and the rays of the sun made delicate patterns in the mist, accentuating the ridges along the side of the gorge in places, obscuring others, forming a contrasting background for the 4 m.-high wild-rose clusters that line the trail as it begins to descend along the side of the gorge. As a result of recent wetting, they perfumed the whole landscape.

It was only 4.15 when we arrived at our Senkaber camp-site among the St John's Wort trees. The Swedes had arrived shortly before and had already set up camp. The sun continued and we had plenty of time to enjoy escarpment views and watch birds. A jackal appeared and circled the camp. Our men slaughtered their second goat and prepared a big fire for roasting it. Amare, the Senkaber game-guard, put on his best uniform and set out for Debarak for the funeral. Shifferaw would remain here, in charge. While we were finishing dinner at dusk, a large group of people came past on the trail. When they saw the light of our fire, they blew a trumpet and when they came nearer they shouted greetings and stopped to talk. They were all going to Debarak for the funeral. A funeral is an occasion not to be missed and everyone goes. The party included women with babies on their backs and children accompanying their parents. The night was clear and there was a bright moon. After Geech with its freezing nights, we felt warm in the open air, so we sat around the fire and asked Teshager more questions about the life of the region. The name Senkaber, he said, meant 'Thieves' Gate' and the place used to be notorious as a haunt of bandits, but they were no longer a problem since the park had been set up and the camp established here. Local people appreciated the change. Every half-hour or so we would hear another trumpet in the distance and soon a party of funeral-goers would appear. Some stopped. Some hurried on, chattering, occasionally singing. The atmosphere was almost festive. We slept warm and well, but all through the night we kept hearing trumpet-calls and groups of passers-by coming up to ask our men, sitting around their fire, who we were and where we had been.

By dawn a huge mass of cloud had gathered over Amba Ras, blocking the sun. The Swedes packed and departed as we had breakfast. They were eager to reach Debarak in time to catch the 3 o'clock bus to Gondar. As we began packing, a Lammergeier circled the camp several times, flying lower and lower. He was zeroing in on a goat-bone lying on the turf nearby. He swooped down and snatched it in his talons and zoomed away towards the escarpment like a small jet. He had spotted the bone from a great height and carefully calculated his seizure of it. He would carry it off to break by dropping it from above onto an exposed rock face. Several bone-breaking sites of the Lammergeier have been identified in this area.[11]

Two horses ran off as they were being loaded and delayed us half an hour. People kept passing on the trail. It was 9.30 when we finally got our caravan moving and the sun had come out. I took time to make a final visit to the viewpoint off the trail where, *en route* to Senkaber, we had first looked out directly over the escarpment. Morning light gave the landscape different outlines. Teshager joined me and the two of us brought up the rear all the way back along the Serekaka Gorge and on towards Mindigebsa. The flowers were especially fresh and attractive after recent rain and Teshager, unlike many of his countrymen, knew local names for all of them as well as medicinal uses for some. We talked again of market-days and distances. Wednesday is market-day in Debarak, Monday on Amba Ras. From Debarak to the top of Ras Dejen one must allow four days on the trail. A trail down the full length of the Serekaka Gorge starts at Kabah, but there are also other trails into the gorge at points farther south along it. There is no practical trail down the escarpment between the Key and the Wolkefit Pass. Teshager recalled with pleasure his travels with wildlife specialists Leslie Brown and Geoffrey Boswall. I never ceased to marvel at Teshager's huge, broad feet. He went barefoot during the entire trip. I asked him if he owned shoes. He said he did, but did not like to wear them.

We all assembled again at Mindigebsa at one o'clock on the slope above the church grove. Women brought *korefe*. We sampled it, but preferred packaged lemonade made with Geech spring-water. *Kosso* trees dotted nearby hillsides, most of them heavy with bunches of bloom. They formed the whole outer ring of the church grove on both sides of the dry-stone wall that circled the church. Inside there had been many cedars, but most of them had been cut down, we discovered on entering, for a major church-rebuilding project. Mindigebsa Maryam was an old thatched round church, rather small, with low outer walls of stone and a main door so low one had to stoop to get through. There were several outbuildings, but none appeared to have been occupied recently. The two-storey thatched gatehouse had been badly damaged by one of the cedars when it fell across it. We had not been in the churchyard long when several men appeared, some priests, others laymen. They explained that they had been rebuilding their church for more than a year. All the local farmers worked on the job when their fieldwork was finished. In one section of the yard lay half a dozen large cedar beams being hewn out of logs. They were being decorated with curve lines and geometrical designs. How long would it take for the rebuilding of the church to be completed? Only God would know. At least another year or two. There was a sense of timelessness about it. No one was in a hurry. The new church would be much more impressive than the present one, with higher walls and a large door. They still planned a thatched roof. Corrugated-tin roofing has not yet penetrated far into the Semyens, it seems. We gave one of the elders a donation to be used towards renovation expenses and set out again down the trail.

We passed a party of priests from Amba Ras Medhane Alem taking their processional cross to the funeral. It was an intricately made brass one and they held it high for us to examine. Black clouds back towards Geech made us thankful for the fine weather we had enjoyed while camped there, but as we reached the final rutted descent down to the Zengwa River, rain mixed with hail overtook us and we got a cold drenching. The trail here, bad enough when we had climbed it on the way out, was close to impossible. Heavy traffic, rain, and animal droppings had turned steeper sections into treacherous mud-chutes. One of our mules tumbled overhead down it, but got up unharmed. We followed detours local people had made, but these were rapidly turning into mud-streams too. In the season of heaviest rains travel over this route must come to a standstill at times.

At the Zengwa ford we met a party of three Britons setting out into the mountains. We answered their questions about trails and travel times and wished them better weather than we were having at the moment. On the edge of Debarak, Teshager was met by his young son and daughter. The rain had stopped. As we entered the town, we overtook a church delegation from Argeen. A priest in rose robes was carrying a large processional cross, a group of attendants marched leading a riderless horse with embroidered red trappings; two riflemen escorted the group. As they came into the market-place, attendants unfurled the glistening, silver-embroidered ceremonial umbrellas, another sounded a trumpet, and the riflemen got into step and marched smartly beside the priest holding the cross high. The sun came out as if expressly to light this magnificent medieval scene. Marching along beside this group, we felt we were returning in triumph from our excursion into the mountains.

In Debarak, paying off our Ethiopian travelling companions, photographing Teshager and his children and everyone else, loading everything into the landrover, saying goodbye over and over again – all this took an hour. Darkness overtook us on the last part of the drive back to Gondar.

At Gondar the Itege Menen's hot showers worked well, but the dining-room had been thrown into confusion by the arrival of a busload of German tourists. We needed the showers more urgently than we needed dinner. Slow service at the dining-table gave us plenty of time to reflect on our recent days in the Semyens. We had heard a good deal of talk about the problems of getting the Semyen National Park established,[12] the frustrations of the foreign advisers, the failure of the government to live up to its alleged promises to construct a road from Debarak to Senkaber, the continual spread of cultivation and the cutting of irreplaceable heather- and St John's Wort-trees, the desirability of moving the people out of Geech and letting the area return to nature. Having seen all these places first-hand, we found it was difficult to be quite so dogmatic as *ferenjis* often were in Addis Ababa. It was true that we had seen newly ploughed land in the Jinbar valley and evidence of recent cutting of heather and St John's Wort in places, but the situation did not seem to be out of hand. We concluded that our party as a whole had seen at least 20 different walia. Considering the relative ease with which we had found these, it seemed difficult to believe that they were quite so rare in the park as some people had maintained.[13] At least there seemed to be a chance that they were now holding their own, if not increasing slightly. Gelada baboons seemed extraordinarily plentiful, so much so that with more protection they are likely to increase to the point where they will have to have their numbers reduced. Semyen foxes (*Simenia Simensis*) were another matter. We had only seen two. If Leslie Brown is correct in assuming that the foxes feed primarily on rats, then their decline would help explain the abundance of rats. The plentiful Lammergeier, buzzards, and eagles must, however, also feed on rats.

Having done the trail into the mountains on horse/mule and foot, we found it difficult to get aroused about the fact that the road, talked about now for several years, had not yet been built. We felt that the park needed more time to get organized to deal with even the modest increase of tourists a landrover-track would bring. Eventually, of course, a road will be built to Senkaber and then probably on to Geech, but we could see little reason to regard it as the key to the success of the Semyen National Park.

Gondar – Castles and Churches

The Italians expended a good deal of effort on Gondar during their brief occupation and the centre of the city still shows it. Unfortunately most of their buildings were of the heavy, angular style favoured during the late Fascist period. Earlier Italian styles would have blended into the low green hills of the regions much more attractively. The setting is reminiscent of Tuscany. Gondar became the capital of Ethiopia in the seventeenth century when the Emperor Fasil (1632–67) chose it as his residence and built a large castle near the centre of the city in neo-Portuguese style. Two kilometres away he built a smaller castle surrounded by a moat. It now sits in a park and is called the Emperor Fasil's Bath. Gondar had its golden age from the middle of the seventeenth to the middle of the eighteenth century when it was an important commercial as well as governmental and cultural centre. Muslims and Jews settled here as well as Christians. Subsequent emperors followed Fasil's example and built castles of their own in the same walled imperial compound.[14] It contains six of them, a number of smaller buildings, and several churches. We spent a leisurely hour visiting the castles. They have suffered a variety of vicissitudes during the past three centuries and could do with a bit of restoration, but when they are eventually renovated, they will lose some of the special charm which results from their present partly ruined condition (Pl. 43a).

We found some of the churches of Gondar in need of repair too. There are 44 of them in all. At least a dozen are of major historical significance and have noteworthy paintings and manuscripts. The most famous of all is Debra Berhan Selassie – 'The Church of the Trinity of the Mountain of Light'. It is situated in a stone-walled compound with an impressive gate-tower and several other towers on top of a small hill in the north-eastern part of the city. Nuns and monks live in the towers and in small stone habitations along the walls. By north Ethiopian standards this church is recent, having been built by Emperor Iyasu (1682–1706) at the end of the seventeenth century. By that time most churches were being constructed in circular form. Debra Berhan Selassie is rectangular like the oldest Christian churches in Ethiopia, but it lacks many of the characteristic features of Axumite architecture. Inside it consists of a large high-ceilinged hall with the *qiddus qiddusan* at its eastern end. Entering through the tall wooden doors, one is struck immediately by the ceiling – its thick beams are all covered by angels looking down. We noticed that some had been damaged by leaks in the roof but were still quite repairable. The walls of this great hall, except for spaces occupied by doors and windows, are entirely covered by paintings. There are 82 of them in all and they cover the full range of Ethiopian religious subjects. The naïveté and freshness of earlier Ethiopian styles still predominate in these paintings. We had this beautiful church all to ourselves during our first half-hour. Then busloads of tourists arrived and photo-flashes began going off at the rate of four or five per minute. We went to visit a Falasha village.

Falashas get more attention from foreigners in Ethiopia than their numbers or current cultural significance merit. If these famous Black Jews were not in a condition of advanced decline, they could capitalize off their popularity and lay a sound basis for cultural revival. There are very few signs that this is occurring. It is too bad. Falashas used to be much more numerous in northern Ethiopia than they are now and in medieval and early modern times they were politically important. Falasha kings and queens ruled large areas north and east of Gondar and sometimes held the balance of power between Christians and Muslims. Old and some relatively recent maps and travellers' accounts provide evidence of Falasha villages in the Semyens, but Falashas in the high mountains seem now mostly to have migrated or to have been assimilated. In the area immediately to the north and east of Gondar, Falasha settlements have maintained their separateness to this day and several thousand Falashas practise their special form of Judaism and adhere to their ancient customs.[15] There can be no doubt about the ancientness of the Jewish ties. Physically, however, the Falashas are indistinguishable from other northern Ethiopians and if they ever spoke Hebrew or anything related to it, which seems doubtful, they long since ceased to do so. They appear once to have spoken Agau dialects, but most now speak Amharic. Their holy books are written in Ge'ez, like those of Ethiopian Christians. Everything connected with the Falashas requires further study, but it is curious to realize that what evidence there is leads to the conclusion that the Black Jews are really less Semitic than the classic Ethiopian Semites, the Tigreans and the Amhara, by whom they have been largely absorbed.[16]

We spent a busy hour in Wolleqa, a Falasha village just off the main road a few kilometres north of Gondar. The village has a synagogue and a school which had received some Israeli assistance. The enthusiastic schoolmaster, Ato Abebe Berhane, had studied in Israel and spoke Hebrew, which was being taught at the school. He proudly told us that his Hebrew name was Ya'ir ben Uri. He gave us each a yarmulka to put on our heads when we entered the synagogue. It was a round, thatch-roofed building like any simple Ethiopian country church, but it had a wooden Star of David rather than a cross at its peak. Inside there was grass on the clay floor and a table with a Torah, Menorah, and a few pamphlets. Services were held regularly, Ato Abebe said, and the local people kept the Sabbath.

The main attraction of Wolleqa was its pottery market near the highway (Pl. 45a). Making pottery has long been a Falasha speciality. The tourist market has influenced the objects made: turtles, lizards, dogs, birds; unusual round-faced figures of men and women; composite groups of people eating around a *mesob*; a couple lying together in bed. The market also had many kinds of pots, vases, jugs, and dishes with the six-pointed star as a prominent decorative feature. Like all Ethiopians, the Falashas were good bargainers, but business was not too brisk this morning and with a little patience we bought objects for a third to a quarter of the asking price. The problem with all this Falasha pottery, we soon found, was that it was extremely fragile. Some pieces broke from the vibration of the vehicle on the road. The smooth black surface was deceptive – there was no strength beneath it. We later treasured the items we had transported safely back to Addis Ababa simply because we had managed to get them back intact. In 1971 the Peace Corps started a project to teach Falashas how to mix clay and fire pottery well enough to make it reasonably durable. Since this is one of their main sources of livelihood outside of agriculture, it is to be hoped the project succeeds.

We could not stay long enough on this occasion to visit the loveliest of Gondar's castles, that of the Empress Mentaub at Qusquam, but on another visit to Gondar six months later I had time for Qusquam. Empress Mentuab, whose name means 'How Beautiful!', was a descendant of the obscure Emperor Minas (1559–63) according to the official chronicle and was discovered by courtiers who had been sent out to search for the most beautiful girl in the region as wife for Emperor Bakaffa (1721–30).[17] The chronicler recounts how the future Empress's mother, Princess Yolyana

> . . . selected clothes of silk from among her treasures and dressed her daughter with them; she anointed her with perfumes, put a ring of gold on her finger and sent her off with great pomp. Mentuab entered into the chamber of the king, and when the King of Kings Bakaffa saw her he was very happy because she was so completely beautiful; he said to her, 'You have no fault at all!' Then he made her sit beside him on his right hand, and had delicious foods brought and they ate and drank together. That day he knew her as Adam knew Eve . . . and she conceived that day.[18]

A more romantic legend relates that Emperor Bakaffa became ill while travelling in a remote area and was nursed back to health by a beautiful farmer's daughter. The maiden not only restored his health but won his heart and was later summoned to become his partner on the throne. It is probable that neither story is true, but both illustrate the Ethiopian penchant for entertaining tales which persists to this day. What cannot be contested is the fact that Empress Mentuab, whatever her origins, rapidly became one of the dominant personalities of her time.

Bakaffa died after only a nine-year reign and an even briefer marriage and his young son, Iyasu II, inherited the throne with his mother as regent. The energetic Empress, politically and culturally active until late in life, played a major role during her son's 25 years on the throne and outlived him. Apparently rather early in Iyasu II's reign, she chose a low rounded hill south-west of the capital for her residence. It was next to a church of which she was patron, Debra Tsehay, 'Mountain of the Sun'. The church, recently rebuilt, crowns the crest of the hill. It has a high stone wall with towers and a spacious tree-shaded park on all sides. Monks were raking *gesho* spread out to dry on sheets on the lawn in front of the main entrance when we walked in. A priest greeted us, explained with pride that the church renovation had only recently been completed, led us inside and up a stairway and then through a small door into a tiny room containing a dark wooden coffin with a glass lid. Inside was the skeleton of the Empress Mentuab herself. Nearby is a room from which the Empress used to watch church services in private with two little windows looking down into the church. We climbed down through one of them into the main circuit of the building. The place smelled of wet plaster and paint. The priest said they were hoping Emperor Haile Selassie I would donate enough money on his next visit to provide new paintings for the bare walls.

We walked out through the back of the churchyard into the grounds of the castle (Pl. 43b). The castle has several arched gateways, an intact round tower, and a great hall which must have been as impressive during the time of the Empress's residence as many great castle halls in Europe in medieval times. The roof has fallen in and a section of walls has collapsed, but there is still enough of the structure standing to give an idea of its elegant proportions. We found many other features of the architecture worthy of attention, for they bear out the Empress's reputation as a devout Christian and humane patron of the arts with a keen eye for detail. Above doors and windows, crosses are carved in red volcanic stone. Representations of elephants, lions, horsemen, saints, and other figures can be seen in other parts of the ruined building. The basic stone is a grey-tan tufa, but red stone insets are used for contrast in door- and window-frames and on arches.

The life of Empress Mentuab is a subject awaiting a biographer. Her private prayer-book, a delicate little parchment volume bound in soft blue velvet, was acquired a few years ago by the Museum of the Institute of Ethiopian Studies in Addis Ababa. It is illustrated with miniature religious paintings in bright colours, 70 of them in all. All of them are still as bright as when the Empress admired them over 200 years ago.

The area north-east of Lake Tana through which we passed again on our return from the Semyens has historical associations of many kinds. The road from Gondar south is paved as far as Azezo and good gravel after that. It leads across the flat Dembiya Plain where many Ethiopian armies have marched and fought. The Portuguese who came to Ethiopia in the sixteenth century were active in this area. They built the castle of Guzera for Emperor Sarsa Dengel at the end of the sixteenth century and nearby are the ruins of one of many Portuguese bridges which survive at several places in the highlands. The highway passes close to the Monastery of Saint Galawdewos (Claudius) situated in a luxuriant wild olive-grove.

I had read in the *Ethiopian Herald* of the 'discovery' of a particularly attractive and well-preserved old church in the mountains east of Lake Tana. Called Sendaba Yesus, it had been visited by the Emperor himself shortly before. Aside from being a measure of its historic and artistic merit, the fact that the Emperor had visited it made it likely that a landrover track had been built up to it. At exactly 80 km. from Gondar we found a pole with a small white flag placed beside the road on the left. A line of white-painted stones marked a track with faintly visible tyre-markings. A farmer confirmed that this was the route to Sendaba Yesus. The mountains in this region are not very high, but make up for their lack of height by their exotic formations. From the highway at least a dozen high volcanic cores are visible in as many miles. They rise like thick columns of poured stone, bluish-tan in colour, and many have vegetation on top. Most of them appear unscalable by any but advanced mountaineering techniques. Nevertheless, some have served as prisons and places of refuge in centuries past. The track to Sendaba Yesus goes back into country like this, with two huge mountain towers at first in view, but stops short of the most rugged terrain after 6½ km., where the old church is situated on a projecting spur with a good view over lower country. The news that our landrover was making its way up the twists and turns of the last part of the track spread quickly and a small group of priests and deacons had already assembled in the churchyard when we drove up. Boys were scurrying off to summon others and a couple of dozen local laymen also came to greet us. There were none of the problems often encountered trying to get into country churches. Doors were unlocked and the local people – clergy and lay – stood by to await our expressions of pleasure as each striking feature of this remarkable old building was drawn to our attention.

Sendaba Yesus is a large round church in an excellent state of preservation. Its thickly thatched roof had weathered to a deep brown colour, but showed no signs of fraying and there were no signs of leakage. The edge of the roof-line was firm. The outermost circuit of the portico was screened by bamboo. The outer walls were *chiqa* and stone. Men opened the doors wide. The richness of the paintings first caught our eye – clean, bright, eighteenth-century Gondarine style. But as we walked around the inner square enclosing the *qiddus qiddusan*, it was the basic architectural features of the building that impressed us most – the thick, skilfully squared walls which look as if they had been built by men accustomed to working in heavy, well-cut stone or at least to imitating models built in this way. Then there were the doorways and windows of the inner structure – perfect Axumite style, with interlocking frames made of large wooden beams confidently placed in the walls. On the back the frames were bare. On the front they were painted in bright colours.

We asked one of the priests how old the church was. 'It was built at the time of the Master', he said, meaning at the time of Christ. Others asserted the church was as old as their Christian faith. This, of course, is patently impossible, but there is nothing to be gained from arguing an issue such as this with a country priest. His sense of time is very different from ours. The 'Time of the Master' is only yesterday to him. To almost anyone in this setting, including ourselves, it seems much less remote than one knows it to be. The 'actual facts' about this church are exciting enough. It appears to have been built about 600 years ago, which is very old for a round thatched church in such good condition. It is reputed to have been constructed during the reign of Emperor Dawit I (1382–1413) by a Falasha carpenter named Gideon. There is nothing to indicate that it has ever been extensively remodelled and, unlike so many old churches, it appears to have been maintained well and repaired before the need became drastic. What happened to its earlier paintings, if it had them, is unknown, but not necessarily unknowable. Local traditions, perhaps manuscripts hidden somewhere in the church or in its *eqabet*, may provide clues.

The elders of the church were eager for us to stay and sent for *talla, injera,* and *wat* so that they could entertain us properly. We had set ourselves a schedule that left no more time, so we said goodbye and hurried away. Half-way back along the track to the highway, we were intercepted by a group of fast-running young men, including a priest, who held a tray of food and containers of *talla* for us to sample. The requirements of country hospitality made it imperative that we take a moment to eat and drink a little, so we did.

NOTES

1 Semyen means north in Amharic. The term appears to have been applied to the high mountain area for several hundred years, though the region was not to the north, but to the south-west, of the area where Ethiopian civilization first developed. It has apparently always been the northernmost part of the area inhabited by Amhara. Increasingly the designation Semyens, or High Semyens, has come to be used only for the highest mountains of the region and it is so used here.

2 *Ethiopian Episode*, London, 1965, 31–80.

3 Issued only in a small edition and, unfortunately, no longer available for purchase.

4 See Haroun Tazieff, 'The Afar Triangle', *Scientific American*, February 1970, 32–40.

5 The first of these, a young Welsh-Canadian with a Japanese wife, has published an account of his adventures and misadventures during the years 1967–69: Clive W. Nicol, *From the Roof of Africa*, New York, 1972. It is an extremely informative and honest book, though occasionally rather intemperate in tone. The PCV whose tour of duty in the Semyens overlapped that of Nicol was also gone when we made our visit. At that time there were no foreign advisers in the park.

6 *The Alone-Stokes Short Manual of the Amharic Language*, Madras/London (Macmillan), 1966.

7 One of them, H. C. Maydon, produced a good description of the Semyen landscape and its wildlife: *Semien, Its Heights and Abysses*, London, 1925.

8 Semyen names are notoriously varied in the renditions different writers give for them and Ethiopians themselves provide no clear guidance. We took Teshager's versions as the most reliable, for he seemed to have the clearest feel for language of any of the Ethiopians we had with us on this trip. His pronunciation of this particular location was quite clearly Kabah or Khabah; other writers render it Khabar, Khabau, Qaba. Variations of other common Semyen place-names include: Debarak, Debarek, Divarik; Kadadit, Kadardit, Qadahdit; Emetgogo, Mietgogo, Metagogo; etc. etc. The local inhabitants love to explain the meanings of place-names and many curious etymologies are given, some of which cannot possibly be correct. All this confusion probably arises in part because the Semyens were originally inhabited by Agau peoples among whom there was a large Falasha element. Scholars could no doubt uncover many traces of earlier Semyen history through study of place-names.

9 Living normally in Addis Ababa at 2,500 m. we were all accustomed to altitude. We were also in good physical condition from frequent outings in other parts of the Ethiopian highlands, so 10 hours of continual exertion at 3,500–4,000 m. was no strain. It could be for those not acclimatized to Ethiopia.

10 Most of the 'lion's manes' sold to tourists in Addis Ababa and Asmara are actually from Gelada baboons.

11 Cf. Leslie Brown, *African Birds of Prey*, Boston, 1971, 58–61.

12 It was officially proclaimed in October 1970.

13 After a 1971 visit, when he counted 25 walia in two days of casual viewing, Leslie Brown expressed optimism about the prospects for the walia in an article in *Safari* magazine, August-September 1971.

14 Ghiorghis Mellessa, 'Gondar Yesterday and Today' and Richard Pankhurst, 'Notes for the History of Gondar', *EO*, XII, no. 3, 1969, 164–227.

15 A Falasha-related Agau group who live north and west of Gondar, the Qemant, have

been described in a recent monograph by Frederick Gamst, *The Qemant, a Pagan-Hebraic Peasantry of Ethiopia*, New York, 1969.

16 The classic nineteenth-century account of the Falashas is Henry A. Stern's *Wanderings among the Falashas of Abyssinia*, London, 1862. It is richer in enthusiasm for the Falashas than in specific information about them. Wolf Leslau's *Falasha Anthology*, New Haven, 1951, records researches among the Falashas in the late 1940s. The best synthesis of present knowledge of the Falashas is given in Ullendorff, *Bible*, 115–18.

17 Son of Iyasu I, Bakaffa spent his early years, like so many royal children of that time, atop the prison-mountain of Wehni in the district of Belesa south-east of Gondar. Thomas Pakenham's *Mountains of Rasselas*, London, 1959, gives a good account of this mountain and the practice of isolation of royal princes.

18 R. K. Pankhurst (ed.), *The Ethiopian Royal Chronicles*, London/Addis Ababa, 1967, 123.

7 The Province of Harar

Roads East

Eastern Marches

The conquest of Harar in January 1887 was one of the greatest events in Ethiopian history. For nearly a thousand years the territory which now constitutes the huge provinces of Harar and Bale had been a menace to the Christian highlands. Harar may originally have been a Christian city. Too little is known about its early history for anyone to be sure.[1] After it was converted to Islam in the tenth or eleventh century, it became a base for Muslim expansion towards the west and south. Eventually a whole series of Muslim kingdoms – Hadiya, Fatajar, Yifat, Dawaro, Bali – encompassed the eastern plateau. During the reign of the warrior emperor Amda Tseyon (Pillar of Zion; 1312–42), the Christian Empire reasserted itself and stemmed Muslim expansion,[2] but not for long. A powerful new Muslim kingdom, Adal, centred in Harar, grew to dominate the region. In 1531, the energetic ruler of this kingdom, the Imam Ahmad ibn Ibrahim, known as Grañ (The Left-handed), began the conquest of the highlands and during the next ten years destroyed a large part of the Ethiopian Christian heritage. His name still lives in the memories of the inhabitants of the central and northern highlands, and sites of towns, forts, and, above all, churches devastated by him are pointed out as if these catastrophes had occurred only yesterday. Ahmad Grañ was defeated in 1543 thanks to the assistance of the Portuguese, but the Ethiopian Empire had been so weakened by his assault that it was powerless to pursue the Muslims back into their own eastern territories. Instead it was the pagan Galla advancing from the south who inherited the old Kingdom of Adal. Life in the region fell back into a semi-nomadic pattern, though Harar itself continued to exist as a relatively prosperous city-state, preserving its unique Semitic language and urban traditions.[3]

Harar became a symbol of inaccessibility, mystery, and Muslim fanaticism. No one was even sure of its exact location. When, in 1855, Sir Richard Burton became the first European to reach Harar and return to publish an account of his adventures,[4] he travelled to the city disguised as a Muslim, but once in it identified himself as an Englishman and was respected for his audacity. The city was then in decline, but the Ethiopian conquest would probably not have come so soon had it not been for the Egyptian occupation which began in 1875. Egyptian adventurism disrupted remaining traditional political links in the region and facilitated the advance of Menelik II. When the army of the weak Harari Amir Abdullahi, who took power when the Egyptians withdrew in 1885, was routed at Chelenqo in the Chercher Hills, Ras Makonnen, one of Menelik's favourite lieutenants, was appointed Governor of Harar and set about consolidating Ethiopian control over the surrounding Galla and Somali tribes.[5] The conquest of Hararge was completed only in 1900. Meanwhile Ras Makonnen's son, Tafari, the future Emperor Haile Selassie I, had been born in Ejersa Goro, a mountain village[6] outside of Harar, in 1892 and large numbers of Christian Ethiopians had come to Harar to settle as a new ruling class.

The new arrivals developed a strong sense of attachment to their new home as well as a good deal of respect for the traditions of the area. Native Hararis, natural traders, benefited from the new commercial opportunities that stable Ethiopian rule brought. The old city, so long a threat to the existence of Ethiopia, quickly became an integral part of the revivified Christian Empire. It would be impossible to write the history of modern Ethiopia without reference to Harar. Ethiopia's military academy is located there. The country's foremost agricultural college is at Alemaya, between Harar and Diredawa. The largest Christian pilgrimage site in Ethiopia, also frequented by Muslims, is at Kulubi in the Chercher Hills. Ethiopia's first modern link to the sea, the Franco-Ethiopian Railway, was begun in 1897, crossed the frontier in 1900, and reached Diredawa in 1902. Diredawa, now third city in the Empire, owes its existence to the railway which finally reached the capital in 1917.[7] In either direction the railway trip is still one of the great classic journeys of the world. The sounds, sights, and smells are much as they were when Evelyn Waugh described them in the 1930s.[8] The full journey takes 24 hours of more or less continual travel, but one can leave Addis Ababa in the morning and reach Diredawa by evening, travelling comfortably in first-class, with stops at busy stations and long scenic stretches through the open game-plains on both sides of the Awash.

From Awash Station northward the Awash River forms the boundary between Shoa and Hararge. On the plains, on both sides of the river, oryx and gazelle still graze in large numbers and there are zebra, kudu, and Somali wild ass in remoter areas (Pl. 46a). On clear days, which are frequent, the western horizon is dominated by the blue wall of the Great Escarpment, while in other directions the volcanic peaks that dot the plain attract the eye: Fantalle (2,007 m.), Dofan (1,151 m.), Ayelu (2,145 m.), Kumbi (1,451 m.; south-east of Awash Station), and the huge bulk of Assebot (2,539 m.), highest of them all. All these mountains are lower than the average altitude of the plateau, but the Awash Plain falls below 600 m. in this region and declines much more farther north, so the relative height of these mountains is not inconsiderable.

The High Road and the Low Road

There is not much plain between Awash Station and Mieso. The terrain is rolling thorn-forest and when I last drove it in 1971 and 1972 the route was still an ordeal because instead of bridges most of the watercourses had cemented fords which were sufficiently concave to give a vehicle a good jolt at any speed above 20 k.p.h. Undergrowth through the thorn forest is mostly prickly pear cactus which here bears a burgundy-red fruit. This energetic shrub, a native of

America, was introduced into Ethiopia less than a century ago. It has spread alarmingly. Danakil and Galla inhabit this region and keep large herds of cattle and camels which can often be seen watering at pools in stream-beds.

Mieso is a dusty place which must owe its existence to the railroad, but is now equally important as a road junction. The high road turns south here and climbs past Asbe Tafari on to the long spur of the eastern plateau known as the Chercher Hills. They extend all the way to Harar. For practically the whole distance of about 175 km. the well-built highway rides the crest of these 2,600–2,900 m. mountains. It is a true skyline drive, for in many places one looks in quick succession out over the plains to the north and then over deep valleys to the south. Originally the highest parts of these mountains were forested like the mountains of Arussi and Bale. Individual old cedar and podocarpus now stand as sentinels in the midst of durra- and corn-fields. Thatch-roof villages perch on ledges, but there are few churches. The area is preponderantly Muslim and mosques are a feature of each of the new roadside towns that straddle the highway every 20 or 25 km. *Chat* orchards become more and more common towards the east. This tough little tree produces numerous small branches like an ornamental shrub. The newer leaves are reddish when they first bud out and remain a vivid, waxy olive-green until they harden. The older leaves are deep dark green and remain glossy. The new growth is cut and tied in small bunches. Chewed, it is a mild narcotic much appreciated by Ethiopian Muslims.[9]

Towards their eastern end the Chercher Hills broaden into expanses of true plateau. We had already driven more than 450 km. since leaving Addis Ababa in the morning when we neared Kulubi about 5 p.m. Our first realization that it was near was a splendid view of the great pilgrimage church, high on its hilltop above the village, reflecting the rays of the afternoon sun like a many-faceted jewel. The opportunity for a respite from driving was welcome, so we turned off at the stone cross at the centre of the village and followed the track that leads for about 2 km. to the church. Here, above 2,700 m., the setting felt alpine with green fields spread over with a luxuriant growth of blue forget-me-nots and a tinge of smoke in the crisp evening air. The sun was struggling to penetrate rapidly shifting masses of cloud in the western half of the sky. A *zabanya* raced up to let us in the rear gate of the churchyard and we walked around to the front of the church. It is made of a warm, tannish-yellow stone which reflects sunlight well, but the architecture, like that of most modern Ethiopian churches, is undistinguished. A mosaic of Gabriel, the patron saint, decorates the wall above the main door and there are good roof crosses. We heard singing inside. An evening service was getting under way. We took off our shoes and entered. The interior gave the impression of great spaciousness. Huge chandeliers hung down from a blue ceiling with gold stars. A dozen priests and deacons were filling the church with evensong. Some nodded a welcome to us. When the time came to bring out one of the church's processional crosses from an inner cabinet, it was held high for us to admire. We left an offering in the collection box and departed, for dusk was already discernible and we still had 54 km. to go to reach Diredawa. I resolved to return to Kulubi at the time of the great pilgrimage in December when over 100,000 people, both Christian and Muslim, assemble here.

The skyline drive continues through cultivated plateau 30 km. beyond Kulubi and meets the paved north-south highway that links Diredawa and Harar. Countryside mosques with bulky minarets and *chat* orchards are the distinctive features of this region. An immense terraced area planted with *chat* forms the head of the valley down which the highway descends to Diredawa (Pl. 46b). Before going on to this enjoyable city, however, let us go back and trace the lowland route. It turns off at Mieso and a sign warns the traveller that it is suitable only for 4-wheel-drive vehicles. Such signs are so unusual in Ethiopia that one's reaction is that this must be an extraordinarily bad road, not passable at all. When I took it in December I found it far from the worst road I had travelled in Ethiopia, though recent rains had had their effect on it.

Between Mieso and Afdem we passed through cultivated country and the road was in excellent condition. The whole way to Diredawa we were close to the railroad, but until we crossed it, we were seldom aware of it except at the little station towns (map, p. 192). From Afdem to Erergota we had to cross dozens of small watercourses – deeply eroded beds of torrents coming down from the Chercher Hills. The terrain here is loosely consolidated sand, rock, and volcanic debris. Every heavy rain loosens thousands of tons from the hillsides. We needed our 4-wheel-drive. Among the few travellers we met was a party of vacationing Frenchmen from Djibouti on their way to the highlands in a group of three vehicles. We went through areas so thickly overgrown with prickly pear that there was room for nothing else among them. Apparently un-inhabited, the region looked as if it would adapt well to cultivation. The streams could be drawn on for irrigation. Late in the afternoon we saw a pair of foxes with deep rust-red coats and black and white markings on their heads and bellies.

Beyond Afdem we had views to the north of the road of Mt Afdem, a complex volcanic massif that rises to 2,125 m. To the south we had even finer views of the Chercher range with clusters of white cloud along its whole crest. Before Erergota we crossed two well-established streams with a steady flow of clear water. One had an old road-roller buried in its bed, but it was so well rusted and so banked with sand that it seemed as natural as the boulders near it. Then we entered a hilly region where road and railway crossed each other several times. Erergota is the centre of large citrus and banana plantations. Muddy, rutted side-tracks led off through the well-tended groves with deep brown soil exposed under lush green trees. Our map showed an improved road from Erergota to Diredawa, so we hurried on, anticipating dinner at the Omedla.[10] But the road continued muddy and rutted and when darkness overtook us, we camped along it in the acacia forest. Birds serenaded us all through the night – sharp, piercing calls from some, long-drawn-out melodies from others, but there were none to be seen in the morning, so we were unable to identify any. Heavy dew left our tent drenched. While it dried in the new sun, we had time to explore a nearby stream-bed. It was a broad avenue of pink sand, absolutely flat and smooth for 400 to 500 m. at a stretch between descents over shelves of volcanic rock. There was no evidence of heavy flow in this stream-bed for a long time. Its sand must absorb all but the heaviest downpours. The sandy surface was a rock-collector's delight. We all came back with pockets bulging with chunks of rose quartz and white and blue jasper.

The route on to Diredawa became gaunt a short distance after we left our camp-site. Charcoalers and woodcutters had eliminated all the big trees. Ten kilometres before Diredawa we saw flights of large birds soaring and diving and, stopping by the roadside, discovered that we were at the disposal area of the Diredawa meat-processing plant. Carcasses and offal are dumped over a large area of cactus and thornscrub and all of this provides rich livelihood for thousands of vultures and marabout storks as well as hyenas and wild dogs. Together, these scavengers are so efficient that they consume everything within hours of its arrival. There were no bad odours, only acres of bleaching bones, picked clean. In many parts of the world all this material would be chopped and ground for fertilizer and feed, but in Ethiopia there is yet no demand for such by-products and it is more efficient to discard the waste and concentrate on processing the meat.

Diredawa

In addition to its meat-processing plant Diredawa has a textile-mill, a cement factory, and a Coca-Cola plant. It also has a modern airport which serves Harar too. The railway station, a tall building in late nineteenth-century style, is the most impressive structure in the city next to the Emperor's Arabian Nights-style palace which occupies a slight rise on the north side of the flat, sandy river-bed that divides the city in two. The 'European' city, on the north side, is expansively laid out in rectangular blocks. Streets are wide, mostly paved, and lined with flame-trees and acacias. Comfortable houses, some now old enough to have acquired an air of tarnished elegance, sit in shaded, flower-filled gardens. The commercial district consists of several streets with solid one- and two-storey buildings with verandas and arcades. At 1,160 m., Diredawa has a balmy climate that makes people accustomed to the highlands feel indolent, but Frenchmen from Djibouti flock to Diredawa to enjoy the altitude. In the summer months more French can be heard on the streets than English.

On my first visit to Diredawa we drove from Addis Ababa in a single day, eleven hours and 524 km. via the high road. We stayed at the Hotel Continental because Evelyn Waugh had stayed there in 1935 and it was said to have retained much of the atmosphere it had then. Sentimentality turned out to be a poor basis for choice of hotel, however, for dinner in the Continental's dining-room our first night led us to resolve to avoid eating there again. The beds were like hammocks. They sank to the floor in the middle and had soft rubber-foam

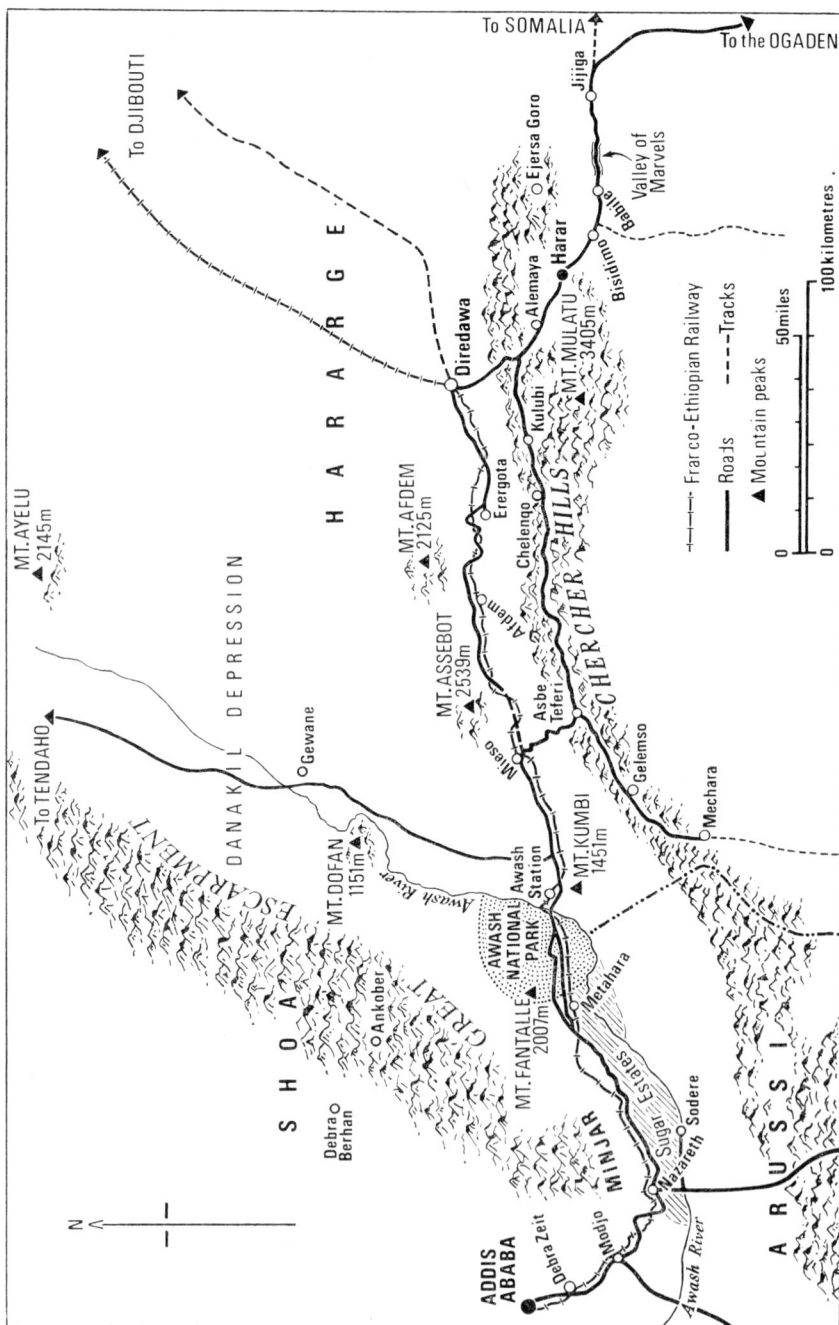

FIG. 21 Roads East

mattresses, undersize sheets, and not much else. The toilet in the bathroom was not bolted to the floor and swayed precariously when sat upon. The rooms all had ceiling fans which, fortunately, worked and we would have had a reasonably good night's sleep if people had not sat on the veranda outside and chattered all night while mosquitoes came in through the glass-slat windows and bedevilled us. Still, the old hotel had its charm and there is nothing wrong with it that a burst of energy and organization on the part of its Greek manageress could not set right. Fortunately Diredawa offers some choice in both hotels and eating-places. Every block or two in the commercial area there are pastry shops that serve excellent *capuccino* and a large array of bars that cater to all desires. The railway station, especially in the early evening, is the liveliest place in town. Continuing a custom that probably dates from the early days of the railroad, people congregate to watch the daily passenger trains arrive and depart and linger afterwards to gossip while young men hawk watches, cigarettes, tape recorders, jewellery, whisky, French wines, and hashish. One has the impression that there is nothing that cannot be bought in Diredawa for a price, and the prices are often not very high.

Though apparently no older than the European city, the 'Somali quarter' on the south side of the river seems like an old town with its main avenues lined with tightly packed Middle Eastern-style buildings painted in bright colours, its cobbled alleys filled with people, animals, traders, and craftsmen. Somali men wear bright cotton skirts, Arabs longer robes; Somali and Galla women like colourful dresses, bright headscarves, and wear large amounts of jewellery. Diredawa as a whole has a population nearing 70,000. Though most industry is on the northern edge of the metropolitan area for easy access to the railroad, the southern part of the city, which forms a 'native quarter' unique among Ethiopian cities, must be growing fastest. All around its edges, and in some open areas along the river, incoming country people build hemispherical Somali houses. In their original form these consist of a framework of curved poles over which finely woven and often intricately decorated straw mats are hung. In Diredawa sheets of tin have replaced the matting. The result is sturdier but much less attractive (Pl. 51c).

The Somali quarter has several mosques with Ottoman-style minarets and many markets. Wherever butchering takes place, colonies of vultures gather in nearby trees. Camels bring loads of firewood from the countryside each morning. The central market is a large, walled area with roofed masonry stalls. A friendly, smartly uniformed Amhara policeman chased away a mad beggar who attached himself to us as we entered and then accompanied us from stall to stall to ensure that fruit-sellers gave us fair prices. Women were offering tangerines, oranges, guavas, bananas, limes, and custard apples. The custard apples were unusually good, with pulp the flavour and texture of soft vanilla ice-cream. The policeman had to abandon us to go and disentangle two donkeys loaded with tin water-cans. One had tried to mount the other and the struggles of both had caused a ferocious clamour and much amusement for everyone in

7—EJ * *

the market-place. The policeman regarded it as an unseemly spectacle, apologized to us for it, and set out angrily to find the donkeys' owners.

Diredawa gets hot and languid by early afternoon. We cooled off by driving up onto the plateau to visit the HSI University College of Agriculture at Alemaya, an institution modelled after an American mid-western agricultural school. The college's campus and experimental fields are situated on the eastern side of Lake Alemaya (2,068 m.) opposite the town of the same name which fronts on the western side of this small, clean lake with its large population of ducks, geese, herons, and ibis. On both sides of Alemaya the main highway is lined with the tallest stands of old eucalyptus in Ethiopia. They must have been planted in Menelik II's time when the tree was first introduced.

Harar, by Day

Harar is least impressive from the direction most modern visitors approach it – over the excellent highway that links it with Diredawa. Until the Italian occupation most of the city remained within the walls. The Italians did a great deal of building at the north-western end of the old city, outside the Gate of the Duke, where there had been some Ethiopian construction after the conquest. There has been further construction in this area since the Liberation. It now contains municipal and provincial government offices, the military academy, the Ras Hotel, a monumental new Orthodox church, and many villas as well as more modest housing. Most of Harar, however, is still contained within its walls and there has been no significant building beyond them on the northern, eastern, or southern sides. A Harari account says of the city:

> Since Harar was built a very long time ago, it is counted among the cities of antiquity. As it is told, in former days there were seven very small villages. Of these . . . two were called *tuxun ge*, 'the city that will be', and *isxanti ge*, 'the city that might have been'. In the end, these seven villages were united and Harar was created. The city is entirely surrounded by a wall. The wall is a barricade of stone. It was built at the time of the Amir Nur. At the time the wall was built, they opened five gates to serve as exits and entrances . . . Each of the gates had a gatekeeper. He closed the gate at night and opened it at dawn. He administered the merchants and the merchandise that came in and went out. A merchant coming from outside late at night spent the night outside with his merchandise. At dawn, when the gate opened, he paid his duties, entered the city, sold what he had to sell and bought what he had to buy. This situation existed seventy years ago, up to the time of Amir Abdullah. Today the closing of the gates has been abandoned and the number of the gates has increased from five to seven . . . Beginning right at the gates, the whole countryside surrounding the city is green . . .[11]

From the east Harar comes into view miles away on the Jijiga road (Pl. 47a). The walls have a rich reddish-tan colour. Many of the buildings are whitewashed and reflect the sun's light sharply. Rising from its surrounding gardens and orchards, the old city is like an illustration from a medieval manuscript. Most of the old eastern walled cities have long since been enveloped by recent suburban growth. Harar has undergone much change during the nearly ninety years it has been under Ethiopian rule, but the ancient city has remained intact and its original relationship to its surroundings has been preserved. Preserved too have been its own Semitic language, its religious traditions, its architecture, customs, and crafts. The walls, when seen close up, have no continuity of design and look thoroughly patched together. They looked this way when Burton came over a century ago. He observed that they would be unlikely to withstand serious siege. They apparently never had to. They served primarily to keep the city sharply delineated from the surrounding Somali and Galla tribes and preserve its character as a commercial and religious centre, an outpost of Islamic and Semitic urban civilization on the edge of what, to its inhabitants, appeared to be a barbaric African world.

Since it is concentrated in a small space but grew with little plan, Harar is not an easy city to get around in. We drove first through the walled city and around the outside of the walls to get a feel for the place; we then parked near the Shoa Gate and set out on foot. Close at hand was the Christian market, which, like all markets of Harar, has some activity every day, but reaches its height on Saturday when thousands of people come in from the environs. There was a great deal for sale: live chickens, grains and herbs, coffee, salt and *gesho*, oranges, lemons, bananas, and many kinds of small fruits and seeds we could not identify. But the people were far more interesting than their goods. Most of the women were dressed in rich oranges and yellows, several shades of red, blue, and green. These light cotton shawls and skirts grow even more attractive as they fade, soil, and age and the colours mellow. Many young girls had marigolds in their hair, a sign they were newly married. Some of them were distinctly pretty, but the legend that all the women of Harar are outstandingly beautiful has little basis in reality. Compared to other parts of Ethiopia, Harari women are on the average rather weak-faced, not particularly distinguished in figure, and far too many of them are flawed by prominent buck teeth. There must be something about the way girls are dealt with as children which causes so many buck teeth, for they are not common among the men. Some of the Somali men in from the country were particularly striking, with good physiques and full heads of curly hair. Most of them wore short cotton plaid skirts, the standard traditional male attire among Muslims all over the eastern part of Ethiopia. The nearby livestock market, next to the wall south of the Shoa Gate, was a male gathering-place, but there was little of interest going on there, so we asked a boy to lead us to the Muslim market in the centre of the city. In Harari it is called *Gidir Magala*, the 'main market'.

Our agile young guide took us down into the old city through a maze of alleys too narrow for vehicles, some of them no more than stony pathways between walls of house compounds. Here we were in the world of medieval Islam.

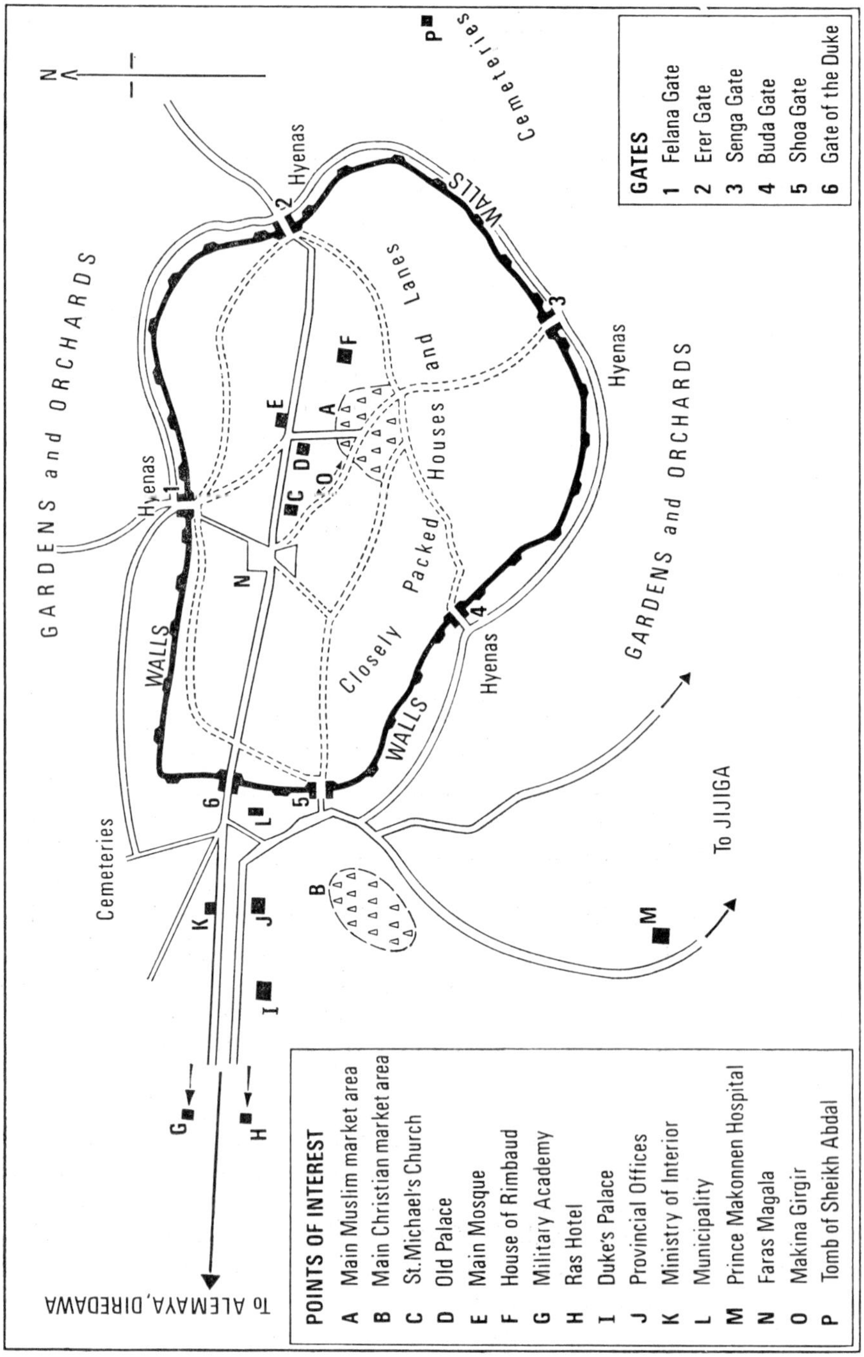

FIG. 22   Harar

GATES
1 Felana Gate
2 Erer Gate
3 Senga Gate
4 Buda Gate
5 Shoa Gate
6 Gate of the Duke

POINTS OF INTEREST
A Main Muslim market area
B Main Christian market area
C St. Michael's Church
D Old Palace
E Main Mosque
F House of Rimbaud
G Military Academy
H Ras Hotel
I Duke's Palace
J Provincial Offices
K Ministry of Interior
L Municipality
M Prince Makonnen Hospital
N Faras Magala
O Makina Girgir
P Tomb of Sheikh Abdal

GARDENS and ORCHARDS

WALLS

Closely Packed Houses and Lanes

Hyenas

Cemeteries

To JIJIGA

To ALEMAYA, DIREDAWA

N

Through carved wooden doorways we looked into rectangular houses built of stone with well-proportioned rooms furnished with tables, chairs, rugs, cupboards. Many had courtyards with green plants, pots, benches, and that sense of peace and order in a small space which is so often characteristic of traditional Islamic life. We were jolted into the modern age when we stumbled over metal water-pipes which come up above the surface of the streets. The old city has piped water. We also noticed that it is supplied with electricity. Wires strung on crude short poles stick up from the corners of houses and compound walls. We encountered many colourful people on our way (Pl. 48), but they were insignificant compared to those we saw when we finally reached the market itself. It is an open area with tall masonry buildings for shops in the centre, a small white mosque on one side, and permanent shops all around the edges and along the many streets that converge here. At 11.30 on a Saturday it was throbbing with life and sound. At least five languages are regularly spoken: Amharic, Harari, Somali, Gallinya, and Arabic. The women were even more colourful than those in the Christian market. They also had more jewellery: finely worked silver in many forms and – most noticeable of all – amber bracelets and necklaces. Many carried goods on their heads in baskets and others carried bundles on their backs and under their arms. Men predominated in the small shops and stalls. Women sellers had their wares spread out around them on the pavement. We had noticed a few men in the Christian market with their mouths caked with green scum. There were far more in the Muslim market: chewers of *chat*. Bunches of freshly cut *chat* were being sold everywhere by young girls. New baskets of all sizes were piled around women who were selling them. Some were of fine design, but most were rather crude and reinforced with leather stained with the deep magenta cactus juice. Basketry has developed into an art form in Harar, but the best baskets are not sold in markets but only in small shops in private houses.

An asphalted street which permits vehicles to come down to the *Gidir Magala* leads up past Ras Makonnen's old palace to the paved vehicular street that crosses the old city from the Gate of the Duke to the Erer Gate. We walked along it, noting basket houses for return visit later in the day, and looked in on a local school where both boys and girls, packed together in a partly roofed courtyard, were reciting the Koran. We then returned to the *Gidir Magala* and spent an hour among the cloth-shops that line the lower part of the narrow lane that goes up towards the *Faras Magala*. This lane is called *Makina Girgir*, 'machine road', because of its sewing-machines. Tailors (all men) working at their machines along the street will sew up newly purchased cloth while the customer waits. While shopkeepers competed to persuade my wife to buy their finest and brightest Indian cottons, I roamed up and down the *Makina Girgir* to observe other buyers. A group of dusty, sun-scorched Somali women in from the country wearing black and red headscarves with well-aged homespun cotton wound tightly around their muscular figures were bargaining for cloth too and were thus, in terms of clothing, entering the machine age. Two young men with fuzzy hair, shaped Danakil-fashion with wine-red earth rubbed into it, moved from shop to shop searching for friends or relatives. They were ill at ease in the city and kept glancing from side to side to see who might be watching them. Brightly-dressed Harari mothers with babies at their waists filed by. Some wore velvet pantaloons, but few wore slippers. Bare feet can grip the rounded cobblestones more easily. While most of the native Hararis seemed to be quite light, the people in from the countryside had darker skin than the average one sees in highland Ethiopia.

In the late afternoon we went basket-shopping in earnest. Entering through the carved doorway of a classic Harari house (Pl. 49a) near the Erer Gate, we were welcomed into a reception room (Pl. 49b) filled with baskets, jewellery, wooden bowls and spoons, horn beakers, even a tray of Christian crosses at astronomical prices for French tourists from Djibouti. This main room[12] was about $4\frac{1}{2}$ m. high with a ceiling made of poles with smaller branches laid crosswise to build a solid roof, covered with beaten clay on top, though many old houses now use tin. The ceiling, like the walls, had been painted white. On both sides of the room stairs led to upper rooms. Other carved doors led from the reception room back into storerooms. An old grandfather clock occupied one corner of the foot-high raised platform (called *nadaba* in Harari) that took up more than half of the floorspace. The basic purpose of this platform, which has its counterpart in many parts of the Middle East, is to provide clean separate space for the family and their visitors to lounge and talk. People traditionally remove their shoes before stepping on to it. We had a good opportunity to examine older baskets and new ones made in imitation of older ones. The original bright colours of the older ones, woven in intricate patterns, age to muted shades of rust, brown, and grey. The black remains unchanged. Many weavers now make new baskets, too, of colours like those that result from natural ageing, but the straw is much glossier and the new dyes more intense.

We went next to an old wooden house above the Muslim market which had been pointed out to us in the morning. A short, jolly plump lady received us in a large room on the second floor. From pegs on the walls she took down old tray-baskets, cowrie-decorated carrying baskets, *agilgils*, basketry milk-jugs, small incense baskets . . . A cabinet had silver jewellery, wooden spoons, coins, horn drinking-cups, and a large wooden chest held brass and copper ware. We looked through it all and watched a pretty young girl (one of the most beautiful we saw in Harar) weaving a new basket in one of the few open spaces on the floor of the room. What quick, sharp movements go into the weaving! What careful calculation to keep the design consistent and to keep all the ends of the basket straw woven into the courses of core straw in such a way that when it is finished, nothing protrudes. This new basket was being carefully done to resemble an old one. Nevertheless, the more we looked at the old ones the more attractive they seemed. Eventually we settled on three, including one with the unusual flame design. The lady said all were twenty or thirty years old. The leather edging on all of them, though intact, looked it. Each had loops for hanging and a few decorative cowries. From an asking price of E$110 we settled on E$87 for the three. Hararis do not do much bargaining.

On Sunday morning we resumed our exploration of Harar, coming in through the Gate of the Duke and going down a shop-lined avenue to the *Faras Magala*, the real central square of the old city. The name means 'horse market', but horses are no longer traded here. It is a centre for buses and taxis and a parking area for cars. Ras Makonnen's old palace, nearby, was in the process of being restored as a library and museum, but it was closed. The Church of Medhane Alem was open and a loud Sunday School class was in progress. This church was built after the conquest on the site of a mosque which the Egyptians had put up during their occupation. It is a round masonry building. Red poinsettia bushes in the grounds match the red trim on the church itself. We walked on past the Ras Makonnen Hospital, a good-looking building, and the Juma Mosque, less impressive close up than when its double minarets are seen rising above the city's skyline from outside the walls. We looked for the house in which Rimbaud had lived in the early 1890s and walked into the courtyards of several other attractive houses. We found a couple of hundred people in the Muslim market, but the place had a Sunday feeling about it and most of the shops on side-streets were closed. Such is the Christian influence on this old bastion of Islam . . . We finished our first visit to Harar by driving around the full length of the walls again, stopping at the gates to watch the human and animal traffic in and out of them (Pl. 47b). When I returned a few months later, I revisited all these scenes by day, but the best part of my second visit was the night.

To Jijiga

The road to Jijiga descends through country that becomes increasingly wild and barren. Beyond Babile, whose mineral springs supply eastern Ethiopia with bottled water, comes the Valley of Marvels, an area of unusual volcanic formations, mostly columns of red rock, some of which are capped by separate boulders. The Somalis of this region keep thousands of cattle and camels. Skirted men carry spears and knives. Somali women who do not have babies on their backs carry wooden milk-containers in wooden frames strapped to their shoulders.

Going no farther than the Valley of Marvels the first time out, I went all the way to Jijiga the next time. The Emperor was visiting Harar. He opened the new library-museum in his father's old palace and then went out to Bisidimo, half-way to Babile, to dedicate additions to the leprosarium which had been built with German aid funds. Harar had been full of flags and bunting and crowds and special policemen were keeping everything moving smoothly. The Jijiga road all the way to the Bisidimo turn-off was lined with soldiers in their best uniforms with polished arms – one every 100 or 150 m. Just before Bisidimo we were motioned by one of them to pull to the side of the highway and got out in time to hail His Imperial Majesty as he passed in a green landrover identical to our own. The ceremony was over and other cars came streaming out behind. A man dressed in a black suit and white shirt flagged us down, waved goodbye to a little Fiat filled with nuns, and asked whether we would take him to Jijiga. He was a Polish doctor from Krakow who had now served fourteen months as director of the government hospital there. He had come to attend the ceremony at the leprosarium, but had to rush back to duty because most of his Ethiopian medical assistants were off on the pilgrimage to Kulubi. He was starved for contact with Europeans and talked like a tape-recorder turned to maximum speed for the rest of the 75 km. and two hours that it took us to reach our destination. He had a camera and jumped out whenever we did to take pictures which he said he then sent home and would not see until he returned to Poland in two years. He had signed a three-year contract and alternated between giving the impression that he felt himself in bondage and, on the other hand, taking pleasure from the life he was leading. When we met local people, he addressed them readily in Somali. His English was deceptive, for he understood less well than he spoke and spoke more rapidly than grammatically. We stopped in the Valley of Marvels and walked back to see some of the columnar red-earth termite hills that occur here which we overlooked on our first visit because of preoccupation with rock formations. Beyond we travelled through rolling country covered with thorn and cactus scrub. The doctor said it was full of game of all kinds, including lion. He had done a lot of hunting. We stopped to eat lunch on the crest of the final range of hills before Jijiga. The doctor told us about the limitedness of life there. There were only three *ferenjis* in the town, himself, a Bulgarian doctor also assigned to the government hospital, and an Italian who owned the local hotel and was involved in other enterprises. The doctors stayed at the Italian's hotel. They missed varied food and longed for vegetables, for they lived mostly off macaroni. We happened to have a jar of Aunt Jane's Polish Dills in our lunchbox along with liver *pâté* and *knäckebrot*. It was a banquet for the doctor. Duty in the hospital confronted him with continual challenges, but the major part of his work consisted in treating men for knife- and gun-wounds, he said. Quarrelling is always at its worst after the rains have brought the grass out, he told us, for the cattle fatten then and the people are strong from drinking rich milk. Somalis live mostly off milk. During the dry season when there is less milk, they are less belligerent.

From the distance Jijiga looked insignificant, a dark splotch in the grey-green plain. We found it more substantial when we reached it. It covers a large expanse on both sides of the straight highway which goes on into the Ogaden. Streets are laid out in rectangles and there are many permanent buildings as well as Somali round huts covered with mats. We saw two filling-stations, a good-looking school, the towers of two or three mosques, and a new church on the north side of the road. The Muslim quarter south of the road is the larger and more active part of the town. Every day is market-day in Jijiga. People stream in from the countryside on foot, by horse, donkey and bus. The main market area takes in several blocks, though there is a separate women's market where food, jewellery, and small hand-made items are traded. Smiths were forging knives in stalls at the edge of this market and men were cutting sheaths to fit them while the knives cooled and the customers waited. They were retailing at E$1.25 to E$1.50 with sheath. We had not got far before we were surrounded by an army of children and young men. Foreigners seemed to be rare enough to attract a great deal of attention. Soon sellers were pressing in to offer us amber necklaces, wooden combs, silver jewellery, all at exorbitant asking prices. A tall, bony old lady who had a house off on a side-street had the best amber of all, but she enjoyed the bargaining process even more than most of the other people in this town of keen bargainers, so settling on a price for her necklaces of randomly shaped natural amber – some lemon yellow, some golden, some butterscotch tan, and some almost brown, took time. In between we visited several permanent shops specializing in beautifully woven mats. Then we set out on a sightseeing tour.

There are few sights, as such, to see – a neat white mosque near the market area, grain warehouses, several small hotels, many coffee-houses, a few moderately affluent-looking houses in walled compounds . . . But it was impossible to escape market activity – the whole town seemed caught up in it and, along with military considerations, trading is apparently the only reason for the existence of the place. We had bought a few hand-carved wooden spoons. Half a dozen people now came to offer us more. The old lady with amber returned with a necklace she had just got a commission to sell. It was a superb piece – alternating hollow silver balls and huge tan amber beads 2 cm. across, a dozen of each. Great puffs of white cloud had filled the sky, occasionally obscuring the sun, which was getting low. In between it shone brilliantly on groups of women *injera*-sellers dressed in reds and oranges who carried their product in double baskets on their heads – a bowl-shaped basket with a foot on the bottom, another slightly smaller one turned upside-down to form a cover on top. We had planned to get back to the Valley of Marvels for sunset, so we settled down to bargaining with the amber-lady in earnest and got three necklaces for half of what she had originally asked. As evening approached, market activity in Jijiga seemed to intensify instead of easing off, as it does in most Ethiopian markets. Fending off eager sellers, we returned to our landrover, but as we drove out a crowd of people rushed up carrying a large Somali milk-jug in wicker rack, complete with a wooden bowl as a cover on top. The jug, a splendid specimen, which would hold at least 12 litres, was cut from a single piece of reddish wood. We bought it for E$12. The sun had already begun to set.

Harar, by Night

We were overtaken by darkness on the way back from Jijiga. The sky was clear and there was a full moon when we reached Harar. We passed the Gate of the Duke and took the road beyond the police compound along the north side of the walls, for I recalled places where we might pitch our tent with a view over the old city by night. It is an area of cemeteries, fields, and open meadows cut by deeply worn trails. But a cool, brisk wind had come up and all possible camp-sites were too exposed. We drove down a gully outside the Felana Gate. Here, 200 m. beyond the gate, was an ideal camp-site – sheltered, with a few tall trees and a good view of the walls where the first sun would strike in the morning. We drove on to the grass and got out to take the tent down from the luggage rack. Children rushed up and asked if we had came to see the hyenas. We said we had come to camp. They looked puzzled. We stumbled over backbones of cows, thighbones, and ribs and off in the shadows saw hyenas gathering – it was indeed not a camp-site but a hyena feeding-ground! Other spectators (mostly Ethiopian tourists who had been to Kulubi) drove up and a young man came out with a basket of meat scraps and began calling the hyenas. Soon about thirty had emerged from thickets at the edge of the gully. All looked fat and sleek in their spotted coats, but they varied a good deal in courage and daring. Some readily came to take meat and bones from the feeder's hands, retiring only a short distance to devour it. Others took a long time deciding to make the dash to pick up a scrap from the ground. The feeder had names for them all: '*Gureza! Mandefro! Taferra! Abebech! Negisti*'! He also had a series of calls, some of them quite musical, which served as signals for the animals. After an active round of feeding when each of them had secured a piece of meat and drawn back, he chanted, '*Telah-telah-telah-telau-u-u-uu*', and the hyenas positioned themselves for the next phase of the feeding. Stragglers emerging from the gully made barking, snarling noises. The others were all silent. The feeder lay on the ground and two of the animals took bones from his mouth. He made others dash and leap for choice morsels. When the meat was finished, the hyenas drifted back into the shadows, the feeder collected coins and dollar notes, and we resumed our search for a camp-site.

We drove around a bend in the walls below the Erer Gate and found ourselves in another hyena feeding-ground. The entire area outside the walls was active with the animals emerging from gullies and thickets. They were not disturbed by passing vehicles. We realized that finding a camp-site in the shadow of Harar's walls meant avoiding direct paths of hyenas. Eventually we found exactly what we were looking for – a flat area in front of the gate of a large cemetery. The stone wall of the cemetery gave shelter from the wind. The main track was 50 m. in front of us and beyond were fields and hedges. The hyenas would be likely to stay on the track and would have no reason for coming close to the cemetery, we calculated. The calculation proved correct.

The moon was so bright we needed no lanterns. We had the tent up in a few minutes and built a hearth of large stones. Local boys came to help get our fire going by raiding a nearby thorn hedge for kindling and soon we had a sizzling, wind-fanned bed of coals on which to heat dinner. After dinner our two teenagers went into the old city while the rest of us had leisurely coffee beside the fire and watched hyenas lope by. Tourists continued to come to the feeding-area near the Erer Gate until nearly 10 and local people continued to walk by, but by 10.30 only the hyenas remained. The air was crisp and so clear and clean that every sight and sound could be seen and heard from afar. The wind died down. The moon lit up the mountains around Ejersa Goro far off to the east and closer in bathed gardens and orchards outside Harar in frosty light. To our left were the walls of the old city. They loom high here at their eastern end and they seemed to sparkle in the moonlight. Behind us, twisted trees and tombstones in the cemetery cast sharp shadows. Just as we were becoming concerned, our boys came back escorted by two Harari teenagers who had invited them into their house where they had spent an hour and a half drinking coffee, discussing Harari life, and comparing interests. They were thrilled with the experience and the Hararis invited us all back the next day. They returned inside the walls and we all retired to our sleeping-bags, thankful for their warmth, for the temperature had gone down to about 5°C.

Acacia logs served us well here, both for warmth and for the cautionary effect the fire might have on overly curious hyenas. All night long the beasts walked back and forth along the track east of our tent, calling to each other from time to time. But it was not the hyenas who were the most unusual feature of the night, but the drumming. There had been none when we fell asleep, but as I half-awoke during the night, I became aware of drumbeats from several different directions: slow, steady beating, then accelerated, complex rhythms. The drumming sounds came from two or three directions at once, then after pauses, sounds came from only one direction as if drummers at different points around the circumference of the city were communicating with one another. At other times there was no co-ordination between any of them. I was not sure it was not a dream. Here outside the walls of this ageless and formless city anything seemed possible during the middle of the night. The moon had gone low, but a very gradual dawn compensated for it. I got up and stepped outside as the drumming reached a crescendo – rapid changes of beat, steady, heavy pounding with different tones. The loudest reverberations seemed to be coming from a cluster of trees beyond the end of the cemetery wall. The air was chilly but still. The hyenas had gone. There were no people. The drumming rose to a frenzy of rhythm and stopped. Like echoes, drumming from other points around the walls could be heard in a similar final burst. Then absolute stillness – broken only by the flutter of birds in the trees in the cemetery.

The sky was totally clear. First there was bluish-yellow light over the eastern hills, then it turned orange and pink. A golden sun-disc gradually emerged, so soft one could look directly at it without discomfort. It was huge as it separated from the crest of the eastern hills, then grew slowly smaller. Soon the walls of the city were gilded and the roofs inside the walls reflected the sun's first rays. For a brief interval, the old city was even more magnificent than it had been by moonlight. People began to appear by ones, twos, and threes: a man driving a donkey down a path into the countryside; boys going to orchards, still sleepy and cold; women with water-pots. Soon large numbers of women dressed in the reds and purples and golds the Hararis like so well were passing by. A few people drifted out of the cemetery where they had spent the night. We followed a group of turbaned old men down a path beyond the cemetery and discovered the source of the drumming – an *awliya*, the shrine of a Muslim saint. A walled compound had a whitewashed domed tomb at its centre. A dignified old gentleman came up and told us it was the tomb of Sheikh Abdal and invited us to a nearby building, a large, high-ceilinged hall. There was a small entry area beyond the high carved and painted door. The rest of the room was elevated about 30 cm. above the entry, a *nadaba*. The keeper of the shrine, who wore an embroidered skull-cap, took us to the right front corner of the hall and proudly showed us his drums. Yes, he had been playing them all through the night. There were eight of them, starting with a large *kabaro* and going down in size to a small flat-bowl type, the *atamo*. Their heads were cowhide with the hair still on it. The old gentleman tapped them and they gave out good tones. Men gathered in this building on the evening of each Friday holy day, he said. He reached back behind the drums and brought out his sword – a sharp curved blade in an old tooled leather scabbard. Would we photograph him with it? He posed brandishing it as if to strike an enemy, with the great carved doorway as a backdrop. He pointed up to the Arabic inscription across the top of the door-frame and told us it declared, 'There is no God but God and Mohammed is His Prophet'. We made a donation for the upkeep of the shrine and returned to our tent-site for breakfast. The city had meanwhile come to life. Streams of people were pouring through the Erer Gate in both directions. Herds of cattle and flocks of sheep were being driven by. The air was filled with sound and warmth.

Kulubi Gabriel

When Ras Makonnen set out from Harar to help Menelik II repulse the Italians at what became the Battle of Adowa in 1896, he stopped at the modest little church of St Gabriel at Kulubi and vowed to the saint that he would endow a major shrine for him there if he returned victorious. In a country where the origins of most holy places are lost in antiquity and where even churches with no great claim to ancient beginnings often pride themselves on legends that link them to early Christian history, it is curious to find that what has now become the major pilgrimage site has barely eighty years of tradition behind it. There are other anomalies about Kulubi. It is not in Christian territory. This region may have been Christianized in early times, but it was overrun by Islam more than a thousand years ago. There has been considerable settlement of Christians in the region since the conquest of the late nineteenth century, of course, and probably some conversion among local inhabitants. But the shrine at Kulubi is not revered by Christians alone. Muslims are fond of the Archangel Gabriel, so they make the annual pilgrimage to Kulubi too. Emperor Haile Selassie I was eager to draw Ethiopian Muslims into national life. His patronage of Kulubi

contributed to the steady expansion of appeal of the shrine. Since St Gabriel
was so responsive to Ras Makonnen's vow, other Ethiopians have been making
vows ever since. There are few concerns that cannot be the cause of a
vow – *silet* – at Kulubi, though appeal to St Gabriel is thought to be particularly
efficacious for people suffering from barrenness. Until it became easy for large
numbers of people to reach Kulubi by road and by air, the yearly pilgrimage on
28–29 December was a modest affair, so it is only in the last decade that the
annual gathering there has reached mammoth proportions. In 1971 the official
estimate of attendance was 120,000.[13]

Western-educated Ethiopians who will have set foot in a church during the
year only to attend a wedding or a funeral will take leave from their jobs to go to
Kulubi. Some will join fully in the religious aspects of the pilgrimage. Some will
be there primarily to see who else is there and be seen themselves. A third of the
attendance each year probably consists of people from Addis Ababa. Another
third, including many local peasants, come from Hararge. The rest come from
all over the Empire. The pilgrimage has aspects of a national ritual and carnival
combined. It is essentially a gay and exciting occasion, though for some who
come performing such penances as carrying a rock on their heads over the trail
from Diredawa or covering long distances on their knees, it is the most earnest
experience of their lives. A comparison with Canterbury in medieval England is
apt. Colour, humour, pathos, tragedy, elegance, pretentiousness, bawdiness,
pettiness, and extreme piety are all present here and all combine to form a rich
tapestry of Ethiopian life with aspects as old as the time of the Queen of Sheba
and others characteristic of the last half of the twentieth century almost
anywhere in the world . . . Foreigners come to Kulubi in considerable numbers,
not only curious white *ferenjis* from Addis Ababa, but Italians, Greeks, Indian
and Filipino schoolteachers, Yemenis, a few other Africans. They are welcome
but inconspicuous, for what goes on at Kulubi during the great pilgrimage, as at
all Ethiopian religious festivals, has nothing to do with entertaining foreigners.

Some years it is dry at pilgrimage time, but these are exceptional, for the
Chercher Hills reach their greatest height – 3,405 m. – in Gara Mulata 25 km.
south of Kulubi and the area seems to attract precipitation. The end of 1971
was unusually wet. We came up from Diredawa the morning of the day
preceding the 29th,[14] but saw little evidence of activity until we were within a
few kilometres of Kulubi because most of the walking pilgrims take the 30-km.
overland route directly uphill (1,500 m. of ascent) from Diredawa. As we caught
sight of the church in its saddle high above the village, we could see a steady
stream of walking pilgrims making their way up to it on the foot-trail. The
village was filled with buses, cars, and pedestrians. We turned off on to the
muddy road to the church and proceeded without hindrance past the battalions
of beggars who lined the route.

The slope below the walled church-site was covered with temporary buildings, tents, and stalls sheltered by awnings. Sound trucks blared out the virtues
of various kinds of aspirin, patent medicines, and drinks. The three big

breweries – Meta, St George, and Melotti – all had large tent beer-halls. There were Coca-Cola gardens, bright with red umbrellas over their tables, and many improvised *tejbets*. We rounded the curve that leads up on to the flat area around the church and realized that what we had seen of this great temporary city so far was only its 'suburbs'. The whole spur of the mountain had been transformed. There were several sections of campers' tents, huge parking areas, large temporary structures made of green reeds, poles, and tin which were used as *tejbets*, eating-houses, and police stations. Policemen and soldiers were directing new arrivals to parking lots, campers to tent-sites, keeping local peasants from settling down on roadways. A loudspeaker rattled constantly from a communications centre upon the hillside, announcing the names of people who were looking for each other: from Asmara, Debre Berhan, Debre Zeit, Harar, Diredawa, Jimma, Gondar . . . It was about 3 p.m. by this time. We drove to a grassy parking area that was filling rapidly with cars, parked, and then walked through the tent area nearby (Pl. 52a). It was occupied 99 per cent by Ethiopians in every conceivable kind of tent, including elaborate foreign ones with porches, separate rooms, and complex camping furniture. There was no place to pitch our tent easily, so we deferred a decision on it and were happy when the rains came later that we had. Large numbers of people had already concentrated around the church. Three donation booths were open along the south side of the church compound wall – one to receive money, one for jewellery, one for other valuables. Livestock donated to the church were gathered in a fenced area below the compound walls. Beggars' cries were audible wherever we went, '*Sila Gabriel, sila Melaku Gabriel, sila Yesus-Christos!*', and hands were thrust towards us for alms. Some Ethiopians take a vow to give a centime to each beggar they meet. They need a large bag of centimes. Great masses of cold, grey cloud floated in and rain began to fall. We retreated to the landrover to sit it out.

Like everyone who comes to Kulubi we had promised to meet several groups of Ethiopian and foreign friends who were also coming, so when the rain stopped, we set out to find them. More and more vehicles had poured in, more walkers kept arriving, and the crowds were thicker everywhere. Beggars, some moving on all fours, shuffled through the mud. Some sang little songs blessing the giver of alms, some muttered long prayers. Some displayed diseased limbs. Gallas, Hararis, Somalis huddled around their camp-fires, drying their *shammas*, absorbing the smoky warmth. On our way down to the 'entertainment district' below the church, we passed rows of itinerant traders offering long beeswax candles, pink-and-blue flowered holy cloth, incense, sacred pictures. Boy- and girl-scouts were assisting old people across roads, helping man refreshment stands, and collecting donations for the National Literacy Campaign. Monks and nuns were selling St Gabriel pennants and packets of Kulubi earth. Music, accordians mostly, and occasional singing could be heard from some of the *tejbets*. In the tents where beer and soft drinks were sold, Radio Ethiopia blared from loudspeakers. A tent at the far end of this section featured the rock rhythms of James Brown over its speakers. We stood in the muddy roadway absorbing the sounds and watching the people pass. A voice called a greeting from behind us. It was an Ethiopian friend from Addis Ababa who had just arrived with his wife. They had brought a special offering for the church, a replica of an old painting of St Gabriel from one of the Tana churches. We all moved into the Meta beer-tent for a drink and discovered another group of friends eating *injera* and *wat*. They had spent a week travelling through the desert from the north via Bati, Tendaho, and Gewane. While they told us about their travels, the light of day faded. People kept streaming up the hillside as buses continued to arrive and disgorge more pilgrims. We walked back to the church compound where preaching monks were now delivering sermons to impromptu groups. All around the huge stone church itself people were standing, both men and women, some clutching the walls in deep prayer, others burning candles which melted down into thick gobs of beeswax on the door- and window-sills. The donation booths were now closed. Gallas were dancing around their camp-fires. There had been no more rain, but the air was damp and cold and stray clouds grazing the mountain-tops combined with the smoke of candles and fires to give everything the quality of being seen through a veil. A large screen had been set up against the hillside south of the church and a continual programme of films was being projected on to it. In between advertisements, old news features and educational films, various embassies' offerings, were shown. The documentary on HIM's 1969 visit to the United States was among them. We walked among journalists' tents and joined friends in *ouzo* and roast goat. The talk was of the abominable weather, the size of the crowds, the scheduled arrival of His Majesty the following morning at 11 o'clock. He was already in the Selam Aderash palace in Diredawa. But would he come if it rained more and the roads became impassable?

By mid-evening the *tejbets* were filling up, musicians were warming to their instruments, and *tej* and *katikala* were flowing freely. We looked in on several and then stayed for more than an hour in one constructed of green branches with a canvas roof. The floor was strewn with freshly cut hay and guests sat on low wooden benches. Sprightly young ladies in white traditional dress with bright headscarves and dangling earrings brought drinks and an *azmari*, a traditional minstrel, improvised songs and accompanied himself on an accordion. There was a feel of medieval warmth and gaiety about the place. When our turn came, the *azmari* serenaded us with a long ballad about *ferenjis* braving bad weather and bad roads to come from Addis Ababa for the great celebration at Kulubi. We thanked him and were welcomed to another *tejbet* where a traditional orchestra with *masenko*, *krar*, *bagana*, and *washint*, was causing the tent to billow out with its sound. By this time the temperature had fallen still farther and more and more people were consuming drink for warmth as well as conviviality. We were not surprised when we set out to visit another *tejbet* to encounter men swaying from one side to another along the muddy paths. It was midnight now and sounds of singing and dancing could be heard from the church. We climbed the hill and the steps of the front gate and stood in the huge doors. The immense chandeliers shone brightly through the smoke of candles and incense. Services were under way and the church was filled with pilgrims, mostly women on the right side of the centre aisle, mostly men on the left. Policemen moved people aside so we could go down to the front. The warmth was welcome after the chill night air. Most of the people inside the church were clearly Christians. Muslims appear to remain outside seeking the blessing of the saint from a distance. People were coming and going constantly, though some gave the impression of having settled into choice corners for the night. Nevertheless, only a small portion of those who come to Kulubi can spend much time in the church, for even when they are packed in tightly, it can hold no more than 1,200 people at a time. We went back to the landrover again and cooked a pot of coffee over our camp stove. The whole encampment was still alive with movement, though it was now past 1 a.m. Occasionally the moon, nearly full, was visible among the clouds. We set out again to explore areas we had not yet seen. A whole new series of camp-sites had sprung up since afternoon on the slopes that extend towards the village and fires twinkled from it. Beggars were still active, but more and more pilgrims were rolling up in their *shammas* and lying down to sleep beside paths and hedges and under trees. The mud had almost dried on the main roads and the air felt warmer, perhaps the effect of the smoke and fog holding the warmth in. Music was pouring out of the temporary *tejbets* and James Brown was still being played loudly at the end of the road.

Some time after 3 a.m. we returned again to the church. Singers, dancers, and drummers had got their stride. Steady rhythms and full bursts of sound were pouring forth. All the church's processional crosses – many of them of solid gold – had been brought out and were being paraded through the congregation. People pressed up to kiss them and, when there was space, bowed and prostrated themselves before them. Censers accompanying each cross poured out blue smoke. Periodically the curtains hiding the *maqdas* were drawn aside to permit the faithful a glimpse of the candles, crosses, chalices, and holy books that surrounded the *tabot* stand. High above, from the front wall of the church, Italianate mosaics of the principal saints, all of them with distinctly white and European faces, looked down ... A group of *debteras* roused themselves to a frenzy of enthusiasm and put on a tremendous display of dancing – shaking their *sistra* in unison, swaying to one side and then another, shouting out Ge'ez syllables to the beat of the *kabaros*, smiling with joy all the while, varying the rhythms subtly after each section of song, springing and leaping gracefully during the final climax of sound and action. It was past 4 a.m. by this time. We took another tour of the churchyard. A few pilgrims still clung to the walls and a few small candles still burned on window-sills, but rows of sleeping bodies, most totally shrouded in *shammas*, lay packed together over the whole area north of the church to the wall of the adjoining cemetery. In front, new arrivals were still coming up the steps to the main gate, sighing, kneeling, and touching the pavement with their foreheads on reaching the top. By 5, energy was waning. Singing and drumming continued inside the church and from the *tejbets* strains of *azmaris'* songs were still audible, but sounds of vehicles had ceased, public address systems were silent, the sky was clear, and the air cold. We returned to the landrover and dozed off, wrapped in jackets and blankets.

The clatter of rain on the roof woke us. The day dawned leaden and rain fell harder and harder. The church was visible only occasionally; nearby trees and ridges were hidden entirely. Masses of blue-grey cloud drifted in and reduced visibility to 5 m. Drenched pilgrims, covered with dripping *shammas*, raincoats, pieces of paper and cardboard, many of them shivering, passed by on their way to cars, under cars, or looking for space in police huts or *tejbets* or other people's tents to sit out the rain. Everybody connected with our party packed into the landrover. Pools of water gathered on the grass and the rain clashed down harder and harder on the roof. It did not stop until 9.30. We jumped out to limber cold, stiff muscles. Roadways and paths were streams of mud. It was like walking on grease. But the Ethiopian pilgrims were irrepressible. As soon as the rain stopped, everything came alive again. *Shammas* were held over fires to warm, if not to dry. Some of the beggars were completely covered with mud which only intensified the energy of their demands for money, their insistent blessings on passers-by. '*Sila Melaku, sila Gabriel . . .*' The sun shone through briefly. The ridges and trees became visible again. Soon there was sunshine in full force and big patches of blue in the southern sky. But what about the roads? Would HIM be able to make it? Perhaps he would have to come by helicopter? Word soon passed that he could be expected at 11 a.m., on schedule . . .

The little old church next to the wall of the new one was in business for baptisms. Yowling babies and sizeable children were being passed in above the heads of the crowd and passed back again. One wondered how parents could be sure they got their own babies back. Children born as a result of vows at Kulubi are doubly favoured if brought back to Kulubi for baptism. The donation centres were doing brisk business too. We looked down into the money-pit – coins and notes a metre thick covered the entire floor. From under the cedars along the south wall of the church compound we watched the steady stream of humanity passing by on the crossroads below: Hararis in their bright-coloured cottons, monks in red blankets, fashionable young Ethiopians in boots, mini-skirts, and bright jackets and hats, portly Amhara ladies who had just descended from newly arrived buses trying in vain to keep their white skirts mud-free, civil servants in blue and grey suits, Galla women leading troops of children, pilgrims just off the Diredawa trail . . .

Imperial Bodyguard officers began placing their men along the track and word came that HIM was soon to arrive. The sun shone from a cloudless sky and the mud had begun to dry. We heard the sound of rapidly moving vehicles approaching in cavalcade and there was the Emperor, sitting stiffly in his landrover, smiling and gesturing in response to the cheers of the crowds, followed by a dozen other 4-wheel-drive vehicles. We rushed over to the front steps and arrived just as HIM disembarked and climbed up them. We found ourselves face-to-face with the Crown Prince who was in high good humour, talking animatedly to the Crown Princess as they followed the Emperor up the steps. Other members of the imperial family and palace retainers followed. We joined the group and were passed easily along with them right up to the front of the church. The *tabot*, accompanied by Abuna Tewoflos, Patriarch of Ethiopia since May of that year and formerly Archbishop of Harar, was waiting at the front door, ready for the procession around the church. HIM and the *abuna*, side by side, went three times round. There was a sense of great excitement, much ululating by women, chanting and singing by the priests, beating of drums and jangling of *sistra*. Perhaps as many as five thousand people were in the churchyard during the procession, but police and soldiers at the gates kept more from pressing in. Otherwise, there were no obvious security precautions. When the *tabot* went back into the church, HIM took his seat on a portable throne, against a red and gold backdrop, to the left of the church door, with the Crown Prince seated beside him and the *abuna* next to him. Crosses and banners were held high behind the group, glittering in the sun. Other civil and religious dignitaries rated seats near the imperial party, but everyone else had to stand. *Ferenjis* were permitted to stand within 6 m. of the throne to observe the proceedings. HIM was chatting animatedly and seemed to be enjoying the whole occasion. Several of the religious dignitaries made brief speeches and the *abuna* concluded by making an appeal for money to pave the road up to the church. He gave E$100 from his own pocket, placing it in a gilt-edge inverted ceremonial umbrella and this and other umbrellas were then passed through the multitude and quickly filled with notes.

The gates of the compound were opened again and everyone who wanted to come in was permitted to do so. Within 15 minutes the number of people inside must have doubled. HIM and his party went into the church for the final service. Beggars began to make their rounds again. Pilgrims with rocks on their heads passed by. Women continued to arrive and prostrate themselves at the top of the main stairway. Every imaginable kind of Ethiopian passed through the main gates. I recognized several friends as well as monks I had met at religious festivals in other parts of the country. Policemen and soldiers who kept the crowd under control showed tolerance for everybody, only moving to push beggars aside when they attempted to settle themselves in the middle of the path HIM and his party would have to take to return to their vehicles which waited in front of the gates. The services inside were broadcast over loud-speakers. A long series of amens caused the crowd to stir, but the services, actually rather short by Ethiopian standards, were still not over. There were further sermons, further hymns, further prayers, and further amens. Light and shadow played across the valley between the church and the village as clouds floated up again. Hundreds of vultures and ravens soared overhead anticipating scraps of food. Some settled on the towers and crosses on top of the church and squawked down at the crowd. A dozen senior police officers, generals, and other dignitaries paced up and down the steps, awaiting HIM's exit. There were amens again, then silence, finally a flutter of activity around the church door. At a quarter to two, he came out and walked briskly down the pavement in front of the church and then alone and unattended down the steps – 23 of them in all, still covered with mud. For an 80-year-old, HIM showed no stiffness of legs and jumped up from the landing onto the step of his landrover and inside. The rest of the party followed and the whole group was quickly on its way down the muddy road back to the village and on to the main road to Diredawa.

With the ceremonies successfully capped off by the return of the sun and HIM's visit, the preoccupation of just about all of the 120,000 pilgrims who had come for St Gabriel's feast shifted quickly to the problem of departure. At least 300 buses were mired in fields along the route back to the village. Three thousand cars were packed into the area around the church. Everyone tried to move at once and confusion ensued, followed by total deadlock. Eager drivers in a position to do so had moved from parking areas out on to roads, clogging them all. Everyone honked horns. No movement. Everyone raced motors. No movement. At 4 o'clock everything was just as it had been at 3. We found a perch on top of the front wall of the church where we could survey the whole scene. We had had friends reserve a camp-site in the garden of the Ras Hotel in Diredawa, but chances that we could extricate ourselves from Kulubi seemed slim. Far off towards the village buses were being pushed and pulled from their ruts – one by one; it looked as if it might take days for all of them to be cleared out.

Below where we sat on the wall a group of monks had established themselves at its base. One was cutting chunks of meat which he carried in an old cloth bag, apparently preparing for the next day's feast, since this day was a Wednesday and, St Gabriel's day or not, was a fast-day. Another was counting his take from begging. He had a thick wad of notes. Whenever another monk approached, he rolled up his money in a rag and stuffed it under his skirts, anxious that no one see how affluent he had become. He was unaware that we were watching everything he did from above. Two or three monks were gathering firewood and hay from leavings from pilgrims. A violent argument developed when one accused two others of having stolen his hay. He picked up a bundle and stomped away with it. Another grappled with him, but no blows were exchanged. At 5 we walked back to the landrover, resigned to staying for the night. No sooner had we reached the parking-lot than we heard sounds of real movement. We drove up into a line of vehicles and pressed forward at every opportunity. Before long we were slithering down the gully north of the church heading for a line of cars moving slowly along the road back to the village. Police and boy-scouts were keeping traffic lines merging smoothly. It took an hour to get to the village and thousands of pedestrians and several dozen horsemen passed us (the horsemen had it best of all, for they could move and still stay clear of the mud), but finally we were out on the main road joining a great parade of vehicles moving eastward. Dusk turned into rain and fog, mixed at times with dust. We crawled along at 20 k.p.h., dripping fine mud. It was nearly 8 when we reached Diredawa and claimed our camp-site. The lobby of the Ras Hotel was full of fashionable people from Addis Ababa. The crowning Kulubi social event was taking place that evening – the grand ball. At the Omedla's dining-room, a new dinner party was being seated the moment a table was vacated, but the management was up to the challenge and the food was excellent. Even if it had not been, we might not have cared, for it was our first regular meal in 48 hours. It was also our first regular sleep in 48 hours, so after a brief look in on the grand ball, we retired to our tent. It mattered little that the camp-ground was noisy with other arrivals all night long, the grand ball continued until the first signs of dawn, and cats – which are plentiful in Diredawa – kept scurrying and fighting all around us. We slept well.

NOTES

1 Cf. J. S. Trimingham, *Islam in Ethiopia*, London, 1952, 68.
2 The Chronicle of Amda Tseyon's reign has been translated into English by G. W. B. Huntingford, *The Glorious Victories of Amda Tseyon, King of Ethiopia*, Oxford, 1965.
3 This history has most recently been dealt with by Jean Doresse, *Histoire Sommaire de la Corne Orientale de l'Afrique*, Paris, 1971.
4 *First Footsteps in East Africa*, London, 1856; reissued in London, 1966.
5 Richard A. Caulk, 'The Occupation of Harar', *JES*, July 1971, 1–20.
6 Amharas believe that the higher a prospective mother goes the easier the birth will be. By the standards of the Shoan Manze nobility Harar at 2,100 m. was rather low and it was natural for the future Emperor's mother, who had had bad luck with earlier children, to seek an easy birth and successful survival of the child by going to the highest location in the vicinity.
7 Richard Pankhurst, *Economic History of Ethiopia, 1800–1935*, Addis Ababa, 1968, 304–37.
8 *When the Going Was Good*, London, 1946; Penguin editions, 1951 ff.
9 Bob G. Hill, 'Chat (Catha Edulis Forsk.)', *JES*, July 1965, 13–23.
10 This unassuming little hotel, named after the town of the Sudan border where Emperor Haile Selassie I and British forces re-entered Ethiopia in 1941 and began the Liberation, has one of Diredawa's best restaurants.
11 Wolf Leslau, *Ethiopians Speak, Studies in Cultural Background, I. Harari*, Berkeley and Los Angeles, 1965, 2–5.
12 Called *gar eqad*, 'front room', in Harari. Leslau, *Ethiopians Speak . . .*, 46–61, describes the classic Harari house.
13 Very little has been written about Kulubi. Few travellers have commented on it. This omission has recently been filled in part by a kaleidoscopic novel which presents a remarkable series of insights into modern Ethiopian life and character against the background of the Kulubi pilgrimage: Edmund P. Murray, *Kulubi*, New York, 1973.
14 The festival always occurs on 19 Tahsas EC. It fell on 29 December in 1971 since the preceding year had been an Ethiopian leap year. In non-leap years it falls on 28 December.

8 · Middle Earth

Unfinished Journeys in Bale

During my time in Ethiopia a coloured map of J. R. R. Tolkien's 'Middle Earth' hung in the big grey stone house above Dincho which served as headquarters for the 'Proposed Bale Mountains National Park'. The PCVs who put it up had in the same style lettered in 'Bale Mountains' before the vaguely Celtic 'Middle Earth' title so that on first glance the map appeared to be an official issuance. The better acquainted I became with Bale, the less whimsical I regarded this map. The PCVs who worked to chart out the new national park quickly sensed the uniqueness of the province. It is an area to a great degree still removed from time, far from the modern age, with a pristine quality that can be found in very few other places in the world. It is an example perhaps of what all of the Ethiopian highlands were like before the cedar forests were cut and the natural ground cover cleared and burned and turned into ploughed fields and grazing land. Almost exactly the same size as England, 130,000 sq. km., Bale is the least populous province of Ethiopia.[1] It is not without its history, however.

Known in late medieval times as Bali, it was often referred to by Muslim and European travellers as an important Muslim kingdom,[2] though no traveller who actually visited medieval Bali left an account which has yet come to light. The area appears to have been part of the original homeland of the Galla and seats of *abba muda*, the traditional Galla tribal high priests, are reported in Bale. Islam penetrated this region early, but pagan Galla practices persisted. Many earlier beliefs were gradually merged into Islam and one still does not need to look very hard to discover pre-Islamic survivals.[3] The basic population of highland Bale continues to be Arussi Galla. The lower country is sparsely populated by Somali who lead essentially nomadic lives.

The Webe Shebelle

Near its sources, the largest of south Ethiopian rivers differs from its tributaries only in the greater depth of its valley. The new road into northern Bale is well constructed and all of the streams are bridged. The bridge over the Webe Shebelle rises high above the stream-bed and provides a good view down the valley which here is almost entirely without vegetation larger than bush size. A bit farther on, where the old caravan trail fords the river between Asasa and Dodola, the valley has stands of large acacia and cedars. I camped in a cedar-grove above the Asasa-Dodola ford one night in early December. Though the day had been warm and the altimeter registered only 2,330 m., the temperature fell rapidly during the night and our tent was coated with frost in the morning. The night had been so clear and the moon so bright that we had seen the whole central Arussi plateau across the river to the north with Mts Kakka and Enquolo clearly outlined as well as the long saddle between them. We were awakened in the morning by flocks of Egyptian geese splashing noisily in the river far below us.

For a thousand kilometres, all the way to the Somali border, the Webe Shebelle forms the northern and eastern borders of Bale. It gathers in hundreds of small streams that drain the northern slopes of the Bale mountains. The fact that these mountains still retain so much of their natural vegetation makes them a great reservoir for precipitation.[4] The streams flow swift and clear the year round. Beyond Sheik Hussein, the great Muslim pilgrimage-site near the point where Arussi, Bale, and Hararge converge, the river drops into gorges. It receives the drainage of the north central section of Hararge and then flows on through the Ogaden, past Gode, where the IEG is developing a modern town, to Mustahil, near the Somali border. Like the Awash, the main river of central and eastern Ethiopia, this great southern river never reaches the sea. It comes much closer than the Awash but, after 1,500 km. of flow, it is still no wider at Afgoi, north-west of Mogadishu, than it is on the plateau. The Webe eventually loses itself in the plain behind the ranges of dunes that line the Somali coast. It has a great potential for irrigation both in Ethiopia and Somalia, very little of which has been realized, though surveys carried out by the French in recent years have produced realistic plans for development of the valley.

The highway into northern Bale seems at first to be running parallel to the forested mountains which dominate the southern horizon, but gradually it comes near to them. They are a splendid spectacle: forested with tall trees with green meadows covering the foothills. Through valleys and gaps in the first row of peaks, higher mountains, even more thickly forested, can be seen extending on towards the south. Lumbering in these mountains has already begun and a collection point for logs has been established along the main highway near Adaba. Cedar and podocarpus trunks are usually piled here by the hundreds for transport to saw-mills. The foothills jut out close to Adaba, the main town of this region. It sprawls over a large area with no buildings of distinction, but it has a large market on Tuesdays which draws thousands of Arussi from the rather thickly settled surrounding region.

Beyond Adaba the highway begins a gradual climb into the foothills, dipping every 3 or 4 kilometres to cross acacia-lined mountain streams rushing down to join the Webe Shebelle. Not wishing to go over the mountains after dark, we set up camp at 2,750 m. along one of these streams at the point where it emerged from forest into meadows. Local farmers had been cutting cedar posts for house-building and had left a pile of knots and joints which fuelled our camp-fire. We had a dozen visitors, all shy young men, in the morning. Some were coming to work on a new field which had been cleared on a steep slope at the edge of the forest. The angle of the slope was about 45 degrees. The soil was thick and rich with the accumulation of millennia of humus. Nevertheless, with open meadows at hand, it seemed absurd to be turning forested hillsides into fields. It is the same process that has denuded so much of the Semyens. Fortunately I saw very few examples of this kind of expansion of cultivation in Bale.

Across the Mountains to Goba

As we drove up into the mountains, tall trees ceased at about 3,400 m. and heather and St John's Wort, ranging from bush to tree form, took over. The long spur which the highway follows in its ascent is at first separated from the main central mountain mass to the south by a broad valley, cultivated in its lower reaches, then thickly forested. Above the tree-line it merges into the central highland region of heather moorland. This magnificent expanse of alpine uplands, dotted with peaks and knobs and outcroppings of rock, all volcanic in origin, stretches on to the south as far as the eye can lead, forming the second highest mountain massif in Ethiopia, variously called the Batu, Dimtu, and Mendebo range. The next year, after I had become familiar with parts of this region first-hand, I could stand beside the highway and pick out the route from Dincho to Batu, but on my first journey to Bale nothing was familiar, all was new and different, as entrancing a landscape as I have ever seen (Pl. 54).

The high point on the road is 3,650 m., but there is no obvious pass. The highway makes its way along a series of crests and divides with views over the mountains to the north and east as well as the south. The vehicle's motor is a better indicator than the eye of when the descent begins. The whole region is a natural flower-garden. The Bale mountains receive some precipitation every month of the year, but vegetation does not necessarily reach its peak of bloom at the same time each year, for variations in amounts of rainfall and sunlight cause shifts of several weeks. Grey-silver, low-growing alpine plants are showy here at all seasons. Not far below its highest point, the highway enters a broad valley which appears to be an old lava and cinder flow that leads all the way down to Dincho. Relatively smooth across its centre and 3–4 km. wide, this valley supports immense fields of red-hot pokers (*cineraria*) as well as many other flowering shrubs and low-growing plants.

Dincho, called Gure on most maps, is an undistinguished-looking little town, so much so that though it was our destination on our first visit, we passed right through it and drove on to Robi before we realized it. After so much mountainous terrain, Robi, situated on a flat plain with tall eucalyptus, looks and feels low, though it is still at 2,620 m. A spur of highway leads back westward out of Robi to Goba, capital of Bale. It lies under a mountain wall at 2,775 m. A long, grassy rectangle, its airstrip, forms the centre of this town which has about 10,000 people and is by far the largest urban settlement in the province. We drove past the airstrip onto a slight rise to a long red two-storey building with a tower, thinking it would be the seat of provincial government, but found it was a hospital. A peculiar old grey two-storey building beside it was the post office. Behind, across a meadow, was a large compound fenced in with 3 m.-tall

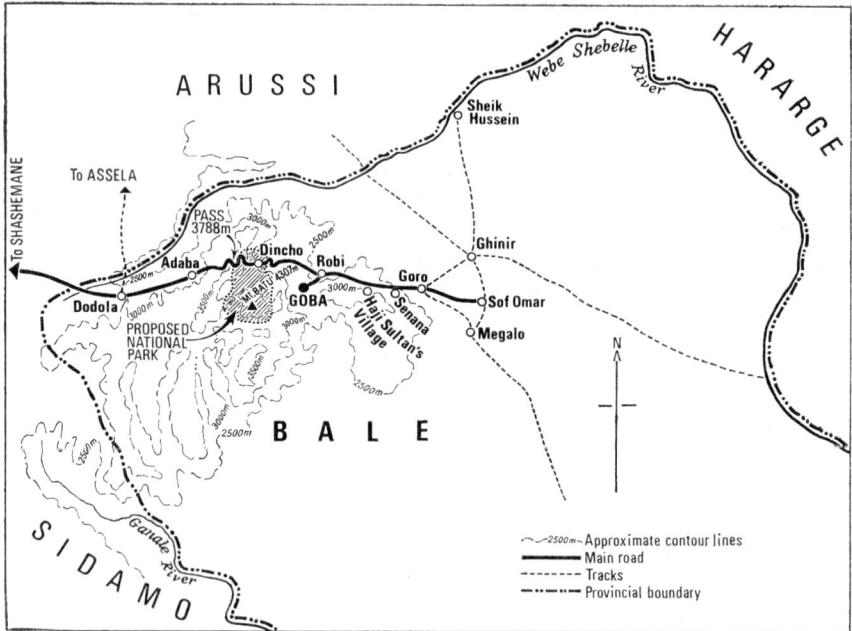

FIG. 23   Northern Bale. Contour lines and heights are from the 'Lake Margarita' sheet of the British/US 1:500,000 East Africa series based on data from the 1930s. They are not entirely accurate, but can be improved upon only when the results of the US/Ethiopian surveys of the late 1960s become available.

upright poles laced together with bands of branches and vines. Inside was the governor's 'palace', a rather simple building. Off to the south, also in a commanding position and directly above the edge of the airfield, was the 'palace' of the Orthodox Patriarch of Bale. It was a long, low house painted in light blue and pink. Near it was the skeleton of what will eventually become a rather grand stone church. Like the governor, the patriarch was not in residence, so our efforts to pay a courtesy call on them were in vain. Our group split up. Some went on eastward; the rest returned to Dincho.

Dincho

A big black-and-white sign in English and Amharic pointed the way to the turn-off to the 'park headquarters' above Dincho. We followed the earth track through grounds that resembled a well-maintained country estate. Undergrowth had been trimmed, grass cut and grazed. As we drew up in front of the stone mansion, Dusty Golobitsch, PCV in charge, came out to greet us and pointed the way to a camp-site down the slope in a grove of cedars, advising us to drive carefully so as not to rut the turf. Our tent glade had lobelias and St John's Wort on one side, giant heather on the other. A servant came to gather dry heather branches and lobelia-stalks to start a fire and then brought down enough cedar logs to last through the night. The sun was soon setting over the western peaks, so we quickly cooked dinner and then went up to the big house to spend the evening with Dusty, a fellow PCV, an entomologist, and a geologist who were staying at the Park Headquarters while doing research in the area. First we had a tour of the house. It was set up like a visitor centre at a national park in the USA: maps, charts, photographs on the walls of the big rooms; displays of nyala and klipspringer horns and skulls; stuffed hawks and lesser birds; shelves with collections of rocks, plants, bones. Smaller rooms had shelves and tables where visiting researchers could lay out their work. Dusty had a collection of local basketry hung all over the house. At night the large rooms were chilly at 3,170 m., so after the tour we settled in front of a roaring fire in a small, wood-panelled study and gradually consumed a bottle of brandy as we heard about life in the area and the progress of the park.

The Bale park was a happier experience in its initial stages than the one in the Semyens. There is a wider choice of terrain available for a park in Bale. The unique animal of these mountains, the nyala, appears to be much less endangered than the walia ibex in the north.[5] The Peace Corps played a minor role in setting up the Semyen park. In Bale the Peace Corps took on the whole job of surveying the terrain and developing a plan for the park. Dusty, a tough, realistic young man from Colorado with academic training in conservation, had started work at Dincho in 1968. He had hiked and ridden over thousands of square kilometres of terrain, had surveyed and marked park boundaries, and made drawings of unusual natural features. He had counted nyala and other animals and catalogued flora. He had developed friendly relations with dozens of local officials and hundreds of local people and had got some of them to understand what a national park was about.

A few years earlier a Belgian had secured a grant of land from the Emperor on which to raise sheep. He brought in a thousand Australian sheep to graze on meadows below Dincho and built the stone mansion on the mountainside above the village. The sheep flourished only briefly and then succumbed to liver fluke and other diseases, the effects of which were intensified by the high, cool, damp climate, so unlike conditions under which the breed had evolved in Australia. The big house with its hotel-size kitchen, palatial living-rooms, and long bedroom wing was abandoned. It was ideal as a headquarters for the new park. Just as the concept of a park was taking shape, a group of *ferenjis* from Addis Ababa organized the Bale Fly Fishing Club and had trout fingerlings flown in from Kenya to stock some of the streams near Dincho. The trout were much more successful than the sheep. They grew quickly and reproduced abundantly and now, just three years later, extraordinary fishing was available for payment of a small fee. The PCVs served as local representatives of the trout club.

But three years of developmental work had made Dusty impatient for the IEG to declare the park officially established and provide legal basis for protecting nyala and controlling cutting of trees and ploughing of alpine meadows. He recounted some of his recent experiences persuading local officials to keep farmers from burning heather and shooting nyala. Now that the insurgency problem in Bale had eased, new settlers were beginning to come in from the north. Dusty had developed a deep affection for Bale, but he was also a realist. He knew that progress was made not in leaps but by small steps. He talked about his own dilemma — should he stay a fourth year or go on to some other part of the world, accepting one of several other conservation jobs he had been offered? Brandy consumed and fire burning low, we rose to go out through the chill air to our tent, mulling over the problems of preserving wildlife and natural landscapes in the developing world.

In the morning while two of our party went trout-fishing I hiked up the mountainside above Dincho through a small valley carpeted with ferns, thistle, wild geranium, and a dozen other kinds of ground cover. I roused two klipspringer as I came out on to a meadow dotted with lobelia. It was a relatively low-growing variety with very compact leaf-clusters. Some clumps had put up $1\frac{1}{2}$m. stalks which carried deep purple bloom. Startling a bush-buck from a thicket of St John's Wort, I climbed a low line of cliffs and emerged on to open moorland with vistas stretching away for miles to grey-green mountains. There were cattle grazing on these moors and a few Galla *tukuls*. So far neither the cattle nor the people seemed to be having much effect on the natural vegetation. The warm sun had dried the thick dew and I was tempted to walk on in the hope of coming on nyala when I looked at my watch and realized it was already mid-morning. Turning back towards Dincho, I came upon the most remarkable sight of this walk — a scattered grouping of St John's Wort trees with trunks a half-metre thick. They were 7–8 m. high and had true tree form. St John's Wort grows slowly. These would have to be at least 150 years old, perhaps double that age. Even by Ethiopian standards they are rarities worth preserving. Still, they could fall victim to a farmer's axe almost any time. One could not live here for long without worrying about such things . . .

Coming back to the big stone house, I found Dusty exercising his horses, eight or ten good-looking riding- and pack-animals, on the front lawn. He used them for long trips to the more distant parts of the mountains and they could be hired by visitors as long as they wanted them. It was Tuesday, market-day in Dincho, and Dusty recommended we visit the market where he would introduce us to local people. We could look for baskets and, if we were interested, buy cloth. The market-place does not fill up until noon and for some reason the women who make the beautiful baskets that are characteristic of this part of Bale are shy about selling them. They hide them under their skirts and have to be persuaded to begin the bargaining process by repeated patient enquiries. Were the women not so interesting to observe in themselves (Pll. 56–7) this might be a tedious process. Naturally good-looking — some of them really elegant in face and figure – the local Arussi women wear graceful black-and-white head-dresses and a great deal of jewellery: headbands, earrings, necklaces. Some of the necklaces are monumental assemblages of beads, cowries, metal, amber, buttons, and glass. Some of Dusty's local friends helped us find baskets and others gave us pointers on bargaining for cloth. This market had the largest selection of locally woven cotton I had up until then seen in Ethiopia. We bought fresh white bread from a Yemeni who operates a small general store on the edge of the market-place and then, about 1.30, set out for the return trip over the mountains to Addis Ababa. Bidding Dusty and his friends good-bye, we promised to return in a few months for a trek into the mountains.

Trek to Batu

Other areas claimed available travel time and it was a full year before I returned. Dusty had left. We telegraphed from Addis to his PCV successor, Bob, to have men and horses ready for a 2–4-day trip. He telegraphed back that he would be away, but everything was arranged. There had been a great deal of rain by late May. We were apprehensive that the weather might hamper us, but in the area around Adaba we noticed that streams coming down from the mountains were flowing heavily but clear, a sign that there had been no recent storms. The great expanse of mountain slope beyond Adaba was greener than it had been at the same time the year before and the alpine flowers on the high moors had exploded into new life. Dincho was green, cool, and damp, but the air was so clean and crisp that one felt scrubbed from walking in it. As soon as we had brought our baggage into the big house, Ato Aman Amara, our guide, came to discuss arrangements for departure in the morning. He was a small, wiry man, a Dincho Galla who looked far older than his 25 years because of an entirely bald head, very rare in this part of Ethiopia. We agreed to set out in the morning for a three-day journey to Mt Batu with five horses and another man in addition to Aman. Departure would be between *hulett* and *sost saat* (8–9 a.m.). Horses and men arrived shortly after 8 the next morning. But, as always seems to happen in Ethiopia, one thing and another delayed us and we did not get off until 9.30.

As second man, Aman brought along Sendabo, a handsome, ragged character with an open, friendly manner. He had a long face and a full head of curly hair, no shoes, and shorts that had been patched fifty times, but he knew how to handle horses and baggage and proved not only always to be cheerful, but was usually engaged in some sort of joke or clowning. Forty-two years old, he liked to refer to himself as a *shimagile*[6]. Aman and Sendabo addressed me as *getoch* and my son and our Ethiopian travelling companion as *gash*.[7] After we all became familiar with each other, a process that took only an hour or two, we gave Aman and Sendabo the titles of *Balambaras*[8] and they enjoyed the play-acting. The horses were large, strong animals. Our baggage fitted easily on two of them and we had the other three to ride. With pads, the Ethiopian saddles were not uncomfortable until we had ridden a couple of hours.

It did not take long to traverse the forested area above Dincho. Then we crossed two green valleys dotted with St John's Wort and lobelia, cedars, and *kosso* and set out across the moorland. There were still squatters' houses here and we stopped to talk to some of the people. One man had wooden beakers and flat bowls newly carved of *kosso* wood. We bought a few, agreeing to stop to pick them up on our way back and pay a bonus if the carver would cut designs in them. For the first two hours we travelled westward. From every high point we still looked back on Dincho and the broad valley to the north of it, down which the main highway comes. Then we turned south and, gaining further height, crossed undulating plateau-land covered with heather and tremendous expanses of red-hot pokers. These, we learned, are called *lela* in Gallinya and *yejib shinkurt* ('hyena's onion') in Amharic. Flat areas had clear water standing among clumps of grass. We forded several small slow-flowing streams.

Sendabo talked about many things. His name, he told us, came from a river on the way to Sheik Hussein where his mother had prayed for a child. Both Aman and Sendabo had been to Sheik Hussein, participated in all the ceremonies there, and were proud of their status as pilgrims.[9] Sendabo was a great local patriot and kept asking how we liked Bale. He showed great pleasure at our delight in the landscape. But he lamented what he considered the poor condition of Bale in spite of its natural beauty: 'All the province has is Sheik Hussein and cattle – this is not enough for us to have much of a life. We need factories – there is not a factory in all of Bale!' I was reminded of James Morris's 'Ticket to Huddersfield'.[10] Even here in Middle Earth ... Climbing farther with even broader views across what was becoming apparent as a huge upland basin covered mostly with heather up to 2 m. high, we passed two small huts and a boy herding a dozen cattle – the last permanent habitations we saw on the way into the mountains. The cliffs towards which we had been heading for more than an hour were now directly before us. As we came up under them we found ourselves in a sheltered basin where a sizeable river emerged from a still higher valley and then descended into a deep gorge which went off towards the north. The place was called Turishoma. We drank from the stream and took time to examine the alpine vegetation, much of it in flower.

Beyond Turishoma came the roughest stretch of trail we had to negotiate that day. The path turned into deep, water-filled ruts through tall heather interrupted by strips of bare lava which were even worse than the ruts for the horses, for they were slippery. Riding was mostly a question of hanging on, trying to anticipate upward or downward jolts of the horse while avoiding the lashing of the larger heather-stalks. We climbed 200 m. through this kind of terrain, dismounting to avoid muscle strain and mounting again to avoid stepping into knee-deep holes. We came out into a high, broad valley, edged on both sides by volcanic walls. Patches of higher ground were laced with rat burrows. Where heather had been burned long ago, new growth had come out of charred roots which seem difficult to kill. The new growth often develops as so many tiny shoots that none can dominate and the plant fails to form strong new stalks. Lobelia, absent from the moors we had crossed after coming up out of the first valleys above Dincho, appeared again. Some of the thick old stalks reached 4-5 m. in height, but they were not as impressive as those I had seen in the Semyens. On the other hand, all the lower plants were far richer in their habits of growth than in the Semyens. As this high valley broadened and flattened, we had expanses of red-hot pokers again. They were less vivid in colour than I had seen in other parts of Ethiopia, but nowhere had I seen the plants and bloom-stalks so healthy and the flowers themselves so large and crisp. The walls of this valley became more interesting the farther up we went. The rocks along their rims had weird shapes resembling those in the Valley of Marvels near Harar – pinnacles with rounded tops, boulders perched on top of other boulders. There was no true columnar basalt. Because of the thick vegetation and the moss and lichen, the rocks all had a weathered look. For this reason the Bale mountains give the superficial impression of greater age than other high Ethiopian mountains.

When we entered this upper valley, Aman pointed to the peak at its far end, to the south-west, as Mt Batu (Pl. 59a). After we had watched the light change on it for an hour or more and its outlines became more distinct as we came nearer, Aman and Sendabo came up with the information that the most impressive peak was called *Tinnish Batu* (Little Batu), but that in spite of its name it was really higher than *Tilliq Batu* (Big Batu) behind it. To us it appeared that the peak behind Tinnish Batu was definitely higher. Tinnish Batu's top was a cluster of eroded pinnacles rising from a platform of rock which itself fell off in steep cliffs on all sides. Debris-formed slopes extended up to the first row of cliffs and green grass and bushes were visible on the ledge above them. Looking at these cliffs through binoculars, we concluded that the mountain would not be too difficult to climb, at least to the uppermost shelf beneath the peak. Ascent of the peak would depend on how loose the rock might be. We had been heading for a camp-site called Shaya near a river on the south side of the Batu massif, but Aman said that would be too far to go if we wished to try to climb Tinnish Batu and suggested we camp on it. It was about 4 p.m. We ascended a long, steep slope and stopped beside a huge boulder. A hundred metres above was a 200-m. stretch of cliff with several sections of overhang. From the accumulation of dung around them it was evident that the overhangs were used as shelters for cattle. At one end of the cliffs was a lean-to made of lobelia-stalks and places where two or three camp-fires had burned recently. South of where we stood rose Tilliq Batu, grass-covered to its top. It had two separate summits and lesser peaks on both sides. The area looked as if it could provide several days of good climbing.

Camp pitched, we still had more than an hour of sunlight to explore the area, so each of us took off in a different direction. I made my way down to the meadow to the south-east of our camp-site on the valley floor. Fresh, clear water lay over grass and other small plants in pools. I sank into the soft, humus-laden ground to the top of my boots, but soon discovered that wherever tussock grass grew there was firm foothold. Out in the middle of the meadow where heather had grown and had long ago been burned off, there were hummocks of higher ground covered with *mida*, the geranium-leaved ground-cover, and *alchaba*, the blue forget-me-not. There were a dozen other plants in flower and many kinds of fresh green foliage as well as many silver-grey plants. Back at the camp-site, the men had got the fire going, starting with heather switches and adding damp heather stumps. These burn slowly but with intense heat once they catch. We added some lobelia-stalks, called *tarura* here in Gallinya. At nearly 4,000 m. we could feel the chill of the thin air, reminiscent of Geech at the end of the day but damper, so we first had hot tea and then a swig of Irish whiskey. I tried to explain to Aman and Sendabo where Ireland was, but that proved impossible. They were nevertheless willing to sample what they called *yeferenji katikala*. Between 6.30 and 7 we had a dazzling display of evening light on all the Batus. Stars appeared quickly and the moon was already up, so the darkness was never as intense as it was cold. We cooked our whole dinner in a single pot of boiling water: cans of *cannelloni*, white beans, fruit cocktail, all served boiling hot, followed by hot coffee and chocolate. All this warmed us for a while, but the effect was temporary and by 8 we were eager to take refuge in our sleeping-bags. The men spent another hour next to the fire wrapped in their blankets and sang – great bursts of raw sound: old Galla songs of love, war, and religious devotion. Some time later when I wakened slightly I noted that the singing had stopped and the two of them had crawled inside the tent too.

Day dawned slowly and I was first aware of it not from the light but from the noise of the men stirring the fire. I looked out. We were enveloped in blue-grey fog. It felt raw as it touched the skin. Visibility was about 10 m. We had some hot tea and took a brief walk around the area. The wind came up and the fog rolled over us in billows. We put all our remaining heather-roots on the fire. I walked down the slope to see if the fog might be caused by a cloud that had got stuck over our camp. It was universal. When I came back to camp, there were three men around the fire and a small, wiry horse tethered against the big boulder. The early-morning caller was introduced as Haji Adem, a local man of some consequence who was returning to Dincho from Arana. He had a wife and family in Dincho, it was explained, and another in Arana, a settled region on the south side of the mountains. It took two days' travel on a fast horse to reach Arana. There was good pasture there and rich land tilled by Gallas who rarely came north of the mountains. Haji Adem owned land and had large herds there as well as at Dincho. He was a handsome man about 35, moderately short, lithe, with a lean face and closely-cut hair under a flat skull-cap. We offered him a cup of hot coffee which he drank with pleasure, even taking sugar in it. He invited us to come to call on him when we returned to Dincho, jumped on his horse, and galloped down the valley into the fog.

As we began breakfast, the fog turned to rain and we had to retreat into the tent. Rain fell harder and the wind whipped it against the tent-sides. Aman and Sendabo joined us, periodically going out to bring hot water from the fire. The heather stumps continued to put out intense heat with no effect from the rain. The dampness heightened the effect of the cold which hot tea and coffee warded off for only brief intervals. We huddled in blankets and talked of other things. Sendabo was happy to answer questions about local life and customs. He explained ways in which marriages are arranged and measures that can be taken if they do not work out. If a wife is divorced, she retains few rights and children revert to the father's family. If a husband dies, his brother is obliged to take responsibility for the wife and children, which usually means that he adds her to his own wives. This can cause a heavy strain for a poor man. Sendabo said that he was a very poor man and had only one wife with whom he was happy because she had produced four sons. Sendabo was an admirer of the new Governor of Bale, General Jagama Kello, highest-ranking Galla in the Ethiopian army. He and Aman both described the work they had done for the government two years before in helping put down the Waqo Guto rebellion. Conditions were better now that the rebellion was over, they said. Sendabo kept shaking his blanket off with his lively gestures. He then had to rewrap himself and take another cup of tea (Pl. 55b). Aman was less excitable, but eager to tell us his experiences, so the conversation kept jumping from one topic to another. Rain poured down and wind hit the tent in violent gusts. The conversation turned to wandering holy people. They had healing and other special powers, Sendabo said, and all of them had been to Sheik Hussein, many several times. They lived off the charity of the people. No one would fail to give them food and shelter. They were likely to cause people who mistreated them misfortunes. We looked out to see if the fog might be lifting. It was thicker and darker than ever. The discussion turned to the important men of the area. In addition to Haji Adem, Haji Aliye Aussi and Haji Kassem were mentioned. The two most important tribes in this part of Bale were the Seymena and the Woresha. Most of the people in the region were said to be descendants of Sheik Said . . .

Shortly after 10.30 the fog began to rise and we could see both sides of the valley by 11 o'clock, though the rain continued. Batu would be too soggy to climb for a day or two. We decided to make a quick effort to pack and load to return to Dincho. The horses had strayed during the night, going far down the valley, and the men had to go down to retrieve them. Shortly before noon we set out on the route back with a few small patches of blue beginning to show along the horizon. After half an hour of tramping, I looked back and saw both Batu peaks visible. It was still a mystery which one was higher.

The flowers, in spite of the cold, wind, and rain, were even brighter than they had been the day before and young lobelia plants looked like huge heads of fresh, spiked lettuce. At Turishoma we dismounted and stretched. The sun came out as we had a snack. The afternoon was sheer delight and we would have regretted leaving Batu unclimbed even more if we had not been continually enthralled by the bright sun over the rain-washed expanses of heather and red-hot pokers on the way back to Dincho and the crystal clear views out over the mountains and valleys on all sides. About 4 we stopped at the farmer's house and picked up our carved and decorated wooden items. The horses kept dashing off. They were so happy to be unloaded when we arrived back at the Park Headquarters that they rolled over and over in the grass.

The Park Headquarters was in a state of great excitement. The Governor-General's office had called and announced that he was coming to pay a visit the next day. Kedir, the chief servant, was moving furniture, rearranging exhibits, and adjusting charts, maps, and photographs. We took refuge after dinner in the small wood-panelled study and laid plans to set out for Sof Omar the next morning. This was to be my second visit to Sof Omar, but, like the climb up Batu, it remained unfinished – rain had been early and heavy that year in the low country too. The previous year at just the same time – the end of May – I had got through to Sof Omar without difficulty, though we had not started to go to Sof Omar at all . . .

Sof Omar

Filling our tank and jerricans at the Agip station, we left Robi at noon and struck out across the almost flat plain, entirely given over to pasture and fields except for euphorbia-stockade villages every 3 or 4 km. These resemble settlements in Jirru in northern Shoa, where houses and farmyards are surrounded by tight fences of living candelabra euphorbia, but the Bale villages are much larger. Some of the euphorbia is so tall and thick that it must have taken decades to reach such size. We left the Batu massif farther and farther behind, but a range of mountains ran parallel to the road on the south and the farther east we travelled the greener and lusher these appeared. The final peak of this group, near Goro, is still over 3,000 m. high. Though the land seemed flat, we were actually descending steadily and soon the altimeter was nearing 1,500 m. The air was perceptibly thicker and warmer. Our immediate goal was the old market town of Ghinir, known for its bright-coloured cloth, and from there we intended to go on to Sheik Hussein. We had heard that if we were able to ford the Webe Shebelle near Sheik Hussein, we could possibly take a track that led north through western Hararge and up to Awash Station. In Addis Ababa information on the existence of such a route was conflicting. People who had never been in the area assured us the route existed. Those who had were less sure. The IHA map showed a track from Sheik Hussein to Mechara and Gelemso. The best solution was to go as far as possible and see.

The road was in excellent condition and obviously quite recently built, for many bridges had not been finished and we crossed shallow streams by ford. The vegetation became semi-tropical. We reached Goro, a smallish town with tin roofs and a large market-place, and asked whether the road went on to Ghinir. A group of young men told us it did, so we continued through cultivated country with fields of bright yellow nug in bloom. There were herds

80 (a) *Mida*, low-growing alpine plant, common in Arussi and Bale mountains

(b) *Helichrysum* of creamy white variety grows luxuriantly on high Semyen meadows. A vivid pink kind occurs in Bale mountains

79 (a) Gojjam. Lake Tana, Daga Island. Detail from fifteenth-century Zara Yakob Madonna of Fere-Tseyon

(b) St John's Wort (*hypericum*) occurs in sub-alpine and alpine environments in highlands. In Semyens and Bale it grows to tree size and produces pungent brilliant yellow flowers

78 Gojjam. Priest from Ura Kidane Mehret displays cross and illustrated manuscript

(b) The devil, in church of Azoa Maryam

77 Gojjam (a) St Matthew from Kebran Gospels

76 Gojjam

(a) Monk studying manuscript books on porch of St Gabriel's church on Kebran Island

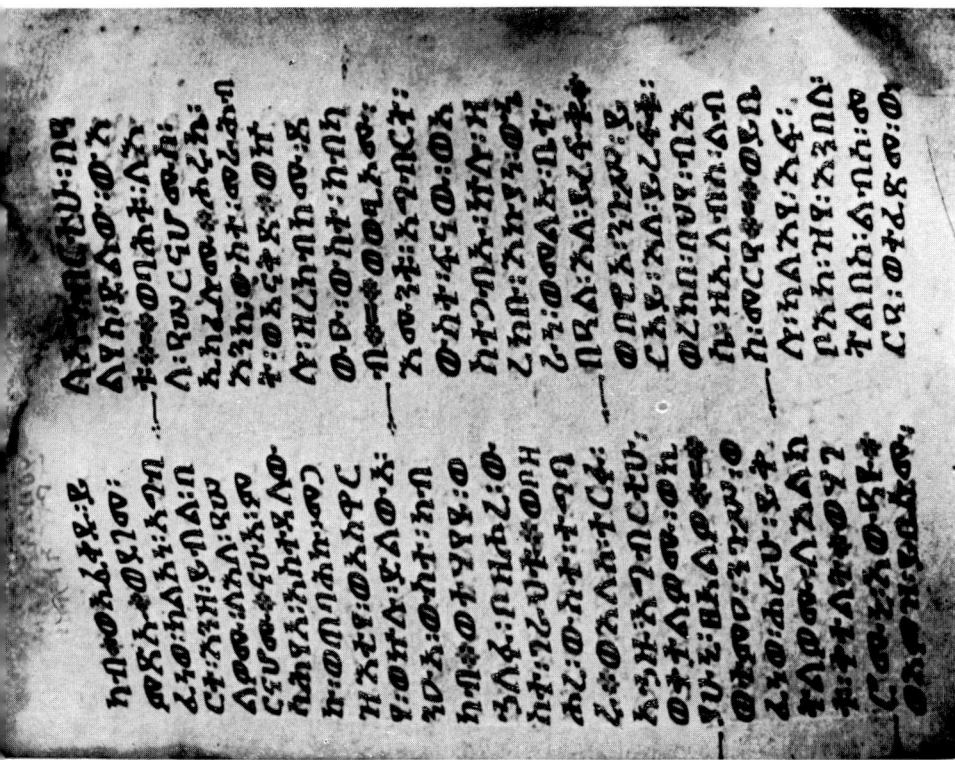

(b) Page from Gospels kept on Debra Maryam island. Though archaic, script differs in no essential way from that currently in use

75 Gojjam

(a) Lake Tana, Narga Island. Land gate leading out of compound of Trinity church

(b) Bahr Dar. One of lions guarding entrance of Imperial palace

74 [*opposite*] It then passes under the First Portuguese Bridge and is confined to a narrow basalt canyon, no more than 10 m. wide in places

73 Blue Nile tumbles over Tisisat Falls (here at relatively low water, in early July), 30 km. from its outflow from Lake Tana

72 Gojjam. Ura Kidane Mehret

71 Gojjam

(a) Jingami Maryam. Eighteenth-century paintings have brilliant colour and sharp outlines

(b) Lake Tana fishermen go out to set fish-trap near outflow of Blue Nile

70 Gojjam

(a) Dima Giyorgis. Some paintings were sketched in long ago, but left unfinished

(b) Lake Tana. Bahr Dar Giyorgis, an example of Neo-Byzantine style modern church architecture

69 Gojjam, Weyname Kidane Mehret. Eighteenth-century paintings of traditional religious themes and details typical of Ethiopian country life

68 Gojjam, Dima Giyorgis. Shutter panels contain portraits of saints in brilliant colours

67 Gojjam, Weyname Kidane Mehret. Portraits of angels decorate door frame
of entrance into Holy of Holies

66 Gojjam

(a) Detail from seventeenth-century *Tamre Maryam* in monastery church of Debra Worq. Predominant colours are red and gold

(b) Lake Tana. St George kills the dragon on walls of St Gabriel's church on Kebran island

65 Gojjam

(a) Dima Giyorgis, after renovation

(b) Jingami Maryam, country church near Felege Berhan

of cattle in pastures and Galla *tukuls*. Then we had a rude shock. We narrowly missed plunging down a deep ditch, unmarked, left open across the road-bed for a culvert which had not yet been placed or delivered. Beyond were more detours around points where culverts were to be laid or bridges built. The road changed to a natural surface of black-cotton soil. There was no more cultivation and no sign of settlement. We were in completely wild country covered with low scrub forest with an almost impenetrable undergrowth of bushes and vines. In between long stretches of black-cotton soil there were rocky ridges and narrower strips of red laterite.

We came to the head of construction on the road. All the work was being done by hand, but since it was Sunday, no work was in progress and the only men visible were occasional guards at workers' camps. We asked one where the road led. To Ghinir? Yes . . . To Sheik Hussein? Yes, but with a more doubtful tone. He asked us if we intended to visit Sof Omar. The name rang like a signal bell – was it near? Before leaving Addis we had talked of visiting it, but were told it was a major undertaking, worthwhile but time-consuming, so we had left Sof Omar low on our list of objectives in Bale. The road-guard said it was not far. We drove on and reached the point where new construction came to an absolute end – ahead was an impassable stretch of stumps where the road-bed had just been marked out through the virgin forest. We roused a guard sleeping in a hammock beside a pile of picks and shovels. How could we go on to Sof Omar? He pointed to a track, barely discernible, that led up a low slope to the north. Did the road lead on to Ghinir and to Sheik Hussein? It did, he said, but Sof Omar was closer. That settled it – Sof Omar became our immediate goal.

The track showed signs of having been worked on long ago. Every time it degenerated into a mere cattle-trail it broadened again after a few hundred metres and we saw faint traces of vehicle-tracks perhaps a month old . . . Vegetation pressed in tightly on both sides much of the time. We saw an occasional cow and passed a few lone Galla. They were all extremely shy and would only nod that the track led on to Ghinir. We saw a few dikdiks and had to stop for a huge land tortoise in the middle of the road. It rushed off with untortoiselike speed into the brush, but we hauled it out to examine it. It had a beautifully polished shell of tannish colour, cleaned and smoothed by crawling through the thick, dry vegetation. It weighed at least 40 kg.

As so often happens when travelling a route the first time, we had the feeling we had been under way for hours and had perhaps strayed far from where we thought we ought to be. To make matters worse, we were not at all sure where we ought to be, for none of our maps showed Sof Omar and only the old Italian map indicated something called *Uluca* which I guessed might be what my Gallinya dictionary[11] gave as the word for cave, *holka*. But it showed it north of Megalo with two tracks branching out from Goro – one going directly to Ghinir and one directly to Megalo. Which one were we on? We concluded that all maps must be wrong and drove on.[12] It was about 4 p.m. when we came to the first break in the landscape.

At the top of a valley in an unusually rocky area we met a small caravan of camels led by one light Galla and a very dark fellow with glistening skin who refused to speak. The camels, like the cattle we had seen before, were sleek and fat. Were we near Sof Omar? The Galla did not seem to know what we were saying. Or perhaps there were local superstitions about not telling *ferenjis* about the location of the holy place. Did the track lead to Ghinir? He nodded that it did. What about Sheik Hussein? We thought perhaps we had strayed off in that direction. The Galla was blank. Where was Megalo? He pointed southward and then picked up his stick and started his camels along a track that led that way. We stood wondering whether he was a bandit or a smuggler. Our track led down into a limestone valley with sharp, evenly defined upper rims and steep sides that dropped to a flat bottom. At the rim our altimeter stood at 1,280 m. As it descended, the track became rockier and steeper and was covered with small bright red and pink zinnias, the first I had seen growing wild. We drove carefully for a few hundred metres and were then confronted by a sharp switchback and a mass of tumbled, jagged rocks. We felt it unwise to drive further unless we could be sure we were on the right route. So we stopped and walked on to where we could see the track descending to the bottom of the valley and then climbing up the other side. Far down below on the valley floor tall red anthills glowed in the afternoon sun under a stand of green acacias. It was an inviting sight, a good place to camp . . . but it seemed foolhardy to take our vehicle all the way down, for there were heaps of loose boulders and it would not be easy to drive back up if we had to retrace our route. So we waited and debated and looked for people to ask, but could find no sign of human beings. Why not go to Megalo – along the track that the camel-driver had followed? In case the Italian map was correct we could go from there back to Goro if we had to by a direct route . . .

Getting our vehicle turned around and back up to the rim of the valley proved to be as time-consuming as we had feared, but at the top we met a Galla who raised our hopes. Megalo, he said, was *saati toko* – one hour – away. One hour for him on foot would mean only 15–20 minutes by vehicle. We made our way swiftly along the smooth track until we reached a shallow valley studded with rock outcroppings resembling a World War II tank-trap. They were all too high to drive over and there was no way through them. None at all. We walked up and down the valley and reluctantly came to the conclusion that we had no alternative but to turn back and retrace our route to Goro. The sun was getting low. If we lingered we might not even be able to find all the twists and turns through the thick scrub . . .

We camped that night on a ridge above an empty stretch of the new road in country that appeared totally uninhabited. Best proof of the scarcity of people was the fact that none of the fallen wood in the thorn forest where we set up our tent had been gathered. In most of Ethiopia all branches and even twigs are picked up by women and used for firewood. The sun set in tones of orange, gold, and mauve behind Mt Batu, more than a 100 km. to the west. With no effort but to throw the dry wood in a heap, we had a roaring camp-fire that must have been visible for miles, if there had been anyone to see it. But it attracted no visitors, though it may have kept some at a distance. The air was soft and warm; the altitude 1,710 m. We felt suspended in time in this virgin, unpopulated region. There were no sounds of birds or animals during the night.

The next morning we drove back to the IHA regional camp at Goro where Ato Debebe, the bright young Amhara superintendent in charge, told us all about roads and roadbuilding in the area and confirmed what we had come to suspect by the time we asked him: the valley we had visited the evening before and where we had decided to turn back *was* the valley of Sof Omar. The new road under construction would cross the valley a little below the caves which were under the very point where we had stopped on the old track and talked to the camel-driver the previous evening. We got out all our maps and Ato Debebe brought out his sketches. He showed how the new road would go from Sof Omar on to Ghinir. It was 55 km. from Goro to Sof Omar via the new road-bed and it would be 35 km. from Sof Omar on to Ghinir. There was a more direct route to Ghinir, but the IHA had routed the new road past Sof Omar to make it easier for tourists to visit the caves . . . It would be possible to drive up to the Sof Omar valley on the new road by the end of the year, Ato Debebe said. We realized that we were very close to being the last of the pioneers on this particular route. Our wanderings of the afternoon before left us determined to go back to see the caves. Before we thanked Ato Debebe, we went over the old Italian map to determine the route to Megalo and learn how other tracks in the area related to each other. The '*Uluca*' on the Italian map was Sof Omar, he confirmed. So all the mysteries were solved . . .

We retraced our route of the previous day and by 11 o'clock were in the glade where we had met the camels. We hiked down to the bottom of the valley with its tall termite mounds. There were remains of old camp-fires and the whole valley floor was crisscrossed with foot-trails under immense acacias and figs. There were several groups of grave-sites. But no people. And where were the caves? The most travelled-looking path led north-westward, past limestone ledges to which fig-trees' roots clung as if poured down over them. We followed it and came to a cluster of shabby *tukuls* along the edge of a high cliff. A few chickens fluttered among them, but no people came out in response to our calls. We walked around a bend of the cliffs and there was the river – broad and clear, shaded by large trees. Birds flitted by in the sunlight and monkeys chattered across the shallow, swift-flowing water. We noticed that the river simply disappeared behind the cliff. Here was the entrance to the caves.

We climbed over a pile of boulders and looked in. It was a splendid sight (Pl. 58) – portals of tannish limestone through which the river, almost smooth-surfaced now, flowed majestically. The stone strata of the cave-walls are almost perfectly flat. As sections wear, they break off in chunks that leave relatively sharp projections and angular edges. The effect is of a series of not quite symmetrical arches superimposed upon each other, rising to great height and eventually coming together in sharp points. We had to climb over more boulders and let ourselves down from a small fig-tree to get inside the entrance. Once in, our progress for the first 200 m. was easy and there was plenty of light from the entrance. We passed through several galleries and eventually emerged into a large chamber which had passage-ways leading in several directions. At each turn we had a whole new array of spectacular sights – thick buttresses widening at the top to form irregular arches, these framing views of further arches reflected in the still surface of the river. As we penetrated deeper, variations in direct and reflected light accentuated the effect of the breaks in the rock. There are no stalagmites or stalactites, no seepage formations. The caves seem to have been formed by the lateral erosion of the river (called the Web), though the river would probably not have shifted its course from the open valley to the inside of the rocky valley-wall had there not been faulting and subsidence.

We noticed light coming in from the opposite direction from the river entrance and moved towards it over ridges of sand interspersed with pools of water that had been left behind from a recent spell of high water. Coming through a broad arch, we faced a 45 degree limestone slope that had been smoothed to a marble-like surface. It was completely dry. Climbing up it we perceived the outlines of an opening 50 m. ahead, but a chamber on the left caught our attention. Pots were lying on the floor around the ashes of fires and wax that had dripped from beeswax candles was apparent on ledges and in niches along the walls. Against the innermost wall stood branches hung with pieces of rag and leather and a few leather pouches with prayers on paper and leather inside. This was a centre of worship and had been used recently, for the ashes were new and the candle drippings had not yet gathered dust. Though the caves are now considered a Muslim shrine and their holiness is attributed to Sof Omar, a Muslim saint who lived here at some indeterminate time in the past, there was nothing Islamic in this worship chamber. It was pre-Muslim and pre-Christian and more basic than either – an old form of earth worship.[13] I was reminded of a visit a few years before to the newly discovered Maya caves of Balankanche in Yucatan where elaborate earth-worship ceremonies had been held.[14]

We hoped to find local people who could tell us something about the religious traditions and ceremonies of the place. We walked on up the smooth rock to the exit. It was now clear that the stone had been smoothed by people coming to ceremonies in the cave over hundreds, perhaps thousands, of years. We came out into the sunlight behind the group of *tuhuls* we had passed when we first came down to the river entrance. A path led down a short distance to a walled-in area shaded by old figs. With a few tables and chairs and a waiter to provide cold beer and Fanta, this would have been a perfect little outdoor refreshment place like those one usually finds near points of tourist interest in most parts of the Middle East. We mused that with the new road and the eventual influx of visitors it would bring, the tables and beer and Fanta would probably not be long in coming . . . But for the present Sof Omar was still firmly rooted to its past. We spotted a few women and children peering out from the *tukuls*, but none would come to us and when we walked over to talk to them, they retreated inside. There were no men.[15]

Gabatas and Guchumas

The collections of the Museum of the Institute of Ethiopian studies at HSIU in Addis Ababa lacked material from Bale. I had already helped Ato Girma Fisseha of the museum collect handicrafts from the Zway Islands and had learned what a good travelling companion Girma was. A Gondari by origin, he has a passionate interest in Ethiopian art and handicrafts and works incessantly to build up the museum's holdings. It was a rare pleasure to go collecting with Girma in Bale, for the province is a treasure-house of native crafts which are still largely uninfluenced by modern manufacturing methods or materials. The Galla of Bale make practically everything they need in their households. Except for an odd tin can, bottle, or jar – glass, metal, paper, and plastic play no role in their lives. They use basketry, pottery, gourds, leather, wood. Everything they make has not only its practical purpose, but also its particular requirements of shape and style and, frequently, ornamentation. Basketry, pots, and items of wood can be bought at markets in Bale, but even at a large market only a few items may be for sale on a particular day and only newly made things are brought to be sold. Women bring milk in elaborate containers that are made of wood, gourd, basketry, leather, and pottery in some combination, but as elsewhere in Ethiopia, they are so reluctant to sell these that it is almost impossible to bargain for them successfully.

We set out on Friday and reached Dincho the evening of the same day. We had scheduled our travel so as to visit the Goro market, which takes place on Monday, and the market at Dincho, which is held on Tuesday. Meanwhile we decided to concentrate on the area around Robi, rich farming country. Coming into this sprawling road-junction town, we asked the way to the *woreda*[16] office, where Girma showed his museum credentials to the local sub-governor and explained our interests. This office was typical of all such places I ever visited in Ethiopia. It gave the impression of being under siege by crowds of people seeking some service, favour, judgement, or advice. We were hustled in ahead of everyone else and the sub-governor, relieved no doubt at the simplicity of the service we asked of him, immediately assigned a man to take us out to the houses of *balabats*[17] who were said to be in a position to assemble good collections of local wares for us to consider buying.

Balabats live well in Bale. We drove over grassy paths about a mile out of town and stopped beside a large compound fenced with euphorbia. Walking inside, we passed long rows of thatched *gotara*, large grain-storage baskets set on legs, and several smaller houses before we came to a big round thatched house with walls of split cedar-stakes. It was over 10 m. in diameter. The *balabat*, a distinguished-looking Muslim in white traditional dress and white embroidered skull-cap, came out and invited us inside where we were seated in a large room which contained only a few three-legged wooden stools on a cleanly swept earthern floor. A $2\frac{1}{2}$-m. high *chiqa* wall separated this room from the other half of the house, which had a cooking-hearth, large storage jars, pots, baskets, beds, stools, and, among them, several women and children who peered timidly through the door and were then shooed back by their mothers. Girma explained to the *balabat* what we wanted and he sent women and boys to bring things. We admired the smoke-varnished ceiling, 6 m. above us, with its intricately woven reeds. It was, in effect, a giant basket seen from the inside. Gradually a fantastic collection of basketry was laid out in front of us. It was all newly made in natural colour. There were two huge *medala*, the teardrop-shaped baskets used for holding grain and sometimes for milk; a large *gabata*, a wooden-footed bowl for mixing dough covered by a peaked basketry lid; several beautiful *tuntos*, tightly woven nursing bottles with horn 'nipples'; half a dozen *chichos*, medium-size milk baskets, made leak-proof with wax inside; and numerous smaller baskets. We lined them up, photographed them, discussed which deserved to be selected for the museum, and slowly came to the point where we felt it was appropriate to start dickering about prices.

The *balabat*'s response was a rude shock – none of these items was for sale! No amount of persuasion could bring him to consider selling even the smallest *tunto*. So we said goodbye and walked back to the landrover. Girma grumbled, 'The fellow is a miser . . . think of having so many fine things and being unwilling to sell any of them even for the Museum!'

At the *woreda* office we exchanged our first guide for a new man, Ato Mohamed, a tall handsome fellow with a white skull-cap. He took us to a house where we made several buys. Here we followed one of Girma's favourite techniques: pay a relatively high price quickly for the first item you really want; this encourages people to get into the bargaining and bring additional items; then take more time bargaining more selectively for the best things . . . We went out to an area called Zeybal, where Mohamed himself lived. His wife, a lady in her way as attractive as he, had a beautiful *medala*, golden with age and redolent of smoke, but with large cowries sewed evenly to its leather carrying-straps and a brass ornament fixed to the top of its horn-stemmed lid (Pl. 60a). Friends and neighbours were streaming in, arms loaded. Coffee was brewed and we had a chance to ask how the different items were made. A medium-sized *chicho* made entirely of basketry took a woman about 15 days, one lady told us. If the lower portion of the *chicho* is made of gourd or wood, it can be made in 10 days. A large *medala* takes much longer – several weeks to finish the basket itself and then the carrying-straps require several days more, especially if they are heavily decorated with cowries and beads. The best basket here was brought in just as we were preparing to thank our hosts and leave. Sturdy and bulbous, covered with smoke and dust, it was called a *kefo*, they said, and used for storing grain. A bit of discussion brought its price down to E$12. The basket may well have been 30 or 40 years old. Every strand of straw was regularly placed, perfectly twisted into the next.

Girma wished to try different collecting techniques, so we took the Goro road as far as the edge of the lowlands and finally turned off on to a field trail leading south towards an immense euphorbia-stockade village which appeared, in effect, to be a 'conurbation' of three or four smaller villages.

'The people in an area like this may be suspicious of outsiders. If we immediately ask to buy handicrafts, they may find the idea so strange that they will not want to sell anything', said Girma. 'Let's first start by saying we want eggs. We will let the people see what we have in the back of the landrover and reach their own conclusions. Then they will bring things to sell to us'.

A woman came to see what we wanted. Girma asked for eggs. She hurried off to get some. More villagers came to see why we had come. Girma told them we were buying eggs and we paid no further attention to them. Soon 25 people had gathered and began peering into the landrover and commenting on the *medalas*, *chichos*, and *tuntos* piled in the back. A man came to ask cautiously if we wanted more such items. I said we might – did he have any *good* ones? Assuredly he did. He disappeared up a euphorbia-lined avenue. More men and women were coming. A sense of excitement was developing. Some of the women in response to shouted instructions from the men turned around and rushed back. Some gave children instructions. In 20 minutes fifty people were crowded around us offering all manner of basketry and items of gourd and wood. Girma was elated. With so much to choose from we could compare and select and reject and bargain. The fact that we did not choose quickly caused more and more people to press their items upon us. There were gourd drinking-cups, *bukes; chichos* half of gourd and half of basketry called *guchumas*. Among the most attractive items here were wooden butter-jars, called *kelas*, stained dark red with geometric ornamentation cut through the red to the creamy white natural wood. Some had had the butter freshly removed. The best of these cost no more than E$1. We spent more than an hour buying and asked the name of the place only as we were leaving. It was called Senana and we later found it noted on the old Italian map. We were back on the main road before we realized that we had never bought the eggs the lady had gone to get!

Driving back westward, we spotted a ring of stones on the edge of a meadow near a neat, medium-sized euphorbia-stockade village. We stopped and walked over to examine the stone circle. We were greeted by a handsome, pregnant Galla matron leading a little boy by the hand. There was an unusual air of elegance and self-assurance about this lady, though she wore no jewellery and had only a thin red band around her black headcloth. We asked about the circle. It was a *mesjid*, she said – a mosque. What was the name of the village? It belonged to her husband, Haji Sultan Amida. Where was he? She motioned across the plain to the south-west where 20 km. of plateau separated us from the forested mountains along the southern horizon. I suggested we camp here for the night, but Girma thought it unwise with the head of the village away. As we discussed the possibility, the lady shouted that she saw Haji Sultan coming and pointed to an almost invisible figure still 3–4 km. away riding towards us. In 10 minutes we were shaking hands with him. He was a fine-featured, broad-faced gentleman about fifty. Girma asked him if we might camp beside his village. The Haji led us through a narrow opening in the euphorbia stockade and down a 'street' to a grassy compound fenced on all sides by euphorbia. It was a night pasture for cattle where the euphorbia fence kept them safe from hyenas. It was also an ideal camp-ground.

A large group of villagers gathered, boys and young men eager to help us set up camp, women and children eager to watch. Most of these people were of the Haji's family and we were introduced to a couple of dozen of them. We soon learned that he had four wives, of whom the one we had met at the *mesjid* was now first in rank. Since various sons and sons-in-law were presented to us, she could not have been the first in time, for she was hardly past her twenties. A couple of trunks of dry *kulkwal* – euphorbia – were brought up and men went to work chopping them. Soon the blue smoke of a camp-fire was rising, silhouetted against the sky by the light of the declining sun. Girma suggested we buy a sheep to treat the villagers. They had already noticed our purchases in the landrover and were beginning to bring up items to offer to us. We bought a good yearling ram for E$10. We suggested the Haji slaughter him so that there could be no question of the meat being eatable by Muslims. After a few bleats – sheep and goats always seem to sense slaughter coming – the animal was quickly dispatched and a group of young men proceeded to skin and clean the carcass. At dusk birds came home to roost among the trees of the village. Cows were driven inside our enclosure and others nearby, but there was so much room – the enclosure was the size of a football field – that the cattle did not interfere with our camp.

We brought out a bottle of vermouth and offered some to the Haji. He declined politely, saying that he took no fermented beverages, not because he was a Muslim but because his great-grandfather had had misfortune in battle because of a *gesho*[18] bush he had grasped when climbing a bank. It had come loose and let him fall back; he was almost overcome by the enemy, though he escaped with his life. Afterwards he swore that he and his descendants would always consider *gesho* cursed and would have nothing to do with it in any form. It would have done no good to explain to the Haji that the vermouth contained no *gesho*, so we offered him a bottle of Coca-Cola which he drank with great pleasure.

The *kulkwal*, which burns quickly, soon formed a bed of coals to which we added acacia charcoal. By the time the charcoal was glowing, the sheep had been cut into roasting pieces. These were placed directly onto the coals. Chairs had been brought from some of the houses and we sat around the fire with Haji Sultan watching the mutton roast. We asked him when he had been to Mecca and he recounted his pilgrimage in some detail. He had gone by bus to Addis Ababa and then to Asmara and Massawa where he had embarked in an

Ethiopian ship to Jidda. It had obviously been one of the high-points of his life, but he confessed he liked Addis much better as a city than he had Mecca or Jidda. He had also been impressed by Dessie and Asmara. He spoke good clear Amharic. Among themselves the Haji's people spoke Gallinya and the women and children seemed to know little if any Amharic.

The meat had been giving off a delicious odour. Soon the choicest pieces were judged ready and were presented to us, the guests. We insisted that the Haji join us too. The meat was tender and delicious though roasted only on the outside. We nibbled off all the roasted parts and returned the pieces to the fire. This seemed to fit the local custom, for as the villagers received pieces, they followed the same procedure. We were soon presented with more pieces from the fire, but not the same ones we had returned for further roasting. Eventually the villagers gnawed every bone clean. We brought out a bottle of red wine and the Haji had another Coca-Cola. The light of day had now been replaced by a nearly full moon and stars. Conversation turned to local life and customs, how much land the Haji had and how various people in the area were related to common ancestors. The Haji ordered a huge pot brought up for coffee-making. The coffee was *jenfel* flavoured in the pot with butter and salt. The result was a rich, steaming beverage more like a Lapsang Suchong tea than coffee. We had two cups each. The villagers were in a very happy mood and burst into song. Both men and women came in close around the fire and sang several sequences. One was a song of welcome specifically for us. They clapped and stomped with sharp rhythms. Gradually women and children drifted away. Then the Haji and the young men said goodnight.

During the hour before sunrise we had continual clatter of birds and lowing of cattle. We came out of the tent as the sun struck the euphorbia on the west side of the compound. Villagers soon had our fire fanned to life again and by the time we had our coffee boiling, people began to come with things to sell. Girma bought a big *gabata* for E\$30. The Haji arrived and greeted us warmly. He suggested we come to see his house. It was a large one in the centre of the village. His compound was busy with early morning activity. A daughter-in-law was milking a cow directly into a *tunto*. When it was half full, she pressed the cap in and her waiting son, about two years old, cradled the nursing bottle upwards in his arm and began to suck energetically at the horn nipple (Pl. 60b). The mother went on milking into a *chicho*. A calf was tethered close to the cow to keep her milk flowing. The Haji's house was divided into the customary two rooms. The front was a men's area, he said, and the rear was used mostly by the women.[19] We went out to admire his *gotaras* and more of his cattle. His first-ranking wife did not appear until some time later, when we had walked back to our tent. We bought several more baskets and wooden items, photographed the Haji with different combinations of his family (Pl. 61a), and finally, about 9.30, packed up and prepared to depart. Getting back through the euphorbia stockade proved to be a major problem, for we could not turn the landrover the same way as we had when we came in. Men had to chop off a large chunk of tough, milky trunk and we still dented the side of the vehicle as we pushed through. We set out across the meadow to the main road with a group of several dozen villagers cheering us on our way.

*   *   *

Goba market with mud and rain . . . Dincho market the next day with full sun. We photographed local beauties, bought cloth and all the new baskets we could find, met Aman and Sendabo who greeted us as old friends. Then over the mountains to Adaba for the Tuesday market there. We tried to find a Qenyazmach known for his interest in handicrafts, but found he had gone off to Goba. A man who claimed to be a friend of the Qenyazmach took us to a country village where he said extraordinary decorated things were available, but we ended up in a roadside *bunabet* being introduced to a couple of scoundrelly fellows who had only contraband leopardskins to sell. Girma threatened to report them to the police and they fled. So did our 'guide'. We drove on. There was a high wind, much cloud and rainstorms were forming over the mountains to the south. Our plan had been to camp near Adaba, but weather looked better towards the west. Girma's enthusiasm for buying more things for the museum had not diminished, though the landrover was packed to the ceiling. After a few kilometres we turned off towards a large settlement on the plain south of the highway. The experience was a repeat of Senana, except that here Girma concentrated on jewellery and in a couple of hours of bargaining assembled a representative collection of bracelets, armlets, neckpieces, necklaces, rings, and head ornaments made of brass, silver, copper, and iron as well as combinations of beads of glass, wood, and metal. The sun disappeared as stormclouds and high winds overtook us (Pl. 61a). The people begged us to camp there, promising singing and dancing during the evening. But we had decided to go on to a forested glade near Kofele and drove away as a rainstorm broke, regretting later that we had not remained.

<h3 align="center">NOTES</h3>

1 There is a curious disparity about population figures for Bale. Mesfin Wolde-Mariam's *Atlas of Ethiopia*, Asmara, 1970, gives Bale's population as 821,000 in 1966–67. The American *Area Handbook* gives a figure of 159,000 on the basis of IEG Central Statistical Office data for 1967–68. The Central Statistical Office's *Ethiopia 1970, Statistical Pocket Book*, Addis Ababa, 1971, gives Bale's population as 194,000. The low figures are difficult to accept, though it is easy to believe that the population of the province cannot be much over 800,000.

2 The earliest European references to Bali are cited in O.G.S. Crawford (ed.), *Ethiopian Itineraries, ca. 1400–1524*, Cambridge, 1958.

3 Haberland, *Galla*, 5–9; Huntingford, *Galla*, 83; Trimingham, *Islam*, 256 ff.

4 Brown, *Episode*, 99–137, gives a good description of the mountains immediately south of the upper reaches of the Webe Shebelle.

5 Brown, *Episode*, 137–43.

6 Amh. 'old man', 'elder'.

7 *Getoch* is the plural of Amh. *geta*, 'master'. Use of the plural makes the word more honorific. Another somewhat more familiar but less-used form of this word is *getaye*,

'my master'. *Gash* means 'shield' and is used to address young men who are felt to be subordinate to the more senior members of a group.

8 A medium-level civil-military title the original meaning of which was 'Chief of the *Amba*', now often granted to minor tribal and regional leaders.

9 Cf. Trimingham, *Islam*, 253–6.

10 *Encounter*, May 1963.

11 E. C. Foot, *A Galla-English English-Galla Dictionary*, Cambridge, 1913. This simple little volume, which I always kept in my landrover, proved valuable over and over again during my travels in Ethiopia.

12 The excellent pamphlet on Sof Omar issued by ETO in 1967, compiled by Christopher Clapham and Eric Robson, with a good map of the Sof Omar caves themselves, was of no use in finding the place, for when it was written, there were only tracks beyond Dincho.

13 See Trimingham, *Islam*, 247–75 on saint worship and pre-Islamic survivals in Ethiopia.

14 As in so many other parts of the world, Ethiopia offers many examples of primitive cave religious sites which have been adapted to later religious traditions. There is a sacred cave at Sheik Hussein. Many monasteries and church sites in central and northern Ethiopia have adjoining caves. There is good reason to believe that the rock churches of Tigre in many instances evolved from or were later built at pre-Christian sacred caves – Christianity in such cases simply pre-empted the earlier religious site as Islam has apparently done at Sof Omar.

15 I did not get back to Sof Omar, but two members of our party went back a few weeks later and made the complete traverse of the caves along the course of the river, about 1½ km. of underground route in all. During the winter of 1971–72 two young American geologists spent several weeks mapping the caves. In the course of their work they discovered many new side-passages and evidence of other caves in this region.

16 A local government unit comparable to an American county.

17 Local prominent citizens.

18 See above, p. 29.

19 There appear to be no rigid prohibitions on where men and women may go, however, and they associate much more freely and naturally together than in some Islamic societies. The veil seems unknown and the foreigner need have no fear about addressing women.

9 The Land of the Blue Nile

Gojjam and Lake Tana

The Great Abbay

The highway from Addis Ababa to Gojjam is one of the best engineered and maintained and one of the least travelled in Ethiopia. Beyond Debra Libanos one may encounter no other vehicle for half an hour at a stretch. The road crosses rolling uplands with distant mountains always in view. Streams in the frequent small valleys all eventually reach the Blue Nile. Parts of the great Blue Nile Gorge system first become visible about 50 km. north of Addis as cracks in the edge of the plateau on the western horizon. Near Debra Libanos, 100 km. out, the road descends to the edge of a broad segment of gorge, the valley of the Jamma River, and the views are a breathtaking foretaste of the awe-inspiring mile-deep main gorge which forms the boundary between the old kingdoms and modern provinces of Shoa and Gojjam. One catches glimpses of the main gorge for half an hour before reaching it, but the descent still comes as a thrill. Beyond Gosha Tsion the highway veers sharply downward at a point where the side-gorge of the River Muger comes in from the south. Twisting around cliffs of columnar basalt, it descends through steep *arroyos* filled with euphorbia and brush. It passes the ruins of old Italian construction and crosses an immense scree slope where broken columnar basalt forms a semi-permanent landslide. A concrete viaduct built to carry the highway over the worst part of this slope had itself begun to slide in 1972 and IHA was building an emergency bypass. There is still cultivation on shelves of the gorge below this slope, but a little farther down permanent habitations cease and the slopes are covered with scrubby thorn forest. So far the descent has been through volcanic and marine strata. Now the sandstone begins.

Red sandstone cliffs averaging 200 m. in height form both sides of a sub-gorge at the bottom within which the river flows between low banks thickly overgrown with forest, though to a height of 4–5 m. the annual floods scrape the river-banks clean of vegetation. At Shafartak, where the highway into Gojjam crosses on a handsome bridge, the surface of the river is more than 1,400 m. below the edge of the gorge at Goha Tsion. Coming down one has descended through hundreds of millions of years of earth history [1] One also descends through rapid changes in temperature and air pressure. I first crossed the Nile in August, the height of the rainy season and coolest time of the year on the plateau. By the time we reached the bridge we were sweltering. The river is at its highest during the period August–November – a raging mass of greyish-tan water. By December it returns to a placid condition, though there is always a fair current. The water in the dry season is clear and the river then merits its name: Blue Nile, *Tis Abbay* in Amharic. [2]

236

Shafartak was the site of a major ferry crossing before it was chosen as the most practical location for a highway bridge. There is only one other vehicular bridge across the main Blue Nile in Ethiopia – at Bahr Dar, where the river flows out of Lake Tana. Two bridges were built by the Portuguese in the sixteenth and seventeenth centuries and both of these have remained in use for local foot and animal traffic. The first (Agam Dildi) is located just below Tisisat Falls, the second (Sabara Dildi) 45 km. farther downstream. When its water is low, the river can be forded at many places and several old caravan routes cross the gorge. These are rarely used except by local traders and few were visited, described, or mapped by outsiders until the British consul at Dangila, Major Cheesman, made his epic journeys in the late 1920s. From Lake Tana to Shafartak, a distance of 310 km., the country on both sides of the gorge is inhabited by Amhara. After Shafartak, as the gorge deepens and the river receives several large tributaries, the people who live in the country above the gorge are Galla and then Shankalla.[3] Throughout much of its course the bottom of the gorge has an evil reputation as the haunt of outlaws and one of the few really dangerous places remaining in Ethiopia for outsiders to penetrate.

For adventurers the entire course of the Blue Nile in Ethiopia is one of the last true frontiers on earth. Attempted several times, it has been successfully and completely navigated only once, by the British Great Abbay Expedition of 1968 which had the help of the British army. It included almost 70 people and was planned with as much care as major expeditions to the Himalayas or the Antarctic.[4] This expedition was successful in covering the entire course of the river in Ethiopia and did useful scientific work.

A great deal remains to be learned about the Blue Nile. It is said to provide 60 per cent of the water which flows down the main Nile to Egypt and a much larger proportion of the silt which through millennia has accumulated to form the Egyptian delta. Ethiopians equate the Abbay with the River Gihon or Giyon mentioned in Genesis 2:13[5]. Legends about its upper reaches and its sources were prevalent in ancient Egypt and intrigued the Greeks and Romans, but almost nothing was known with certainty. As late as the eleventh century A.D. the Egyptians attributed a long famine to suspicion that the Ethiopians had somehow interfered with the Blue Nile. Ethiopian emperors were not above letting Arab enemies believe that they might be able to control the flow of the river, though most of them must have known how hollow such a threat actually was. The first European known to have visited and described the source of the river was the Spanish Jesuit in Portuguese service Pero Pais (Paez), who accompanied the Emperor Susneyos (1607–32) to Sakala in 1613.[6] Credit for discovering the source of the Blue Nile has generally been given, however, to the energetic Scot, James Bruce, who spent the years 1769–71 in Ethiopia and was appointed governor of the Sakala district by Emperor Tekla-Haymanot II (1769–77). He visited the spring which Ethiopians regard as the ultimate source of the river near the church of Gish Mikael in November 1770, and published a detailed account of the site in an immense work which was attacked as full of fabrications.[7] Cheesman, who went to Gish in the late 1920s, found it very much as Bruce described it. The river which begins here is called the *Wetet Abbay* or *Gilgil Abbay* (Milk Abbay or Calf Abbay). Where the highway crosses it north of Dangila it is a modest stream about 15 m. wide in the dry season, a torrent of coffee-coloured water at the height of the rains. It flows into Lake Tana at its south-west corner and is by far the largest of all the streams that supply the lake with water.

*   *   *

To a greater extent than most of Ethiopia, Gojjam remained medieval until very recent times. It had no roads in the modern sense until the 1930s. The first motor car was brought into the province in 1934. Considering its natural isolation, the most remarkable thing about Gojjam is that it became integrated into the Ethiopian Empire so early and that control over it, in some form, could be maintained by most of the emperors down through the centuries. It was not easy and imperial authority was often more nominal than real. Its traditional rulers were kings in their own right. The last to hold this title was Negus Tekla-Haymanot whose son, Ras Hailu, retained his father's authority, but was not granted the title of *negus* by Haile Selassie, whose policy of consolidation of central authority in the country resulted in his deposing this 'last of the great provincial magnates of the old order'[8] in 1932.[9]

Gojjamis are traditionally dissident and rebellious. The province was a major centre of resistance during the Italian occupation in spite of the fact that Ras Hailu joined the Italians. Haile Selassie exerted himself after the Liberation to tie it more closely to the rest of the country. The Shafartak bridge, which linked Gojjam easily and directly to the capital for the first time, was completed in 1948 and the highway across the middle of the province, *Fenote Selam* – Road of Peace – which the Italians had never been able to bring to full completion because of Patriot resistance, was finished.

Gojjam is a province of contrasts. Geographically its densely settled and cultivated eastern highlands contrast with the sparsely populated, primitive savannah country of the west. The Amharas of eastern Gojjam are among the proudest and purest of Ethiopia, but the province also has several groups of non-semitic peoples who have kept their languages, traditions, and separate ways of life: Agau, Weyto, Kemant, Shinasha, Kunfel, and the varied Nilotic groups of the west whom Ethiopian highlanders group together under the term Shankalla.[10] Gojjamis are proud of their old Christian traditions, but the province also has more pagan survivals than any other part of northern Ethiopia.

Gojjam Back Country

Beyond the Shafartak bridge the highway climbs up to Dejen on the Gojjam plateau. It has a partly Muslim population, a main street lined with hotels and bars, and a new school at its northern edge. The road, which except for wash-outs and breaks in the gorge, has been asphalted all the way from Addis Ababa, turns to gravel and continues that way for 342 km. to Bahr Dar. Ten kilometres beyond Dejen near a church called Tig Maryam (St Mary at the Corner) a secondary road branches off to the east. Before we cross the province, let us follow this route up into the country within the great bend of the Abbay. This was the first part of Gojjam to be Christianized during the late Middle Ages. It is now rich agricultural country where the oil-seed *nug* (*guizotia abyssinica*) is a principal crop. It flowers at the end of the rainy season and perfumes the air with its sharp, dry odour. In late October the landscape here consists of irregular patches of bright green grain and dazzling yellow *nug* with splotches of darker green where clusters of trees mark groups of farmsteads or church groves.

Eventually an all-weather road will be built through this country to Mota and from there on to Bahr Dar, completing a second route across Gojjam. In the early 1970s the improved road had gone only as far as Bichena, and all available maps were in disagreement as to where tracks led in the country beyond. Three old monasteries, Dima, Debra Worq, and Mertule Maryam, dominate the religious life of this region. The first two were probably founded in the fourteenth century, though some Debra Worq traditions claim foundation in Axumite times[11] and this church possesses an icon reputed to have been painted by St Luke.[12] Mertule Maryam is interesting because of the ruins there of a carved stone church that shows clear European derivation and is unlikely to be later than the sixteenth century. It appears to have some affinity with another mysterious old ruin on the plateau on the other side of the gorge, Day Giyorgis[13] in Jirru, discovered by Professor Chojnacki in the late 1960s. Having seen Day Giyorgis, I wanted to compare it first-hand with Mertule Maryam, so this latter site was my goal on both journeys I made into this region, at the end of October 1971, and in May of the following year. I never reached it, being prevented by heavy rain from getting through when only a few kilometres away in 1972. But none of this travel was in vain, for highland Gojjam is a treasure-house of art and history which is only beginning to be tapped. One stands a fair chance here of coming across manuscripts, paintings, perhaps even archaeological remains, that may never have been seen or recorded by an outsider before.

Dima Giyorgis

We were unable to find Dima on our first trip north of Bichena. The second time out we realized why so many of the directions we got from local people were contradictory: vehicles are so new to the hinterland of Gojjam that few people know what they can and cannot do. People were telling us about foot- and animal-trails that go where a vehicle cannot. The eastern edge of the plateau is broken by valleys and chasms that drain into the main gorge, whose

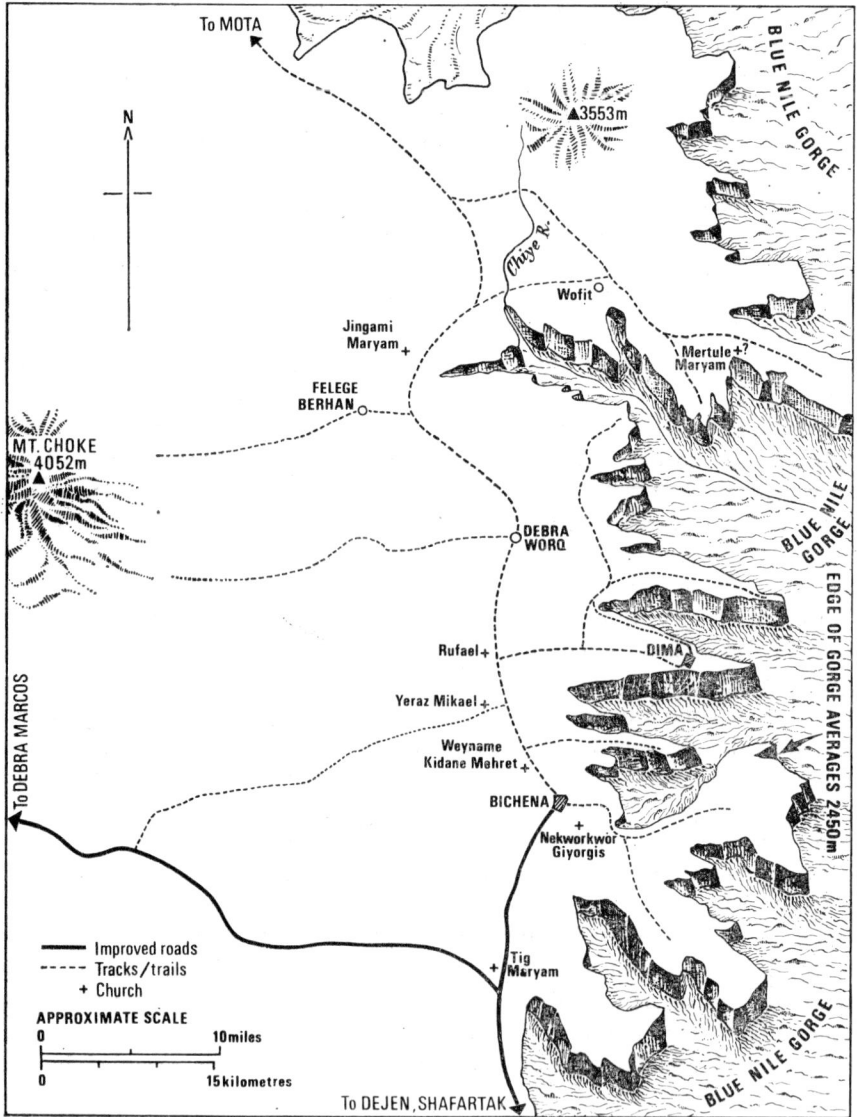

FIG. 24   Gojjam Back Country

bluish edges are visible 20–30 km. eastward. Dima lies above one of these valleys. It is actually not far from Bichena, but can be reached only by driving in a wide arc to the north and then to the east. The key-turn is to the east beyond a church called Rufael 16 km. north of Bichena. The distance from there was only 13 km., but it seemed much farther because we had to go slowly over newly ploughed fields. Gojjam farmers like to assert their claims to land over which tracks pass by ploughing them up each year.

As we passed the first houses of Dima, children scurried away, men bowed; some women bowed, some fled. To reach the market-place we had to cross an expanse of exposed rock. It resembled limestone or chalk, but was a very fine tufa. It lies in layers and can be broken out in flat pieces which rest easily on top of each other; thus it has been much used for building and walls. We came to a stop in the open meadow before the massive church wall. More than 2 m. high, the wall has two clearly defined halves: a bottom section of large volcanic boulders; an upper layer of courses of tufa laid in mud capped with broader slabs of the same stone with a heavy growth of grass as natural thatch. More than a metre thick at the bottom, the wall undulates with the terrain and looks as if it had settled into place long ago. It encloses a huge elliptical compound. The church itself was at first sight a disappointment, for it had recently been renovated on the outside and given a new tin roof (Pl. 65a). Piles of construction debris still cluttered the yard. A section of the main wall near the front gate had been breached to permit vehicles carrying building materials to enter and had not yet been restored.

People quickly gathered around us. A handsome old man, Ato Alemayehu, emerged as a spokesman and a young man with an air of authority, Ato Demissie, volunteered to help us find a camp-site. He turned out to be the seventh of the old gentleman's fifteen children. We found an appealing place on the south side of the church compound wall not far from the edge of the gorge. As we set up the tent, people came to gather firewood for us and a lady brought a gift of a double baker's dozen of eggs. Men connected with the church came to tell us that they would arrange for us to see the church and photograph manuscripts the next morning. We built a rock fireplace and soon had a good fire over which to roast lamb chops and heat pilaff. Ato Demissie and his father stayed to talk after most of the other people had left. We offered them vermouth which they drank with pleasure. Asked how old he was, Ato Alemayehu said he had been born in the year of the Battle of Adowa; he was now 76. He drank to our visit and the day we had arrived – Liberation Day (5 May), the thirty-first anniversary of the triumphal return of HIM to Addis Ababa, saying that Haile Selassie deserved credit for uniting all Ethiopians and making them forget their petty quarrels. We all toasted the Emperor. Ato Demissie's wife brought over a tray of grey-brown, thin country-style *injera*. It would taste good with scrambled eggs in the morning. We asked Ato Alemayehu about the history of the church. It had been established in the time of Amda Tseyon (1314–44), he said. The outside had been rebuilt over the past three years, but the inside was much older and had beautiful paintings. There were hundreds of manuscripts. The next day promised to be interesting.

From somewhere in the neighbourhood we heard music much of the night. A wedding was being celebrated. At 7.30 a.m. a Mass began and we were told that we would have to wait until it was finished to visit the church. Meanwhile we explored the area between the church and the edge of the gorge, south and east of the church compound. Though many people were still living here, the area was in a state of decline. There were many ruins of what had been well-built stone structures. The walls of flat stones hold well because rain does not wash out the mud mortar. The most striking feature of these ruins as well as many of the houses still in use was the arches – large, symmetrical, and true. Someone had taught people to build well here and the church was apparently the centre of a much larger religious community than it has now. When we returned to the churchyard at 8.30, the *qeddasse* was still in progress, so we went to watch a church school. About 40 boys were being taught in a compound with several thatched huts. Most of them appeared to be between 8 and 14 years. Some were learning Ethiopic characters from small paper books. More advanced students were reading from religious manuscripts set out on reading stands, droning out long Ge'ez passages. Four monks were in charge.[14]

When at 9.30 word came that the *qeddasse* was approaching its end, we went into the churchyard and spent the next half-hour examining the outer part of the church. The walls are of thick *chiqa*, built on solid stone foundations. There was no evidence of cracking or settling that had needed repair during the recent renovation. The wood was all in an excellent state of preservation. The frames of the double windows are elaborately carved and painted. Some of them were covered with cloth, but those that were visible featured the full-length portrait of a different saint in each shutter panel (Pl. 68). These saints' clothes are unusually rich in colour and style. The tall doors are beautifully framed and ornamented – their lintels, centre pillars, and their frames have incised designs in the form of arabesques, crosses, outlines of animals, and geometric patterns, some with a light application of colour. Each one is different, but there is a repetition of similar basic patterns.

When the final amens had been intoned, Aleqa Marcos, the blind *memhir*, led by a small boy, came out to welcome us and asked to be photographed. We went inside the church. Its nineteenth-century paintings are undistinguished, but they cover all four walls of the large *maqdas* with strong basic colours. St George, the patron of this church, is prominent and there is a charming young red-robed Virgin. The devil here is very black, though all other faces are light. While we were inside, chanting and moaning had arisen among a steadily growing crowd on the far side of the church. A farmer from the neighbourhood was being laid to rest amid the lamentations of two or three hundred relatives and friends. Until the funeral was over, we were told, we could not see manuscripts . . . Women walked by letting out shrieks, both men and women carried rocks on their heads, people forming the central group at the grave-site sang dirges.

When the deceased was in his grave and the mourners had filed out of the church gate, we were led to the *eqabet* in an enclosure along the western side of the wall. A thick parchment volume was brought out and laid on a mat. It was a *Gadla Giyorgis*, a life of St George. It was inscribed as having been copied in the reign of King Sebastyonos of Shoa at the very beginning of the eighteenth century. Excellently preserved, its paintings were fresh as new. There were about ninety of them, with strong reds, deep greens, and yellows the main colours. The tortures the saint had had to endure had obviously caught the artist's imagination. He is shown nailed to a board being roasted over a fire, suspended from a tree with a boulder lashed to his head, being hacked at with axes, and in a dozen other gruesome situations. He is also shown working miracles, rescuing the faithful from perils, and challenging wicked kings. Most of the detail of the paintings is Ethiopian, but the abstract ornamentation recalls Indian and Persian designs. I photographed all these illustrations in the sunlight as a crowd of local monks, *debteras*, deacons, and townsmen pressed in around us to enjoy them too.

After the *Gadla Giyorgis*, two enormous volumes were brought out, each leather bound, enclosed in a leather case, and wrapped in turn in cloth. These contained the Four Gospels, two per volume. Each was illustrated in identical style and there was a good deal of duplication of paintings, though each Gospel had some unique ones. These volumes were said to have been made in the seventeenth century. I photographed them for the IES archives. Other church treasures were then produced for us to admire and photograph, among them a curious blue enamel plaque with European-style representations of Emperors Naod (1494–1508) and Lebna Dengel (1508–40), done in Limoges between 1521 and 1525. It was well past noon by this time. There were said to be many more manuscripts, including many in a cave, but the monks felt we had seen enough and assured us we had seen their best. We returned to our camp-site where a large crowd had collected. Several people wanted medical attention, so we passed out aspirin, coricidin, vitamin and malaria pills, and doctored a man who had slit his leg open in falling from a ladder. We bought several tiny silver neck-crosses from local people who brought them to sell and departed.

Debra Worq

Dima had eluded us on our first trip into the Gojjam back country, but we had penetrated to Debra Worq in spite of muddy fords and deeply rutted tracks. We had a romantic first view of the old monastery town, whose name means 'Mountain of Gold', at dusk and camped beside a stream beneath the large round hill on which the settlement is situated. In the morning we drove up to the immense market-place dominated at its eastern end by an old fig with an extraordinarily horizontal habit of growth and then climbed on up the uneven, worn-down stone steps to the church. Its compound takes up the entire hilltop and is enclosed by a tall stone wall. The church was a large round structure roofed with thatch, with beautifully cut cedar arches forming its outer colonnade. Its golden roof-cross was complete with seven ostrich eggs. The windows were framed in thick cedar and the tall wooden-plank doors were in good condition. But they were locked. The *memhir* was off in Addis Ababa and none of the many priests and monks who gathered around us could let us inside. The place had an air of lethargy about it beyond the sense of peace and timelessness that usually characterizes remote religious establishments in Ethiopia. The *eqabet*, a well-built high stone tower, was not locked. I looked in the door and saw a handsome, wild-eyed young monk sitting beside a pile of manuscript books, crosses, censers, and umbrellas. He unwrapped a brass – or was it gold? – cross and displayed it to me proudly, but he would not let me touch it. I asked him about manuscripts. He reached over and took a large volume off a peg on the wall and removed it from its leather case. Opening it carefully he held it up to reveal clean parchment pages of beautiful red and black Ge'ez text alternating with splendid paintings in bright yellows, reds, and blacks. Then he shoved the manuscript back into its case and refused to show us any of the other books. . . . He seemed fearful. Someone came and said the key for the church had been sent for. We waited an hour only to be told that the man who had the key had gone off to Addis Ababa. There was something peculiar about the situation here.

When we returned the next May, we were accompanied by Professor Chojnacki and two young assistants, Berhanu and Hailu, from the HSIU Institute of Ethiopian Studies. We were also armed with a letter from the Patriarch of Ethiopia to the Archbishop of Gojjam requesting all churches and monasteries we might visit to permit us to photograph their treasures for the Institute. We had not needed to show the letter at Dima and at other churches we had visited, but we expected it would prove useful at Debra Worq. As we walked through the gate to the churchyard we found that what often seems timeless in Ethiopia does change; the old church was being taken apart and put back together again! The thatch was gone from the roof and tin was in process of replacing it. The wooden arches had been taken down so that their foundations could be rebuilt and the roof structure was being held up by scaffolding. The monks told us that the Emperor had donated E$60,000 for the renovation and the job was being carried out by an Italian contractor who intended to have the new roof completed by the time the heavy rains began. It was good to see that this famous old place was being given the means to withstand the ravages of time for another century or two, but it was disappointing to learn that we would not be able to see the church's paintings on this visit either. They had all been covered with muslin for protection during the renovation.

Again the *memhir* was away. We showed the Patriarch's letter to a group of monks. There was no reaction. Entering the gate to the *eqabet*, we met the same intense young monk who had given me a glimpse of a manuscript on our previous visit. He refused to shake hands and glanced at us suspiciously. We showed him the Patriarch's letter. He said he did not have the authority to comply with the Patriarch's request. Who did? A certain Aleqa Tadde. Where was he? Somewhere in the town. Could he be sent for? Several other church officials entered the discussion. Finally we were assured that someone had been sent to find Aleqa Tadde. We had not seen anyone leave. We strolled around the churchyard, came back, and were told that the *aleqa* could not be found. Curious. It is rare in even a largish Ethiopian country town that anyone cannot be found in 15 minutes, for everyone knows where everyone is . . . We walked back to the market square. Berhanu and Hailu went into the first bar to ask about the *aleqa*. He was inside! He emerged, a grand figure in his clerical robes, carrying a walking-stick which he handed to a young boy accompanying him to hold from time to time. He greeted us like old friends, read the Patriarch's letter, and seemed impressed. We waited in the square while he went up to the churchyard where he said he would arrange everything . . .

Half an hour passed. Berhanu came down and reported that the *aleqa* had been out-argued by the hostile monk. We were not to be allowed to see manuscripts until the *memhir* returned several days hence. We sent up word we were disappointed because we had come so far and had the letter from the Patriarch . . . Berhanu returned again and said it had now been decided that we could see manuscripts if we would allow the church to keep the Patriarch's letter. This, we said, was impossible, since it was not addressed to Debra Worq alone but to the Archbishop of Gojjam . . . Further negotiations required two more trips up and down the steep hill by Berhanu before we all returned to the *eqabet*. There the hostile monk was sulking inside the building. But in the yard outside a mat was being rolled out on which to place manuscripts. Three deacons brought out a large, cloth-wrapped volume and placed it upon the mat. We were told it was too holy for us to touch. They undid it and I saw that it was the same volume the monk had permitted me to glimpse on my first visit – a seventeenth-century *Tamre Maryam*, a book of the Miracles of the Virgin Mary (Pl. 66a).

We felt the tension around us ease as local people pressing in around us enjoyed seeing the manuscript as much as we did and commented to each other on the Virgin's miraculous deeds depicted in the illustrations. Taking a break from photographing them, I took out my Polaroid and photographed Aleqa Tadde and a friendly local *balambaras*, handing them their pictures a moment later. This modern miracle brought forth even greater exclamations of astonishment than the miracles of the Virgin Mary. Everyone wanted to be photographed in the same way. We could have consumed a case of film in an hour. Two priests posed for their Polaroid portrait near the gate. The sulking monk emerged from the depths of his *eqabet* and moved swiftly over to get into the picture with them. They were embarrassed and the crowd was amused. The monk retreated into the *eqabet* again. The sun was getting low and we hoped to see more manuscripts. Debra Worq is reputed to have a library of more than 400 volumes and we were sure there were probably other treasures worth recording for the IES archives. But the monk was sulking, probably embarrassed at his own vanity in rushing to be photographed. The *aleqa* talked to him, followed by the *balambaras*. Other monks were discussing the situation in whispers. Finally a heavy single volume of Gospels was brought out and laid on the mat. We had it carried to a wall where the declining sunlight was better. When we had finished with it, we decided we had pressed our luck far enough. We wanted to get back to Weyname to set up camp before darkness. So we shook hands with the *aleqa* and the *balambaras* and thanked the other monks and priests, but the monk in the *eqabet* continued to sulk inside it and refused to come out to see us off. We walked out of the churchyard feeling a sense of triumph at having photographed the *Tamre Maryam*, but regretting that we had been able only briefly to lighten the tension and unease which hovered over this old hilltop monastery . . .

Weyname Kidane Mehret

Unusual art in Gojjam is not confined to the big monasteries. Some of the best is in small parish churches. I visited many of these and sometimes found nothing worthwhile, or was unable to get in, but two were of extraordinary interest.

On our first trip, after negotiating a hideously rutted section of track north of Bichena, we stopped beside a church grove to find someone to ask directions to Dima. No one was in sight. While we waited for people to come, we pushed through the dense brush, climbed over a dry-stone wall, and made our way up to the church. It was in a state of sad neglect. We entered it by climbing over a collapsed section of its outer wall. The inside was a revelation. The *maqdas* was covered with extraordinary eighteenth-century paintings (Pl. 69). All the classic themes were there: the Flight into Egypt, Christ as a boy descending a sunbeam, Adam and Eve, Abraham sacrificing Isaac. There was an outstanding St George and dragon, a vivid depiction of the cannibal who was saved. The details – people's dress, baskets, pots, household furnishings, weapons, ploughs, and tools – were from traditional Ethiopian country life as it is still being lived in the surrounding area. The main (western) door of the *maqdas* had a garland of heads of angels as fine as any I had ever seen and there were several portraits of standing saints of exceptional quality and individuality. The colours were more effective for being relatively subdued: pastel shades, rusts, grey-blues. They had probably been brighter originally, but weathering had taken its toll. The whole eastern side of the church had fallen in, taking down part of the thatched roof. Birds had been sheltering beneath the roof, sitting on top of the *maqdas* walls, and their droppings as well as water dripping down from the greyed thatch had already loosened and discoloured many canvas sections. Perhaps, in fact, as many as a third of the original paintings – nearly all the upper ones – were already damaged beyond repair. But the rest were worth taking some pains to preserve or, at least, record. The ornamental cross on top of the building was still intact and the door to the *maqdas* was locked. Two boys who came to see what we were doing bowed before it and said that the *tabot* was still inside. I photographed all the paintings within easy reach before we returned to our landrover, where a few local people had gathered. They told us the place was called Weyname and the church was a *Kidane Mehret*.[15] Why had it not been repaired? They shrugged. Where were the priests? In Bichena.

When we returned to Addis Ababa, we found that by curious coincidence other friends, the Spencers and Walter Krafft, had 'discovered' Weyname Kidane Mehret within days of the time we had visited it and were also concerned about doing something to rescue its paintings, for after another rainy season or two they would be lost forever. In the ensuing months a project to save the paintings and perhaps restore the church developed among the Society of Friends of the Institute of Ethiopian Studies. The Patriarch and the Archbishop of Gojjam were contacted and a group visited the church again in March to plan repairs.[16] It was learned that the church had fallen into neglect because during the time of Ras Hailu it had lost land on which it depended for income and now had only a small parish. The parishioners had no appreciation of the quality of the art, but, initially at least, would not consent to having the paintings removed for safekeeping.

We camped beside the wall of the church compound at Weyname the final night of our visit to the Gojjam back-country in May. At dusk birds that make the church grove their home – grey herons, hornbills, doves – came in noisily to settle for the night. A farmer brought a large gourd of milk. Blooming eucalyptus perfumed the whole area. At dawn farmers came with oxen to plough the fields east of the church. As soon as there was enough light we set about photographing all the paintings in detail. Local elders came to discuss the restoration project. No work had yet been done. They had various excuses, but it all added up to the fact that there was little enthusiasm in the parish for the project and the priests who served the church appeared to be an indolent lot. We concluded that if Weyname Kidane Mehret were to be rescued, little help could be expected from the people to whom the old church belongs.[17]

Jingami Maryam

On this same journey we had tried to get through to Mertule Maryam, but instead had spent a wet, cold night at Wofit (Place of Birds) after being drenched by downpours. The next day was sunny and clear, but the tracks were not. The Chiye River was a torrent of brown water. We had to spend an hour rebuilding a ford before we were able to cross it. We had noticed a church grove in the saddle of a range of low hills to the west and decided to go up to have a look at it while the tracks dried.

A man standing by the road told us the church was called Jingami Maryam. This was a local pronunciation of Dingayami Maryam – St Mary of the Rocks. It was named for a rocky outcropping a short distance to the south of the church-site. We took a steep trail up the hillside, verifying the route with the first people we met, a group of women with the usual short cropped hair of the northern Amhara. They bowed low as we passed. Farther on we met a priest. He was the Liqa-Kahenat Wase Kassa, a small fine-featured old man who had just concluded Sunday Services. He was delighted, nevertheless, to turn around and go back with us. He said the church had good paintings, but complained that it had little land from which it could gain income and therefore he and the other five religious men connected with it were entirely dependent upon fees for services for their livelihood. As we came up onto the saddle, the situation was revealed to be every bit as impressive as it appeared from below. Inside the large walled compound were tall, straight cedars. Outside the wall was a grove of eucalyptus that must have had forty years' growth (Pl. 65b). The church was smallish, but well proportioned and well thatched. There was a walkway around the outer circuit, tall slab doors, rather attractive four-part windows with each section arched, two above, two below. The *maqdas* was painted on three sides. There was not as much originality in these paintings as at Weyname, though they were perhaps a century earlier, but they were exceptionally well done (Pl. 71a). The church had been built in the reign of Susneyos (1607–32), Abba Wase said, as he called our attention to a portrait of this emperor on the front wall. He was so eager to be sure we saw all the paintings that he had men carry in a ladder so I could climb up to photograph those close in under the roof. We asked about manuscripts. The priest said most of what the church owned had been stolen some time before. They had since learned that the police had recovered them and were holding them for the church, but for some reason they had not yet been returned. Outside stood a monumental *atronsa* (a bookstand) carved from a tree with its spreading roots making four legs.

We went on to the rocks which give the church its name. They are a pile of massive volcanic boulders with a survival of many kinds of vegetation around them that is now seldom seen in fields. A group of children playing among the bushes were so startled to see a motley mixture of *ferenjis* and Ethiopians approaching that they tumbled down over the hillside to escape, much to the amusement of the local people who accompanied us. Local men described the main features of the landscape. To the west we looked down on the eucalyptus groves of the town of Felege Berhan and towards Mt Choke, highest point in Gojjam (4,052 m.) beyond. Spread out to the south was the flat Gojjam plateau. In the farthest eastern distance, across the Blue Nile, rose the rugged western part of Wollo called Amhara Saynt, a region with even older Christian traditions than Gojjam. In the bluish air and bright sunlight it recalled the ramparts of the Semyens. Closer in to the east lay a broad valley and then a range of smooth hills. Along these they pointed out the exact location of Mertule Maryam as well as half a dozen other churches – to the inhabitants here, as in most parts of the highlands, the most important features in the landscape. We examined these distant groves through field-glasses, but could not penetrate to the buildings themselves. The thought of hiking over to Mertule Maryam, which looked not more than 15 km. away, seized us. Was there a trail? They said a good trail turned off the track we were travelling a short distance south . . . How long would it take to go to Mertule Maryam and back? About eight hours, they decided after discussing it among themselves. It looked closer, they admitted, but it was necessary to go down a deep gorge and climb out again before reaching the church. An Ethiopian country estimate of eight hours would more likely add up to ten or twelve if we spent any time at the church. It was out of the question on this trip.

On the way back down my wife stopped to watch a colourful lizard on the trunk of a cedar. This provoked comment among the now quite large group of farmers and young men accompanying us. 'Look!', one of them exclaimed, 'She is watching the lizard as if it were something important! Of what importance is a lizard to anybody?' We all laughed as the lizard, alarmed at the unexpected attention it was getting, disappeared into a hole in the tree-trunk. A woman finding a lizard interesting was absurd enough to their way of thinking, but they were really nonplussed when Professor Chojnacki, an ardent gardener, stopped to dig up a rare campanula to take back to Addis Ababa and a little farther on pried out a few exposed lily bulbs. He asked the local men the names of these plants. No one knew them. One commented, 'Why would anyone want to know anything so useless as the name of a plant that grows by the side of the path – why does it need a name? Is it good for medicine?' While these people found our curiosity about natural things incomprehensible, there was nothing malicious in their attitude. When we reached the village, one of the group insisted that we all come to his house to have fresh *talla*.

* * *

Before I travelled there I had been told that Gojjamis were dour and unfriendly towards *ferenjis*. I never found this to be the case. Though my fascination with the landscape and the churches never lessened, the more I saw of this province the more interesting I found the people themselves. This will be evident as I describe highlights of travel across the province on the highway which bisects it from south to north.[18]

Across Gojjam

December 1970 was dry, cool, and sunny. Between Dejen and Debra Marcos we drove over almost flat plateau, all farmed but with very few trees. The roadsides supported a heavy growth of acanthus, enormous thistle-like plants, which were covered with red or lavender flowers, each patch confined to a single colour. Debra Marcos is unattractive, though its surroundings are appealing – great groves of eucalyptus which come as a relief after the barrenness of the plateau. It has been the capital of Gojjam for a long time, but this privileged position has not resulted in acquisition of any buildings of distinction. The most impressive structure is the triumphal arch – *Yenitsanet Bir* (Gate of Freedom) – which dominates a formless square. It commemorates Haile Selassie's re-entry into the Ethiopian highlands in 1941 after crossing the Sudan border at Omedla with Colonel Wingate and Brigadier Sandford.

It was 3 o'clock in the afternoon and we were still 275 km. from Bahr Dar. For another 100 km. beyond the provincial capital, the landscape was unchanged: gently rolling plateau, cultivated or in pasture, roadside and stream-beds edged with acanthus, church groves always in sight, deeper stream valleys filled with thicker vegetation and clusters of creamy wild roses. Every 20–25 km. we passed tin-roofed villages with their houses strung out along the roadside. Behind were round thatch-roofed *tukuls*. Countryside scenes were the classic timeless ones: women carrying clay water-pots on their backs from streams and springs, children herding cattle and sheep, brown basenji-type dogs loping along the roadside, men talking animatedly in small groups. In one area boys were selling horsehair fly-whisks by the road and bottles of honey called *tazma*, said to be made by bees who nest in the ground. The road remained excellent, but we raised a good bit of dust.

Before Jiga we crossed two clear rivers and the countryside became greener and more wooded. Monumental *warkas* had been retained and fields ploughed around them. Beyond Fenote Selam we entered Agaumeder (The Country of the Agau), a delightful region with gracefully proportioned, outsize round *tukuls* set in rich green fields. Amharas say Agaus still adhere to many pre-Christian practices. Near Injibara we were entertained by panoramas of spectacular volcanic outcroppings – upthrusts of rock which seem to occur along a broad east-west fault. In this scenic area we passed close to a small lake on the right of the highway which was almost covered with white storks. They were a striking sight in the late evening light against the blue of the water and the intense green of the surrounding meadows. At dusk we reached Dangila.

We still had nearly 100 km. to go to Bahr Dar. Somewhere during the mid-section of this stretch we caught a large pair of warthogs in our headlights as they crossed the road. We passed through several villages, each with its thickening veil of smoke from evening fires. Through the open doors of houses and *tukuls* silhouettes of their occupants were outlined against the light of the fires, occasional candles, and even less frequent gas lanterns. We had to creep to a halt more times than we cared to remember to permit herds of cattle and confused herdboys to sort themselves out and move off the road. From 25 km. away, across desolate uninhabited country, reputed to be the haunt of *shifta*, we saw the bright lights of Bahr Dar. We reached it at 7.30 and were suddenly thrust from the empty countryside on to broad four-lane divided avenues with modern lampposts closely spaced on central islands. At the Blue Nile Springs Motel on the north side of the city, Ato Mammo, the owner, welcomed us warmly.

*   *   *

The next June I crossed Gojjam for the second time from north to south. The countryside was already green and farmers were ploughing their fields, using oxen drawing iron-tipped tree-limb ploughs, cracking their long whips high over the animals' backs. When we stopped to watch them, we heard their continual singsong shouts to the oxen which set the rhythm of the work. Thirty km. south of Debra Marcos we stopped beside the road to eat and afterwards walked to a nearby church grove where we found clergy and laymen concluding a rededication ceremony for their beautiful old thatched church. It had been renovated and contained excellent paintings. It was called Dimbukway Giyorgis.

*   *   *

The next year I again saw Gojjam in the rainy season, traversing it in both directions in early July with a Gojjami friend from Addis Ababa, Assefa, as a travelling companion. We awoke after a night in Debra Marcos's Turist Hotel to find the city a sea of mud. It was a relief to drive out into the vivid green countryside where light clouds obscured the mountain-tops to the east and floated down into the valleys. We crossed the broad Santara plain. Assefa explained that throughout the province Santara is a standard of comparison for anything large and broad – 'big as Santara'. Perhaps 50 sq. km. in extent, it is a communal grazing area. Cattle were being driven down into the plain for the day by children dressed in dirty rags. The cattle looked fat and sleek and the children, except for their shabby clothes, did not look unhealthy or unhappy. A little farther on we passed through Chalga where the Emperor's forces fought an important battle in 1941.

At Fenote Selam we stopped at a roadside hotel, painted a brilliant Mexican pink, and had a mid-morning brunch – huge plates of deep yellow scrambled eggs served on *injera*, a *wat* of lamb with green peppers, and large glasses of hot tea. When we had eaten all we could hold, a servant came in with a censer billowing blue smoke and a *jabana* of coffee flavoured with cardamom. The owner of the hotel, Woizero Tsehay (Lady Sun), a very attractive Amhara matron dressed in a spotless white traditional dress with green border, came to pour the coffee. She held the *jabana* delicately, high above the cups, gave us a choice of sugar or salt, then poured herself a cup and added salt before sitting down to tell us about herself. As well as being a favourite stop for travellers, her hotel was a social centre of the area, for many people came to pay their respects to Woizero Tsehay as we talked to her. After three cups of coffee we rose to leave, but Woizero Tsehay insisted we see her establishment. Behind the main public rooms, a series of low buildings held 25 or 30 single rooms, each with a simple bed and table and chair or two. All had tile floors and looked clean, though the damp of the rainy season gave everything an earthy smell. Woizero Tsehay said she had come in from the country and set up the hotel nine years ago. She had been married twice, the first time at fourteen, and twice divorced. She was too self-sufficient to need a husband now, we sensed. She had plans for expanding her establishment further, she said, as soon as she made more profit. She proudly called our attention to her new red Peugeot parked in the yard. She asked to pose for photographs with us before we departed and I left reflecting that if, 25 years from now, Fenote Selam has a Holiday Inn, Woizero Tsehay will probably have the franchise and make a success of it. With an official 1970 population of 5,190, Fenote Selam is the fourth largest town in Gojjam and at some point in the future will undoubtedly take on a grander appearance than it has now. In the middle of the rainy season its central square was a vast sea of puddles and ruts with a not-yet-completed statue of HIM in the middle.

Near Dangila we stopped to visit Assefa's great uncle, a retired *fitwrari* and decorated Patriot[19] veteran of the Italian occupation. He lived in a small *chiqa* house with tin roof also occupied by a daughter and her family. Several framed medals and citations decorated the wall. The old gentleman received us in bed – not because he was ill but merely staying warm. He was a handsome man in his sixties. He sent a grandson out for beer and to pass word that we had come and soon a whole troop of local residents began streaming in to meet us. Among them was a shabbily dressed, very dark man who stood shyly at the door and then suddenly threw himself at Assefa's feet and repeatedly kissed his legs until the young man, embarrassed, lifted him up and kissed him on both cheeks in the conventional Ethiopian manner. He introduced him to me as Gebre and, after a little hesitation, explained that he had been an old family slave who had belonged to his grandfather. He was a Shankalla from the low country who had been captured as a boy and had grown up with Assefa's father. He knew nothing of his ancestry, not even his original name. Gebre had been officially liberated many years ago and now worked as a handyman around the village. He was touchingly excited and awed at the return of a scion of the family of which he had once been a part. During the next two hours, as other friends and relatives came and went, Gebre stood dutifully in a corner of the room, coming to attention every time Assefa or I moved, pouring beer for us, and serving us parched barley when the women brought it in, walking meekly a few steps behind us when we went outside to greet three of the local priests. We had planned to reach Bahr Dar that evening. The day had been wet, with little sun, so we did not notice the passage of time and it was nearly 5 when we realized we must be on our way. Farewells were effusive. A dozen people who wanted to ride into Dangila or beyond tried to squeeze into the landrover. We took only those who were going to Dangila.

As we let out our passengers at the filling-station (the main part of the town is somewhat west of the highway), Assefa, less sensitive about the subject, recalled that Dangila used to be one of the largest slave-markets in northern Ethiopia. On the road again we were soon forced by a deep purple sky to turn on our headlights even though it was still an hour before sundown. As we drove into a small roadside town which we later learned was called Durabete, a monstrous rainstorm enveloped us, reducing visibility to almost zero. The only thing to do was pull up by the roadside and wait it out. During a lull in the downpour a young man standing in the door of a house beckoned us in. We jumped across a 2-m. wide torrent to accept his invitation. A very friendly fellow, he introduced himself as Kassahun Wolde-Tsadik, said he was from Nazareth in Shoa, a graduate of the Ambo vocational high school, and now was serving as Ministry of Agriculture extension agent for this region. As he prepared coffee, we were joined by another young man, an Eritrean from Asmara who had been teaching here for three years. Kassahun, bubbling with enthusiasm for his work, told us how he was overcoming the conservatism of the local farmers, how he had organized a chicken-raising co-operative and taught women to grind corn for feed that would increase egg production, and then took us across a courtyard to a shed piled high with bags of fertilizer manufactured in South Korea which was being supplied to farmers at nominal cost if they agreed to participate in his crop-improvement programmes. The storm had passed and the sun appeared. We said we had to go. Kassahun insisted we stay for the night, said he would arrange beds for us, and pressed us to drive into the country to see his experimental fields. As the sun set, we walked among plots of local and foreign strains of wheat, barley, maize, alfalfa, and *teff*, with and without fertilizer, each neatly labelled. The fields were on a flat area below a church grove on a knoll. Each Sunday after *qeddasse*, Kassahun said, he gave tours of his plots to all farmers who wished to see them, explaining why some plantings were flourishing better than others, comparing local seeds with others (not always to the disadvantage of the local seeds), and pointing out that care in planting in rows and spacing seeds could also make a difference in growth and yield.

We drove back into Durabete as night settled in and a new rainstorm approached from the south-east. At Kassahun's house the Eritrean schoolteacher was waiting with his bright-eyed Eritrean wife, a teacher herself, to invite us to the schoolmaster's house where, they said, a number of local people would be gathering for the evening. We walked up the street, through a tin-roofed gate in a new eucalyptus pole fence and were met at the doorway by a tall, sharp-featured man in his thirties, principal of the local elementary school. He told us proudly that his house had just been finished and he had moved in only a few weeks before. It was pole-frame plastered with *chiqa*, with clay floor and tin roof. The big sitting-room was lit by a German gas lantern. We were introduced to several men seated around a long table in one corner. The schoolmaster's wife set bottles of *tej* and *katikala* and glasses before us as her husband led us to a blue plush setteee behind the table. From the beginning the conversation was dominated by the *Merigeta* Kifle, an imposing man who was a teacher of morals in the local elementary school. The *merigeta*[20] rose to lead a toast to our health and made a speech thanking us for staying to spend the evening with them, but finished by saying, 'There is only one regrettable aspect of your coming – you have come on a fast-day so we cannot feed you meat!' This was considered a discourtesy by the others who apologized for him. The schoolmaster asked me to excuse him because he was a little fanatic and explained in English (of which the *merigeta* understood nothing) that all schools in this part of the country had one or two church people to teach 'morals' as a concession to the conservatism of the local inhabitants. The *merigeta* claimed to be forty-five, he said, though he was sure he was well over sixty, but no one could prove it and he insisted on the lower age to avoid being pensioned off. Somehow his religious principles did not keep him from lying about his age . . . The *merigeta* went on to say that he rarely saw an American and would like to ask me some questions. The first was, 'What is the difference between communism and democracy?' I gave an extensive answer which Assefa translated and expanded upon to be sure everyone got the basic points I was making and this, in turn, led to many other questions and a lively discussion among the whole group, which by this time had been joined by several more men, both young and old. When we had worked over such questions as the role of religion in society, the nature of religious freedom in America, whether Ethiopia was a democracy (the consensus was that it was not, but they could not agree among themselves on whether it ought to be), I decided to turn tables on the *merigeta* and asked him what he considered to be the most important problem among young people he taught. Without a moment's hesitation he declared, 'Getting them to understand the importance of keeping the fasts and leading a proper Christian life, avoiding sin'. Assefa was appalled and whispered angrily to me that this kind of attitude towards religion showed the depth of the problem of modernizing Ethiopia. The schoolteachers tried to persuade the *merigeta* that there was more to Christianity than fasting and avoiding sin, but it was obvious that this was a discussion they had had often with him before in which no opinions were ever changed.

A servant had been refilling our *tej* glasses every time we drank an inch off the top. Fortunately I was able from time to time to pour a bit of this oversupply of liquor on to the clay floor without being observed. The conversation broke up into groups and roast barley was brought in, but no other food. Kassahun, the agricultural extension agent, drew us aside to say that he and two of the teachers had a chicken stewing at their house – would we come over to have *doro wat* with them when this group broke up? But we must say nothing about it! We made our way through steady rain to Kassahun's house and enjoyed the hot *doro wat* all the more for recalling that the *merigeta* had declared earlier in the evening that people who broke the fast deserved to be stoned and expelled from the village. At 11, we said goodnight to Kassahun, and the Eritrean teacher led us to our 'hotel'. It was a cluster of tin-roofed mud huts around a central courtyard. The rooms were small cells lit by candles. The bed was short, the mattress hard, but the blue sheets were clean, and I slept well with rain clattering on the roof, warmed by the *tej* and *doro wat* as well as the stimulation of the human contacts it had been so easy to establish in this little highland town. The next day we drove on to Bahr Dar.

Bahr Dar

Bahr Dar (Lake Harbour) was a mere village, the site of an old church dedicated to St George, when Cheesman frequented it in the early 1930s. It was not much more than that 20 years later. Then, with the decision to build a power station at Tisisat Falls, it was scheduled for development as a modern industrial town. The Russians agreed to build and staff a technical high school as a gift to Ethiopia. It was opened in 1962. Its attractive modern buildings seem quite out of keeping with the style of architecture favoured by Russian designers until very recently. The Germans helped build a modern hospital nearby. With plentiful electricity and an unlimited supply of good water, Bahr Dar is an ideal location for light industry. A large textile-mill, an Indo-Ethiopian joint venture, went into operation in 1960. By 1970 the city had more than 20,000 people. Plans displayed at EXPO 1972 in Asmara envision a population of between two and three hundred thousand by the end of the century.

The city has been designed for future growth with residential districts separated by wide avenues with school sites at convenient intervals. The business district faces the lake. The airport is now in the middle of this area, but will eventually be moved outside. Flat land south and east of the city provides room for industrial growth. The main avenues are all asphalted, but side-streets are clay and rock. Some lead to settlements of thatched round huts belonging to Galla and Weyto, the primitive original inhabitants of the Tana shores. A large dock serves boat traffic on the lake. Both the IEG Marine Department and a private company, called Navigatana, provide regular service to the most important islands and to Gorgora on the northern shore.

The old harbour at Bahr Dar is still used by papyrus *tankwas* which bring in loads of firewood every afternoon from across the lake. The lake-shores here are all black lava, solid stone in places, but more frequently boulders of considerable size. Enormous sycamore figs shade the landing site. Above it, on a small peninsula, are ruins said to date from Portuguese times. A two-storey tower stands empty, but until recently was inhabited by an old nun. Old Bahr Dar Giyorgis has been replaced by a tan stone modern building in the popular neo-Byzantine style (Pl. 70b). As such churches go, it is quite attractive. Several old trees around it have grown to great height and provide nesting-places for a large colony of black-headed herons who make good watching when they come in from the lake before sunset.

One afternoon I went with a young Ministry of Community Development officer to the headquarters of the fishermen's co-operative he had organized in a building at one end of the market area. We watched the fishermen bring in their day's catch. They carried them suspended from both ends of short poles yoked over their shoulders. Until a few months before, each of these fishermen had gone about his work separately, each going to sell his fish to townspeople as soon as he had caught enough to justify his plying the streets. The co-operative encouraged each man to spend a full day fishing, bringing a maximum catch to the co-operative centre in the late afternoon where they are weighed and credited to his account, and sold directly over the counter to local purchasers, while the excess catch is refrigerated and transported to buyers in more distant locations. The community development officer was hoping to begin flying fish to Gondar soon. His fishermen, he said, had already been convinced by a doubling or tripling of their income of the value of joining together to everyone's mutual benefit. The same community development man had half a dozen other projects under way, including a women's handicraft group and the renovation of an old church in a rural area east of the lake as a tourist attraction.

I drove out twice to the Tisisat Falls, 30 km. from Bahr Dar, once in the evening in January and once in the morning in July. At any time of the day or year they are an exciting spectacle (Pl. 73). From the lake to this point the Abbay flows over a succession of brutal rapids which have proved to be among the most difficult on the whole river for those hardy souls who have attempted to ride out its entire course.[21] Just above the falls, however, the river spreads out into a broad expanse of island-studded smooth water which provides a serene backdrop for the sharp break-off of the falls. There are several separate sections of sheer falls as well as several side-streams which have little or no flow in the dry season, though the main falls always flow. They are best seen from a hillside which faces them from the east, reached on a trail which crosses the old Portuguese bridge, a single tall arch, at the point where the river – all of it! – tumbles into the unbelievably narrow crack in the rock through which it races onwards below the falls (Pl. 74). The road out to the falls from the town is good and goes through cultivated country where, in the rainy season, the local farmers can be seen working in teams, called *wobera* here – a system whereby a group of independent farmers works on the fields of each in turn. It is curious that while the farmers of the area naturally co-operate, the fishermen, without outside initiative, would not have done so on their own. Bahr Dar is well supplied with electricity from the Tisisat generating plant, but the large village that has developed at the falls has no electric service.

On my last visit to Bahr Dar I went to see the Emperor's palace on a hilltop above the river on the Begemder side. It has a full view of the lower bay of the lake, with several of the islands, the city, and the course of the Abbay over its first few kilometres. The Emperor had palaces built in many parts of the country. This one, completed in 1967, is surrounded by formal gardens. It is a large two-storey villa, with the lower storey partly open for parking and storage. A grand staircase with a lion on each side at the top leads to the main living and reception area (Pl. 75b). Bronze-framed glass doors were opened and we were welcomed by the palace-keeper and an assistant who led us from room to room. Everything was spotless, the furniture simple modern style. The floors were ceramic tile in a great variety of patterns and subdued colours, with each room different. The central hall was hung with paintings presented to the Emperor by civic groups and local governments. The keeper explained each one: one from the police with portraits of all the principal police officers; another commemorating the reunification of Eritrea with the motherland. We were shown the bedrooms of the Crown Prince and Princess and Princess Tenagne Worq, but HIM's bedroom seemed to be off-limits, though we were taken into his office. All in all, it was a most attractive residence, but HIM had used it only three days during the preceding year.

Lake Tana

To judge by the legends linked to it, Ethiopian history has revolved around

Lake Tana. Emperor Menelik I, son of King Solomon and the Queen of Sheba, is said to have come to the eastern shore of the lake when he arrived in Ethiopia from Jerusalem bringing the country's first *tabot*. The *tabot* was allegedly kept for 600 years on the island of Tana Cherqos before being transferred to Axum. The Virgin Mary, it is claimed, stopped to rest on the same island during her flight from the Holy Land into Egypt. A rather roundabout route . . . Legend also has it that Frumentius, who brought Christianity to Ethiopia, found his way to Lake Tana, established a church where Jewish rites had previously been observed, and was buried on Tana Cherqos. The legendary twin emperors, Abraha and Atsbaha, are said to have constructed a church on Tana's shores and the less legendary Emperor Gebra Maskal is also said to have come here. Entertaining as they are – and they and many more are still related earnestly by the priests and monks of the Tana churches – none of these legends seems to have much basis in history. From what can be conjectured, it appears that during this early period Lake Tana belonged to the Weyto, the hippopotamus-hunters who still live along its shores and dominate the papyrus-boat commerce on the lake. The inhabitants of the lands around the lake may have been Agau or perhaps even peoples of Sidama stock. Some of these may have been adherents of cults influenced by old Jewish or south Arabian practices.[22] On the other hand, the tradition of early Jewish influence in the area may be a retroactive explanation of purely pagan cults that are known to have survived long after conversion to Christianity.

When did this lake really become Christian? Rather late, in comparison with most of northern Ethiopia, though one of the most diligent of modern Ethiopian scholars has concluded, 'There seems to be no doubt . . that a Christian community existed in the area before the end of the Zagwe dynasty'[23] (i.e., before 1270). The body of Emperor Yekuno-Amlak (1270–85), who restored the Solomonic line, is kept in the *eqabet* of the Church of St Stephen on Daga, but there is no tradition that this church itself dates from that time. The fourteenth century was the great period of expansion of Christianity in the Tana region. The 'glorious victories' of Emperor Amda-Tseyon (1314–44) enabled the church to establish itself so firmly in and around the lake that it could never afterwards be successfully challenged.

Lake Tana receives brief mention from the Portuguese travellers of the sixteenth century, but none seems to have visited its islands. Bruce did little better. A few nineteenth-century travellers reached some of the islands and there were several engineering and survey expeditions in the early twentieth century, but it remained for Major Cheesman to do the first thorough job of exploring the lake in the early 1930s. He did geographic research and at the same time examined paintings, manuscripts, and relics and carefully recorded legends and traditions recited by priests, monks, and laymen.[24] No description of the lake's shores and islands has since appeared which is not deeply indebted to Cheesman and none has even begun to approach his work in completeness.

Heart-shaped, Lake Tana extends for 80 km. from south to north and is

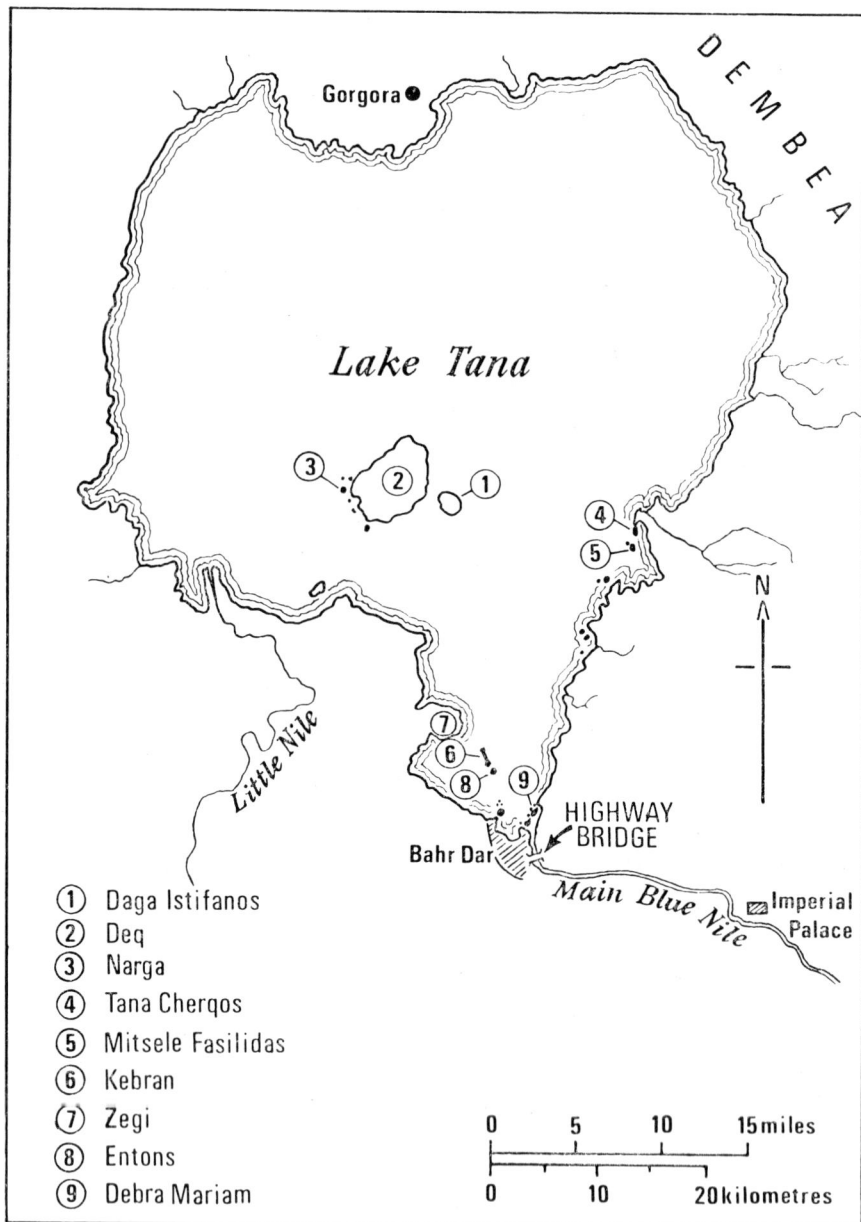

FIG. 25   Lake Tana

about 70 km. across at its greatest breadth. Its total area is about 4,000 sq. km. It is the largest of Ethiopia's lakes, though small compared to many others in Africa. Like so many of the surface features of the Ethiopian plateau, it owes its existence to volcanic action, but it is not a crater. The basin in which the lake lies was blocked off by a heavy flow of lava at its south-eastern corner. The Nile flows out of the lake over this lava dike which seems to be eroding at a geologically rapid rate. Local traditions attest to higher levels of the lake during the period when Christianity was becoming established, probably averaging a metre above the present level. Evidence of old shorelines points to much higher levels a few millennia ago. The mean level of the surface of the lake is now 1,785 m. There is still a good deal of uncertainty about the lake's maximum depth. Cheesman found no greater depth than 15 m. Long stretches of shore are filled with beds of papyrus. The papyrus *tankwas* are punted by long poles. Even when they cross open stretches, which they avoid whenever possible because of the high winds that come up in the afternoon, boatmen use the poles as oars and get a surprising amount of propulsion out of them, though oars would undoubtedly be more efficient. The total amount of water in Lake Tana is calculated to be considerably less than that contained in the deepest of the Rift Valley lakes, Shala, which occupies a series of recent craters. Nevertheless, the flow through Tana is enormous during and immediately after the big rains. The water of the lake is normally a translucent light grey-blue. It becomes tannish as the streams which feed it bring in silt as they swell in volume. Some of this silt is carried on down the Great Abbay, but the huge quantity of silt which this river eventually deposits in Egypt is taken on as the river flows through its own main gorge and receives the silt-laden waters of its dozens of major and hundreds of minor tributaries.

I spent two days on Tana in early July. The way to make best use of a small amount of time was to engage one of the government boats that rent for E$20 per hour of running time. Called the *Deqe Stifa* after a local legendary figure, it was a red fibre-glass 14-footer with a 50 h.p. Mercury outboard motor that ran dependably, but was no longer capable of its rated speed. Our boatman was a competent fellow who had worked on the lake for many years, but did not go on sightseeing voyages often enough to be bored with them. Though it would be pleasant to do one's own navigating on Tana, a great deal of time would be needed and the venture could not be undertaken casually. The lake is full of reefs and shallows. There are no charts that show them and only a few buoys mark the passage out of Bahr Dar into the open lake. The size of the lake and the absence of striking landmarks along most of its rather flat shores would cause a navigator unfamiliar with it a good deal of trouble finding his way into secluded landing-points. One would want to take a couple of Weyto along.

Kebran

The first day we were off by 7 and set a course for Kebran, passing the forested

island of Entons on the way. It used to have a nunnery but is now uninhabited.
At the landing-stage on Kebran we disembarked into an argument between an
agitated monk and three British students. All had long hair and jeans, but the
monk had correctly concluded that one was female and therefore forbidden to
step upon the island and certainly – God forbid – could not be allowed to
proceed up the path to the church. The students, who had no Amharic, realized
what the problem was, but could do nothing about it because they had been
deposited by the early morning Navigatana boat and could not be picked up
again until it returned at 11 o'clock. The monk wanted the young lady to leave
immediately, without being willing to consider how, without a boat, she might
do so. Our arrival provided what to him seemed a rational solution – we could
haul her away and preserve the island from defilement. We managed to mediate.
The monk consented to let the forbidden female sit next to the dock until the
public boat came and we set out up the trail to the church.

Kebran is a heap of volcanic boulders and ash softened by an overgrowth of
trees, brush, and vines. Nearing the top we passed a few small cultivated fields,
coffee patches, and huts of monks. The church, dedicated to St Gabriel, crowns
the top of the island. It is built of red stone with a broad outer arcade. Roofed
with metal, it gives the impression of great solidity which is reinforced when
one steps into the *qiddist* and sees the twelve tall stone pillars, symbolizing the
twelve apostles, which support the roof. In its present form the structure dates
from the reign of Iyasu I (1682–1706) who, according to a manuscript kept in
the church, had it rebuilt with the help of European workmen, for whom stone
and lime for mortar were brought from distant locations.[25] The original church
was established here in the early fourteenth century. We walked first around the
outer arcade where several monks were sitting on the floor reading hand-lettered
parchment volumes (Pl. 76a). They paid no attention to us. A relatively young
monk in a red skirt was the greeter of visitors. He led us to a bookstand beside
the main door where the famous Kebran Gospels were displayed for our
perusal. There was no objection to our leafing through the huge yellowed
volume which dates from the early fifteenth century. It is rare that one can see,
let alone photograph, a treasured manuscript with such ease in an Ethiopian
church. Most entertaining of the numerous illustrations of this manuscript are
the portraits of the four Evangelists composing their respective Gospels[26] (Pl.
77a). Kebran has a large manuscript library which includes books formerly kept
on Entons as well as volumes brought here for safekeeping at the time of
Ahmad Grañ's depredations. We spent a good deal of time listening to the
monk's explanation of the paintings on the *maqdas* walls. They are one of the
most impressive groups of paintings I have seen in any Ethiopian church
because of the richness of their colours, the fineness of their execution, and the
varied subject-matter. The red is bright, but has a light earthy tinge, the yellow
a slight brownishness. In addition to primary colours, which too often prevail in
Ethiopian church painting, there are many intermediate shades and tones. St
George, who looks happy and confident, skilfully dispatches a mauve dragon

(Pl. 66b). A pink-cheeked, richly robed Archangel Gabriel brandishes his sword. Oval-faced medieval patriarchs with full beards and large eyes hold their cross-tipped staffs high and gaze out on the world with self-assurance: Iyasus, Tekla-Haymanot, Hirut, and Betre-Maryam. A large headed, grey-black Satan with round red eyes and a mouth as broad as his face with jagged white teeth reminds the wayward of the fate of sinners. Some of these paintings are on cloth, pasted to the walls, as is common in Ethiopian churches; but others are true frescoes, rare in Ethiopia.

In the yard we examined the church's three bells: one of cast bronze, the second a stone *dawal* made of two different lengths of columnar basalt, and the third, unique in my Ethiopian experience, made of slabs of weathered hardwood designed to slap against each other with a sharp sound like the report of an old shotgun. Worked energetically from high on the island, this bell can probably be heard far out over the lake, certainly on Entons and perhaps all the way to the shores of the Zegi Peninsula, 5 km. away to the north-west.

The Zegi Peninsula

We crossed to Zegi in sun over mirror-smooth water and cruised along shore where every now and then basins had been built among the black rocks for *tankwas*. Our boatman called out the names of churches, pointing to locations up the hillsides through the thick vegetation.[27] Zegi is given over almost entirely to coffee-growing and large trees have been left for shade. Its coffee has been famous for hundreds of years and there is still a good trade in it. We landed at a small jetty. After 15 minutes of hiking through coffee forest, we reached a thatched gate and entered a clearing, in the centre of which rose an imposing thatched church with a bamboo screen around its outer colonnade, Ura Kidane Mehret (Pl. 72). Monks who greeted us said that the Emperor had walked up the same trail three years before at such a brisk pace that he had tired out his whole party. He had been so taken by the old church that he donated corrugated tin for a complete reroofing. We were shown this tin stacked in the *qene mahelet* as we were led inside. No one knew when it would be put on. The thatch on the roof had been a first-class job, thickly packed and smoothly trimmed, but it had turned black and had gathered a thick growth of moss, a sign that it was well past middle age and would soon need attention if the paintings and beautifully carpentered and carved window and door frames were not to be damaged by seepage. There are more paintings at Ura than in Kebran Gabriel, but, taken together, they are not as impressive. One of the most unusual shows a white-bearded old saint, who appears to be Abuna Gebra Manfas Qiddus, brandishing a red spear and riding a hefty red rooster said to symbolize lightning. The *memhir* was a handsome tall man with a very Caucasian face. The other monks were all quite young. As we walked out of the church to the *eqabet*, they told us that Ahmad Grañ had never been able to reach Zegi and treasures had been brought from great distances for safekeeping. Forty *tabots* from churches destroyed by Grañ were still kept in their *eqabet*. This gave a special holiness to the place. Lightning had never been known to strike here and snakes in the vicinity never bit human beings . . . From the *eqabet* they brought three crowns said to have belonged to Emperors Tewodros and Yohannes IV and to King Tekla-Haymanot of Gojjam. They had a good collection of parchment books, two of which we examined page by page: a *Dersana Mikael* and a small prayerbook, both generously illustrated in eighteenth-century style.

Our next stop was on the north side of the peninsula. The coffee forest was somewhat neglected here and so was the church, Azoa Maryam. Its thatch was badly in need of renewal, though no leaks were yet discernible inside. New straw was piled in the outer arcade, evidence of good intentions. The church was richly painted in eighteenth-century style, but only a few paintings struck me as noteworthy: a fierce blue devil sitting in flames with a green snake twined around him (Pl. 77b); a series of faces painted in black and white on a deep ultramarine background – they seemed to be men and women of various ages but bore no labels and the local monks could not (or did not want to) explain whom they represented; and the ornamentation around the doors to the *maqdas*, a succession of black and white block silhouettes of local life, repeated over and over. The Azoa monks, half a dozen and all rather young, were an unattractive lot. They asked for money before agreeing to show us the contents of their *eqabet*. It contained a hodgepodge of odds and ends, a large modern painting of the Crucifixion being the only item of any significance. When we gave the most senior monk E$5 in E$1 notes as we were preparing to depart, stressing that it was to be used for the upkeep of the church, a quarrel broke out among them and rose in intensity until we demanded our money back. This brought a moment of calm, but the argument flared again and they began striking and pushing each other. At this point my Ethiopian travelling companion, a deeply religious man, became offended and intervened physically. He made the two principal protagonists stand out of reach of each other while the others voluntarily drew aside. He then delivered a lecture on Christian virtue, accused the monk who had started the argument of wanting money only to go off and spend the afternoon getting drunk, took back the money, and gave it to one of the non-quarrelling monks with adjurations to all the others to see that it went into the church's funds and not into anyone's pockets.

Debra Maryam

On the lake a light wind had risen, though the sky was only lightly overcast and visibility excellent. Twenty-five kilometres away to the north-east we could make out the low, dark hump of Tana Cherqos along the eastern shore. But our boatman said we could not reach it and still get back to Bahr Dar before the high winds of the late afternoon. So we headed instead towards the south-east, where the Nile flows out of the lake and the old monastery of Debra Maryam dominates the islands along the shore (Pl. 71b). The sun came out and the air grew hot. We cruised in to the landing-site through narrow channels past thick beds of papyrus, called *dingil* in Amharic. The island on which Debra Maryam is located is flat and almost totally cultivated. We walked through a small village where men were mending fish-traps. Dogs barked and children rushed to look at us as we passed fields where men were turning over the black earth with digging-sticks preparatory to planting maize. The churchyard was flat, like a large park, but the building itself was disappointing. The roof thatch was in poorer condition than any of the others we had seen that day. The building has no *qene mahelet*, the roof is held up by gangly tree-trunks. The walls of the *qiddist* are of red stone and the *maqdas* is solidly built. A jolly, shabby old monk appeared from somewhere and opened the large doors, but would not let us enter the *qiddist*. He was happy to bring out the church's Gospels, among the oldest in Ethiopia, with four charming paintings of the four Evangelists done in a cruder and probably earlier style than the illustrations in the Gospels of Kebran. The lettering of the pages of text was perhaps the best I have seen in old Ethiopian books – bold and well formed, clean but with a certain angularity and a greater degree of contrast between the thin and thick strokes in the letters than is characteristic of some later styles of manuscript writing (Pl. 76b). The black and red inks still retained their strong colour on the yellowed pages. The monk showed us a more delicately lettered *Sinkesar* which had no illustrations and a *Tamre Maryam*, to which some illustrations had been added long after the book itself had been written. Then he drew aside the curtains that covered the doors of the *maqdas* so we could see the portrait of St Tadewos which hung beneath them. The saint founded this church early in the fourteenth century. It was rebuilt during the reign of Emperor Tewodros (1855–68), but will need rebuilding again soon if its manuscripts and paintings are not to be endangered by the decay of the roof.

Daga

The next morning we were up before the dawn and on the lake before 7. Storms had gathered during the night and seemed to be concentrated directly over the point towards which we were heading – the highest island of the lake, Daga, more than 30 km. directly north of Bahr Dar. At first it appeared as only a spot on the horizon. Gradually it grew as we cruised steadily for more than two hours towards it. The lake was moved only by swells. By the time we came in under Daga's thickly wooded shores and pulled up at the new concrete dock on the north-east side, the storms had all dissipated. The island of Daga rises 109 m. above lake level, but it seems even higher as one climbs through the thick forest and feels higher when one looks out from the top. The church of St Stephen – Daga Istifanos – on the narrow top ridge was a new experience. It is a thatched rectangular structure of field-stone, but with rounded ends and a low arcade all the way around the outside. The building has settled irregularly and looks much older than it is said to be, for the earlier building was struck by lightning and burned down about a hundred years ago. A morning service was coming to an end as we arrived. The whole island top smelled of incense which was floating up through the thatch, giving the impression that the church was steaming or on fire. We waited outside for the final hymns and amens and were then surrounded by monks and priests. This was by far the most populated of the Tana monasteries we visited. The monks told us they were about eighty.

We entered the church at its western end and stood in a forehall, the *qene mahelet*, from which two wood-slab doors, at least 3 m. high, opened into a large central hall, the *qiddist*. Behind its eastern wall, adorned with many hanging paintings, was the chamber where the *tabot* was kept. The monks were friendly and obliging, ready to take paintings down from the wall so we could examine them closely. The best painting of this church is the so-called Zara Yakob Madonna (Pl. 79a), painted during the reign of that emperor (1434–68) by an artist called Fere-Tseyon (Fruit of Zion), who is one of the few Ethiopian medieval painters about whom anything, though very little, is known.

The *qiddist*, for all its size, had a cluttered look. There were piles of drums along one side, several old benches, bundles of staffs and umbrellas, and cases of vestments. The floor was covered with reed mats and hay and had a generous population of fleas. We were happy to go on to the *eqabet*, a large building made of heavy stones. It had a thatched roof and was partly cut back into the hillside. One is not often allowed inside an *eqabet*, but here we were led directly into an inner chamber where black coffins rested on shelves against the walls. Here lie the bodies of five Ethiopian emperors whose reigns spanned 400 years: Yekuno-Amlak (1270–85), Dawit I (1382–1413), Zara Yakob (1434–68), Za Dengel (1603–04), and Fasil (1632–67). The coffins, the monks said, had been donated by the present Emperor and replaced decrepit old ones. Each had a glass panel through which, with a beeswax candle held beside it, we could look inside. The body of Fasil is much the best preserved. The head appears to be genuinely mummified and the features of a fine long, noble face are clearly distinguishable. His coffin also contains the remains of his young son, Aizor, who died in the process of being crowned. We moved back into the outer room where the monks vied with each other to call to our attention various imperial relics which were piled on shelves and stacked in corners. We saw Fasil's crown, Zara Yakob's sword and shield, Fasil's bed, several crosses, pieces of royal robes, many books which we did not have time to look into closely. We did ask to have a large Gospel brought out into the sunlight. It was the same style as that at Debra Maryam.

Our plan this day was to proceed from Daga to Narga, stop on Deq, and then go over to Tana Cherqos and return along the eastern shore of the lake to Bahr Dar, though we would gladly have remained longer with the friendly monks of Daga. It would be interesting to know whether they still believe that famous personages return after death to live disguised among them. Emperor Zara Yakob is supposed to have been found sitting under a tree on the island seven years after death and left the world permanently only after his body had been brought to Daga and placed in the *eqabet* where it still rests. In the 1920s Ras Makonnen, father of Haile Selassie, was thought to be living on Daga disguised as a monk. He had died in 1906.

Deq and Narga

Rounding the high cliffs which form the north side of Daga, we passed through the channel which separates it from the large low island of Deq. Deq is roughly circular in shape, about 6 km. in diameter and so flat that no part of it rises above 30 m. It is the only Tana island which has a permanent agricultural population. The shore has many reefs and must be approached with caution, so we stayed 400 to 500 m. offshore as we made our way around the island on the south. With field-glasses we could see the neat fields, dotted with huge *warkas*, which cover the island's entire interior. Behind the rocks of the shore there are extensive papyrus beds and meadows where cattle graze. Deq gives the impression of being a fragment of the world suspended in space and time. On its western side the island's shore breaks up into a series of small islands, necks of land, and isolated patches of rock which barely emerge above the surface of the lake. There was little to distinguish Narga from the other lushly wooded islands until we turned and headed for the shore. Before us, behind a small dock, rose a moss-flecked, two-storey stone tower, the Narga water-gate. Square, it is capped by a round dome. We disembarked and climbed the steps, eager to see if Narga still justified Cheesman's enthusiasm for it:

> Even if no more of interest were to be found on the lake, I felt that to see these old gray towers, forgotten on this lonely island, was worth all the trouble taken to get there. At first sight the church suggests the work of Portuguese Jesuit priests, but that is impossible as they had all been expelled from the country when it was built. The architect . . . may have been one of the descendants of the Portuguese artisans who accompanied the priests who received his inspiration from the Gondar palaces. A masonry wall surrounds the precincts. The church itself is round and is built of rock and mortar; a graceful circle of rock-and-mortar pillars with arches surrounds it and supports the thatched roof. All the woodwork is massive and the huge doors are made of one plank cut out of a *warka* tree. Some good paintings of saints adorn the walls, painted on linen and stuck on.[28]

Since Cheesman's time the church has been thoroughly and tastefully renovated and given a metal roof. A marble plaque fixed to one of the pillars states that the renovation was done at the initiative and expense of Emperor Haile Selassie I in the Ethiopian year 1944 (1951–52). It is one of the best restoration jobs I have seen on an old church in Ethiopia and must have required a good deal of effort to bring in materials and workmen.

The church is dedicated to the Trinity (Selassie). It was built at the initiative of Empress Mentuab and she is said to have visited here often. The site has a feel of serenity and elegance characteristic of this distinguished lady. It calls to mind Mentuab's castle at Qusquam.[29]

The pleasant churchyard, green with new grass, was devoid of human beings. We walked through rich greenery to the land-gate on the eastern side of the island (Pl. 75a). This gate is almost an exact duplicate of the water-gate. Beyond, a causeway of lava blocks leads on to Deq. We were concerned that we would be able to find no one to unlock Narga Selassie so that we could see some of its manuscripts and paintings (which include a portrait of Empress Mentuab), so we walked on through papyrus beds into the meadows of the larger island. Seeing cattle, we found a herdsman nearby. He told us that a man of prominence had died in one of the distant Deq parishes and the entire clergy of Narga Selassie had gone to the funeral. They would not return until late afternoon. Was there no one who could let us into the church? He offered to run off to find a man who he thought had a key if we would meanwhile watch his cattle. How long would it take him? Probably two hours. That would mean overnighting on Narga which would also give us the opportunity to see more of Deq the next day, but we also wanted to visit Tana Cherqos and our total time was limited . . . We thanked the man for his willingness to help and walked back through the churchyard to the water-gate and embarked.

The sun was brilliant and the lake smooth, but half an hour later we were watching a huge body of black stormclouds that had gathered over the mountains of Achefer south of the lake. They swept down upon us faster than we thought likely and we were soon being tossed and drenched by both waves and driving rain. The boatman feared the storms would last the rest of the afternoon, so we returned to Bahr Dar.

A period of concentrated bad weather, to be expected as the big rains come into full force, followed and my Tana explorations were at an end. Since the time for my departure from Ethiopia was approaching, I left Tana knowing I would not be able to return soon to see some of the places I had not had time for . . . Not only must I postpone seeing Tana Cherqos, but many others: Gorgora on the north shore and the many historic sites there, Debra Sina, Birgida Maryam, Mandaba; the eastern shore; the mouth of the Little Abbay. Zegi and Deq would be worth several days of exploration. The whole long western shore of the lake seems to have gone unvisited by outsiders since Cheesman was there. The interest of Lake Tana lies not only in its historical and religious associations, but in its birds and fish and hippopotamus and in the Weyto who are bound to be subject to greater pressure for assimilation in the next decades. Remote lakes have always had a special appeal for travellers and researchers and several good books have appeared in recent years on lakes.[30] Tana has not yet attracted such attention. Though I left the lake drenched and shaken up by storms, I think back on this lake as essentially a mild, friendly body of water. Even in the cooler periods of the Ethiopian year, temperatures are always moderate here. Vegetation grows lushly, but there is none of the dankness and sense of oppression often present in the low tropics. Life moves slowly around Tana and seems to have stood still in the monastic communities. But Bahr Dar is astir and the Tisisat Falls are already harnessed to feed the development process. I departed from this area with the comfortable feeling that tradition and development should be able to blend more easily here than they can in most places in the developing world. One hopes that this may prove true of Ethiopia as a whole as well.

NOTES

1 P. A. Mohr, *The Geology of Ethiopia*, HSIU Press, Addis Ababa, 1971, has notes and diagrams on 70–3.

2 *Tis*, also pronounced *chis*, means smoke and signifies a blue-grey colour.

3 The entire length of the Great Abbay from Lake Tana to the Sudan border is approximately 725 km. The river falls approx. 1,400 m. in this distance.

4 Richard Snailham, *The Blue Nile Revealed*, London, 1970. There are good summaries in this book of earlier attempts to navigate the Blue Nile with the exception of two adventures by young Germans. The first of these is described in a book rich in melodrama and self-dramatization: Kuno Steuben, *Alone on the Blue Nile*, London, 1973. It recounts adventures which took place in 1959–60, mentions a few other incidental efforts to navigate the river, and concludes with a brief description of a voyage by two young Germans in 1970 from the second Portuguese bridge to Shafartak.

5 Cf. Ullendorff, *Bible*, 2.

6 Pero Pais, *Historia da Etiopia*, Oporto, 1945, I, 214–21.

7 James Bruce, *Travels to Discover the Source of the Nile*, 8 volumes, Edinburgh, 1804–05. The description of the source is in V, 302–21.

8 Margery Perham, *The Government of Ethiopia*, London, 1969, 359.

9 Cheesman, *Tana*, has excellent descriptions of Ras Hailu and the 'old order' which still prevailed in Gojjam during most of his residence there.

10 It is questionable whether this term has any ethnic meaning at all. It tends to be used for all dark-skinned, negroid peoples of the western border regions and in certain contexts can have distinct pejorative connotations.

11 Taddesse Tamrat, *Church and State*, 202.

12 It was first photographed by Diana Spencer in 1971; see her 'In Search of St Luke Icons in Ethiopia', *JES*, July 1972, 67–96.

13 'Day Giyorgis,' *JES*, July 1969, 43–52; I plan to describe my three visits to it in a subsequent volume dealing exclusively with Shoa.

14 This is the way reading and writing have been learned in Ethiopia for more than a thousand years. Even now church schools play an important role in spreading elementary literacy. Though much memorizing is done, a great deal of historical, literary, and linguistic knowledge is acquired by brighter students. Many of Ethiopia's best modern writers received their initial education in church schools.

15 The Covenant of Mercy, a favourite Ethiopian theme. It refers to a pact between the Virgin and Jesus which entitles her to be merciful towards all she desires to intercede for.

16 Walter Krafft, 'Report on Wayname Kidana Meherat, a Little Known Church in Gojam', *JES*, no. 2, 1972, 70–85.

17 The paintings of this church suffered a tragic end which may in part have resulted from the publicity generated by efforts to rescue them. Early in 1974 thieves tore all the paintings from the walls and soon afterwards fragments of them were being offered to tourists in Addis Ababa second-hand shops.

18 An excellent study of agricultural life in Gojjam contains a great deal of information about the people and their attitudes towards life. Allan Hoben, *Land Tenure Among the Amhara of Ethiopia*, Chicago, 1973.

19 In Ethiopia the term Patriot (Amh. *arbanya*) has the specific meaning of a partisan who fought the Italians during the period 1935–41.

20 A church title meaning 'Master of Guidance'.

21 Cf. Snailham, *Blue Nile*, 135–66.

22 Cheesman was shown a bowl at Tana Cherqos with a Sabaean inscription judged to date from the third century A.D.; *Tana*, 177–8.

23 Taddesse Tamrat, *Church and State*, 190.

24 The most remarkable thing about Cheesman's book, *Lake Tana and the Blue Nile*, is the fact that we have it at all. When he returned from Ethiopia to London at the end of 1934, he had his typescript in a suitcase which was stolen from a parked automobile and never heard of again. He spent the year 1935 rewriting the entire book from notes.

25 Cheesman, *Tana*, 152–3.

26 Fifteen of the illustrated pages from this manuscript are reproduced in accurate colour in *Ethiopia, Illuminated Manuscripts*, published by the New York Graphic Society by arrangement with UNESCO, 1961.

27 I neglected at the time to write down the names of all these churches, some of which the boatman said were no longer in use, for I assumed they would have been recorded by Cheesman. On returning and checking his normally complete descriptions, I found that Zegi had received short shrift and he had apparently visited none of the churches on the peninsula. He mentions, however, that there were seven in all.

28 Cheesman, *Tana*, 135.

29 See above, pp. 182–3.

30 One of the newest and best is Sylvia Sikes's *Lake Chad*, London, 1972.

Glossary

Unless otherwise noted words are all Amharic or Ge'ez. G – Gallinya; T – Tigrinya; H – Harari; I – Italian; F – French; L – Latin.

ababa – flower
Abba – father, priest
abun(a) – bishop
addis – new
adi, T – village
agaza – antelope, deer
agilgil – covered basket for carrying lunch or food on a journey
ahhiya – donkey
alchaba, G – forget-me-not
alem – world
Aleqa – head priest
amba – isolated plateau, mesa
ambatch – water-loving tree belonging to the acacia family with extremely light wood
amole – salt bar
anbasa – lion
aroge – old
atamo – small flat drum
Ato – Mister
atronsa – bookstand
aware – wild animal
awliya, H – shrine of a Muslim saint
awo(n) – yes
azmari – minstrel
bagana – large, ten-stringed lyre played by plucking
bahr – sea, lake
bahr zaf – eucalyptus
bahtawi – hermit, religious recluse
bakela – fave bean
balabat – landowner, freeholder, prominent citizen
Balambaras – commander of a fortress; lower-level civil/military title given to tribal chiefs and locally prominent leaders
baqollo – maize, corn
ber – gate
berbere – red pepper, hot seasoning
berhan – light

269

bet krestyan – 'House of Christians', i.e., building in a church compound where nuns make communion bread

bezu – much, many

betam – very

bira – beer (European type)

birz – non-alcoholic beverage made of honey and water

brindo – raw beef

buke, G – gourd drinking-cup

buluqo – homespun cotton cloth

buna – coffee

bunabet – coffee-house

cheh! – 'giddap!', spoken only to horses

chicho, G – medium-size, tall milk basket made leak-proof with beeswax

chiko – pastry of flour, butter and spices

chiqa – mud, earth, mud plaster

chow – salt

dawal – bell, usually of stone, but also used for large wooden and metal bells

debra – mount, mountain; used only with names of churches and monasteries

debtera – non-ordained church official who specializes in music, dancing, poetry (*qene*) and who may also serve as a scribe

dehna – good, well (of health)

Dejazmach – traditional title meaning 'guardian of the main gate'; often translated as general or count

dildi – bridge

dingay – stone

dink – okay, alright, good

diyakon – 'deacon', acolyte; usually refers to young boys who assist in religious services and may go on to become priests, monks, or *debteras*

doro – chicken

Egziabeher – God

Egzer yistilliñ – Thank you

ehul – grain, corn

ensete, esat – *ensete edulis*, false banana

eqabet – treasure-house of a church, storeroom

faras – horse

fenote – road

ferenji – foreigner, 'European'

fitwrari – a traditional military rank approximating colonel

gabata, G – wooden mixing-bowl, usually footed

gadam – monastery

gadl(a) – account of a saint's life and deeds

gan – large clay beer-pot

gash – shield; used as a title for young men

ge, H – city, town

gebaya – market

gebs – barley

Genna – Christmas

geta, getoch – master, lord; the plural form is used as a very polite form of address to superiors

gesho – *rhamnus prinoides*, a shrub whose leaves are used as a fermentation and flavouring agent in brewed beverages

gidir, H – road

gommista, I – tyre repair-shop

gotara – large grain storage basket set up outside with a top of thatch

Grazmach – traditional title meaning 'guardian of the left flank'

guchuma, G – gourd milk-container with basketry upper part

gumare – hippopotamus

guzo – journey, trip

haik – lake

hail(e) – power, force

haymanot – religion

holka, G – cave

indemin – how

injera – flat bread

Ityopya – Ethiopia

jabana – coffee-pot

jenfel – coffee brewed from the husks of the bean

jib – hyena

jibara – lobelia

kabaro – large tall drum

karne, F – carnet, ticket

katikala – gin-like distilled liquor

kefo, G – bulbous basket for storing grain or flour

kela, G – wooden butter-jar

kirb – near

kocho – flat bread made of *ensete* root

korefe – thick country beer

koricha – saddle, riding animal

kosso – *hagenia abyssinica*; tree whose flowers are used as a vermifuge

krar – small six-stringed plucked musical instrument

kremt – 'winter', the main rainy season which lasts from June through September

kulkwal – candelabra euphorbia

lela, G – *cineraria*, red-hot poker

liqa-kahenat – chief priest

magala, H – square, concourse

mai, T – water

makina, I – automobile, machine of any kind, sewing-machine *mangad* – road, path, way

maqdas – inner sanctum of an Orthodox church where the *tabot* is kept; same as *qiddus qiddusan*

mashila – sorghum, durra

masenko – single-stringed fiddle played with a bow

Maskal – cross, Feast of the Cross at the end of September

medala, G – large basket used for milk or grain

Medhane – Saviour

Melak – Angel

memhir – abbot

menoksi – monk, nun

merkato, I – market, market area

mesjid – mosque

mesob – large basketry table for eating

metfo – bad

mida, G – alpine plant with geranium-shaped leaves

miqaber – grave, tomb

muchh! – 'giddap!', used only for mules

nadaba, H – raised platform in main room of Harari house

naw, nachew – is, are

negus – king

negusa negast – king of kings, i.e., emperor

qeddasse – religious service, Mass

qene mahelet – outer circuit of an Orthodox church

Qenyazmach – traditional title meaning 'guardian of the right flank'

qes – priest

qey – red

qiddus – saint, holy

qiddus qiddusan – Holy of Holies, same as *maqdas*

qiddist – inner circuit of an Orthodox church; feminine form of *qiddus*

qolfe – key

qolo – parched grain

qorqoro – tin

quanta – dried beef

Ras – head; also traditional title equivalent to prince or duke

ruq – far

saat – hour

selam – peace, greetings

Senbet – Sabbath

sende – wheat

shamma – cotton shawl wrapped around shoulders and much of the body, toga

shay – tea

shimagile – elder, old man

shimbera – chickpea

shinkurt – onion

shola – kind of fig-tree

sila – for the sake of

silet – vow

Sinkesar – church reference book devoted to information on principal Ethiopian saints and instructions for observance of their anniversaries in church calendar

sint – how much, how many

sistrum, L – *tsanatsel*, metal rattle used in church music

tabal – sacred pool or spring

tabot – sacred tablet in which holiness of a church rests, kept in *maqdas* or *qiddus qiddusan*

takul – half an hour

talla – barley beer

tankwa – papyrus boat

tarura, G – lobelia

teff – *eragrostis abyssinica*; a native Ethiopian grain

tej – mead, hydromel

tejbet – traditional drinking-house

Tena yistilliñ – greeting used for both hello and goodbye

tid – *juniperus procera*; highland cedar

tilliq – big

Timqat – Epiphany, baptism

tinnish – little

tiru – good

tis – smoke

tsehay – sun

tukul – native round house; though widely used by foreigners in Ethiopia and understood by many Ethiopians, this word is not Ethiopian in origin

tunto, G – basketry nursing 'bottle' with horn nozzle

wada – to, towards

waga – price

wanz – river

warka – kind of large fig-tree

washint – flute

wat – stew, sauce

weha – water, stream

wetet – milk

wayna tej – 'grape tej', i.e., wine

weyra – *olea chrysophylla*; wild olive

Woizerit – Miss

Woizero – Mrs, Lady

woreda – local government unit

yellem – no, there isn't

zabanya – guard, watchman
zenab – rain
zigani, T – stew, northern equivalent of *wat*
zigba – *podocarpus gracilior*; a large alpine tree related to the cedar

AMHARIC NUMERALS

1	and	8	simmint	60	silsa
2	hulett	9	zatañ	70	seba
3	sost	10	asir	80	semana
4	arat	20	haya	90	zetena
5	ammist	30	selasa	100	meto
6	siddist	40	arba	1000	shi
7	sebat	50	hamsa		

Bibliography

This bibliography lists a small number of basic or outstanding works which are frequently cited in the text and includes, in addition, a representative selection of books on Ethiopian history and a few specialized subjects which I have found especially useful. Many additional works are cited in the footnotes.

Abir, Mordechai, *Ethiopia, the Era of the Princes*, London, 1968.

Alvares, Fr Francisco, *The Prester John of the Indies*, 2 vols, Cambridge, 1961.

Beckingham, C. F., and Huntingford, G. W. B. (eds), *Some Records of Ethiopia, 1593–1646*, Cambridge, 1954.

Brown, Leslie, *Ethiopian Episode*, London, 1965.

Budge, Sir E. A. Wallis, *A History of Ethiopia – Nubia and Abyssinia*, London, 1928.

Buxton, David, *Travels in Ethiopia*, 3rd edn, London/New York, 1967.

——, *The Abyssinians*, London/New York, 1970.

Cheesman, Major R. E., *Lake Tana and the Blue Nile, an Abyssinian Quest*, London, 1936.

Clapham, Christopher, *Haile-Selassie's Government*, London, 1969.

Crawford, O. G. S. (ed), *Ethiopian Itineraries, ca. 1400–1524*, Cambridge, 1958.

Doresse, Jean, *Histoire Sommaire de la Corne Orientale de l'Afrique*, Paris, 1971.

Gerster, Georg, *Churches in Rock*, London, 1970.

Haberland, Eike, *Galla Süd-Äthiopiens*, Stuttgart, 1963.

Jones, A. H. M., and Monroe, Elizabeth, *A History of Ethiopia*, Oxford, 1962.

Leslau, Wolf, *Amharic Textbook*, Berkeley and Los Angeles, 1968.

Levine, Donald, N., *Wax and Gold*, Chicago, 1965.

Nesbitt, L. M., *Desert and Forest*, London, 1934.

Pankhurst, Richard K. P., *An Introduction to the Economic History of Ethiopia*, London, 1961.

——, *Travellers in Ethiopia*, London, 1965.

——, *The Ethiopian Royal Chronicles*, London/Addis Ababa, 1967.

——, *Economic History of Ethiopia, 1800–1935*, Addis Ababa, 1968.

——, *A History of Ethiopia in Pictures*, London/Addis Ababa, 1969.

Pankhurst, Sylvia, *Ethiopia, a Cultural History*, London, 1955.

Perham, Margery, *The Government of Ethiopia*, London, 1969.

Powne, Michael, *Ethiopian Music*, London, 1968.

Rasmusson, Joel, *Welcome to Ethiopia, a Tourist Guide*, Addis Ababa, n.d. (c. 1967).

Taddesse Tamrat, *Church and State in Ethiopia, 1270–1527*, Oxford, 1972.

Trimingham, J. S. *Islam in Ethiopia*, London, 1952.

Ullendorff, Edward, *The Ethiopians, an Introduction to Country and People*, London, 1965.

——, *Ethiopia and the Bible*, London, 1968.

Walker, C. H., *The Abyssinian at Home*, London, 1933.

Wylde, Augustus B., *Modern Abyssinia*, London, 1901.

Index

Abbreviations: Ch – Church, Emp – Emperor, I – Island, L – Lake, Mtn(s) – Mountain(s), R – River, St – Saint

Printed in Great Britain by
The Garden City Press Limited,
Letchworth, Hertfordshire SG6 1JS